JAMES AGEE IN CONTEXT

JAMES AGEE
IN CONTEXT

NEW LITERARY, VISUAL, CULTURAL, AND HISTORICAL ESSAYS

Edited by Michael A. Lofaro

THE UNIVERSITY OF TENNESSEE PRESS / KNOXVILLE

First Edition.

Library of Congress Cataloging-in-Publication Data

Names: Lofaro, Michael A., 1948- editor.
Title: James Agee in context : new literary, visual, cultural, and historical essays / edited by Michael A. Lofaro.
Description: First edition. | Knoxville : The University of Tennessee Press, [2022] | Includes bibliographical references and index. | Summary: "This collection of new essays exploring the life and cultural significance of James Agee grew largely from the scholarship of The Works of James Agee series under the editorial guidance of Michael A. Lofaro. The present volume's eleven essays concern Agee's relation to authors as diverse as Wright Morris, John Dos Passos, William T. Vollmann, Stephen Crane, and Ernest Hemingway. Furthermore, it sheds fresh light on Agee's career as an artist, critic, romantic and modernist, reviewer of books, film, and photography, journalist for *Fortune* magazine, and, uniquely, explores the author's personal writings through the lens of his father's life"—Provided by publisher.
Identifiers: LCCN 2022037195 (print) | LCCN 2022037196 (ebook) | ISBN 9781621907428 (hardcover) | ISBN 9781621907435 (pdf)
Subjects: LCSH: Agee, James, 1909–1955—Criticism and interpretation. | Agee, James, 1909–1955—Influence. | American literature—20th century—History and criticism. | Authors, American—20th century—Biography.
Classification: LCC PS3501.G35 Z734 2022 (print) | LCC PS3501.G35 (ebook) | DDC 818/.5209—dc23/eng/20220826
LC record available at https://lccn.loc.gov/2022037195
LC ebook record available at https://lccn.loc.gov/2022037196

FRONTISPIECE: Photograph by Florence Homolka.

TO NANCY

CONTENTS

ILLUSTRATIONS

PREFACE

It is hard to overestimate the impact of the many new works by James Agee uncovered and then published in the last twenty years. These previously unknown primary works have, in turn, encouraged a parallel explosion of critical evaluation and reevaluation by scholars, of which this volume is but the latest contribution.

This collection of new essays, whose authors investigate the work, significance, and life of James Agee in multiple contexts, also serves to document growing realization of the promise of the scholarly edition of The Works of James Agee. It adds newly annotated, revised, and corrected scholarly versions of those texts previously available to the numerous new works in print for the first time; and with these editions in hand, scholars are drawn to the investigation of these materials. The volumes now available include scholarly editions of *A Death in the Family, Complete Journalism, Let Us Now Praise Famous Men, Complete Film Criticism*, and the screenplays for *The African Queen* and *The Night of the Hunter*. All contain never before seen materials. Soon, the "Complete Poetry" and "*The Morning Watch* and Short Fiction" volumes will likewise appear and, one hopes, excite similar critical attention. Samples from these works are included here in Appendix 1 by co-editor Jesse Graves ("Three New Poems: James Agee's "The Darkened Cage," "[A deer went down to water]," and "Eureka") and in Appendix 2 by co-editor Michael A. Lofaro ("A New Story: On the Brooklyn Waterfront—James Agee's 'Freighter's Sailing Day'"). Finally, volumes covering the remaining screenplays, Agee's complete correspondence, and a miscellany of his works will appear, the last devoted to works either discovered after the publication of the most appropriate volume for their inclusion or ones that simply did not fit well into existing categories. When complete, the eleven volumes of The Works of James Agee will more than double his catalog of works.

The eleven essays on Agee that comprise this collection feature many approaches and present multiple contexts for the evaluation of his writing. There are comparisons to and influence studies of authors as diverse as Wright Morris, John Dos Passos, William T. Vollmann, Stephen Crane, Ernest Hemingway, and many others, as well as of Agee's collaborations with Walker Evans and Helen Levitt. While these essays do not cover the entire scope of Agee's canon, they do bring the reader to the streets of James Agee's New York and from Alabama to Hollywood to Havana, explore overlapping and sometimes unique subjects, themes, and accomplishments (or lack thereof), and highlight the diversity of interest that Agee's equally diverse writing inspires. Five essays deal with *Famous Men*; five with varying aspects of the visual; two with his "commercial" journalism for *Fortune*, *Time*, and *The Nation*; and one with his father, the title subject of Agee's *A Death in the Family*. The essays likewise probe themes of poverty, populism, realism, anti-authoritarianism, aesthetics, art, ethics, elitism, bohemianism, regionalism, the commercial, the effect of heritage, and the nature of culture. They focus in addition upon Agee's careers, temperament, and collaborations as an artist, critic, journalist, and reviewer of books, film, and photography, both as a romantic and as a modernist.

Given their varying subjects and viewpoints, it should surprise no one that the present authors differ in their conclusions about Agee's writing. As a longtime appreciator and critic of Agee, David Madden opens this book with a near whirlwind of compared pairings of James Agee, Walker Evans, and Wright Morris, whose literature and photography he discusses from a personal, mainly New Critical stance. For example, he says that, in relation to *Famous Men*, Agee was "primarily a fact-finding journalist," while still acknowledging that the secondary emphasis on Agee himself, on his "amorphous lunging of personality," and on his indulgence in "pure lyrical rhetoric for its own sake" is more often what catches the eye of his readers. In the "The Case Against Language," Michel Jacobs takes a different tack on *Famous Men*, noting that Agee, like Dos Passos, pioneers "the development of modernist documentary literature" by integrating "modernist poetics and journalistic narrative techniques."

The next two essays likewise deal with *Famous Men*, but in quite different ways. Agee himself is the centerpiece for Jeffrey Folks's "James Agee's Legacy of Cultural Repudiation," which begins with Agee's agonized self-inquiries in Alabama and extends those views forward into his life and to other authors and works in the latter half of the twentieth century. He illustrates the continuity of the anti-authoritarianism that Agee espouses in his focus on freedom—both intellectual and moral—that in turn alienates the author in his tangled search for an acceptable relationship between self and art. Andrew Crooke's "Confessions of Inadequacy" highlights some of the same themes by examining Agee's influence upon William Vollmann's *Poor People.* His focus upon elitism versus populism in their writing reveals a shared need to assert the visual in prose as well as in photography in the quest for realism.

Several of these views and themes again come to the fore, as in Michael A. Lofaro's investigation of Agee's book and movie reviews of works that deal with the South. It is a region that inspires ambivalence for Agee; a place of which he says, "I a great deal more than loved this country," despite the fact that much of his life is lived elsewhere. The reader may wish to tie Paul Brown's historical essay "James Agee's Father Before *A Death in the Family*" into these reviews of the South, given Agee's long-standing preoccupation with the Appalachian side of his family tree. Brown's work features a wealth of previously unmined materials that should further illuminate the impact of Hugh James Agee and his death upon his son.

Much of the latter part of Agee's life and work emphasizes a devotion to visual arts, a path that leads him to writing screenplays and also writing about Helen Levitt's photography and film. In "Stephen Crane through the Admiring Lens of James Agee," Jeffrey Couchman shows how and why Agee sought to bring *The Blue Hotel* and *A Bride Comes to Yellow Sky* to the screen. Couchman's conclusions find support in Caroline Blinder's analysis of Agee's collaboration with Levitt that results in *In The Street,* a film that she notes "allows a rare insight into how a pre-war documentary aesthetic in photographic terms was transformed into a post-war cinematic aesthetic" and as well demonstrates how "Agee sought to redefine the visual through the still *and* the moving image." Needless to say, both of these articles add much to the previous ones by Madden, Crooke, and Lofaro, which also concern the visual.

Agee's salaried writing in the 1930s for *Fortune* magazine is specifically taken up in two essays that discuss his articles on cockfighting and tourism to Cuba ("Havana Cruise"). The first, Lofaro's "Cock and Bull Stories," compares Agee's article to one in the second issue of *Fortune* by Ernest Hemingway on bullfighting. Both had to wrestle with Henry Luce's model for the magazine, a "distinguished and deluxe monthly magazine" marketed to and priced for the "most wealthy people." Both *Fortune* articles also engage the issues of class and race that these two blood sports reveal as well as an expected evaluation on a business/economic basis. Replete with detail, Paul Ashdown's examination of "Havana Cruise" provides a wealth of information about Agee at this point in his life, his thoughts on the passengers and the middle-brow, the act of vacation cruising itself, and cruising as a volatile business, in what he rightly terms a "Panoramic View." Like Brown's previously mentioned, fact-laden piece on Agee's father, Ashdown's essay gives readers many new facts and fresh contexts.

In addition to connecting with the other articles on *Famous Men*, Hugh Davis's "Tidmore and the Negro" both presents an excluded chapter of the book and yields another example of how Agee so often sought to aestheticize a realistic scene into art through his dual lens of anxiety and perception. It likewise ties to the two appendices, which, as noted, also offer the reader samples of the newly edited manuscript materials that will appear in The Works.

It seems sound to allow Agee the space to add his voice to introduce those of the contributors and to explain some of his own aesthetic, which resonates with the articles and materials already mentioned. What follows is a transcription of Agee's previously unpublished broad comments on poetry, culture, and life of his time in a short, undated manuscript. It presents his rather sweeping conceptions of poetry and writing and life, many still applicable today. The piece has the working title "Agee on Poetry and Life."[1]

> Poetry is a matter of life itself—of greed and the love of gain, of pain and the joy in it and the escape from it, of the love of ruling and the hatred of being ruled.[2] It is not *for* these things or *against* them. It has nothing to do with their *effects*.
>
> Its first & greatest intention is *not to reform*: it tries to understand and record change as well as it can: it tries to distinguish good from evil; but it does not attempt to *cause* change, any more than it attempts to *cause* a sunrise or to *be thunder*.[3] There is nothing profound in the relation between poor and rich, between oppressor and oppressed. It is a thing you may, as a person, become angry about: but as a writer you are concerned rather with the fact that equality is the dream of the human race and that power is necessary to the race and that power—and law—are things which the h. r. [human race] has never for long decently handled.
>
> The human race evolves slowly and certainly, and no man can truly say that any development is for the better. The thing to remember is that human beings remain human beings: there is a constant and forever unchangeable leaven of evil and injustice; that no change on earth will eliminate it.

> More than finality, any change is a matter of passionate necessity: and more than a matter of passionate necessity, a matter of inevitability. The race builds awry, the pattern continues to change, because of certain constancies in the human soul: and *they* are the business of poets—as well as poets can find them out. The effects are of worth to him only insofar as the human soul is involved and changed by them—which is very little indeed.[4] And only insofar as they *assist* and *supplement* his findings. Only insofar, in fact, as he finds them an intrinsic part of the human soul. And he finds this best, not by try[ing] to *change* that soul, not by wandering into effects and shouting, but by watching that soul, very patiently. And as he records it best by recording only that, by learning his art, by making use of whatever he finds best to make it clear and to make it beautiful. And if, as is said, the great issues of the race are now social & economic—that's too bad for the race, that's all. The truly great issues of the race at any & all times is: what *is* the race?[5] And it is, incidentally, better for the race if a few people continue to realize that.
>
> You are, to a certain extent, obstructed by your training, by what you think you ought to feel and think. But you must not further obstruct your lens with all the fallacies you can pick up on the ground that then are *contemporary*.[6] As a poet your business is to live in eternity as well as in the present: and the only eternity you find in the frantic bellowings of a Communist is the fact that the human soul hates oppression. Therefore don't bellow yourself.
>
> Your own mind is a mirror and a lens as honest as you can make it. You will not gnarl this lens with the eccentricities of a day or with the turmoil that shall resolve into the next thousand years. You shall keep it patiently concentrated upon the essential quietudes of the human soul.

James Agee gives us all much to contemplate.

Acknowledgments

I should like to express my sincere appreciation to all those who have assisted and encouraged the preparation of this volume. Scholars who work with Agee have benefited from the kindness and cooperation of the Rev. Paul Sprecher, trustee of The James Agee Trust, through his permission to use the author's works. I am grateful for grants from the Better English Fund, established by Dr. John C. Hodges for the Department of English, the College of Arts and Sciences, and the Office of Research, all of the University of Tennessee, which supported the research necessary to complete my contributions to this book.

Special thanks is due as well to my colleagues, especially Drs. Hugh Davis, Paul Ashdown, and David Moltke-Hansen, who have generously provided sound advice, suggestions, and criticism. Thanks also to Drs. Allen R. Dunn and Misty Anderson for their assistance. The support and interest of all these people, along with that of my adult children, Ellen and Christopher, and, as always, my wife Nancy, has aided my continued investigation of a man whose life and work always repays the effort. Any shortcomings or errors of any sort, however, are certainly my own.

Notes

1. Four handwritten pages constitute this manuscript (University of Tennessee Special Collections MSS 2730, box 8, folder 17). In the order found in the folder, the first two pages seem a near final text, with the last paragraph recorded above written in the left margin and beginning two lines lower than the preceding paragraph. These pages are given as the base text transcribed above. The third page of the manuscript is best described as random working notes and thoughts; the fourth has more finished statements, some of which replicate—or are expanded versions of—the first two pages and some of which are essentially different. Those five separate statements on page four are separated by Agee's lines across the page, are each initially indented as a paragraph, and are recorded below in subsequent footnotes placed in or near their "proper" place, in the estimation of the editor. The author's original underlinings for emphasis are rendered in italics. It is impossible to know if the five statements are preliminary to the base text or additions/supplements to it that Agee was considering. Likewise, no exact date can be established for the manuscript. Agee's handwriting indicates only that it is from his mature years, from the 1930s forward. The manuscript has been given the working title "Agee on Poetry and Life" by its editor, Michael A. Lofaro.

2. This second separated statement on page four seems to expand on Agee's first paragraph, although it moves away from his thoughts on the function of poetry: "Our government is inactive: our society is rotting away; our people claim more and more to despise gain and wealth; we have suffered because we loved it. We still love it. Every man for the State is not a bit better than Every man for himself."

3. The third separated section of page four reads: "The business of the poet is not to reform and not to build or tear down but to attempt to understand and try to record. This is the first distinction he must make: the second is, *what* he is to understand."

4. The first separated section on page four may be an earlier draft of the preceding part of this paragraph and of the previous paragraph: "The human race evolves slowly and certainly: degrades to conditions of evil too practical for itself to bear—and thus changes. Such changes are necessary and inevitable; but they do not go deep: a changed structure of society may change the ways of daily life, to some extent: may even change some of the everyday thinking of some person; but it doesn't change the essential parts of human conduct. No more than [here the passage ends]."

5. The fourth and longest separated passage both expands and overlaps the paragraph in the base text. Also, in the left margin, Agee has written the phrase "the *existence* of," but does not indicate a place for its inclusion. This section reads: "You talk about divorcing art from life. Will you tell me first what life is? Whether it is not, most importantly of all, the nature and destiny of the race? Whether this is not most intimately and thoroughly studied in the short time we have, in watching human beings as they move and think and live—*not* in trying to move them or make them think or change their lives. True art has nothing to do with changing life simply because it *is* life—at its best. The most valuable thing in life so far as we know it. [New paragraph] The matter of who rules and with what justice or injustice is a part of the destiny of the race but (a) it is not the most stable part and (b) it is not the business of the poet to encourage or discourage it. He is to watch it and try to understand it and when he thinks he understands, try to make comments."

6. The fifth, shortest, and last separated passage reads: "Poetry should have passion? O.k. The quickest passion, beyond lust, is anger; and it is easier to write angrily than even lustfully—and *very* easy to write badly."

JAMES AGEE IN CONTEXT

FIGURE 1.1 The Old Mansion by Walker Evans.

FIGURE 1.2 The Erosion by Wright Morris.

ONE

A Writer's View of James Agee, Walker Evans, and Wright Morris

Three "Ways of Seeing"

DAVID MADDEN

Although I edited one of the first four books on James Agee, published four essays and two works of fiction about him, and two books and many articles on Wright Morris, it is more as creative writer than as critic that I embark here upon a comparison of James Agee's and Walker Evans's *Let Us Now Praise Famous Men* and Morris's photo-text books *The Inhabitants* and *The Home Place*.[1] What more can I say? The process of re-seeing, of comparison, has resulted in information that is new to me and in new insights, and consequently a deepening of earlier insights. I have written so much about Morris with a focus upon the art of fiction that I draw upon some of that previous work.

Walker Evans and Wright Morris: Photographers

Because the effect of Walker Evans's sensibility, insights, and photographs upon Wright Morris and James Agee was so deep and lasting, it is relevant to begin by conducting a short comparison of Evans's photographs in *Famous Men* and Morris's photographs in *The Inhabitants* and *The Home Place* before comparing Agee's prose and Morris's prose, from the perspective of a creative writer whose interest in photography is also deep and lasting. What may seem to be negative judgments now and then are intended to be descriptions of similarities and differences as one way to illuminate the works of Evans and Morris.[2]

Evans began photographing seriously in 1928. In 1935, Morris set aside the fiction on which he was working to "buy a camera and take some pictures." As of 1940, thirty-eight of his photographs had been exhibited. "The photography grew out of the writing, not the other way around."[3]

Evans's thirty-one photographs for *Let Us Now Praise Famous Men* appeared in 1941; for the new edition in 1960, he added twenty-nine more. From 1946 to 1992, Morris published seven collections, drawing upon two hundred of his photographs. "Sometimes I wonder how on earth I did so many books," Morris said to me in Venice. "Maybe I didn't do them on earth."

Morris was flattered that Walker Evans chose his photograph of one of the chairs from his novel *The Home Place* for a book called *Quality*, published in 1969.[4] But he objected to his photograph being compared to Evans's photograph of a chair, because "his view is usually that of the commentator, the acute social historian. We each selected the same chair, but for palpably different reasons." Evans stated that the chair "is expressive of the cruelty of rural environment, its stark shearing off of what is minimally human . . . but to my eye and my nature the poignancy of that derivation is moving and appealing. I *love* the chair. Other and more expressive forms lacking, I would accept it as an icon." The chair "arouses in me more complex responses than a sign or a symbol . . . [The] very American blending of facts and artifacts is at the core of my mingling of words and pictures."[5]

For all their similarities in raw material, the differences between Evans's photographs and Morris's are immediately apparent to the eye interested enough to compare them. Evans precedes Morris with images of classical purity that are essentially revealing reports on people and places that the Depression era projected. Morris followed with images that conveyed the purity of revelation. Evans fulfilled assignments; Morris's predisposition was to respond to the mysteries of common objects and places that common people had experienced, and thus inhabited. Evans collected the artifacts, especially signs, that he photographed. "If I have the photograph," says Morris, "I can dispense with the artifact" (*Time Pieces* 91).

True, in very different ways, for Morris and for Agee and Evans is the epigraph for *God's Country and My People* by Samuel Beckett, "From things about to disappear, I turn away in time. To watch them out of sight, no, I can't do it."[6]

In describing his own, Morris describes Evans's perspective as well. "First we make these images to see clearly: then we see clearly what we have made" (*Time Pieces*, 76), By contrast to Morris's and, perhaps, to Evans's, Agee's effort is to remember exactly; then what he remembers is what memory has made.

Morris faced, he said, "the peculiar problem of the photographer of taking pictures of an empty place."[7] But while writing prose vignettes for his book of photographs *The Inhabitants*, he was working on *The Works of Love*, the mystical beginning of which is "In the dry places, men begin to dream. Where the rivers run sand, there is something in man that begins to flow."[8] Agee filled the empty spaces of the three tenant families' landscape and simple lives with aspects of himself, while Evans "recoiled from" both commercial stance and artistic posture."[9] His attitude, working for himself or for *Fortune, Vogue*, and other publications, was about the job itself—to do it or reject doing it.

Evans's photographs of people are among his most memorable. Only one person appears in all of Morris's photographs, except those in his Venice book. Perhaps because of the scope of Evans's work for hire and his overall documentary sensibility, there is much greater subject variety among his photos than among Morris's. The street faces in Evans's Chicago series look more like faces in almost any other city, at that time, that era, than a capturing of faces that situates the viewer in that particular city. But his New York subway portraits, "The Passengers," taken with a hidden camera, are more convincing expressions of compassion than he would ever take later on.[10]

Evans and Morris sometimes took on the same general subject. Evans's 1948 six-page feature for *Vogue,* "Faulkner's Mississippi" is composed of stereotypical exterior scenes that convey little sense of Faulkner's works.[11] Morris's single photograph, "Faulkner Country, Near Oxford, Mississippi, 1940," the second one in *The Inhabitants*, showing massive erosion in the foreground, with a lone decayed house in the background, is far more effective.

Morris, Evans, and others who stick with black-and-white images agree on the effect of color photographs. Morris said that "the color photograph forces upon us the ultimate banality of 'appearances.' That is why we tire of them so quickly. The first effect is dazzling: the total effect is wearying."[12] Walker Evans wrote in an essay that "Color photography is vulgar."[13]

Aside from the fact that the color photographs clash with the full gallery of his other photographs, too many of those in Morris's *Love Affair—A Venetian Journal* (1972) are almost snapshots merely, somewhat inferior in quality, and often of people; it is a minor work in every respect. But he chose a few ancient houses that provide interesting comparison and contrast with his black-and-white works, and the one-page prose pieces touch upon his recurring interests. He called those houses "The unsigned murals of Venice, hung in plein air."[14]

Although Morris planned to use his photographs in a quintet of novels, they appear in only one more work after *The Inhabitants*, in his third book, *The Home*

Place, a novel; a photograph appears opposite each page of a continuous narrative, and with no chapter breaks, rather than short epiphanies, except for a gallery of eleven that ends the novel. In his second, *The Man Who Was There,* and in later novels, he describes in prose a goodly number of photographs.[15] *Origin of a Species* (1992) consists of fifty-five photos from *The Inhabitants* and *The Home Place*, without prose. Morris never reprinted in a collection the close-up image of the wagon wheel that appears in *The Home Place* on page fifty-two, but it turns up, upside down, on the cover of *Ceremony in Lone Tree.*

Remarkably, many of Morris's most famous photographs appear and reappear in seven different books and editions. Morris must have had a wonderful experience choosing photographs for *God's Country and My People*, juxtaposing photographs from *The Inhabitants* with those from *The Home Place*, and imagining new voices, new epiphanies, for each photograph. The lone farmhouse, plate nine, from *The Inhabitants* is the first plate in *God's Country,* with a different epiphany. Did he hunt for a picture for each of the repeated epiphanies? Or did he hunt a photo to fit each text?

Sometimes the reprinted photograph is more complete and of better quality. Many of the photographs in *The Inhabitants* are cropped at the top and on the sides. It is startling to see, in *Wright Morris: Origin of a Species*, "White Barn, Connecticut, 1940" cropped at the top again. That print in *Wright Morris: Photographs and Words* is finer than in *The Inhabitants*.[16]

Morris re-assembled photographs in new sequences for new books over decades. By comparing two prints of the same photo, with a different text for each, we may see and feel the ways the text inspires us to see and feel differently. As one moves about among the seven books of photographs, experiencing Morris's mind, imagination, and consciousness overflowing with images, one may envisage him, with great concentration and deliberation, making selections and positioning, juxtaposing, reversing, and cropping, setting new tasks for himself, imagining the effect on former and on new viewers of each photograph. *God's Country and My People*, says Morris, is "a reconsideration and reappraisal of my photographs"; "both the writer and the photographs undergo a sea change"; "many of the photographs are the same, but the writer has changed."[17] In his works, Agee does not evolve; he seeks the "thing itself," to fix it in amber.

To fit the format for the novel, Morris cropped the photographs (none of which had appeared in *The Inhabitants*) in *The Home Place* (137). One of the best examples, "Dresser with mirror, Southern Indiana, 1950" reappears in *God's*

Country, as the last image listed, showing a dresser with a lamp and a snapshot of a girl, a mirror reflection of a bed in the next room, and a curtain.[18] In *Photographs and Words*, he sacrifices the curtain to favor the reflection of the bed.[19]

About cropping, Evans said, "Stieglitz wouldn't cut a quarter-inch off a frame. I would cut any inches off my frames in order to get a better picture."[20] When cropping, Morris's stress was upon getting, not a better, but a different photograph. Cropping is a form of revision, of editing, and sometimes, as with Dorothea Lange's "Plantation Overseer and His Field Hands, Mississippi Delta, *June 1936*," of deception. She cropped to give the impression of a white man lording over a group of black men.[21] Locked onto a Morris photograph, one is not likely to feel deceived by possible cropping.

Photographer James Alinder asked Morris why he reversed some photographs in later works. "I once actually believed that by reversing information (words, numbers, advertising, etc.) I was rejecting that information."[22] He discovered that, on occasion, he "liked the reversed print better." The magic, he said, was in the darkroom, not in what he saw when he took the photographs, especially after twenty years and reproducing them for *God's Country and My People*.[23]

Evans's declined to call his photographs documents as such, preferring the terms "documentary style," a sense of art hovering unseen. "I lean toward the enchantment, the visual power of the aesthetically rejected object."[24] "The real thing that I am talking about has purity and a certain severity, rigor, simplicity, directness, clarity, and it is without artistic pretension." It is "lyric documentary."[25] Looking at a Morris photograph, one is immediately aware that it is, first and last, a work of art. Evans's photographs, sometimes of the same objects as Morris's, are as intentionally literal, in the highest sense, as classical sculpture and architecture. Examine, for instance, Evans's photograph: "the family standing as if in a frieze on the porch."[26] Morris's photographs convey a mystical aura.

Like Evans, but unlike Agee in his prose, Morris's personality, which suffuses his fiction and nonfiction, is nowhere to be seen in his photographs, his voice unheard. What you see and read are works that convey a sense of anonymity, of impersonality. The unblinking camera eye shutters, the emulsion takes hold, the artist acts, then withdraws. What looks real is merely a distant relative to reality, as if excavated among ruins. Paradoxically, the photograph is not overtly art *per se*, while the accompanying epiphanies are indeed works of prose art.

Unlike with Evans, there is no what, when, where, why, or how in Morris's photos; they do not refer or allude to facts. Morris says, "In aesthetic terms, facts are those sensations that have been convincingly processed by the imagination. They are the materials, the artifacts, so to speak, that we actually possess."[27] His photographs convey spiritual qualities. " Much of what the inhabitants are, their particular ways of life, their values, their feelings, can be rendered by the visual aspect of the material things among which they live and die . . . The objects, imbued with the personalities of the inhabitants, become, in essence, inhabited and holy; their factuality reveals a spiritual quality."[28]

His discussion of the effect of Evans's 220 photographs in *First and Last* (1978)[29] suggests that Morris thought long and hard over time about Evans's photographs.[30] He describes lucidly the nature of Evans's work. But the collection itself gives no information. "In Evans's book we need words to clarify what it is we see and to inhibit much that we might imagine. . . . Words can be as intrusive in their absence as in their presence . . . Some of Evans's photographs are familiar to people who couldn't care less who took them: the portraits in *Let Us Now Praise Famous Men*." For instance, "The images will never be free of the Great Depression. Nor will the photographs themselves ever resolve or clarify their conflicting impressions." They "do not speak to Americans of human realities but of social conditions to be remedied." They "have helped shape our image of what is real, and as this image hardens to a cliché, it now obstructs the emergence of what is actually there."[31]

I have always thought of Evans's many photographs of signs, standing alone or with people, among buildings, and in poverty, serving as contexts for social criticism—punning, ironic, paradoxical signs—the same way I have thought of most photographs of signs, as being too easy, shallow, and somewhat cheap. Very few signs show up in Morris's books, but they are a kind of fetish for Evans, favored as the last page in *Evans at Work.*

"The similarities of all photographs are greater than their real or imagined difference," Morris declares.[32] As tough guy novelist James M. Cain used to say to me, "Good, Madden. If true." To my eye, Morris's photographs are not like any others. The best gauges for me of differences between Evans's photographs and Morris's are those that are similar. The eyes of both Morris and Evans were drawn to many of the same types of images, to similar exterior and interior scenes, and to objects, or artifacts; kitchen views, old and simple churches, closed doors, doorways, mysterious windows, gates, litter, junk, building facades, vernacular houses, small buildings, such as outhouses, many types of chairs, old shoes, graves, shacks, grand houses in ruin, hanging clothes, curtains, fire plugs, steps, grain elevators, windmills, Jute boxes, water buckets, eggs, and pin cushions, among numerous others.

Compare a stove in Nebraska in Morris's *The Home Place,* page twenty-six, to a stove by Evans in Nova Scotia.[33] To Evans, photographs of tools and townscapes were evidence of things abandoned. Morris favored mirrors. He brought photograph and text back together for the first time in thirty-two years, but only one, "Reflections in Oval mirror, *The Home Place*, 1947: plate 37:" it is the same image for each chapter of his final novel *Plains Song*.[34]

Evans pointed his camera at many junky, old cars to illustrate as factual evidence the regrettable conditions of poverty; for Morris, cars were, to borrow Evans's own memorable phrase, "radiant raw material." Another such Evans phrase is "visual mindedness." Although Evans took a formal photograph of a single, very old, small truck against a white house background, somewhat similar to Morris's such shots, his photograph of many similar black cars parked fender to fender on both sides of a wide avenue in Saratoga Springs—one of my favorites—suggests more interest in decorative, compositional values than in a feeling for cars. Morris would never have taken such a shot.

Evans's faces and bodies, solo or in groups, look in some ways like the rustic architecture in the background or the landscapes or an interior object. A haunting example is an image in the twenty-seventh photograph in the 1960 edition of *Famous Men* of a pathetic woman, cropped to isolate her to expose her misery as a fact of poverty, alone, wearing a ragged homemade tent-like garment. Considered as an object, she resembles the bed in which she sleeps. As an expression of the sleeper, Morris would focus only on the bed itself.[35]

On the *Famous Men* panel at St. Andrews Episcopal School near Sewanee during Agee Week in 1972, I said, and reaffirm, that it were better had Agee taken photographs himself, or left them out, the book itself being heavily loaded with his prose pictures. Great though they are, in this context, Evans's photographs seem artificial."[36] Partly perhaps because Evans's photos have the look of someone having been sent there to take photographs. They fit that aspect of Agee's passages that derive from his basic journalistic fact-fixation, but are alien to the spirit of his lyrical passages. The effect of that disjunction is compounded by the addition in 1960 of twenty-nine photographs, as previously noted. One of the differences between the thirty-one photos in the first edition and the twenty-nine Evans added in the second is the shift away from the two farms to the towns, an attempt perhaps—ill-considered—to create context. Agee himself devotes relatively little space to his trips in to town.

In *Famous Men*, Agee talks a great deal about photography and often imagines metaphors and similes from photography (11). "The importance and dignity of actuality and the attempt to reproduce and analyze the actual . . . [the] still and moving cameras are the strongest instruments and symbols" (245). As one wonders whether it so happens that Agee describes in his prose some of the same images that Evans photographed, one may wonder whether Agee watched Evans take photographs, and then saw developed photographs during the time he was writing the prose. Agee describes things similar to what we see in Evans's photos, but does not comment on the photographs directly. Agee may seem to comment on an Evans photograph, but he may have contemplated the scene before Walker took the photograph.[37] A phrase in the footnote that appears on page 201—"much better recorded in photographs for which there is no room in this volume."—is rather odd considering `it is unlikely that Evans was assigned after Agee wrote this footnote.

I am inclined to modify a statement I made in 1981. "A touchstone combination is Walker Evans's cool eye and James Agee's 'burning heart.'"[38] Evans's photographs record images. Journalist Agee's words record facts "of the case" (his phrase), even as he also employs similes, metaphors, and other rhetorical devices.

In 1948, Evans was mentoring photographer Helen Levitt at the same time as Agee worked with her and her sister Janice Loeb shooting a sixteen-minute silent movie "In the Street" in the Spanish Harlem section of New York City. Imagining what Agee brought into his participation in the filming of that movie, out of his interest in photographs and moving pictures, enhances in yet another way an understanding of his temperament and sensibility. Images nabbed from that movie would make a haunting book. One sees in his works that Agee was profoundly interested in the effects of photography, but I found no record of his having taken pictures, not even snapshots, himself. That he was one of three cinematographers who captured moving images for "In the Street" would suggest his photographic ability, if only we knew which images were his.[39] Likewise, mindful of the cross-pollination of the two mediums in *The Home Place*, one may see what Morris means when he says that, as he writes fiction, he uses a "camera-eye voice," attempting "to see what the camera would see."[40]

The Visions of James Agee and Wright Morris

Before taking up the major topic, the art of prose, comparing Agee and Morris as to their visions of morality, religion, politics, intellect, art in general, and journalism will provide contexts for my comments and insights. And again, what may seem like negative comparisons are intended to be descriptions of similarities and differences as one way to illuminate the works of Agee and Morris. For me, "Only what is abusable is usable."[41] Let us fully enjoy the paradox that the contradictions, pretensions, and all the other elements conventionally considered as faults in a writing, are *experiences* for the reader that contribute to the overall magnificence of *Famous Men*.

Agee would have seen reviews of Morris's works in *Time* and *Newsweek*. Having read the 1941 *Famous Men*, Morris was predisposed to be responsive to the spell Agee cast when talking to a group. Morris memorably met him, at one of those times when Agee was famously holding forth with insights and anecdotes at a gathering.

> One humid summer evening, Double-dukes [a writer friend] escorted me to the apartment of a friend who taught at Columbia, where I would meet James Agee. They were discussing, quietly but intensely, Celine's *Journey to the End of the Night*. Agee admired it extravagantly. His friend's appreciation was qualified. They were so much at ease with this writer and his book, I was reluctant to intrude on their discussion. Agee was very Southern, to my eye and ear, a poet in every vibrant strand of his nature. He was wearing a blue work shirt, khaki pants, and the rough farm work shoes of a sharecropper. I liked his quiet manner, his fine sad eyes, his well-bred face. *Let Us Now Praise Famous Men* had not as yet been published, but this brief event with Agee would contribute much to my reading.[42]

Morris credits the photographs in *Famous* Men with stimulating an understanding of his own photographic ventures: "A few years later, when I had read James Agee's *Let Us Now Praise Famous Men* and saw Walker Evans's accompanying photographs of sharecroppers, I would fully appreciate the wide range of impressions I had just experienced" (*A Cloak of Light*, 63). Agee's effect on young Morris was so lasting that, as Joseph Wydeven insists, he gave to the title character of *The Man Who Was There* the name Agee, who made a profound impression upon all who met him, and later even people who only heard others talk of him, that paradoxically he was most the man who was there when he was missing in action, a hero to his witnesses.[43] Much about this Agee suggests to me Morris's own childhood and young manhood.[44]

Agee lived (for free, taking along his pet goat, at the house of a friend's in-laws) at 179 St. James Place, in Clinton Hill, Brooklyn, for a few months in 1938–1939, while at work on "Brooklyn Is: Southeast of the Island: Travel Notes."[45] In 1941, finishing *The Inhabitants,* Morris lived at 196 Columbia Heights in the Brooklyn neighborhood where Hart Crane, Thomas Wolfe, and Agee had lived.[46] Maybe Morris's encounter with Agee happened in Brooklyn Heights.

Morris himself was a memorable talker. Critic Granville Hicks remembers the first impression Morris made on him. "He hadn't been in the house half an hour before Dorothy and I knew that he was one of the best talkers we had ever encountered, remarkably well informed in literary matters and completely serious about his work, but a great man for laughter." And Hicks, a champion of Morris's writing, had great praise for his way of giving a talk at a conference.[47]

In *The Inhabitants* and *The Home Place,* and ever after, Morris posed for himself, quite personally, "the perennial question, What is an American?" By contrast, the question that obsessed Agee was "What and who am I?" Morris acknowledges that, as Americans, "Nothing interests us quite as much as ourselves."[48]

Similar moral questions also arise often in Agee's *Famous Men* and in Morris's fiction and nonfiction. They worried about violating privacy, Agee in agony, Morris as a serious consideration, especially involving rural folk.

Both Morris, in a sort of Midwestern, improvised way, and Agee, within Episcopalian structures, were very religious in their youths, and retained strong religious and moral attitudes in unconventional ways in life and art. In adulthood, they remained profoundly, although not overtly, religious. His old friend Robert Fitzgerald remembered Agee as having "a religious sense of life."[49] In "Part Three, Inductions," Agee quotes, "I will go unto the altar of God . . . Upon the harp will I give thanks . . . " (359–60). Throughout *Famous Men,* Agee engages in religious terminology—direct and metaphorical. He calls one section "Introit," a psalm or antiphon sung or said while the priest approaches the altar for the Eucharist (393). He invokes Jesus, "And seeing the multitudes, he went up into a mountain," where he delivered the Sermon on the Mount (81). He ends that section with the Lord's Prayer. Near the end of the book, he quotes the "let us now praise famous men" passage from Ecclesiasticus (445).

A motif in Agee's works and in Morris's photographs and prose are images of mirrors that are mystical in personal ways for Agee throughout *Famous Men* and evocative of the lives of characters in Morris's works. In "On the Porch: 3," Agee invokes a mirror image: "like the exchange of two mirrors laid face to face" (463). It appears also in Agee's "The Truce."

> So we look, and so love passes:
> Take two flat quicksilvered glasses,
> Press each to each the mirroring planes,
> You naught can see, but much remains.
>
> "Where two pities stand displayed, /Shade shall mirror endless shade."[50]

Mirrors are a major feature later in *The Morning Watch*: "reflecting like mirrors locked face to face."[51] He looks deep into himself at "good and evil, as if they were mirrors laid face to face" (79). "The bureau, squared on a corner, and its blind mirror receiving, reflecting, the blindness of the bed" (84). "Reflecting like mirrors locked face to face" appears also in *A Way of Seeing*.[52] Agee's second wife, Alma Mailman, quotes the mirror image as representing Agee's relationships with his mentor Father Flye, whom she neither liked nor trusted, and with Walker Evans, with whom she was shy and afraid, but she said that the image did not represent her own relationship with Agee.[53]

In *The Morning Watch*, one of the most overtly religious works of fiction in American literature, Agee comes closest to creating a work of art. Its flaw is that its fine style is overwrought on a level too much higher than its juvenile protagonist's mind. Agee's longtime friend Dwight Macdonald said that the style of *The Morning Watch* is far too preciously poetic, like some passages in *Famous Men*. The narrator's *agenbite of inwit* makes it less a companion of *A Death in the Family* than of *Famous Men*, about which Father Flye told Agee, "I call it in a true sense deeply religious."[54]

In *Famous Men*, Agee tells us that, as a child at St. Andrews, he stood "at the altar at earliest lonely Mass, whose words were thrilling brooks of music and whose motions, a grave dance: and there between spread hands the body and the blood of Christ was created among words and lifted before God . . ." (89). Father Flye read that long paragraph at Agee Week at St. Andrews.

Very like Agee often in *Famous Men*, but in no way like Morris in his memoir *A Cloak of Light*, the boy Richard feels an "almost worshipping delight and awe" (*Morning Watch* 108). "Who wants to be *good*. *I* do, he answered himself" (42). Agee expressed the same desire to Father Flye. Richard feels an "affectionate scorn" for his vanities and vainglory (51). He identifies with those who betrayed

Christ (66). Doubting his feeling of contrition, he desires absolution (52, 59). He feels "self-esteem" fall from him (78). He cries out for forgiveness (118). He makes a "tally of the sins he must soon confess" (61). But he fears that confessing may be "pride . . . a mortal sin" (93). Even so, Richard thought that "he himself might aspire to actual sainthood," aware that it was "an inordinate ambition" (48, 38). "*I've got the wounds*!" he cries, exulting (77).[55]

Morris, too, had a saintly period, when he was a teenager, working at the YMCA in Chicago. The director's "feeling was that I was chosen" for a future in Christian service. "Boys just naturally looked up to me." Those few who did not envied his "Christian character."[56] He would have understood Richard's pride in *The Morning Watch*, but not his esoteric agony. "I just naturally assumed that when they all knew better they would be reading the Bible my way."[57] He briefly attended a Seventh Day Adventist college. "A budding Evangelist myself, I enjoyed making converts. Here at the college my audience was captive."[58] Regarding him as a disruptive influence, the dean asked him to leave. He did not want to, but he returned to the Chicago Y. Although compassion is often assumed, implied, or quietly alluded to throughout much of his fiction, a good many of Morris's protagonists achieve what I call "the moment of compassion." Compassion is the constant, prevailing or pervasive thematic expression on almost every page of *Famous Men*.

In "The Young Dickens," Graham Greene declares that "the creative writer perceives his world once and for all in childhood and adolescence, and his whole career is an effort to illustrate his private world in terms of the great public world we all share."[59] That statement is true of both Agee and Morris.

Agee refers to himself and Evans as spies. "God's spy" is a more apt term for the overall transcendent effect of his achievement of a mystical dimension (xxi). The sex in *Famous Men* never quite rises to the level of the mystical, certainly in the mediocre poem that ends with "O thou girl's breasts." Novelist Frederick Manfred was so moved by the passage that begins "All this while something very important to me is happening, and this is between me and Louise" (400) that he read it performatively at Agee Week (400).[60] Early in the book, Agee imagines group sex with Emma Woods and George Gudger and himself and Walker (62).

Agee and Morris were lukewarm on political passion. Agee's cranky political responses to the *Partisan Review*'s May 1939 questionnaire, "Some Questions Which Face American Writers Today," is flippantly entitled: "Intermission: Conversation in the Lobby" (349–57). The overall tone and some of the self-righteous comments render this section God-awful; or, to put it more moderately, embarrassing. Why he suddenly included a name-dropping list only he and God knew: "Christ, Blake, Whitman, Crane, Melville, Kafka, Joyce, Gide, Beethoven, Eisenstein, Chaplin, Miller, Evans, Levitt, Celine, Swift," adding family albums, postcards, Brady's photographs, "everybody's letters," and race records (353).

Agee states, "I am a communist" (249). Later, he writes, "'I find in retrospect' that I have forms of allegiance or part-allegiance to Catholicism and to the communist party. I felt less and less at ease with them and I am done with them" (355). Agee declared that he was anti-politics, but he was deeply, intellectually, critical of politics. "Workers of the world, unite and fight. You have nothing to lose but your chains, and a world to win." Then Agee declares, "Neither these words or the authors are the property of any political party, faith or faction."[61]

Morris's nonfiction is full of direct and indirect political concerns, but his only fiction that deals directly with politics is *The Huge Season*, especially the sections that focus on Foley, the "professor of dead languages," and the McCarthy hearings of the 1950s.[62]

Thinking about Agee and Morris, I quite naturally think of F. Scott Fitzgerald's test of a first-rate intelligence: "The ability to hold two opposed ideas in the mind at the same time and still retain the ability to function."[63] Reading *Famous Men*, we are witness to Agee's sustained but fitful struggle to pass such a test. Reading Morris is to see at work a mind that seems already to have passed Fitzgerald's test, at least with a C+.

Morris's phrase "the resonant density of the mind of James" might apply not so much to his own mind as to Agee's. "An impression, for James, is nothing less than the thing itself." In "an act of possession," James created something that had "an anonymous air of permanence."[64]

In *Famous Men*, Agee makes many fiercely anti-intellectual declarations. Even so, the last line of his collection of poems, in a note, is in the intellectual vein: "to preach seems valid and obligatory" (179). The fingerprints of intellectual ecstasy are all over *Famous Men*. He describes his conception of the book and his task writing it, and, repeatedly, his hostility toward art and intellect, in very abstract intellectual terms: "the simultaneity in existence of all of its rooms in their exact structures and mutual relationships in space" (183) is "a symmetry sensitive to so many syncopations of chance" (230). "This asymmetry now seems to us to extend itself into a worrying . . . " (231). Generally, one feels a simultaneity of Agee's expressions of his personal feelings and his journalistic descriptions of the actual scene.

Artistic technique informs the creative personality of the writer, as with Morris. With Agee in *Famous Men*, force of personality silences questions of technique. Reading Morris, the reader hears a voice that the craft of fiction created. Reading Agee, one hears his actual voice, lucidly, as it sounded memorably, his friends tell us, in his life.[65]

The three "On the Porch" sections are very personal, subjective interludes, in which Agee ponders theories of art. He expresses his opposition to art as fervently, but intellectually articulated, as he rails against the intellect (15). "Above all else: in God's name don't think of it as Art" (11). More calmly, wittily, Morris, too, was intolerant of the so-called pretenses of art, but did not go so far as Agee went. "If I could do it," Agee says, "I'd do no writing at all here. It would be photographs; the rest would be fragments of cloth, bits of cotton, lumps of earth . . ." (13).

Commenting on excessive sentimentality in *Famous Men*, James Ward Lee, on a panel during Agee Week, said, paraphrasing J. D. Salinger, that Agee seemed to be "more concerned with God's creatures than God is."[66] The fundamental ambiguities arising from his dual spheres of interest may incline one to wonder whether the operative word is "seemed." In Morris, sentimentality is not detectable, and even nostalgia is organic in *The Inhabitants* and *The Home Place*.

"The artist in exile wants to feel akin to the folks left behind," writes Morris, "but returning, he is still an outsider." For Uncle Harry and Aunt Clara, Clyde Muncy (Morris), as a living artifact of their past, lacked authenticity.[67] In his relatively few works, Agee was obsessed with Tennessee and Alabama country experiences, real and imagined. In his twenty-nine works of fiction and nonfiction, Morris was perhaps even more obsessed with his rural and small-town Nebraska's real and imagined experiences. "*The Inhabitants* and *The Home Place* grew out of the plains just as I did, and they are an experiment in the way I am also an experiment."[68]

In a tone of desperation, Agee writes, "I certainly felt that they were my own people, and wanted them to be, more than any other kind of people in the world"—and he hopes they feel the same. That had been for a long time his feeling about his family, which produced a longing to write "the Book" or "This Book," as he called the autobiographical narrative of his life; *A Death in the Family* is but a part of it.[69] One feels that kind of longing, subtler, in Morris's *The Home Place*. "All through school, I was apt to confuse Grandfather Cropper [a train fireman] with all the Greek heroes. . . . I suppose an epic is how you feel about something."[70]

Agee's original title of his article for *Fortune* magazine, *Three Tenant Families*, emphasizes his primary role as journalist, compared with which the title *Let Us Now Praise Famous Men* seems limited, if not contrived.[71] Does he really praise tenant farmers, who should, I suppose, be famous as well as praised? Morris's four journalistic articles for *Holiday* are firmly in the stylistic fabric of his fiction. The fabric is nowhere rent, not even when he gets into literary matters in four books: *The Territory Ahead* (1958) *A Bill of Rights, A Bill of Wrongs, A Bill of Goods* (1968), *About Fiction* (1975), and *Earthly Delights, Unearthly Adornments* (1978).

Coming upon them in a cranky mood, one might feel that some of Agee's all caps subtitles are pretentious: RECESSIONAL AND VORTEX (212), INTROIT (393), INDUCTIONS (361), A DEFINITION (454). "Part Two: Some Findings and Comments" takes up "Money" and other documentary subjects for 245 pages, with intellectual interludes now and then (113–358). For instance, "Clothing" is the title of a list with commentary on some of the clothes the members of the families wore (255–98). Agee's calling a section on a page by itself late in the book "WORK," and then beginning it with "To come devotedly into the depths of a subject . . ." and quickly returning to the theme of his "shame" in failing to do it justice and his "unworthiness" for the task anyway is a usable example with which to examine and understand his dual purpose in the book: agonized autobiography and pure journalism (319). Eleven pages later, he gets to work as a journalist, taking up aspects of the work in "Cotton Farming": planting, cultivation, and picking.

Agee inveighs early against what people call "honest journalism." "The very blood and semen of journalism . . . is a broad and successful form of lying" (235). I think that very thing is what he strives to achieve throughout, to lift journalism to a higher level, while suffusing it with his own complex emotions (7). "All of this, I repeat, seems to me curious, obscene, terrifying, and unfathomably mysterious," but then he sets about doing it anyhow (8).

Agee's offering "the facts as they are" consorts with "the effort to perceive simply the cruel radiance of what is" (11), as if his vocation were to follow "a lure set out by God."[72] "Agee tried," said Robert Coles, James Agee Professor of Social Ethics at Harvard, to render "an actuality that only God can."[73]

"Persons and Places" is another of Agee's lists that reminds readers of the original journalistic assignment (xxi). He offers a two-page-long Whitmanesque catalog of sensations (227–28). "Notes and Appendices" offers as documents lists of books, projects, photographs, and "other Anglo-Saxon monosyllables," two pages of words, and many famous quotations, without attribution. "One thought fills immensity." "Everything that is is holy" (447, 456–59). Agee's lists and the documents are incongruous but also totally appropriate to his underlying purpose, out of his obsession to get down as a record all the facts of his own experience, not just those of the tenant family members. One finds no lists in Morris's works.

His commentary on Helen Levitt's *A Way of Seeing*, written in the late 1940s, published ten years after Agee's death, reveals that Agee, as anti-intellectual, is ultra-intellectual, speaking of "a new and different kind of reality: aesthetic reality." In the photographic graphic image "the actual is not at all transformed; it is reflected and recorded, within the limits of the camera, with all possible accuracy."[74] But each image is also a record of the fact that two women and one man made choices, decisions, in the late 1940s—juxtapositions of one photo to another, the drama of what to cut, what to keep, and so on. "The artist's task is not to alter the world as the eye sees it into a world of aesthetic reality, but to perceive the aesthetic reality within the actual world, and to make an undisturbed and faithful record of the instant in which this movement of creativeness achieves its most expressive crystallization"[75] This task is true to the viewer of photographs and text in *Famous Me*n as well: "the static work is generally the richest in meditativeness" (5). This is simply interesting: "the volatile work is nearly always lyrical" (5). And so is this: the photographs convey "a quality of mystery" (6). The "pure spontaneity of true folk art" is true of the people in the movie, but not of filmmakers (5). Agee compliments Helen Levitt. "Like most good artists Miss Levitt is no intellectual and no theorist." But that is what Agee himself effectively is in this essay.[76]

Agee does not comment on photographs in *Famous Men*, but he comments directly, although lyrically, on many of Helen Levitt's photographs in *A Way of Seeing*. He begins commentary slowly, then in the final pages takes up and quickly describes photographs of people in clusters, as in a quickened dance: "Dancing, indeed, is implicit in nearly all that they do—as in the heroic frieze of [19] [stet] and the centrifugal, fire-dance fury of [21]; or with the exquisite dignity of the greatest of dancers, in the image of the solitary duelist [23]."[77]

In his on-screen written preface to the silent movie "In the Street," Agee stresses imagery. "The streets of the poor quarters of the great cities are above all a theater, and a battleground. There unaware and unnoticed, every human being is a poet, a masker, a warrior, a dancer." He projects "an image of human existence. The attempt in this short film is to capture this image."[78] Meanwhile, in 1948, Wright Morris was caught up in a swarm of imagined and actual images, living in

Haverford and later in Wayne, Pennsylvania, writing *The Home Place*, *The World in the Attic*, a new draft of *The Works of Love*, and taking photographs at his Uncle Harry's farm in Norfolk, Nebraska.[79]

Writing a good deal about the camera and moving pictures, Agee comes up with many camera metaphors: "it is emerging like a print in a tank" (87). In turning away from "digestion into art," one finds salvation in the camera, "the central instrument of our time" (11). He advocates "the importance and dignity of actuality and the attempt to reproduce and analyze the actual," to achieve which "the still and moving cameras are the strongest instruments and symbols," a new "way of seeing" (245). Mindful of Agee's argument, one might think, as one looks at a Morris photograph, that Agee has described the nature and effect of Morris's work. But no, Morris's literary choices and photographic takes convey simultaneously a purity and a mystic quality, not simply "the radiance of what is."

Agee and Morris and the Art of Prose

Comparing themes, techniques, including style, and other elements in *Famous Men* and in *The Inhabitants* and *The Home Place* is a fundamental way of seeing some similarities and differences between Agee and Morris as writers of prose. There is enough agreement that *Famous Men* is a major work of what has been called creative nonfiction for six decades now to justify my comparing it with Morris's fiction.[80]

After seventy years of doing New Criticism in many works of criticism, some of it innovative, I am still doing it. I simultaneously write here as a critic and a fictionist. But I call upon Mark Schorer to set the course. In "Technique as Discovery," his famous essay that has influenced both writers and critics, Schorer wrote,

> When we speak of technique, then, we speak of nearly everything.
>
> For technique is the means by which the author's experience, which is his subject matter, compels him to attend to it; technique is the only means he has of discovering, exploring, developing his subject, of conveying its meaning, and, finally, of evaluating it.[81]

And, "Although Morris never takes his eyes off the berserk elements in the American character," I wrote in 1967, "the style he uses . . . is the most perfectly controlled in contemporary American literature."[82]

Looking at and reading any of Morris's works of fiction, one feels certain that he wrote out of a well-articulated and lucid concept. Except maybe for his movie scripts, Agee does not seem to have worked from an orchestrated conceptualization of his raw material. In a work of art, structure and all other elements and technique derive from vision. One can readily see and follow in all of Morris's works a "vision-structure." In Agee, one finds no governing vision. Rather than visions, Agee seems to have been enamored of interesting notions, as his long list of projects in his Guggenheim application illustrates. Agee's structure by the application of labels in *Famous Men* may divert readers from the fact that instead of the developing of a concept and vision, we witness the amorphous lunging of personality. "With subjective, poetic language, Agee groped painfully, shame-ridden, for a metaphysical concept about the Alabama sharecropper, his landscape and artifacts."[83]

Many of Morris's characters attempt to maintain connection with the past, or with something permanent, through artifacts. Archetypal activities such as ceremonies, funerals, singing, and bullfights, and ritual and gesture, elements that provide a means of making connections among people, permeate Morris's works. "The unity of elements in his novels depends upon an organic structure for which time is the generative principle."[84]

The first and very important technical decision the fiction writer must make is what point of view to employ; it determines all other technical elements, especially style. "Every writer who is sufficiently self-aware to know what he is doing, and how he does it, sooner or later is confronted with the dictates of style."[85] Most of Morris's fiction is rendered in what Henry James calls "third person, central intelligence," from which he very seldom deviates, in a style that fits the point of view character. In first-person narratives, such as *My Uncle Dudley*,[86] his first novel, *The Home Place*, his second, and *Love Among the Cannibals*[87] his ninth, very different vocabularies fit the age and character of the narrators.

The omniscient narrator is unbound. Oddly, although Agee's first-person narration certainly derives from his high style, his rhetorical mind, and rhapsodic poetic sensibility, it is as rich as the finest fiction omniscient narrators I know—Dickens, Melville, and Woolf in the "Time Passes" section of *To the Lighthouse*. But Agee too often seems to indulge in pure lyrical rhetoric for its own sake, so that what we experience is a mind in action, not its subject. "Here we have two, each crucified, further crucify one another upon the shallow pleasure of an iron bed and instigate in a woman's belly a crucifixion of cell and whiplashed sperm"

(102–03). The style is excellent, but one may feel that exalted language describing the poor robs them of their actual humanity and dignity.

William Gass once severely stressed the all-important function of style when he held a large audience of major writers spellbound with a two-hour lecture on Gertrude Stein's use of the word "and," and further said of his own fiction, "I don't write novels, I write words." Stepping out from under the shadows of Shakespeare, Spencer, Donne, Gerard Manly Hopkins, and Hart Crane, among others, Agee the young poet made a great lunge at poetic art that bewitched the Yale Younger Poets judge Archibald MacLeish. For the reader, *Permit Me Voyage* can be, however, simply a deep immersion in language.[88] Morris cautions that "Immersion is immolation."[89] Immersion in the past or in oneself is immolation. No writer I know ever immersed himself so deeply in his own consciousness (and unconsciousness) as Agee, but "immolation" is perhaps too strong a word.

I "throw light on the tension it is the nature of writing to examine and relieve . . . ," says Morris. "So I believe in shearing off. In working and in traveling light, I like a minimum of words arranged for a maximum effect."[90] Early in my reading of Morris, I told him that his underwriting sometimes left me adrift. "Underwriting—which seems to be a species of underwater swimming—has its many disadvantages, and that is one. Is the pool empty? That is how it often looks"[91] was his answer to me.

Superlatives such as this one—"the streets under their lifted lamps lie void of eternity"—contradict Agee's stress on "what is." Both Morris and Agee play upon words and phrases, Morris both seriously and playfully, but Agee is almost always serious.

Both Agee and Morris are masterful image-makers. A needle is an artifact to Agee. The wall and the mantel "create a shrine and altar" (162). "On a cloth at center, a small fluted green glass bowl in which sits a white china swan" (163). "In a split in the bottom of the drawer, a small bright needle, pointed north, as the swan above it is" (169). "[T]he swan, the hidden needle, hold their course . . . The whole home is lifted before the approach of darkness as a boat and as a sacrament" (220). Elements similar to Agee's word image are seen in a photograph on page 118 of Morris's *The Home Place*: three large needles, in one of which is threaded thick black thread, stuck in a large, ragged-edged, burlap-textured, homemade cushion, amidst a constellation of pin heads. Opposite, Morris, as is his general practice, lets an old woman, who perhaps has made the cushion, talk, making no reference to the improvised pincushion. The effect is that we are looking at a supremely practical artifact that enhances not only what the old woman says but also the effect of all the other images in the novel.

Although Agee repeats certain images throughout, each of them appears in isolation; lacking cohesion, they are mere repetition. He does not create a pattern of images, metaphors, and similes as motifs that contribute incrementally to an overall effect. In each of Morris's works, as in any fiction that is a work of art, what I call a charged image, discharges its power gradually, activating and reactivating all the other techniques and elements as the story unfolds.[92] For *The Home Place*, Ed's sagging bed in a photograph and text is a cogent example of a charged image (*THP* 134–35).

Morris embraces clichés, but in order, within a prepared context, to resurrect their original vitality rather than simply record them. While one may search Agee in vain for a cliché, the Morris technique of transforming the cliché would probably strike Agee as another violation of the purity of "what is." "It is style that sets the cliché," says Morris."[93] "Cliches, bless them, both destroy life—and make it possible."[94] "Character . . . is primarily an imaginative act, a fiction. . . . It is the fiction that shapes the facts."[95] "The cliché told the story." "I seek to make my own what I have inherited as clichés." "Every cliché once has its moment of truth. At the moment of conception it was a new and wonderful thing"—the word made flesh.[96] The cliché serves "the purpose of almost every technical device: it characterizes, enhances mood, evokes time and place, points up dialog . . . expresses modes of transformation, revelation, and resurrection; it is revealed in gesture and in informal ritual; and it acts as a structural aid." [97] The most moving example of a spoken cliché comes when Mrs. Porter in Morris's *The Deep Sleep*, having shocked other survivors of her husband's death with her apparent lack of grief, says, barely within hearing of her grieving daughter, "I'm going to miss your father."[98]

An excellent visual cliché is deceased Uncle Ed's sagging bed in *The Home Place*. "'That's Uncle Ed's room,' I said. My wife stepped up to look at it. Then she backed away, as if she saw someone in the bed." The cliché becomes something more to Clyde Muncy's city-bred wife, Peg, who has denigrated images of life on the farm. "Without saying a word, or snapping her knuckles, my wife turned away" (*THP* 135). Peg's sensibility transforms the cliché into a moment of revelation. In *God's Country*, Morris's authorial voice, characteristically in a serious play upon words, speaks a different epiphany for the same photograph of the bed. "There's little to see, but things leave an impression. It's a matter of time and repetition. As something old wears thin or out, something new wears in."[99]

Certain elements in Agee's style in *Famous Men* and *A Death in the Family* resemble Wolfe's, James's, and Faulkner's, but, unlike those three, and Morris, who minted a single, unvaried style, Agee conjured superb phrases and images, but he had no overall style *per se*. Agee's most abstract passages transcend philosophy, and his most specific style transcends journalism, making *Famous Men* different from any other meditative memoir. We experience the brilliance of Agee's phrasing in these passages: "these wild fugues and floods of grain" textures (145): "the patternings and constellations of the heads of the driven nails" (146); "all surrounding the unlighted lamp which stands in the bare delight in the beauty of a young nude girl" (182); "the state of being we distinguish as 'life' than in the state of being of a stone, the brainless energy of a star" (226). And this perfect simile: "the cow let out a comment like a giant wooden flute" (406).

Some passages may remind one, fifteen years before *The Voyeur*, of Robbe-Grillet's geometrical style. The house, writes Agee,

> stands just sufficiently short of vertical that every leaf of shingle, at its edges, and every edge of horizontal plank (blocked, at each center, with squared verticals) is a most black and cutting ink . . . each texture in the wood, like those of bone, is distinct in the eye as a razor: each nail-head is distinct: each seam and split; and each slight warping; each random knot and knothole. (142)

Another example: "Half between the barn and house, symmetrical to the axis of the house, the henroost and the smokehouse face each other across a bare space of perhaps twelve feet of dirt" (132).[100]

Joseph Conrad wanted "before all, to make you see."[101] Imagery is the soul of fiction (although I tend to say that about every other element of fiction), and both Morris and Agee are in that regard almost equally soulful. Agee cautions against description, "a word to suspect" (238). Again, he often does what he believes a writer should not do. One of the most memorable images in *Famous Men* is of Agee writing. "It is late in a summer night, in a room of a house set deep and solitary in the country; all in this house save myself are sleeping," as he writes with a soft pencil in a child's tablet, "but just now I am entirely focused on the lamp, and light" (49). Smoking Cheroots and occasionally stroking his cat Carbon Copy, Morris kept strictly to an all day, every day, regular, ordinary, and practical writing routine.

In the three books, Agee and Morris take up many of the same subjects, with characteristic differences. Given Morris's early preoccupation and later return to rural and small-town life on the Great Plains and Agee's preoccupation with tenant family life in rural Alabama during roughly the same time period, their attention to and expressions of the meanings of artifacts reflects ways in which their sensibilities and temperaments are both similar and dissimilar.

In *Time Pieces*, Morris includes a photograph I had never seen before: a bench in the foreground, an old model T at the curb behind it, a building behind that. The photograph itself is an object, an artifact, created by the imagination of a writer, that defies the viewer to imagine a person sitting on the bench or driving the car.[102] "Boxes, Western Nebraska, 1947" is a photograph of artifacts that itself becomes an artifact. I had not remembered seeing it before, until I compared plate 45 in first edition of *The Inhabitants* with the same image in the second edition. It replaces a photo of a western fence and church.[103]

The effect of the rural environment upon "the city Muncys" gives rise to a humor that depends upon the quiet collision of ways of life going in opposite directions. Morris's works are full of comic gestures, syntax, and wit, but no satire. I find many successful instances of wit, but I find little humor in Agee. His efforts at satire seem forced and verge on extended sarcasm.

The folksiness of the artifacts Morris photographed and wrote about is merely superficial, more the work of the viewer-reader than of the creator. Self-absorbed, Agee was mainly interested in each of the artifacts he described as yet another occasion to fix upon some aspect of himself. Even so, neither he nor Morris strives to convey the conventional nostalgia that many people seek to satisfy. Both Agee and Morris were afflicted with what I call "a *terrible* nostalgia."

Alfred T. Barson is one of the few Agee critics to speak of Morris's fiction as "more than the *nostalgia* Wright Morris finds common to American writers."[104] That word only *seems* to apply to Agee and Morris: Agee pursued and apprehended the facts of "the case"; Morris's artistic conception of his raw material ameliorated the shallowness of mere nostalgia. Even so, on one level, Agee's phrase fits the Morris of the photo-text books well: "a pleasing, nostalgic drift of memory and imagination" (225). "When I was a kid," says a voice in *The Inhabitants*, "I saw the town through a crack in the grain elevator, an island of trees in a quiet sea of corn" (np). Objects "made on the plains . . . what few there are on the plains, acquire a dense symbolical significance, and certain simple artifacts have a functional and classic purity. . . . They speak for themselves. They would rather talk than be talked about."[105]

Agee and Morris consistently place importance upon artifacts, often describing them in homey or holy or mystical terms. Walker Evans includes a close-up photograph of worn work shoes on bare ground, and Agee, likely wearing work shoes himself, describes such things as shoes, beds, and overalls. "Overalls. They are pronounced overhauls." That line is Agee's, from his super-factual perspective. In the next line, he shifts into lyricism. "Try—I cannot write of it here—to imagine and to know, as against other garments, the difference of their feeling against your body" (265). Further along, Agee's metaphor verges on the mystical. "A new suit of overalls has among its beauties those of a blueprint and they are a map of a working man" (266). Agee continues, as is his habit, to work on getting the artifact in focus through yet another metaphor, this a folksy one. "So that in these new work clothes a man has the shy and silly formal charm of a mail-order-catalogue engraving" (266–67). Not yet satisfied, he tries again. "The changes that age, use, weather, work upon these . . . they are changed into images and marvels of nature" (267). Then he moves on to close-ups of shoes and hats.

In his introduction to *Wright Morris: Photographs and Words*, photographer James Alinder quotes Morris: "'A pattern for living, the blueprint of it, can be seen in the white stitches of the denim, the timepiece stamped like a medallion in the bib of the overalls. Between wearing something in and wearing it out the line is as vague as the receding horizon, and as hard to account for as the missing hairs of a brush.'"[106] Somewhat expressive of Agee's attitude about the three tenant families, Morris wrote, "I saw the American landscape crowded with ruins I wanted to salvage. The depression created a world of objects toward which I felt affectionate and possessive. I ran a high fever of enthusiasm and believed myself chosen to record this history before it was gone."[107]

In *The Home Place*, Morris's full-page photograph of a farmer's roughly worn shoes resting on an old kitchen chair, a flowered worn carpet underneath, appears opposite a page of the narrative that does not refer directly to the shoes but is a meditation on all such artifacts pictured before and after. "Was there, then, something holy about these things? If not, why had I used that word? For holy things, they were ugly enough . . . whatever it was I was feeling, at that moment, was what I expect a thing of beauty to make me feel. To take me out of my self, into the selves of other things" (*THP* 138–43).

Saul Bellow, sitting beside me in the back seat of a car passing through the slum buildings of Cincinnati asked, "Aren't they beautiful?" Having had my character Cassie, a sickly young Harlan, Kentucky girl who fills her room with scavenged junk, say, "It's something about junk that thrills a body's soul,"[108] I was responsive to Bellow's nostalgia. The first line in Albert Camus' first notebook, in 1935, sounds a similar note, "One can, with no romanticism, feel nostalgic for lost poverty."[109]

Agee ponders the distortions of art while granting "the clarifying power in this effort of the memory and the imagination . . . they do both at the same time, clouding in one way the thing they are clearing in another" (232). This phrase has been very meaningful in my own life and writing: the "seining of experience," which art embodies, but Agee declares "for its own, not for art's sake" (233–34). But "Art . . . has nothing to do with life" (366) is the opposite of my own conviction as a writer.

It is the *imaginative act*," says Morris, "—not the action of events, that reveals the artist of stature."[110] Agee says, "What could be more moving, significant or true: every force and hidden chance in the universe has so combined that a certain thing was the way it was" (41). Morris looks at the thing itself as "an act of possession" to achieve and convey a sense of anonymous, impersonal "air of permanence."[111]

Agee the journalist gathering the facts of "the case" laments the "deifying of the imagination" (241). Morris does that, out of sheer character and sensibility more than conscious effort. Journalist as a recording angel, Agee does not imagine. Morris's photographs do not activate imagination. Nor do they record facts. Facts as record seldom survive the first look. Agee's failures lie in his using the imagination only as ways to frame the facts, and he employs his style only to express the personal. His shadow in his image of Ed's car is the only instance of Morris's presence in his photographs—as if simply to say, I was the man who was there—in contrast to Agee, whose presence is everywhere in *Famous Men*.[112]

Morris added a two-page preface to the 1969 reprint of *The Inhabitants*, in which he comments on the effect of the short prose epiphanies that appear opposite each photograph. "I have heard from readers distracted by the photos, and from lookers distracted by the reading, each testifying, inadvertently, to the separate faculties it is the intent of the book to join." That he juxtaposes earlier prose epiphanies to new images supports the idea that the thoughts he imagined neither refer directly to nor depend upon the subjects of the photographs and what they convey. Many or all the epiphanies are first-person, Morris's own voice, it seems, as in *God's Country and My People*. Simultaneously, there is a hovering sense of God too, as spirit and as cliché.

In Boone, North Carolina, I worked on my book about Morris in such a house as the one in the ninth photograph in *The Inhabitants* called "Farmhouse in McCook, Nebraska," and Agee worked on *Famous Men* in such a house—a lone house on the plains, close up to the very grain, my own favorite, to be seen on the wall of my study. In *God's Country*, it is the first photograph, and sets the vision. The tone of the reprinted photograph is lighter, perhaps deliberately. The epiphany for the first one is vernacular, a first-person country voice, that alludes only indirectly to the photograph. "The thing about Grandpa," after he left the plains, "is all you see is where he is from."[113] The second photograph is more expressive of Morris's sensibility, very lyrical, mystical, opening with a somewhat direct comment. "Is it a house or an ark? . . . the last tenants went thataway with the Okies—except for those who stand, immaterial, at the windows, or move about with the creak of hinges. The land has tired of the house but it will not soon be free of the inhabitants."[114] Again, the epiphanies, even those few that most directly allude to the photo opposite, do not make literal contact with the photographs. The photographs retain their own meta-reality.[115]

Given various kinds of reuse, the question arises, Did Morris reuse the same epiphany for different photos, dealing cards out of the same deck? If not, he could have, each coming out of the unbroken flow of his mind for almost fifty years.

Morris "intended the relationship between text and pictures to be poetic, not journalistic." "This novel [*The Home Place*] is almost entirely one of sensibility, of character. Unity lies in viewpoint, attitude, and overall mood."[116] One of the most evocative examples of Morris's photo-epiphanies is the white barn in *The Inhabitants* (np, seventh plate).

> My cane has the carved head of a dog, smooth hollow sockets are his eyes. Walking, I keep my fingers there. I can feel him check me at a rise and lead me where objects fall away. Space is a thing we lean upon. We can feel my son's new love affair as he stoops and tips my head to shave. My wife's patience rises from her hair. We can read a storm and hear a color glow, and in the rain we can smell a sparrow's fear. But to see, they say, is a thing we do not know.
>
> What is there between the branch and the apple when it falls?
>
> We have seen it—we would recognize it anywhere. Yet of an evening we are told nothing is there.[117]

Morris photographed only one person, his Uncle Harry, and only a few times, and always from the back or with his face obscured. "It is my feeling that the absence of people in these photographs enhances their presence in the objects—the structures, the artifacts, even the landscape suggests its appropriate inhabitant."[118] *The Home Place* opens with a frontal image of Uncle Harry, but with his head down, coming out of a barn, holding an inner tube; fifty pages later, we see him from the back, standing, hands clasped behind his back, as if wondering what next needs to be done; then fifty pages from the end, he is sitting at rest in the doorway of the barn, his face in the shadow his straw hat casts. The novel ends with a rear view of him stepping over the threshold into the barn (*THP* 127).

Above each epiphany in *The Inhabitants* appears, in bold, a line in a continuous commentary that begins "It's getting to be harder than ever to tell what an American is—."[119] A view of the ends of logs that suggest a monumental pillar is the last photograph. Below the phrase "What it is to be an American," the epiphany begins with "There's no one thing to cover the people, no one sky."[120] Morris places the same image as the eighth in *God's Country*, shifting to a first-person epiphany, which begins, "At eighty-six, when I first set eyes on him, he stood erect."[121] Having placed it ninth in *The Inhabitants*, Morris came to realize a greater effect for "Farmhouse near McCook, Nebraska, 1940," putting it first in *God's Country*, but it is plate 25 in *Photographs and Words*, where it is sharpest by far.[122]

The photographs in *Structures And Artifacts: 1933–1954* (1975) and *Wright Morris: Photographs and Words* (1982), appear without epiphanies. "Words" refers to a long narrative about Morris himself. All of the following images are also in *The Home Place*, except that three images of a Model T cluster nearly midway (plate 20, plate 21, plate 22): plate 2, clothes on hooks; plate 4, reflections in an oval mirror, which appears repeatedly in *Plains Song*; plate 14, straight-back chair; plate 46, White barn, Connecticut, 1940; plate 48, Faulkner Country, near Oxford, Mississippi, 1940. No page numbers are given for those plates.

Such dilapidated tenant houses as he literally contemplated, inside and out, spending the night in them, sleeping on the inhabitants' beds, inspired Agee to know that kind of beauty of which Victor Hugo famously made the world aware. Having lamented "what I can hardly hope to bear out in the record," Agee then enters into the record that "there can be more beauty and more deep wonder in the standings and spacings of mute furnishings on a bare floor . . . than in any music ever made" (134). Agee raises the vexing question, in a style both formal and poetic, "Are things 'beautiful' which are not intended as such, but which are created in convergences of chance, need, innocence or ignorance, and for entirely irrelevant purposes?" "It is my belief," Agee wrote, "that such houses as these approximate, or at times by chance achieve, an extraordinary 'beauty.' . . . To those who own and create it this 'beauty' is, however, irrelevant and indiscernible . . ." (202–03). Agee is totally in character when he agonizes over whether he is permitted even to declare such perceptions. "But consider this merely as a question raised: for I am in pain and uncertainty as to the answers, and can write no more of it here" (203). A footnote follows immediately, as the agony grows more intense. "The 'sin,' in my present opinion, is in feeling in the least apologetic for perceiving the beauty of the houses." While they would recognize in essence Agee's feelings as their own, neither Hugo nor Morris experienced any such pain for having, in their cases, such convictions. Agee ends "Beauty" with his expressive, perhaps excessive, declaration: "[A]nd the partition wall of the Gudgers' front bedroom IS (sic.) importantly, among other things, a great tragic poem" (204).

A rural farmhouse was an icon for Morris, an image of himself for Agee. Agee, I imagine, would have recognized his own feelings in the epigraphs to Morris's two photo-text books, as expressed in these lines from Henry James in *The American Scene*, which served as epigraph to *The Home Place*: "[O]bjects and places, coherently grouped, disposed for human use and addressed to it, must have a sense of their own, a mystic meaning to give out. . . ." For *The Inhabitants*, Morris chose two epigraphs. Thoreau: "What of architectural beauty I now see, I know has gradually grown from within outward, out of the necessities and character of the indweller, who is the only builder. . . . " Rilke: "Love consists in this/ that two solitudes protect,/ and touch, and greet each other."

From *The Home Place*, here is Morris's own expression of those feelings. "What is it that strikes you about a vacant house? I suppose it has something to do with the fact that any house that's been lived in, any room that's been slept in, is not vacant anymore. From that point on it's forever occupied" (*THP* 132).

The themes Morris and Agee develop in the three books are, again, both similar and significantly dissimilar. In the works of Morris, the predominant thematic concept that gathers around it all other themes and elements is that of the hero and the witness. The hero bewitches those who witness his or her unconventional speech and acts; they become in some ways transformed; the hero seldom benefits. In *The Home Place*, the land itself is the hero. We find no such pervasive theme-structure in *Famous Men*, although Agee is certainly a witness, but very differently. To the extent that the book made Agee a cult hero, one may argue that he was the hero of the land itself and of its people.[123]

The American dream and nightmare and the American east-west conflict is a major Morris theme; he springs out of that concept into an image of the consequences in rural Nebraska. Some old buildings "faced to the west—a row of old men with their hands tied behind them, with blindfolded eyes—facing the firing squad, the careening globe, and the impending flood."[124]

Out of the hero-witness relationship, motivations of nostalgia often devolve into nausea, but the end result may be transformation and resurrection, of the past, into the present, an apprehension of the eternal moment, sometimes with a resolve to face and become a vital part of the future, as with the composer of popular songs witnessing the vitality of a woman he calls The Greek in *Love Among the Cannibals.*[125]

One can readily list the themes and elements in the photo-text works and the novels and short stories of Wright Morris: audacity, resurrection, and transformation, archetypes, artifacts, ceremonies, clichés, stereotypes, visionary concepts, the power of imagination, improvisation, impersonality, living in and out of this world, local color, regionalism, time, mythic elements, mysticism, the Midwest as the navel of the world, nostalgia-nausea, privacy, permanence and impermanence, multiple and alternating points of view structures, the immediate present, the promise and failures of America, the transformation of raw material, technique, style, ritual and gesture, satire, romanticism, rural-urban conflict, social problems, stripping to the essentials, symbolism, the territory ahead, technique as discovery, vision, travel, wisdom of the body, textures, faces, the texture of walls close up, rusty sculpture, fact and fiction, risk, revelation, realism, the real McCoy, connection, Joycean epiphanies, the American character, the American dream, the American scene, the hero and witness relationship, suppressed emotions, gesture, identity, historical forces, life imitates art, love, memory, matriarchy, the Great American Desert, the Great American home, the Great Plains, comic elements, the hero as magnet to witnesses, male-female conflict, and the technical power of prose fragments.

One may, with more effort, derive a similar list from *Famous Men*, but what makes for difficulty in getting a fix on the techniques, themes, and other elements in Agee's book and in his fiction and poetry, excluding the movie reviews and nonfiction articles, the goal of which is immediate clarity, is the journalistic impulse at the core of the book, which works against craft. What controls Morris's imaginative use of themes and elements is indeed craft.

Morris and Agee are similar in their description of beds. For Agee, see page 176, ending with "they spend a third of their lives getting the refreshment and rest of sleep." In "Privacy as a Subject for Photography" (1951), Morris shows two of the photographs he took of beds in rooms on two different farms, one of which showed a white "night pot polished by use, under a bed sagging with invisible sleepers," raising the quandary of "the blurred gap between revelation and exposure." "There is either revelation –or there is invasion." Making a choice, he labeled the one with the pot "rejected," the other, without a pot, "accepted."[126] In *The Home Place*, a similar bed, without a night pot, appears in one of the finest passages in all Morris (*THP* 135). Forty-one years later, without apology, Morris includes both photographs in Wright Morris, *Origin of a Species*, plates 32 and 34. The first photograph ignited a cheap shock of the sacredness of privacy. Some may judge even the second an invasion, but Morris felt that it rose to the level of revelation, and the inclusion of that photograph, with an epiphany opposite, in *The Home Place*, enables the viewer-reader to experience a sense of revelation (*THP* 134–35). To support his argument, Morris cites the work of Evans in *Famous Men*: "[W]here the extremities of privacy are confronted with boldness and delicacy . . . privacy is the subject, and revelation, sometimes nearly intolerable, is the result."[127]

Morris drew upon the phantom circuits of light and time as conductors of revelation. Revelation "becomes . . . the problem of stating what remains unsaid,"[128] somewhat as in this passage, in which Agee and Evans lay on their "backs about two feet apart in silence, our eyes open, listening" ("On the Porch: 2" 228). Agee's awareness of his behavior as "spy" and Evans's as "counterspy" is pervasive. "I am being witness to matters no human being may see" (136). Sometimes Agee deliberately invades the privacy of the families, as when he sneaks into the Gudger house and touches, even sniffs, their bed and clothes, then seems to justify his act by a religious reference to their clothes as "cerements" (169). "Those garments whom I took out, held to my lips, took odor of, and folded and restored so orderly, so reverently as cerements" (188). Agee's mission, seems to be less revelation than benign exposure of himself, even when self-revelation may be his intent. "I am not interested in 'expressing' 'myself' as an 'individual' except when it is suggested that I 'express' someone else" (356). In "On the Porch-3," he ends that section with a seven-page focus on himself and Walker (471).

In two of his works of nonfiction, Morris has Agee and Evans on his mind, as in "Let Us Now Praise Famous Men" (1941), "James Agee/Walker Evans" in *About Fiction*. "Agee welcomes the collaboration of the camera to make visible what defies description," "the consecration of an object through use," which he regards as an artifact. "In Agee, the burden of this intent is religious."[129] And in "James

Agee," in *Earthly Delights, Unearthly Adornments,* Morris writes, "Words have seldom received such a charge of emotion to no other end than a reverence for life. . . . Revelation on this scale is embarrassing, and many readers find the book intolerably poignant. . . . the words evoke the unheard music."[130] Agee often invokes the word "music" to express what he strives to create. "Agee's word picture is detailed and vibrant in a way that exceeds the lens of the camera."[131] "His purpose is liturgical, to exalt in a ritual of purification."[132] He expresses "a reverence for life that is at once earthbound and transcendent. . . . The true reader of Agee is compelled, as in an act of communion, to an expansion of consciousness."[133]

As one of the people involved in creating the celebrated movie "The Quiet One," in *Famous Men,* Agee argues that it is wrong-headed education that blights potential. "The so called natural teachers . . . are at best the servants of unconscious murder" (291). He describes the education of tenant children, attacking specific passages in textbooks (xx, 298–307). "'Education' as it stands is tied in with every bondage I can conceive of" (308). Despite repeated attacks on art, his attack on education includes the lament that "The 'esthetic' is made hateful and is hated beyond all other kinds of 'knowledge'" (311). "In every child who is born, under no matter what circumstances, of no matter what parents, the potentiality of the human race is born again" (289).

If *Famous Men* were a novel, the term "meta-fiction" would fit neatly; even as nonfiction it may be apt. Agee teaches us how to read what he is at the moment writing. "The text was written with reading aloud in mind . . . . Continuously, as music is listened to or a film watched" (xv). In four of his books, Morris tells readers how to read Agee, among other fiction writers. Ironically, few of the folk about whom Agee writes could read his book.[134]

In a long, richly textured passage, Agee shifts his unbearably unachievable task to the reader. Having declared that " . . . it is beyond my power to do," he "leaves to you much of the burden of realizing in each of them what I have wanted to make clear of them as a whole." He invites "you," as his collaborator, to eschew art. "For I must say to you, this is not a work of art or of entertainment, nor will I assume the obligations of the artist or entertainer, but is a human effort which must require human co-operation" (110–11). The agony of the effort to do due justice to writing about *Famous Men* is almost as great as Agee's was in writing it.

Agee insists that "it is important that you should so far as possible forget that this is a book" (246). Well, one may try to, but fortunately, he failed to make readers forget, for millions have long remembered. The pages of his book as a book testify against Agee's declaration. Then comes an Archibald MacLeish "You, Andrew Marvel" kind of lyric: "in the short yet extreme winter of that shadow of itself through which a continuous half the earth twists its surface" (246).

Having told his readers how to write the book, Agee invokes an ending. "But there must be an end to this: a sharp and clean silence: a steep and most serious withdrawal . . . " (99).

Agee not only talks directly to the reader, in "Part Three, Inductions, First Meeting," he speaks directly to members of the families. "Walker had picked up talk with you, Fred" (361). "I must excuse myself this apparent digression because you of whom I write are added to the meaning of this song." Morris very seldom speaks to the reader.

Morris surprised me one day when, sitting in Howard Johnson's the first day I met him, he watched a typical tourist family in Bermuda shorts file into the restaurant. "There go my readers." Who obviously were not. Farmers to whom I lent *The Home Place* showed little interest, including my landlady for the house and shed in the mountains where I wrote my book on Morris. About the reader of fiction, Morris is rather avuncular. "Let's say the reader has bought the book . . . and has set himself down . . . to read it. What makes him think he *can*?" (*About Fiction* 85)

James Agee, Walker Evans: Journalists Wright Morris: Prose Artist

James Agee was primarily a fact-seeking journalist. Wright Morris was an artist, as fiction writer and as photographer. Walker Evans was a master, fact-fixing photographer. Agee and Evans often stated opposition to the intellect and to art but neither fully developed a case. They merely alluded repeatedly to their belief that intellect and art are defective when engaged in a rendering, in words and images, of real life. Ironically, Agee was indeed an intellectual; he was not an artist. Motivated by the mission of the documentarian, Evans, ironically, made images that are works of art. Wright Morris never set out to make a case against intellect or art, but he made rather off-handed, almost parenthetical, negative allusions to intellect and art, while he engaged effectively in sustained intellectual explorations and consistently achieved art in his photographs and fiction. As we read, we feel that Agee inhabited *Famous Men,* in ways that could not be said of Morris and his works, who, the reader may feel, was deeply moved always, but who was always more objective than subjective. Both Agee and Morris were myriad-minded, but Agee was more of a Renaissance man reaching for every medium in which to deploy his thinking and articulate his emotions, while Morris, as writer, stayed pretty much within what Henry James called the House of Fiction.

Notes

1. James Agee and Walker Evans, *Let Us Now Praise Famous Men* (Boston: Houghton Mifflin Company, 1960). I have used the more widely available 1960 edition of *Famous Men* because it contains the order of pictures to which I often refer. Citations to *Famous Men* will be noted parenthetically. Wright Morris, *The Inhabitants* (New York: Charles Scribner's Sons, 1946); Wright Morris, *The Home Place* (New York: Charles Scribner's Sons, 1948); hereafter, I will cite this novel parenthetically as *THP* and give page number(s).

2. Because Morris's seven books of photographs are not as well-known as they deserve, I'll list them here: *The Inhabitants,* 1946; *The Home Place,* 1948; *God's Country and My People* (New York: Harper & Row, Publishers, 1968); *The Inhabitants*, 2nd ed., facsimile reprint (New York: Da Capo Press, 1972); *Love Affair—A Venetian Journal* (New York: Harper & Row, Publishers, 1972); *Structures and Artifacts: 1933–1954* (Lincoln: Sheldon Memorial Art Gallery, Univ. of Nebraska, 1975); *Photographs and Words* (The Friends of Photography, 1982); *Origin of a Species* (San Francisco: San Francisco Museum of Modern Art, 1992). For repeated appearances of Morris and Agee, twice in the same issues, in *New Directions*, see "Text-Photography," 181–82, in "Selected Bibliography," David Madden, *Wright Morris* (New York: Twayne Publishers, 1964).

3. Clarus Backes, ed. *Growing up Western* (New York: Harper Perennial, 1991), 104.

4. Louis Kronenberger, ed. *Quality, Its Images in the Arts* (New York: Atheneum, 1969).

5. Wright Morris, *Time Pieces* (New York: Aperture, 1989), 46–47. Morris identifies neither his chair, from among nine in the novel, nor Evans's.

6. Samuel Beckett, *Molloy* (Paris: Olympia Press, 1955), 14–15.

7. David Madden, "The Great Plains in the Novels of Wright Morris," *Critique* 4 (Winter 1961–62): 13.

8. Wright Morris, *The Works of Love* (New York: Alfred A. Knopf, 1952), 3.

9. Jacket copy of 1960 edition of *Let Us Now Praise Famous Men,* found in paragraph 6. Walker Evans, *Walker Evans at Work* (New York: Harper and Row, 1982), 58.

10. *Walker Evans at Work,* 186–89. Houghton Mifflin published in 1966 a selection of these photographs, made in 1938 and 1941, under the title *Many Are Called,* "With an introductory note written in 1940 by James Agee." *Walker Evans at Work,* 152–61.

11. *Walker Evans at Work,* 170.

12. Wright Morris. *Structures and Artifacts 1933–1954* (Lincoln, NB: Sheldon Memorial Art Gallery, 1975), 117.

13. Quoted in *Walker Evans: Depth of Field,* eds. John T. Field and Heinz Liesbrock (New York: Prestel Publishing, 2015), 310.

14. Wright Morris, *Love Affair--A Venetian Journal* (New York: Harper & Row, 1972), 12.

15. Wright Morris, *The Man Who Was There* (New York: Charles Scribner's Sons, 1945), 63–83, 136–38.

16. Wright Morris, *Photographs & Words*, ed. and with an introduction by James Alinder (The Friends of Photography, in Association with Matrix Publications, 1982), plate 46, "White Barn, Connecticut, 1940."

17. Morris, *Time Pieces*, 30, 89, 90.

18. Morris, *God's Country and My People*, n.p.

19. Morris, *Photographs & Words*, plate 59.

20. Evans, "Katz-Evans Interview," *Walker Evans at Work*, 139.

21. Karen Becker Ohrn, *Dorothea Lange and the Documentary Tradition* (Baton Rouge: Louisiana State UP, 1980), 57–61.

22. Morris, *Time Pieces*, 141.

23. Ibid., 143.

24. Quoted without reference from *Yale Alumni Magazine* in *Walker Evans at Work*, 220.

25. Walker Evans, lecture, 11 March 1964, Yale University, *Walker Evans at Work*, 238.

26. David Madden, "'The Cruel Radiance of What Is': Thoughts on Photographs and the South," *Southern Eye, Southern Mind* (Memphis, TN: The Memphis Academy of Art, 1981), 83.

27. Morris, *Time Pieces*, 47.

28. David Madden, "The Hero and the Witness in Wright Morris's Field of Vision," *Prairie Schooner* 34 (Fall 1960): 267.

29. Walker Evans, *Walker Evans. First and Last* (New York: Harper & Row, 1978).

30. Wright Morris, *Time Pieces*, 61–63.

31. Ibid., 62

32. Ibid., 62.

33. Morris, *Home Place*, 26; *Walker Evans at Work*, 224.

34. Wright Morris, *Plains Song* (New York: Harper & Row Publishers, 1980).

35. "Sharecropper's Wife, Hale County, Alabama, 1936," *Walker Evans*, intro. John Szarkowski (New York: Museum of Modern Art, 1971), 96.

36. David Madden, ed., with Jeffrey J. Folks, *Remembering James Agee.* 2nd ed. (Athens: U of Georgia P, 1997), 122.

37. For instance, see 197, and photos 39; 442, and photograph 11 in the 1961 edition.

38. Madden, "Cruel Radiance of What Is," 82.

39. See "In the Street," https://www.youtube.com/watch?v=z7sfvo38seA

40. Wright Morris, interview, "The Art of Fiction," CXXV, *The Paris Review* 120 (Fall 1991): 91–92.

41. Madden, "Cruel Radiance of What Is," 91.

42. Wright Morris, *A Cloak of Light, Writing My Life* (New York: Harper & Row, 1985), 77.

43. Joseph J. Wydeven, *The Man Who Was There* (New York: Twayne Publishers, 1998), 57.

44. Warren Eyster, one of the editors who prepared the manuscript for *A Death in the Family*, and the silent editor of the two volumes of Agee movie criticism, talked about Agee's effect on people in "Conversations with James Agee," *The Southern Review* 17 (Spring 1981): 346–57.

45. James Agee, *The Collected Short Prose of James Agee* (Boston: Houghton Mifflin Company, 1969), 177. It appeared first in 1968 in *Esquire* as "Brooklyn Is," and, on my recommendation, as a hardcover book, *Brooklyn Is Southeast of the Island: Travel Notes* (New York: Fordham UP, 2005), preface, "Agee's Brooklyn" by Jonathan Letham.

46. Morris, *Time Pieces*, 128.

47. Granville Hicks, *Part of the Truth* (New York: Harcourt, Brace & World, 1965), 280, 286.

48. Wright Morris, "Made in U.S.A.," *The American Scholar* 29 (1960): 483.

49. Agee, *Collected Short Prose*, 23.

50. James Agee, *The Collected Poems of James Agee* (Houghton Mifflin, 1968), 132–33.

51. James Agee, *The Morning Watch* (Boston: Houghton Mifflin Company, 1950), 7.

52. Helen Levitt, with essay by James Agee, *A Way of Seeing* (New York: The Viking Press, 1965), 7.

53. Repeated searches leave me unable to find that quotation again.

54. James Agee, *Letters of James Agee to Father Flye* (1962; Boston: Houghton Mifflin Company, 1971) [previously unpublished letter of Father Flye to Agee]. For ten interviews about Agee, including with his aunt, at the house where my wife and I lived during the first year of our marriage and where, as a kid, Agee often spent the night, see Ross Spears's documentary film *Agee* (1980).

55. One may well wonder whether Agee intended to include *The Morning Watch* in "This Book," his reference to the long autobiographical novel he had planned. Seems so, so see his outline, in *A Death in the Family: A Restoration of the Author's Text*, ed. Michael A. Lofaro (Knoxville: U Tennessee P, 2007), 579.

56. Wright Morris, *Will's Boy* (New York: Harper & Row, 1981), 109.

57. Ibid., 163.

58. Ibid., 167.

59. Graham Greene, "The Young Dickens, *The Lost Childhood, and Other Essays* (New York: Viking P, 1952), 54.

60. Madden, *Remembering James Agee*, 2nd ed., 117–18. Here, on a panel about *Famous Men*, Manfred quoted three sentences from the passage on page 400 in *Famous Men*; later, on another occasion, he read the whole passage.

61. Agee, *Famous Men,* third unmarked page after page xvi.

62. For more by Morris on politics and on social issues, see his *A Bill of Rights, A Bill of Wrongs, A Bill of Goods* (New York: New American Library, 1968).

63. F. Scott Fitzgerald, *The Crack-Up,* ed. Edmund Wilson (New York: New Directions Books, 1945), 69–84.

64. Wright Morris, "Henry James's The American Scene," *Texas Quarterly* 1 (Summer–Autumn 1958): 36, 29, 31.

65. About the time of the breakup of his first marriage, Agee wrote the narration for the movie *The Quiet One,* his voice narrating. But regrettably, Gary Merrill's voice replaced his. *Billboard* published Agee's script for "The Quiet One" in full. https://www.billboard.com/music/magazine. With Helen Levitt's permission, I passed on to the Special Collections Library at the University of

Tennessee, Knoxville, a good copy of her print with Agee's voice narrating. And his voice may be heard on "James Agee—A Portrait," first released in 1971 on two vinyl records and still available (Caedmon Records TC 2042). Moderated by Alistair Cook, Agee debated historian Allan Nevins about his Omnibus Lincoln movie, March 29, 1953, two years before his death, in May 1955. *Omnibus: James Agee's Mr Lincoln and the Civil War.* My impression of Agee's responses do not match Bergreen's; he goes so far as to say there were tears in Agee's eyes; 369, 373–74.

66. Madden, *Remembering James Agee,* 2nd ed., 108.

67. Madden, "Cruel Radiance," 86.

68. Stanley J. Kunitz, ed. *Twentieth Century Authors*, first supplement (New York: H. W. Wilson Company, 1955), 691.

69. James Agee, *A Death in the Family* (New York: McDowell, Obolensky, 1957). In his correspondence and notes, Agee also refers to *Death* as "the book'" in addition to the larger project of his entire life.

70. Morris, *Home Place*, 65.

71. Hugh Davis, ed., "Cotton Tenants" ("The Three Families), in *LUNPFM*, 565–636.

72. "James Agee—A Portrait" (Caedmon Records).

73. David Madden, "The Test of a First-Rate Intelligence: Agee and the Cruel Radiance of What Is," ed. Michael Lofaro, *James Agee Reconsiderations* (Knoxville: U of Tennessee P, 1992), 38.

74. Levitt and Agee, *Way of Seeing,* 4.

75. Ibid.

76. Ibid., 73.

77. Ibid., 75–78.

78. John Wranovics, *Chaplin and Agee* (New York: Palgrave MacMillan, 2005), 79–80.

79. For more about rural life as depicted in *The Home Place,* see Morris's autobiographical short story "The Rites of Spring," in *Real Losses, Imaginary Gains* (New York: Harper & Row, 1976), 165–72.

80. I created the term "creative nonfiction" in 1958 during my first year of teaching. For Agee's and Morris's similarities and differences as fiction writers, a full-scale comparison of Morris's *The Deep Sleep*, how a family dealt with the death of a beloved father and husband the day before his funeral, and Agee's *A Death in the Family* would be so revealing that I am well into doing that in another essay.

81. Mark Schorer, *The World We Imagine* (New York: Farrar, Straus and Giroux, 1968), 3.

82. David Madden, "Wright Morris's *In Orbit*: An Unbroken Series of Poetic Gestures," *The Poetic Image in Six Genres* (Carbondale: Southern Illinois UP, 1969), 160.

83. Madden, "Cruel Radiance," 89–90.

84. Madden, "The Great Plains in the Novels of Wright Morris," 20.

85. Wright Morris, *The Territory Ahead* (New York: Harcourt, Brace and Company, 1958), 137. Morris discusses facets of the art of fiction throughout.

86. Wright Morris, *My Uncle Dudley* (New York: Charles Scribner's Sons, 1942).

87. Wright Morris, *Love Among the Cannibals* (New York: Harcourt, Brace and Company, 1957).

88. James Agee, *Permit Me Voyage* (New Haven, CT: Yale UP, 1934).

89. Wright Morris, "Letter to a Young Critic," *The Massachusetts Review* 6 (Autumn–Winter 1964–1965): 97.

90. Kunitz, ed. *Twentieth Century Authors*, 691.

91. Wright Morris, "Letter to a Young Critic," 95.

92. David Madden, *Revising Fiction: A Handbook for Writers* (New York: New American Library, 1988), 216–17.

93. Morris, "Made in U.S.A.," 487.

94. Ibid., 490.

95. Ibid., 483.

96. Ibid., 488.

97. David Madden, "Character as Revealed Cliché in Wright Morris's Fiction," *The Midwest Quarterly* 22 (Summer 1981): 322.

98. Wright Morris, *The Deep Sleep* (New York: Charles Scribner's Sons, 1953), 302.

99. Morris wrote brief comments for each photograph in his friend Jim Alinder's book *Picture America* (Boston: Little, Brown and Company, 1982). All Alinder's photographs, mostly of groups of people, are totally different from Morris's, as are Morris's own texts for the book. Morris provides pedestrian words that refer directly to Alinder's photographs. For instance, "Photographing, Aspen, Colorado" (78) shows a young couple at a lake. Right, the man, his back to us, is holding a baby, while, left, the woman is squatting by the water, taking a snapshot. Morris provides three seemingly slap-dash lines that begin: "It's hard to take a bad picture." (78)

100. For more on Agee's Robbe-Grillet–like passages, see *Famous Men,* 142, 145, 146.

101. Joseph Conrad, *The Nigger of the 'Narcissus'* (New York: Doubleday, Page & Company, 1926), xiv, 8.

102. Morris, *Time Pieces*, 32.

103. Ibid., 74.

104. Alfred T. Barson, *A Way of Seeing* (Amherst: U of Massachusetts P, 1972), 136.

105. Kunitz, *Twentieth-Century Authors*, 691–92.

106. Alinder in Morris, *Wright Morris: Photographs and Words*, 10.

107. Ibid., 8.

108. David Madden, *Cassandra Singing* (Knoxville: U Tennessee P, 1999).

109. Albert Camus, *Notebooks, 1935–1942* (New York: Alfred A. Knopf, 1963), 3.

110. Morris, "Letter to a Young Critic," 98.

111. Morris, "Henry James's The American Scene," *The Texas Quarterly* (Summer-Autumn 1958), 29, 31.

112. Morris, *Wright Morris: Photographs and Words*, plate 20.

113. Morris, *God's Country and My People*, n.p.

114. Ibid.

115. Morris, *Time Pieces*, 89.

116. Madden, quoted on the back cover of the U of Nebraska P reprint of *The Home Place*, 1969.

117. Morris, *The Inhabitants*, n.p., plate 7.

118. Morris, *Structures and Artifacts*, 4.

119. Morris, *The Inhabitants*, n.p.

120. Ibid.

121. Morris, *God's Country*, n.p.

122. Morris, *Wright Morris: Photographs and Words.*

123. Madden, "Great Plains," 8, 12.

124. Morris, *The World in the Attic*, 178–79.

125. Madden, "Great Plains," 21.

126. Wright Morris, "Privacy as a Subject for Photography," *Magazine of Art* (February 1951): 54. If I were screwed down on a rack, I doubt I could utter even a half-hearted lie about why I think Agee devoted four pages of the climatic final twenty pages of *Famous Men* to a reprint of a lightweight newspaper article praising young, very famous Margaret Bourke-White and her new book of photographs that depicted rural poverty among blacks and whites in the Deep South called *You Have Seen Their Faces* (1937), text by Erskine Caldwell, her husband and author of *Tobacco Road.* Something, perhaps, about wife and husband having violated the privacy of their subjects and making money doing it.

127. Morris, "Privacy as a Subject for Photography," 55. A "reworked" version of this article was reprinted in Morris's *Time Pieces*, 107–10.

128. Morris, "Privacy As a Subject for Photography," 55.

129. Morris, *About Fiction*, 167–68.

130. Morris, *Earthly Delights*, 155.

131. Ibid.

132. Morris, *Earthly Delights*, 159.

133. Ibid., 161.

134. Maybe their descendants will be prepared to read it. See Dale Maharidge and Michael Williamson, *And Their Children After Them* (New York: Pantheon Books, 1989). One of the descendants is said to have read it. See this video for interviews in which a woman depicted in the book speaks of reading it: https://www.youtube.com/watch?v=Qw50BeKyb1c.

TWO

The Case Against Language

Agee, Dos Passos, and Modernist Amalgamation

MICHAEL JACOBS

James Agee and John Dos Passos are without question pioneers in the development of modernist documentary literature, a form that integrates modernist poetics and journalistic narrative techniques in the representation of human actuality. In many ways, Agee's and Walker Evans's *Let Us now Praise Famous Men* (cited hereafter as *Famous Men*) stands as a model for the amalgam of art and fact in this context, as it goes further perhaps than any other work of its kind in effecting the union of reported observation and artistic imagination to communicate more faithfully not only the lives of its subjects, but their humanity as well.[1] Moreover, the nonfiction sections of *U.S.A.*,[2] Dos Passos's three-novel "counter-epic" on the advent of the American century,[3] which is otherwise classified as a work of fiction, function collectively as a fulcrum of sorts between the aesthetic and humanist ambitions of the so-called high modernists and both *Famous Men* and the more experimental examples of the *New Journalism* of the 1960s and 70s. Despite such intersections, however, Agee and Dos Passos are rarely mentioned in the same scholarly texts, and when they are, only in the most tangential of terms: footnotes in an otherwise separate existence, both biographically and artistically. Yet these writers, or rather their most celebrated works, represent conjugated parts of a continuum within the master narrative of twentieth-century American literature. In juxtaposing Agee and Dos Passos, there is salient alignment in myriad frameworks, particularly in their respective goals of nullifying otherness through similar documentary methods.

A proper investigation of this alignment begins with the writers' dissatisfaction with conventional language on many fronts, for it is this frustration that catalyzes the cultivation of their aligned techniques. First and most apparent is contemporaneous nonfiction's representation of the human subject, specifically the objectifying, often sensationalistic approaches of journalism and documentary (in their many forms) in ostensibly illustrating the reality of one's existence—often as it relates to the most marginalized people or groups. Agee directly rebuffs journalism throughout *Famous Men*, calling into question its capacity to convey "more than the slightest fraction of what any even moderately reflective and sensitive person would mean and intend by those inachievable words, [who, what, where, when and why (or how)]" (189). In Agee's estimation, journalism is a clear "falsehood" because it prioritizes the attainment "of almost unanimous public approval" over representational honesty (*FM* 7, 189). For Dos Passos, this failing extends to a fundamental and pervasive disconnect between the sociocultural reality of early twentieth-century America and the language of mass culture meant to signify it. Such discontinuity is demonstrated throughout the trilogy, but nowhere as much as in "The Camera Eye (50)," where the narrator laments, "America our nation has been beaten by strangers who have turned our language inside out who have taken the clean words our fathers spoke and made them slimy and foul . . ." (*USA* 1157).

On an even more basic level, both *Famous Men* and *U.S.A.* show authorial discontent with the representational limitations of conventional written forms (i.e., the failure of traditional nonfictional *and* literary modes to adequately represent lived experience). Agee explores this idea extensively, noting that both the distinct and collective identities of his subjects—their "particularities"—"are exactly themselves beyond designation of words" (*FM* 84). And, within this unfortunate reality, all parties are complicit, for the writer, "as part artist . . . feels the strength of need to select and invent," while the reader "is so used to the idea that art is a fiction that he can't shake himself of it" (*FM* 195). Dos Passos is equally interested in "[destroying] inherited, ossified language," in the name of cultivating an honest and temporally relevant means of representing human actuality.[4] In this respect, both writers echo a pervasive modernist displeasure with aesthetic and linguistic status quo; readers must therefore examine the *modernist* documentary methods and philosophies by which Agee and Dos Passos aim to reconcile these inadequacies in the name of countering the misrepresentative, often duplicitous, and inept character of contemporaneous language.

Despite efforts to construct a fixed and absolute definition of modernism, literary scholarship as a whole has never been successful in effecting a consensus on a singular aesthetic ideology to delineate the movement. Quite the contrary;

a multitude of modernisms has emerged, each reflecting its own formal and thematic principles. While a comprehensive aesthetic formula appears inconceivable, the identification of a general modernist zeitgeist is not. In "Pound/Stevens: Whose Era?" Marjorie Perloff presents an appropriate, albeit broad, definition of modernism. She states simply that modernism is an act of "rupture, not with the distant past," which one might reclaim and "reassimilate" (what might be considered a purposeful and productive nostalgia—or a "usable past"),[5] but with the aesthetic and philosophical conventions of one's own time.[6] Ultimately, rupture is tantamount to Pound's famous edict "Make it new," and exists as a means of *reconciliation*. In other words, rupture is an apparatus through which one declares that the conventions of language are no longer suitable to the purpose of making sense of, representing, or rectifying contemporaneous problems.

More than any other modernist work, James Joyce's *Ulysses* embodies Perloff's notion of rupture, for not only does it endeavor to cultivate a new language capable of illustrating both the modern human condition and the modern hero, but also works throughout its entirety to affirm the limitations of traditional literary and linguistic modes of representation. It is in this enterprise that the root of alignment between *Famous Men* and *U.S.A.* is located.

Toward the end of the "Cyclops" episode of *Ulysses*, the reader finds Leopold Bloom in a heated exchange with the Citizen, an aging, physically debilitated sermonizer of nationalistic rhetoric. What begins as a relatively unremarkable situation—men in a pub talking politics, sports, and gossip—devolves into chaos wherein the Citizen attempts to inflict serious bodily harm upon Joyce's protagonist for, among other things, Bloom's proclamation that "Christ was a jew like me."[7] The central narrative voice of the episode belongs to an unnamed, first-person narrator who functions as an eyewitness to the ensuing action. While not completely unreliable, his cynicism and largely biased perspective are obvious, and his judgments against Bloom—and there are many—are fueled by misinformation and hearsay, and thus largely miss the mark; central to such obtuseness is the narrator's chagrin over his mistaken belief that Bloom has won big at the Gold Cup horse race yet has not offered to buy a round. Compounding the complexity of the episode's narration is the fact that it features a dizzying array of alternate narrative voices that run the gamut of rhetorical styles. The reader is presented with a narrative interpolation in which Joyce implements dozens of literary and discursive modes to chronicle the late afternoon goings on of Barney Kiernan's pub. These stylistic parodies range from the demonstrative prose of sentimental and romantic literature to legal jargon, Biblical verse, advertising copy, scientific discourse, epic poetry, and more. In short, these are the conventions of language—the standard, primary means of linguistic representation in Joyce's time—and, by juxtaposing these modes with the limited perspective of the central narrator, Joyce means to reveal their shortcomings.

Amid the chaos of the Citizen's attempted assault on Bloom emerges a specific narrative voice that parodies the vapid style of a dispassionate newspaper story. On the surface, this device produces a perplexing and humorous effect in that it implements a reserved, haughtily aloof journalistic tone to convey the anarchic events of the episode's conclusion. For example, Bloom's near beating and the scorn he solicits from more than a few of the pub's patrons is "characterised by the most affecting cordiality," while the Citizen's biscuit tin-turned agent of attempted murder morphs into a "gift of a silver casket."[8] Joyce's aims in this context are not merely stylistic, however. In conveying the crisis at hand with incongruously temperate, if not benign language, he presents his readers with a metaphor that permeates all of *Ulysses*. This moment of Bloom's journey is but one of many in which conventional language fails to represent actuality. As stated, the language of objective journalism is not the only parodied mode of representation in "Cyclops" that proves insufficient in this sense. But in this moment of disarray, when Leopold Bloom asserts his identification with Christ, Joyce shifts to the fourth estate, mass culture's language of the phenomenological, going so far as to identify Bloom as "the distinguished phenomenologist."[9] Such a stylistic shift is no mere coincidence. Throughout *Ulysses*, Joyce works through the whole of English literary traditions, beginning with Naturalism, the dominant novelistic style of his day, and dismisses them one by one as a scientist dismisses invalid hypotheses, until he arrives at a language suitable to his purposes.[10] And, among these seemingly countless modes of representation, journalism is positioned as a principal agent of fraudulent language.[11]

As Joyce does with *Ulysses*, Agee and Dos Passos overtly, and often antagonistically, challenge the conventional means of written representation of their era. Agee is unambiguous in this undertaking, for his is an endeavor in representing the genuine humanity of his subject, "not just to amalgamate him into some invented, literary imitation of a human being" (*FM* 194). While Dos Passos's ire in this specific sense is a bit broader in scope than Agee's, for he rails against an epidemic of fraudulent language in mass culture, both writers mean to expose not only the often condescendingly dehumanizing practices inherent to the journalism of their day, but also the intrinsic flaws of so-called objective news in general.[12] Certainly they find, investigate, and work to overcome the limitations of art as well, but journalism—in its culturally accepted position as the broker of unmitigated truth—is dealt with much more severely.

In *A History of American Literary Journalism: The Emergence of a Modern Narrative Form*, John Hartsock argues that the surge of the mass-circulated newspaper, coupled with transformative scientific developments in the late nineteenth and early twentieth centuries, gave rise to a common belief that total objectivity in the conveyance of actuality was an attainable means of grasping verifiable truths of the human condition.[13] In their respective works, Agee and Dos Passos reject this idea, believing that such truth, if at all within reach, can only be sought through the writer's own subjectivity or imagination. Objectivity is an alienating constituent as it distances not only the writer from their human documentary subject, but also the reader. In other words, the endeavor toward objectivity limits the reader's ability to engage actively with the text. They become a passive onlooker who must accept the veracity of the textual construct at face value. And when such an approach concerns the representation of human actuality, the story's subject is usually positioned as object, an ontological other with whom the reader cannot identify.

Hartsock adeptly accuses objective journalism of assuming the truth of its own observations. He challenges the prevalent belief that objective reporting, the ostensibly impartial conveyance of the *who, what, where, when, why,* and *how*, provides an unequivocally evenhanded, dispassionate view of the actual world. Hartsock's focus is not stylistic or rhetorical (although these two elements are explored to some extent), but rather epistemological. In its assurance of "cold facts," he argues, objective journalism endorses a positivist philosophical stance—the idea that through the ingestion of said facts, one will come to some universal truth. Thus, objective news possesses not only an unfathomable power to persuade, but also stymies the reader's imaginative participation in the reception of factual news.

Interestingly, such a hindrance is found in sensational and muckraking journalism as well. On the surface, this assertion seems a dubious parallel, for it presumably belies the accepted notion that muckraking and sensational (or "yellow") journalism not only employ biased language, but are also largely agenda-driven. For Hartsock, however, it is precisely these constituents that connect muckraking and sensationalism with objective news, for they work to imbue readers with a sense of moral, ethical, and logical *certainty* that is often tested by the mercurial nature of reality.

Of even greater concern to Agee and Dos Passos are the ways in which the people whom sensational journalism endeavors to represent must invariably conform to a position of other; that is, the very goal of sensationalism is to deliver fodder for exhibition and spectatorship. In this way, the reader comes to view Agee's sharecropper or Dos Passos's political radical, immigrant, or factory worker as distanced significantly from their own cognitive and emotional perspective. Thus, they solicit an objectification not unlike that which can be found in objective news. Conversely, *Famous Men* and *U.S.A.* strive to *narrow* the gulf between the objectified world (or object) and the reader's (and writer's) subjectivity.

Agee is indeed cognizant of journalism and documentary's tendency toward sensationalism and exploitation. The exposé's inherent (and *invented*) condescension thrust upon the marginalized subject leaves Agee, like his high modernist counterparts, wary of the fraudulence of written language, especially language implemented under the guise of represented actuality. Hence the assertion, "Journalism is true in the sense that everything is true to the state of being and what conditioned and produced it" (*FM* 189). From the very beginning of the book, Agee makes clear that his is not to be a work of journalism because the genre, in both form and practice, is unsuited to his purposes. In the first lines of the "Preamble," the writer takes to task his employer, *Fortune*, for its "obscene and thoroughly terrifying" (and profit-driven) attempt "to pry intimately into the lives of an undefended and appallingly damaged group of human beings, an ignorant and helpless rural family, for the purpose of parading the nakedness, disadvantage and humiliation of these lives before another group of human beings, in the name of science, of 'honest journalism' (whatever that paradox may mean) . . . " (7).

Agee's real gripe with journalism, however, is its pretentions to objectivity and certainty. Coinciding with Hartsock's notion of "objectified news," Agee is not simply critical of conventional journalism's inability to deliver truth to its readers; he disparages its overt claims to do as much. "Journalism is not to be blamed," he concedes, "no more than a cow is to be blamed for not being a horse." But whereas "few cows have the delusion or even the desire to be horses," journalism suffers from "its own complacent delusion . . . that it is telling the truth," and even worse, possesses the "enormous power to poison the public with the same delusion" (*FM* 190). Therefore, it is not merely that journalism *does not* offer truth; it simply *cannot*. Hence Agee's assertion that "Journalism can within its own limits be 'good' or 'bad,' 'true' or 'false,' but it is not in the nature of journalism even to approach any less relative degree of truth" (*FM* 190). On an even more primal level, he expounds to this end that "The very blood and semen of journalism . . . is a broad and successful form of lying. Remove that form of lying and you no longer have journalism" (*FM* 190).

For all of his wariness of journalism, Agee seems equally mistrustful of art, in this case literature, to authentically represent the lives of the tenant families. His stated intention is to present a "non-'artistic' view" that seeks to "suspend or destroy imagination" (*FM* 10). Throughout *Famous Men*, the reader encounters myriad explicit challenges to art and its ability to signify human existence truthfully. From his command, "Above all else: In God's name don't think of it as Art" (*FM* 13), to the subsequent confession, "it is their texture I want to represent, not betray, nor pretty up into art" (*FM* 194), to the matter-of-fact conclusions "Art . . . has nothing to do with Life" and "I don't care for art, and I shant much bother" (*FM* 299), Agee consistently observes the limitations of aesthetic creation when it comes to representing the real lives of real people.

But what is Agee's specific grievance with art as an agent of represented actuality? The crux of his argument posits that art attempts to make tidy the disarray of real life. It "honors" and thus quells the "fury" of life (*FM* 13). It attempts to "pretty up" the "savage and dangerous and murderous" nature of human existence.[14] For Agee, this is especially true in the literary arts, where the conventions of narrative closure abound. T. V. Reed identifies in *Famous Men* a challenge to art's "illusion of a self-contained aesthetic universe" too distant from the tangibles of everyday reality.[15] There is nothing "contained" in the writing of *Famous Men*. Unlike Evans's photos, the narrative is not cast in closed form.[16] There is no discernible arc, no central conflict, and certainly no resolution. It is open ended, for it possesses the DNA of the phenomenological, which in a time and place marked by existential and ideological uncertainty (such as the age of modernity or the Great Depression—or both) implies limitless, unknowable probabilities. Such is the impetus for the exhaustive cataloguing and meandering observations of the book: the hundreds of pages describing the sights, sounds, odors, and various other sense impressions to which Agee is privy. For the writer, art is a compromise; it "accepts the most dangerous and impossible of bargains and makes the best of it" (*FM* 193). Agee has no designs on making such concessions, no desire to compromise on the representation of the lives of his subjects, no will to "dab at them here, cut them short here, make some trifling improvements over here, in order to make you worthy of The Saturday Review of Literature" (*FM* 299).

Agee sees journalism and art as complicit and congruous as they both purport to present truth while leading us (often quite destructively) further away from its realization.[17] Toward the middle of *Famous Men*, the author asserts, "[A]nything set forth within an art form, 'true' as it may be in art terms, is hermetically sealed away from identification with everyday 'reality'" (*FM* 194). The same can be said of journalism, as it also promotes a distanced, often escapist approach to the reader's engagement with the phenomenological. And so Agee's task is to do with words what, from his perspective, has never been done: to represent "the cruel radiance of what is" "*in its own terms*" (*FM* 10, 189).

By themselves, the conventional representational modes of art and fact possess far too many limitations to suit Agee's purposes. The writer's goal is to establish the humanity of an indigent people for a reader who has been conditioned to see such people as other. Yet the aesthetic and journalistic conventions of his day only serve to widen the ontological divide between reader and subject. Agee's intended audience is a jaded, modern readership that has been conditioned by traditional journalism to gaze upon the poor and disenfranchised with a cynical and condescending perspective. The writer therefore struggles to document and adequately represent the bleak existence of three sharecropper families without serving them up for the amusement of a privileged readership seeking not merely edification, but entertainment. To avoid such trappings, Agee works within an inter-formal aesthetic while constructing a method for conveying his brand of modernist humanism. In short, his decided task is to get his relatively affluent reader to identify with the existence of his destitute subjects, and success to this end is ultimately to be measured by the degree to which the former can ascertain the humanity of the latter.

To circumvent the limitations of individual forms to this end, Agee endeavors to combine them. What has been referred to here as "art and fact," Agee calls "art and *science*." Throughout *Famous Men,* these terms are paired more than a dozen times. In the context of this book, both constitute modes of depicting specific human existences. Art is a mode born of the imagination while science attempts to deliver the observable world.[18] Neither, individually, support his commitment to using language to represent the real, for they "merely describe" the truth (or attempt to do so) while "human beings and their creations and the entire state of nature, merely *are*, the truth" (*FM* 193). Agee's approach to overcoming the limitations of these representational modes is best expressed in a two-part question posed by the writer, himself: "Isn't every human being both a scientist and an artist; and in writing of human experience, isn't there a good deal to be said for recognizing that fact and for using *both methods*" (*FM* 195; italics added). Agee's method combines art and fact, attempting to absorb their merits and expel their detriments.[19]

Such combinations of art and fact run throughout the text; they exist in the various instances when Agee's meandering interior monologue gives way to precise physical descriptions of people, landscapes, domiciles, and possessions, only to return to his stream of consciousness. They are also found *within* those descriptions, as Agee unobtrusively shifts between objective and subjective observations; one of the best examples of this shifting is found in a lyrical subsection simply titled "Overalls." In describing this most recognizable garment of the sharecropper, and the way it fits on his body, Agee cannot help (nor would he want to) but conflate scientific observation with artistic invention, noting in one passage, "The shape, particularly along the urgent frontage of the thighs, so that the whole structure of the knee and musculature of the thigh is sculptured there; each man's garment wearing the shape and beauty of his induplicable body" (*FM* 217).

Perhaps the most noteworthy example of such amalgamation comes in the "Shelter" section of the book. While Agee roots through the withered and seemingly valueless possessions of the Gudger home, he comes across "a scissored hexagon of newsprint" to which he has transitioned seamlessly from the Gudger children's clothes (*FM* 138). In this moment, Agee accomplishes precisely what he has set out to do: establish a connection between the real world of the reader and the represented world of his sharecropper families; and it is through this connection that the reader will, in part, come to identify with the *real* existence of the documentary subject.

The passage begins with a fragment of the "scissored newsprint," a construct overtly resembling the Newsreels of Dos Passos's *U.S.A.*:

> GHAM NEWS
> hursday afternoon, March 5, 1936
> Price: 3 cents
>   in G
>   (else

Thousa
are on d
througho
cording its

for the Birm

(over two photographs:)
Glass and night sticks fly in a strike. (*FM* 138)

After another caption fragment, Agee offers his own descriptions of two accompanying photographs, "both flashlighted night scenes" (*FM* 138). Each is written with the sparse, objective concision of an experienced newsman, save for the interpretive observations that the policeman's "face signifies uh-huh" after striking down a picketing laborer with his nightstick.

Not simply sociopolitical rhetoric, this passage calls attention to a bloody conflict between the police and their proletarian victims. Agee is connecting the social upheaval of the day, and the actual world of his reader, with the represented world of his subjects. He is calling upon both art (interpretive representation) and fact (the found document) to signify the human actuality of the Gudgers. In this act, he avoids the limitations of art, specifically its tendency to promote an "illusion of a self-contained aesthetic universe" in two ways. First, he offers his reader fragments. She is not privy to a discursive or narrative whole. There is no certainty to the narrative bits before us, no dénouement to give us closure. Rather, Agee provides a construct that adequately represents the uncertainty and limitless possibilities of human actuality; the reader is given a form to match the text's content. And Agee has effectively embedded this uncertainty—what Bakhtin would call the "inconclusive present day reality"[20]—into not one, but four interconnected worlds: the writer's, the Gudgers', the reader's, and the police and workers'. Through journalistic documentation and intertextuality, he has successfully challenged the representational limitations of art.

Here, Agee also avoids the positivist pretentions of mainstream journalism in that he calls attention to the actual *form* of the news article, the tangible paper and ink before him. He artistically arranges the fragments, and thus announces them as constructs. To the same effect, he chooses to *describe* the news story's accompanying photographs rather than include them in the text as a found/

arranged document. And he is careful to highlight the news text's identification of the presence of a "cameraman [who] was right o[n]" the scene to snap the photographs, therefore alerting to his readers that the text and image before them are not reality, but merely *representations* of reality. All of this acts as demystification, for it reveals, in part, the process behind the *creation* of news. More than that, however, it calls attention to Agee's own processes. In this elucidation, Agee has engaged the reader in ways that journalism cannot.[21]

Like *Famous Men*, *U.S.A.* is an overt and comprehensive experiment in the amalgam of art and fact. Interwoven with its fragmented fictional narrative are three recurring nonfiction segments that, themselves, blend experimental documentary, biography, and memoir with modernist literary poetics. Framing the fictional narratives of the collective protagonist, which invoke history in their implementation of American vernaculars and historical figures and events, are the juxtaposed fragments that comprise the Newsreels, the lyrical biographies of important historical figures, and the impressionistically autobiographical vignettes of The Camera Eye. *U.S.A.*, in its "creative treatment of actuality,"[22] is every bit a documentary text as it is a work of fictional prose. The structure of *U.S.A.* underscores Dos Passos's understanding that singular conventional forms of written representation cannot achieve his goal of representing the real. Thus, the trilogy works to dismantle representational conventions to expose their inner workings and, in doing so, positions the reader as an active participant in the process.

In *U.S.A.*, Dos Passos, like Agee, is explicit in his indictment of conventional journalism as an agent of dehumanizing fraudulence. Really, his scope in this context comprises the broader language of mass culture, but it is easy to see that news media, as typified in the fifty Newsreel sections that pervade the trilogy, is the most significant. This position was established with even greater emphasis in Dos Passos's 1935 address to the American Writer's Congress during which he remarked, "American writers who want to do the most valuable kind of work will find themselves trying to discover the deep currents of historical change under the surface of opinions, orthodoxies, heresies, gossip and journalistic garbage of the day."[23] While Agee largely *tells* his reader of journalism's shortcomings, however, Dos Passos works with decades' worth of newspaper text, juxtaposing it with the trilogy's three other modes of representation, to *show* us.[24] More than that, *U.S.A.* demonstrates the alarming disconnect between conventional language and the reality it means to represent—a disconnect that *Famous Men* endeavors to reconcile.

U.S.A. is, in large part, a work of experimental prose fiction that relies heavily on historical events and phenomena to shape its narrative. More important, it is a text that, to a greater extent than any other work of literary modernism, implements the palpable, historical documents of American mass culture in the early twentieth century. Just as Agee fixatedly sifts through the minutiae of the sharecroppers' milieu, describing in exhaustive detail their economic conditions, domiciles, clothing, schooling, and livelihood, Dos Passos leaves virtually no stone unturned in the vast landscape of American culture. Political campaign slogans, newspaper headlines, Vaudevillian catch phrases, working class vernacular, sensationalist news blurbs, patriotic maxims, and an abundance of advertising copy—largely found in the Newsreels but featured in the other three sections as well—work in concert throughout the trilogy of novels to project the fragmented narrative of the new American century. Dos Passos depends on the documented stuff of cultural discourse, for it lends to his vision the requisite authority to define American culture. In *U.S.A.*, the reader encounters a culture in crisis. America's imperialistic and capitalistic aspirations lay waste to its innocence. The social and humanist ideals forged in the doctrine of Jeffersonian Republicanism and fortified in the abolition of slavery in the previous century are betrayed by an economic system based on labor exploitation and a populace that subsists on excess and unchecked ambition. The fictional characters of *U.S.A.* suffer from a profound sense of existential dislocation. Specifically, they are disconnected from one another, a metaphor for modern alienation, as demonstrated in Dos Passos's use of a collective protagonist adrift in storylines that only minimally intersect. Thus, just as the culture is fragmented, so, too, is human connectivity.

But this crisis belies the fact that the language of the culture in *U.S.A.*, specifically in the constituents of mass communication of its Newsreel sections, tells a completely different story. The language found in American newspapers and magazines, on billboards and advertising pamphlets, communicates a society on the rise, one promising unlimited prosperity and happiness for all those willing to work hard and believe in the greatness of America. Much of *U.S.A.* works to reveal the disparity between the goings-on of human actuality and the language that shapes our perception *of* that actuality. Such a revelation is Dos Passos's attempt to provide his reader with the means of cutting through the fraudulent language pervading modern American society. This language, along with the political, economic, and technological developments of modernity, is for Dos Passos a dehumanizing entity, for it works to turn individual, free thinkers into mindless conformists—or, in his words, "automatons."[25] Dos Passos's attempt to deconstruct the language of mass culture is therefore also a humanist endeavor, a platform from which the reader navigates beyond misleading rhetoric and journalistic claims of honesty to a real understanding of the national identity; in this, they can circumvent fraudulent language and reclaim her human individuality and free will.

While Agee reserves his powers of probing, comprehensive analysis for his documentary subjects, Dos Passos works methodically to scrutinize the very language that both writers seek to overcome. Through Dos Passos's deconstruction of the headlines, news stories, song lyrics, advertising slogans, and gossip of America, the reader sees a comingling of sociopolitical criticism and humanist ambition. The fundamental challenge for Dos Passos is that the cultural discourse, which largely occupies the pages of the nation's newspapers, is the language of hegemony, and just as Agee is quick to note the incompatibility of profit and truth, particularly in his rebuke of *Fortune* in "Preamble," Dos Passos reveals that for the dominant strata of American culture, truth is bad for business. Nowhere in *U.S.A.* is this more apparent than in the Newsreels' indirect criticism of news itself.

In "Newsreel XLIV," the first of its kind in *The Big Money*, such criticism plays out within a confluence of headlines, news snippets, and song lyrics that work in concert to reveal a troubling milieu:

Yankee Doodle that melodee
COLONEL HOUSE ARRIVES FROM EUROPE
APPARENTLY A VERY SICK MAN
TO CONQUER SPACE AND SEE DISTANCES
but has not the time come for newspaper proprietors to join in a wholesome movement for the purpose of calming troubled minds, giving all the news but laying less stress on prospective calamities
DEADLOCK UNBROKEN AS FIGHT SPREADS
they permitted the Steel Trust Government to trample underfoot the democratic rights which they had so often been assured were the heritage of the people of this country
SHIPOWNERS DEMAND PROTECTION
Yankee doodle that melodee
Yankee doodle that melodee
Makes me stand right up and cheer

only survivors of the crew of the schooner Onato are put in jail on arrival in Philadelphia

PRESIDENT STRONGER WORKS IN SICKROOM

I'm coming U.S.A.

I'll say

MAY GAG PRESS

There's no land . . . so grand

Charles M. Schwab, who has returned from Europe, was a luncheon guest at the White House. He stated that this country was prosperous but not so prosperous as it should be, because there were so many disturbing investigations on foot

. . . as my land

From California to Manhattan Isle. (USA 775–76)

Here, Dos Passos has positioned journalism, patriotism, laissez-faire capitalism, imperialism, catastrophe, war, and class warfare in the same bricolage to communicate something important about the trajectory of American society soon after the Armistice. While there is much to unpack, perhaps the single most significant bit of text in this section is that which urges newspaper publishers to calm "troubled minds." The suggestion here is that newspapers, the primary means by which early twentieth-century Americans acquire information on current events, downplay misfortune for the purpose of maintaining a sanguine and subdued population.[26] By itself, the inclusion of this snippet says much about Dos Passos's wariness of conventional journalism. However, when juxtaposed with the other constituents, one finds an even broader indictment of American culture and the language that helps shape it. *U.S.A.* is a trilogy primarily focused on the intersections of language and sociopolitical/economic power. Like Agee, Dos Passos sees the hegemonic implementation of language as antithetical to his humanist ideals. Specifically, he believes that those who represent the dominant social strata have hijacked pure language, twisting and perverting it until it is no longer recognizable. Just as *Famous Men* endeavors to restore the humanity and agency of its marginalized subjects, *U.S.A.* is Dos Passos's attempt to restore the agency of the American people through the reclamation of their language.

While Dos Passos is not nearly as explicit as Agee on the limitations of art in representing the truth of human actuality, he really need not be; *U.S.A.*, in its amalgam of realism, reportage, objective journalism, impressionistic memoir, and experimental bricolage is an attempt to "bridge the gap between history" and artistic imagination for the purposes of countering the insufficiencies of both artistic and journalistic representation. Dos Passos lamented such inadequacies as early as 1917 while serving in France as an ambulance driver during the First World War. There he struggled to write about the horrors he witnessed, noting in his diary, "I'm dying to write—but all my methods of doing things in the past merely disgust me now, all former methods are damned inadequate."[27] While writing *The 42nd Parallel*, Dos Passos published a piece in the literary journal *Bookman*, in which he argues that the form of the conventional novel is found wanting, for the novelist is little more than "a second-class historian of the age he lives in."[28] Like *Famous* Men, *U.S.A.* eschews the familiar constructs of the novelistic plot. The minimally intersecting storylines of the collective protagonist present no resolution, no closure. Moreover, all four sections of the text(s) confront history in all its brutality. Nowhere does *U.S.A.* attempt to "pretty up" the "savage and dangerous and murderous" nature of human existence (*FM* 13). For Dos Passos, any writer attempting to cut through the fraudulent language of mass culture, the myopic lens of objective journalism, the half-truths of sensationalism, and the consumer ads and "crackpot notions" pervading newspapers and magazines must move beyond such conventions. He must be a "truffle dog digging up raw material which a scientist, an anthropologist or a historian can later use to permanent advantage."[29] Ironically, though not coincidentally, while Agee professes no such desire for his investigation of the three families to be used in this way, history has had different plans.

In their mutual indictment of conventional written representation, namely the fraudulence of journalism and inadequacies of literature as well as their attempt to counter such hindrances through formal amalgamation—all in an effort to represent human actuality more faithfully—*Famous Men* and *U.S.A.* are indeed aligned in meaningful ways. In terms of their humanist ambitions, however, the texts diverge significantly. Whereas Agee largely strives to get his readers to see the humanity of the Gudgers, Woods, and Ricketts families—to position his "defenseless" and dehumanized subjects before the collective lens of an ontologically distant, bourgeois readership in such a way as to effect not sympathy, but empathy—Dos Passos is much more focused on illuminating the conditions that led to their very dehumanization.

This is not to say that there are no instances in *U.S.A.* where Dos Passos endeavors to reconcile directly the marginalization of individuals. "The Camera Eye

(49)" and "The Camera Eye (50)" are the two sections of the trilogy in which the writer works to effect an ontological identification between his reader and his documentary subjects, Nicola Sacco and Bartolomeo Vanzetti, two Italian-born immigrants who, in May of 1920, were falsely arrested for robbing and murdering a paymaster and guard for Slater & Morrill Shoe Company in Braintree, Massachusetts.[30] It is here that the writer uses himself—his first-hand recollections, fears, hopes, feelings of failure and defeat—to align his abortive efforts to stay their execution with the victimization of two innocent men. Dos Passos interprets their deaths and their effects on the crowd outside of the Charlestown jail through his own experiences. He was there, in the streets with the crowds of lamenting protesters, and this first-hand experience, along with the host of thoughts and emotions it cultivated within him, provides the means by which Dos Passos can use his own humanity to establish that of his documentary subjects.[31] Here, through the eyes of a slightly younger (though much more idealistic) Dos Passos than he who penned *U.S.A.*, the reader finds Sacco and Vanzetti positioned as Christ figures—martyrs whose deaths ostensibly promise to take the power of language back from the oppressors and return it to "haters of oppression" (*USA* 1157). For a moment, it seems that the "men in the death house" have not died in vain, for "they made the old words new before they died" (*USA* 1158). Dos Passos's journey has thus come full circle. In his 1926 article on the Sacco and Vanzetti conviction, he makes clear the idea that language is power, and those who currently control that power have effected the perversion of a once-pure and righteous language that formerly stood in opposition to oppression, not in line with it. Thus, in 1920s America, "the wrong set of words means the Chair."[32] In "The Camera Eye (50)," however, "the old American speech of the haters of oppression is [made] new" through the public outrage elicited by the Italian immigrants' executions. The writer's faith in this context is reflective of his vulnerability, which effectively represents the vulnerability of the condemned men. His desperate search for meaning in their deaths helps lessen the otherness most readers would ascribe to Sacco and Vanzetti, men largely positioned for the public as other via what Dos Passos sees as the fraudulent language of the mass media.[33]

In the end, however, Dos Passos's ability to humanize Sacco and Vanzetti for his reader is limited, for he never actually knew them. He never met with them face to face, interviewed them, or shared a common experience with the pair (nor most of the other important documentary subjects of *U.S.A*). Therefore, his attempt to make common cause, and thus bridge the gap between his reader's subjectivity and his documentary subjects, never comes to fruition. Ultimately, The Camera Eye is the closest Dos Passos comes to truly and reflexively engaging his subjectivity with his documentary subject. No other section provides the level of reflexivity, a thorough exploration of the writer's personal place within his documentary milieu, adequate to the humanist purposes of nullifying otherness.

In contrast, immersion into the lives of his subjects is fundamental to Agee's humanist methodology and success in *Famous Men*. Such an approach affords him the capacity to not simply observe and engage with the three families, but also come to connect with them on existential and spiritual levels. And this feeling of kinship catalyzes innumerable confessions, ranging from his love (and lust) for the subjects of his documentary, to his deeply felt fear of inadequacy as a writer—all of which establishes Agee's vulnerability among the group of "defenseless" sharecroppers and tenants. Ultimately, Agee's alignment with the Gudgers, Woods, and Ricketts allows his reader, who is presumably of the same socioeconomic strata as the author, to identify with these marginalized subjects—a far different result than that achieved by Dos Passos.[34]

Despite its humanist limitations, the importance of *U.S.A.* in establishing a framework for Agee's documentary method is undeniable. While little is written of Agee's engagement with the works of Dos Passos, his correspondence with Father Flye (in 1927) reveals that he admired the novelist's "brilliance" and thought him to be a "marvelous writer."[35] Moreover, Linda Wagner-Martin is keen to note that *Famous Men's* innovation "draws upon a quantity of devices and themes from the high-modernist experimentation of William Faulkner, Thomas Wolfe, and John Dos Passos."[36] Indeed, it must be noted that *U.S.A.* investigates and exposes the limitations and detriments of conventional journalism and cultural discourse on semiotic and societal levels so thoroughly that Agee, who would not venture down to Alabama until the very year that the final novel in Dos Passos's trilogy was published, can largely assume the truth of his own assertions on the subject.

It is clear that *Famous Men* and *U.S.A.* succeed in presenting novel ways of elucidating unprecedented times. The convergence of modernity in all its exciting and terrifying forms, America's foray into imperialism, and the Great Depression produced a precarious, often calamitous, and unequivocally dehumanizing milieu. With their respective works, Agee and Dos Passos recognize that amid crisis, conventional systems of representation are inadequate, and this recognition engenders new approaches to representing human actuality that continue to inform our perception of the world.

Notes

1. James Agee, *Let Us Now Praise Famous Men: An Annotated Edition of the James Agee—Walker Evans Classic, with Supplementary Manuscripts*, ed. Hugh Davis (Knoxville: U of Tennessee P, 2015). All page references to *Famous Men* will be parenthetical and indicated as *FM*.

2. John Dos Passos, *U.S.A.: The 42nd Parallel, 1919, The Big Money* (New York: Literary Classics of the United States, Inc., 1996). All page references to *U.S.A.* will be parenthetical and marked as *USA*.

Permeating U.S.A. are three distinct structural devices that intersect and contextualize the loosely connected fictional narratives of the three novels: *The 42nd Parallel* (1930), *1919* (1932), and *The Big Money* (1936). The Newsreel sections comprise a complex arrangement of headlines, song lyrics, and textual fragments (including advertising copy and news stories), which establish both a chronology and means of investigating the national culture. The Camera Eye sections are autobiographical vignettes written in stream of consciousness that chart Dos Passos's life from childhood to 1929; they too parallel the chronology of the fictional narratives. Rounding out the trilogy are twenty-seven biographical sketches focused on noteworthy icons of early twentieth-century America; they chronicle the contributions, triumphs, and failures of both heroes of the people and perpetrators of avarice and iniquity.

3. Michael Denning, *The Cultural Front: The Laboring of American Culture in the Twentieth Century* (New York: Verso, 1997), 163.

4. John Trombold, "From the Future to the Past: The Disillusionment of John Dos Passos," *Studies in American Fiction* 26, no. 21 (1998): 240.

5. In response to *SOME QUESTIONS WHICH FACE AMERICAN WRITERS TODAY*, Agee takes issue with the idea of a "usable past," noting that "things are 'usable' only by second-rate people and worse. To those who really perceive them they are too hot to handle in any utilitarian way" (*FM* 312–13).

6. Marjorie Perloff, "Pound/Stevens: Whose Era?" *New Literary History* 13, no. 3 (1982): 498.

7. James Joyce, *Ulysses* (Oxford: Vintage International, 1990), 342.

8. Ibid., 343.

9. Ibid.

10. Stephen Sicari, *Joyce's Modernist Allegory: Ulysses and the History of the Novel* (Columbia, SC: Univ. of South Carolina Press, 2001), 17. Sicari argues that Joyce is successful in this endeavor, as evidenced by the "Ithaca" episode in which Stephen remarks that Bloom is "the traditional figure of hypostasis." Here, Bloom is aligned with Christ, and his consistent demonstration of Christian virtue (most notably love) positions the protagonist as representative of the ideal in human behavior—a hero for the modern age. He is at once made human *and* something beyond human—better than human. He is "Everyman or Noman."

11. This idea is equally present in the "Aeolus" episode in which the reader encounters, among other symbols of the wayward and destructive nature of newspaper journalism, a haggard and "bowed" typesetter. Here Bloom considers the detriments of an entire career spent having to sift through reports of the cheerless goings on of everyday life that pervade daily periodicals: "Queer lot of stuff he must have put through his hands in his time: obituary notices, pubs' ads, speeches, divorce suits, found drowned." The absence of anything remotely uplifting—something to transcend the downward pull of reality—has a decaying effect on the ancient typesetter. Thus, as Bloom notices, he is "Nearing the end of his tether now" (468).

12. For a detailed analysis of the patronizing and exploitative practices of 1930s documentary literature, see William Stott's *Documentary Expression and Thirties America* (Chicago: Univ. of Chicago Press, 1986). In contrasting *Fortune's* stylistic expectations—particularly in the "Life and Circumstances" series in which the sharecropper piece was to be included—with Agee's documentary sensibility, Stott argues that *Fortune's* bourgeois readership "would be bored by the lives of average folk were they not made quaint and amusing" (262). One example of the condescending treatment of such subjects offered by Stott is the article, "Success Story: The Life and Circumstances of Mr. Gerald Corkum—Paint Sprayman at the Plymouth Motor Plant." Featured in this story is a "close-up photo of a newspaper, a *Saturday Evening Post*, and a *Webster's Daily Use Dictionary* on a living room table" (262). The underlying caption, which reads, "The Corkum Library," not only suggests that this is the extent of the subject's reading material; the positioning of the items also implies that Corkum needs a dictionary to understand the newspaper and *Saturday Evening Post*. It should be noted that Margaret Bourke-White took this photograph. Agee and Evans criticized Bourke-White for taking patronizing and exploitative photos of vulnerable documentary subjects.

Stott does much to distinguish the various modes and techniques of 1930s documentary literature. In doing so, he identifies the pervasive sentimentality and exploitation in most of the era's socially-minded reportage, even those texts that explicitly sought to dignify their unfortunate subjects. The problem, as Stott sees it, is that while the writers of these works "cared deeply" about the disadvantaged victims of both circumstance and (often capitalistic) exploitation of whom they wrote, they "cared more about moving [the] audience" (178). What is remarkable in Stott's analysis is the revelation that both radically-social and conservative documentary texts succumb to the same practices of exploitation and objectification.

13. John C. Hartsock, *The History of American Literary Journalism: The Emergence of a Modern American Form* (Amherst: Univ. of Massachusetts Press, 2000).

14. Ibid., 13.

15. T.V. Reed, "Unimagined Existence and the Fiction of the Real: Postmodernist Realism in *Let Us Now Praise Famous Men*," *Representations* 24 (1988), 162.

16. There is much to be said of the role of Evans's photographs in *Famous Men*, but such an analysis is beyond the scope of this essay. It is worth noting, however, that Agee sought to do with words what he felt Evans achieved with pictures. Agee admired Evans's approach to his subjects as it afforded them dignity. Evans took very few (and published even fewer) candid shots of the sharecroppers and their families. In all but a few photographs in *Famous Men*, the subjects have

posed themselves. This approach is analogous to the documentary technique of implementing dialogue—letting the subjects speak for themselves. In this way, Evans provides his subjects a degree of agency. What is more, he completely avoids extreme high or low angles, which often yield distorting, sensational, and grotesque effects.

17. Thus it remains that one of the most remarkable elements of this text is Agee's ability to deconstruct the aestheticized reification of human being—some forty years before the most notable achievements in postmodern and poststructural theory.

18. To emphasize the idea that science is also a product of human invention, and thus unreliable in representing actuality, Agee refers to it as "scientific art" (*FM* 193).

19. T.V. Reed sees such an amalgamation as the genius of *Famous Men*—the defining characteristic that establishes the text as a canonical work of American literature. In "Unimagined Existence and the Fiction of the Real," Reed positions Agee's and Evans's work as a response to the limitations of any single literary form to adequately represent "the real." He notes that while "representational systems are always inadequate," *Famous Men*, in its merger of profound realism and aestheticism, comes closer to delivering the representation of reality than any prior attempt (157). Reed's monumentally incisive argument posits that the "ossified" (159) representational categories and practices of its time (or any time, for that matter) need to be subverted and ultimately shattered if one is to successfully "capture the real" (161).

20. M. M. Bakhtin, *The Dialogic Imagination: Four Essays* (Austin: U of Texas P, 1981), 39.

21. Such engagement begins in *Preamble* where Agee questions the reader's purpose and authority in exploring his investigation (*FM* 8).

22. John Grierson, *Grierson on Documentary* (London: Collins, 1946), 13. Grierson coined this definition for documentary cinema in 1926. While the interpretation was conceived for a different medium, it is no less applicable to documentary literature.

23. Michael Spindler, *American Literature and Social Change: William Dean Howells to Arthur Miller* (London: Palgrave Macmillan, 1984), 184.

24. As established, not all content in the Newsreels consists of headlines or news stories. However, the song lyrics, slogans, and advertising copy were largely culled from newspapers, and their inclusion here suggests both the relationship between such elements and journalism as well as their conflation in the reading experience.

25. Dos Passos employs this metaphor in a number of well-known works, including *Three Soldiers* (1921) and his poem "They Are Dead Now," *New Masses* (October 1927): 7.

26. Such a position would continue into the next decade as much of the devastation of the Great Depression was marginalized or ignored by newspaper editors who feared that close coverage of what seemed like the total collapse of the economic system would inspire riotous panic among the masses. It should also be noted that editors and publishers largely sympathized with big business and were thus hostile to those entities "making the most noise about the depression," (e.g. labor unions; Norman Sims *True Stories: A Century of Literary Journalism* (Evanston, IL: Northwestern UP, 2007) 134. James Boylan argues that such obfuscation was readily referred to as "newspaper leadership" by editors who partook in the practice. Thankfully, this self-imposed myopia waned after the first few years of the depression, leading to debate and infighting among

the nation's "big-city editors," and eventually more thorough coverage of the fallout. See "Publicity for the Great Depression: Newspaper Default and Literary Reportage," *Mass Media Between the Wars: Perceptions of Cultural Tension, 1918–1941*, ed. Catherine Covert and John Stevens (Syracuse, NY: Syracuse UP, 1984), 162.

27. James McGrath Morris, *The Ambulance Drivers: Hemingway, Dos Passos, and a Friendship Made and Lost in War* (Boston: Da Capo Press, 2017), 29.

28. Ronald E. Martin *American Literature and the Destruction of Knowledge: Innovative Writing in the Age of Epistemology* (Durham: Duke UP, 1991), 320.

29. Ibid., 321.

30. On September 1, 1920, the pair was indicted for first-degree murder; Sacco and Vanzetti were found guilty in July of 1921 after a six-week trial. They both received death sentences. The conviction and death sentences of Sacco and Vanzetti sparked public outrage and a wave of demonstrations by artists, writers, laborers, immigrants, and political radicals (many of whom fell into one or more of these categories) in both the United States and abroad. Most who opposed their prosecution cited Sacco and Vanzetti's radical politics (they were both anarchists) and ethnic heritage, not the evidence, as leading to guilty verdicts. In fact, in the subsequent petitions, motions, and appeals made on Sacco and Vanzetti's behalf, evidence apparently exonerating the two surfaced but was largely ignored by the state and federal authorities to whom it was presented. On August 23, 1927, Sacco and Vanzetti were electrocuted. Dos Passos staunchly assailed Sacco and Vanzetti's conviction and sentence. Just two days before their execution, he was even arrested outside of the Massachusetts State House for his part in the public protest.

31. The Camera Eye is narrated from the perspective of the author at the time of the events being depicted. In this case, we are privy to the viewpoint of a twenty-five-year-old Dos Passos—who would not begin work on this final installment of the trilogy for seven years.

32. John Dos Passos, "The Pit and the Pendulum," *New Masses*, 1926, qtd. in Donald Pizer ed., *John Dos Passos: The Major Non-Fictional Prose* (Detroit: Wayne State UP, 1988), 89.

33. Dos Passos, as Joyce does with Bloom, aligns the wrongfully prosecuted immigrants with Christ, positioning their deaths as instruments of salvation. In this way, he seeks to ennoble them, to humanize them, for a middle class readership that, through consumption of mainstream journalism, had come to see them as little more than foreign terrorists.

34. Michael Jacobs, "From Cotton Pickin' to Acid Droppin': James Agee and the New Journalism," *Let Us Now Praise Famous Men at 75: Anniversary Essays*, ed. Michael A. Lofaro (Knoxville: U of Tennessee P, 2017), 343–65.

35. George Braziller, *Letters of James Agee to Father Flye* (New York: James Harold Flye and the James Agee Trust, 1962), 29.

36. Linda Wagner-Martin, "Let Us Now Praise Famous Men—and Women: Agee's Absorption in the Sexual," *James Agee: Reconsiderations*, ed. Michael A. Lofaro (Knoxville: U of Tennessee P, 1992), 44.

THREE

James Agee's Legacy of Cultural Repudiation

JEFFREY FOLKS

James Agee was an important influence on what Roger Scruton has called the culture of repudiation, or what, in a positive light, might be called ethical disengagement from authoritarianism of any sort. This aspect of Agee's writing is inseparable from his cult-like standing in the years after his death and his growing reputation in the 1960s. In this paper, I will study the anti-authoritarian nature of Agee's writing, especially *Let Us Now Praise Famous Men,* and its influence on an increasingly skeptical and detached public culture.

That an Agee cult did and continues to exist is undeniable, despite the efforts of several contemporary critics, whose dismissal of the importance of this issue would seem to mask an attempt to suppress both the reasons for the cult following and the impact of that following since Agee's death.[1] I would suggest that the intense interest in Agee since his death has had much to do with the ersatz Christ-like tenor of his life, a life that nonetheless set itself defiantly against established religion, and that the continuing cult-like interest may be grounded in the extent to which American liberal culture has moved toward similar goals of secular materialism over the last sixty years. Much like Fredrich Nietzsche, who passionately sought a source of compelling meaning in existence even as he declared the death of God, Agee was a "seeker" who had broken with conventional religion but was obviously motivated by a spiritual quest. Rather than being an issue of merely biographical or "historical" importance to present readers, the Agee myth is crucial to any thorough understanding of Agee's reputation. Agee was obsessed with the idea of pressing his existence to the dangerous margin and beyond, and he understood that he was offering up his life in the service of a cause. If the legacy that he created, in the form of the Agee myth, is unimportant because it transgresses into the biographical fallacy, then it is difficult to make a case for Agee's lasting influence. Understanding the exact nature of this martyrdom, and especially of the "cause" for which Agee died, is crucial to an assessment of his importance as a writer and cultural figure.

Agee never expressed sustained interest in social or political reform. Instead, he rejected all forms of human community and sought perfection as a solitary critic of society who repudiated all institutions by which ordinary persons define their existence. Agee was hardly original in this antagonism, having modelled it from Joyce, Zola, Pound, Kafka, O'Neill, Brecht, Proust, Stein, Russell, Dewey, and a host of other modernist writers and intellectuals. Like Bertrand Russell, Agee aspired to be a "free intellect, an intellect that will see as God might see, without a *here* and *now*, without hopes and fears, without the trammels of customary beliefs and traditional prejudices."[2] That sort of moral and intellectual freedom was the goal of writers and artists from Flaubert to Joyce and beyond, so it is not surprising that Agee should ascribe to a similar ethos. Many writers in this tradition might be described as radical in their commitment to art. Flaubert famously spoke of being "regular and orderly in your life, so that you may be violent and original in your work," but Agee differed from his predecessors in the degree of his alienation. For Agee, the precondition of his originality was, apparently, a life that was even more violent and original than his art. The fallacy of Agee's conception of art pointed the way toward writers such as William S. Burroughs and Jean Genet, who were even more self-destructive.

Perhaps the most important element of modernism was the separation, or defection—and inevitably antagonism—of the writer and intellectual from the common life of man. Ibsen's contempt for the masses was apparent in his comment to his friend Georg Brandes: "Under no circumstances will I ever link myself with any party which has the majority behind it."[3] In Agee's case the elitism so obvious in Ibsen takes the form of defiance of the common rules and institutions shared by the majority of mankind: marriage, family, religion, labor, patriotism, and the like. This antagonism toward ordinary life is apparent in so many mid-twentieth century intellectuals that it is hardly necessary to cite examples. In many cases, it was not simply a matter of rejecting conventionality but also of a violent dislike and wish to mock and bring harm to those viewed as representatives of everyday life. This alienation of writers and intellectuals, though it continues still, reached a sort of culmination in the radical days of the 1960s. It was not coincidental that *Let Us Now Praise Famous Men* was republished and achieved its first broad circulation in the Ballantine paperback edition of 1966. Unlike the 1941 first edition, which sold poorly even in a small print run, the 1966 edition sold well and was well received: the antagonist culture had spread to college campuses and a new generation was better prepared to read Agee.

The common man may not have possessed intellectual skill, but he had the majority on his side as well as the material benefits that flow naturally from stable careers and social acceptance. As the antagonist culture grew in strength during the twentieth century, it garnered the means of exercising control of the ordinary citizen, whether through the tyranny of a Stalin or Hitler or through FDR's Brain Trust and subsequent American presidents' reliance on academic "experts." While Agee had little interest in governance, he displayed a similarly elitist attitude toward art. Whether in his film reviews, in which he lectured the public concerning the bad taste of popular Hollywood films, or in *Let Us Now Praise Famous Men*, in which he outlined a theory that removed art from the reach of the masses, Agee was consistently disdainful of everyday American taste. As Roger Scruton wrote in *Modern Culture*, "For a long time now it has been assumed that there can be no authentic creation in the sphere of high art which is not in some way a 'challenge' to the ordinary public. Art must give offence, stepping out of the future fully armed against the bourgeois taste for kitsch and cliché. But the result of this offence is that offence becomes a cliché."[4] Certainly, Agee's "offence" against bourgeois art is apparent in his characterization of tenant existence as "delicately fragrant as a paradise, and, like all that is best . . . loose, light, casual, totally *actual*."[4] The alienation of art and artist from everyday life, a development in which Agee played an important part, has had serious consequences both for art and the public. Just as artists have disdained the public, the public has come to disdain art and so has been deprived of a crucial means of cultural understanding. The growing divisiveness of Western society is surely the result of the public's lack of subtlety and imagination, itself a result of the abandonment of common experience on the part of artists such as Agee.

That kind of retreat from common existence was appealing to the generation that came of age following WWII, and Agee's example was that of a martyred bohemian who died for the cause of uncompromising honesty. Agee was just as antagonistic toward religion, government, business, education, and marriage and family as he was toward conventional art. Even the best of teachers, he asserts, "are at best the servants of unconscious murder" (237)—what would he have thought of the *average* public-school teacher? It is impossible, however, to reside in a state of complete antagonism and retain sanity: as Alasdair MacIntyre shows, rationality requires a definite structure of thought organized around enduring principles. In Agee's case, the basis of self-definition centered on his conception of himself as an artist. Agee had, in effect, dropped out of respectable society and set himself against the norms of conventional middle-class America, but he sought to conform quite closely to the ways of the bohemian artist as defined by the late-Romantic ideal of Art. The fact that this ideal was already quite outmoded by the time Agee adopted it is beside the point: it served as a means of organizing his life and establishing his identity, just as it did for other late Romantics such as H. G. Wells, Jack London, Ezra Pound, Virginia Woolf, Sherwood Anderson, Hermann Hesse, Henry Miller, Thomas Wolfe, Dylan Thomas, Lawrence Durrell, and Tennessee Williams. Agee abandoned every other responsibility of life but never that of Art, which offered him both status and redemption. Judged from a conventional perspective, Agee was a failure at nearly everything, even at book publication (other than his early poems, he published only the short novel *The Morning Watch* and *Let Us Now Praise Famous Men* during his lifetime); but in one respect he excelled: he consistently sought an ideal state of life and art beyond any that could be achieved, and he sacrificed his life in the pursuit of that impossible ideal.

If Agee despised the middle class, as indeed he did, his sense of his own failure aligned him with the underclass. In the long passage from *Let Us Now Praise Famous Men* in which he traces the life of the tenant, and by extension the lives of all the "two billion now living" on earth, most of whom consisted of the poor, Agee presents an image of human beings as terribly fragile, helpless, victimized, and at risk. From birth "this tender and helpless human life" (90) grows through agonies of pain and disappointment to adulthood and on to old age, battered and worn down by life's burden until it expires almost unnoticed in some barren corner of some miserable shack. Agee's view is the opposite of that of Sophocles in *Antigone*, Scene 1 ("Wonders are many, and none is more wonderful than man"), but then it was precisely the inheritance of classical and European civilization that Agee had rejected as false and hypocritical. Indeed, Agee fantasized his own self-creative, godlike powers precisely because he had rejected the cultural creations of others. Having dismissed his cultural inheritance, it was necessary to begin from scratch and create his own standards and values. Certainly, the Alabama tenants appeared to Agee to be similarly without a cultural inheritance, however far from the truth this was, and Agee viewed them as fellow travelers on the road to self-creation. They were living at the level of necessity that Agee also wished to achieve, beyond society and the deathly influence of respectability. If their lives were brief, painful, and miserable, so be it: that was the price one paid for the sort of freedom that Agee sought.

Another element of the Agee cult was the ideal of authenticity that he adopted from Romantic writers and that became a crucial element of antagonist writing in the 1960s. What strikes one in his letters to Alma Mailman, published in *James Agee Rediscovered*, is not just the typical lover's lament over being separated by distance and by the fact that Agee was married at the time to Olivia Saunders, but an aspiration that transcends the possibilities of either Agee or Alma as lovers. What Agee seeks is simply "joy," a quality he equates with the highest form of art but which he also detects in "that delicate stage of love when a girl . . . first begins . . . to use her light slow frank hands upon your head and body" (381). The bluntness of Agee's expression, no less so than that of Henry Miller or Lawrence Durrell, expressed a repudiation of conventional sexual norms. Like other late Romantics, Agee sought an unachievable authenticity in the sexual act. The difficulty is that there are values other than authenticity, many such as faith, courage, and responsibility of far greater consequence to society. To base one's ethics solely upon the authenticity of one's actions dangerously distorts the nature of the moral order.

Certainly, Agee appears to have derived pleasure from the familiar game of *frapper la bourgeoisie*, but at a deeper level he seems to have sought to vanish altogether. It was not, as a number of critics including Mark A. Doty have written, that Agee sought to *discover* his identity: oftentimes, he wished to *disappear* without a trace, taking his fragmentary but authentic writings with him. What is disturbing about this ambition is not just its destructiveness but the fact that, at the moment he is writing these long and rather bizarre missives to Alma, Agee is still married and that what he has to say about his spouse, predictably perhaps, is dismissive: Olivia ("Via") is conventional and uncomprehending and can never aspire to the romantic dream of the merging of souls and, more darkly, to the level of antagonism that is akin to a suicide pact. In the manner of so many adulterers before and after, Agee informs Alma that Via just doesn't understand him. One might imagine that Agee's promiscuity, not just during his marriage to Via but in that with Alma and later Mia Fritsch as well (and in his "flirtation" with the vulnerable tenant woman Emma Woods in *Let Us Now Praise Famous Men*), would disqualify him as a role model for later generations, but just the opposite is the case. Like James Dean, and like the Beats and other leading cultural figures of the time, Agee's promiscuity was not just overlooked—it was a necessary element of his standing as a cult figure who anticipated the acceptance of promiscuity and "openness" in later decades.

Agee's bohemian protestations can sound rather pointless when read in the context of the economic expansion after his death. For example, his rapture at staying at the Read House, a pleasant hotel in Chattanooga, Tennessee, while on his way to Alabama seems unconvincing because of its self-indulgent fantasy of solidarity with the common man. "The very thought of cheap to middle-price hotel rooms and of the look of the streets of all cities except huge ones can make me as happy as the greatest art."[6] It would seem that Agee had spent too much time at Exeter and Harvard and in Manhattan to understand that, by heartland standards, the Read House was a highly respectable hostelry that during its long history has accommodated such guests as Winston Churchill, Gary Cooper, and Oprah Winfrey.

What readers may overlook is that Agee carried this same attitude of bohemian excess with him to his stay with the three tenant families in Alabama and that repudiation is as much or more the subject of that chronicle as is the life of the Southern tenant farmer. Agee's enjoyment of slumming in the Read House is indicative of the attitude toward the poor that he brought with him to Alabama. Certainly, the life of a Southern tenant family was difficult, but it was not exceptionally harsh in the context of the 1930s. Tenants struggled, but they survived, and their ordeal was not unusual at a time when one quarter of American workers were unemployed and wages and conditions for those still working were poor. Agee and Evans did not present a realistic account of tenantry: they distorted the subject for their particular purposes—purposes that in Agee's case centered on his repudiation of bourgeois values. At the center of this repudiation in Agee's case was the maternal presence that shadowed his life from Knoxville to St. Andrews and from there to New England, a matriarch "worried to death"[8] over her son and a worry he did all he could to amplify. The colossal face of middle-class complacency that loiters behind Agee's bohemian gestures is that of his hovering mother. Evidence of this is Agee's peculiar attraction to uncleanliness and poverty. The inevitable dirt that accompanies the life of the tenants, albeit against their wishes, is for Agee a source of pleasure, even a mark of "holiness." Likewise, the tenant cabins are thought to express a great beauty: "[T]heir esthetic success seems to me even more important than their functional failure" (164). Ragged clothes, dirt, infestation, and body odor are not something that most persons, including tenant farmers, wish to endure, but for Agee they are indications that the rural poor are "on his side" and truly opposed to respectability. He does not seem to realize how eager the tenants themselves are to escape these conditions.

Significantly, Agee himself preserved a version of this degradation in his personal life after returning to New York: his unshaven face, workingman's clothes, and unwashed body were a distinctive, and disturbing, presence to many of his co-workers, and it was his way of asserting his bohemianism against others from his own upper-middle-class background. It bears repeating that Agee was *not* a working-class Southerner whose values were aligned with those of the tenants: he was the offspring of a Midwestern mother determined to afford him a genteel education in preparation for a respectable career and marriage. What Agee wrote of tenantry had less to say about the life of the tenants than it did about his own genteel social background.

Agee's bohemianism was, as I see it, both adolescent and inauthentic, but it was just this immaturity that appealed to the generation that followed. Nor is "bohemian" quite the right word in Agee's case. His bohemianism, as Walker Evans points out in his preface to the 1960 edition of *Let Us Now Praise Famous Men*, was not a "game"; it was deadly serious, infused with something of the anger of the radicals and anarchists who followed in the sixties and subsequent decades, including the Weather Underground, Germany's Red Army Faction, Italy's Red Brigade, the Japanese Red Army, and the antifa movement of our times. Among members of these groups, anger, disaffection, and a totally uncompromising hatred of convention not unlike what Agee expressed is redirected toward radical political ends. Like Agee, radicals such as Fusako Shigenobu have shown a willingness to sacrifice human life in the service of an idea—in Agee's case, a devotion to "art" or "truth" rather than political ends, a fact that does not make Agee's actions less destructive. Agee was in fact "deadly" serious, and not enough scholarly attention has focused on the extent to which he set in motion beliefs that proved destructive to many of his associates and followers, and to Agee himself. Agee was intent on self-harm from a very early point in life, and his anger only gathered momentum as he matured.

Anger of that intensity is different from the merely attention-getting bohemianism of his late-Romantic predecessors. In Agee there was a willingness to sacrifice human beings, even and perhaps especially those closest to him, for the sake not so much of a "cause," and certainly not for a political cause such as communism, despite his passing claim of being "a Communist by sympathy and conviction" (201). What Agee wished above all was for his "reader"—the reader he so often entreats and by which he meant the world as a whole—to join in an indictment of all who are living, even of the tenants themselves to the extent that they remain oblivious of their own victimization, not for the sake of social justice but for the sin of being alive. The horror that Agee had resisted facing prior to writing *Let Us Now Praise Famous Men* is the conviction that all are guilty and that none should live. It was the Manson-like urge to stamp out life and replace it with something pure and untroubled and beyond all control, especially that of "the pigs," whom both Agee and Manson so much despised.

Agee's assertion that the lives of the tenants and their children are hopeless is very much in line with his own sense of despair. As Agee presents it, tenancy is a permanent caste condition that is incapable of improvement. That claim turned out to be false even in the case of individuals such as Louise Gudger, one of the less successful of the tenant children, who nonetheless made her way from tenancy, married, had children, and lived a modestly affluent existence. Personal problems led to Louise's suicide in her thirties, but her children lived financially secure lives far above those of their mother or grandparents. For others, success was much greater, as it was for Carl Albert, Harold Hamm, Audie Murphy, Ross Perot, Harland Sanders, Oprah Winfrey, and hundreds of thousands of others with roots in tenancy.

A cursory look at US GDP figures demonstrates the rise in real living standards in the decades following the publication of *Let Us Now Praise Famous Men*. Adjusted for inflation, US GDP rose from $1,33 trillion in 1940 to $3.23 trillion in 1960 and $13.26 trillion in 2000. While not every individual benefited from this rising tide, Americans as a whole, including the children and grandchildren of sharecroppers, did rise proportionately. From $621 in 1930, per capita income, adjusted for inflation, rose to $1,541 in 1950 and $4,218 in 1970 to $53,658 in 2018, or by a remarkable 8600%.[7] Individuals may have fallen through the cracks, but the vast majority of Americans, including those in the rural South, are now living vastly better than they did at the time of Agee's visit to Alabama. Agee's assertion that the lives of the tenant class would remain unchanged was demonstrably false, and nothing in the sweeping rhetoric of his prose will make it less so.

Agee's very nature displayed an intense quality of pessimism directed at others and at himself, a quality that comes across in the section of *Let Us Now Praise Famous Men* ("Intermission: Conversation in the Lobby") in which Agee prints his response to a questionnaire of May 1939 from the editors of the *Partisan*

Review. "A good artist," he declares, "is a deadly enemy of society . . . " (288). "I feel violent enmity and contempt toward all factions and all joiners," he adds (288), including members of the Communist Party, whose political "means" he appears to find the least unsatisfactory of all parties. In the event of America's entry into another world war, Agee wrote that his preference would be to "Escape from it [presumably, the military draft] by whatever means possible and by the same means continue to do my own work" (288). There were of course many, including Robert Lowell, who claimed to be conscientious objectors and who refused to fight, but Agee's response was different: he specifically dismissed conscientious objector status since he did not believe in any identifiable religion or moral scheme: he simply asked to be left alone. (As it was, it appears that he may have been exempted on the grounds of his claim of homosexuality or bisexuality.)

Agee's degree of pessimism and his fantasy of being "left alone" suggest a destructive attraction to nihilism. Death, after all, is the only prize for one who rejects all connection with society. In a chapter on "Hume on Practical Rationality and Justice," Alasdair MacIntyre analyses the necessity of preserving some basis of shared rationality with others in society: "Withdraw from human beings that reciprocity of shared responses and the consequent possibilities of shared reasoning and you withdraw also that type of social order in which the calm passions and the habits of response which express them restrain and overcome the violent passions. You thereby surrender the social order either to the superstitions of ancient barbarians or the enthusiasms of the barbarous of modern times."[9] I suspect that MacIntyre would have classified Agee as among those "barbarous of modern times," along with Jack Kerouac and the rest of the Beat Generation, yet, like that of James Dean, who died one week after taking possession of his prized Porsche Spider, Agee's reputation only grew after his death. The Agee cult is based on the extent to which he rejected every practical basis for civilization and even for existence, leaving death as the sole alternative.

As he often suggests in *Let Us Now Praise Famous Men*, Agee is "angry" on the part of the tenants at the owners, the authorities, the educational system, and America itself, but the tenants, who wish merely to become part of the system and of America, were not.[10] In the decades following Agee's death, antagonistic rebellion gained a mass following among middle-class youth in the West. Music, films, novels, and television all catered to the taste for sheltered rebellion. At the same time, the youth of the sixties was pursuing college degrees in unprecedented numbers, and would emerge as the most affluent generation in American history.

It was a generation that admired Janis Joplin, Jimmy Hendrix, and Bob Dylan, along with James Dean, J. D. Salinger, and James Agee, but that did not take them seriously, at least not for long. For the Boomers, slumming was recreation, a momentary escape from the otherwise serious business of life. For Agee, since he believed that his very soul was at stake, only a complete repudiation would be sufficient, and, indeed, the conditions that he imagines for his three tenant families have something of this post-apocalyptic quality. The seared expression of "beatitude" that Agee records—"in their eyes so quiet and ultimate a quality of hatred, and contempt, and anger, toward every creature in existence beyond themselves" (29)—is confirmation of the damage they have endured.

Altogether, Agee's appealing personality, his romantic persona, and his repudiation of bourgeois values combined to make him a cult hero after his death, but the serious task of the Boomer generation was earning a living, supporting and raising a family, and securing one's comfort in advance of and in retirement. The Boomers turned out to be no more or less conformist and self-indulgent than any generation before them, although they were fortunate to be raised at a time and place of great affluence and opportunity. The seriousness of postwar culture lay elsewhere, in the tens of millions of families formed or reunited after the war and in the unprecedented level of prosperity and happiness achieved in American society in the postwar decades, not in the culture of repudiation that flourished apart from the everyday life of ordinary Americans. Of this historic economic advancement, Agee was utterly naïve. While the country marched rapidly forward after the war, Agee remained stuck in romantic conceptions of repudiation and the religion of Art, this at a time when most Americans were thrilled with a suburban rancher and a new Chevrolet.

Agee's goal of breaking through to a higher and purer plane of expression—the word "rebellion" seems weakly inappropriate here—is sometimes understood to be a variety of religious aspiration. In reality, it is the very opposite of religion as practiced by the great majority of the world's people. At the center of Christianity and the other major religions is the requirement of humility in the face of divinity. As Roger Scruton puts it, the "essence of the religious life" is "not progress and experiment but the journey back to the place that protects us" (237). Nothing could be further from Agee's conception of "religion," which seems instead a version of Gnosticism, the modern substitution of the divinity of the Self in place of genuine religious experience.

As Agee understood, the alternatives were freedom and death. Agee carried his rejection of all structures of order "to the very edge"—almost his exact description in his Notebooks—but this dangerous effort resulted in enormous harm to himself and to those around him. It was not commendable for James Agee to be married three times and engage in a large number of adulterous affairs or to chain-smoke and regularly drink himself into a stupor, nor was it necessary for him to die at age forty-five. It is a mischievous and destructive culture that celebrates such an individual as a cult hero. Judged from the perspective of enduring ethical standards, from Aristotle's belief in excellence and happiness as natural ends of existence to Aquinas's faith in a supreme good to Wittgenstein's recognition of the redemptive quality of presentness, Western moral philosophy has always privileged goodness, truth, and happiness as enduring goals of human life. Agee set himself squarely against this understanding. Along with many his contemporaries, Agee led modern culture toward an antagonist perspective that was nihilistic, anarchistic, and narcissistic. It should be obvious that this perspective cannot be the basis for a healthy or comfortable life, nor can it be the basis of a stable and productive marriage and family life.

In the generation that followed, this nihilistic drive entered the general culture, culminating in the disillusionment of the 1970s with films like *Midnight Cowboy* (1969) and *Dog Day Afternoon* (1972). It was only gradually that American culture worked its way out of this dead-end of opposition to all that was conventionally valued. The conclusion of *Dog Day Afternoon*, with one bank robber shot dead and the other taken into custody while hostages are happily reunited with friends and family, is a marvelous representation of the contrast between the antagonist culture (acted by Al Pacino) and the mainstream culture represented by police, media, and bank employee hostages. Pacino delivers an unsettling performance as the crazed and damaged antisocial, a young man "just doing the best he can," who in fact is utterly failing by every measure. One cannot help but think of the similarity between Pacino's role in this film and Agee's self-description in his letter to one Dr. Rogers, the Navy psychiatrist Agee contacted with the intention of avoiding military service during WWII. Like Sonny in *Dog Day Afternoon*, Agee repeatedly spoke of the "unsatisfactoriness" of his life, of feeling blocked and unfulfilled, and indeed of not even wishing to find fulfillment, which he regarded as a form of compromise. Like Sonny, Agee was failing in his marriage and, more importantly in Agee's mind, in his art. Like

Sonny, Agee expressed sympathy for others whom he perceived as victims, but in the end he did them little good.

Dog Day Afternoon is one of the most angry, troubling, and repugnant films ever made. There is nothing about the protagonist, or the film itself, that can be said to possess redemptive value. Although Agee's writing represented an earlier stage of this attitude, it was in this direction that his work pointed. As Agee portrays it, there is little about the life of the three tenant families that is attractive except perhaps the beauty of the unspoiled tenant children and of Louise Gudger in particular. It is important to remember, however, that it is not tenant life itself that is inherently nasty—it is Agee and Evans's depiction that strips it of whatever beauty it might actually possess. While the tenant families were not educated, they were literate and they possessed an inherited religious culture that provided a moral framework for behavior—more of a framework, it might be said, than that possessed by Agee and Evans themselves. Those elements of tenant life that Agee mocks, particularly the role of farm owners and authorities of various kinds, including police, business owners, and educators, would have been respected by the tenants themselves. The "Bonny and Clyde" romanticism that liberal culture attached to the lower rungs of Southern culture was absent in the denizens of that culture itself, who could recognize the difference between thuggish criminality and respectable poverty. In sum, *Dog Day Afternoon*, like *Let Us Now Praise Famous Men*, was an expression of a demoralized phase of American culture in which America's elite class was turning against itself.

The 1970s, with so many books and films resembling *Dog Day Afternoon*, could be said to represent the logical culmination of the nihilistic impulse that was central to Agee's art. Agee's misreading of the tenant culture in *Let Us Now Praise Famous Men* casts the tenants as unknowing and natural antagonists when in fact they were simply individuals who aspired toward conventional happiness but were unable at present to achieve it. Within a generation of Agee's writing *Let Us Now Praise Famous Men*, tenancy would largely disappear in America, and most of those whose families had endured the privations of tenant farming had assimilated into middle-class America. Agee accepted the idea that tenancy was a permanent and static condition because he wanted to use his tenant families as tropes in support of his own alienation. Even later, as the antagonist culture became more mainstream, the implications of *Let Us Now Praise Famous Men* can hardly be taken seriously except by individuals who are as fully alienated as was James Agee. Agee recognized that his book, should it find a publisher, would hardly be a popular success. It was his aspiration, in fact, that *Let Us Now Praise Famous Men* not be a success and, one suspects, that it not even be published. After all, the ultimate expression of "not art" was "not book," just as the ultimate expression of nonacceptance of convention was divorce, adultery, alcoholism, and early death. Perhaps the ultimate goal was not to have ever been born, and this of course was not just Agee's goal but that of many others in the antagonist generation. From William Burroughs to Jean Genet, from Michel Foucault to Jacques Derrida, from the Red Army Faction to Islamic extremism, the modern world has followed Agee down the rabbit hole of cultural repudiation. It remains an open question whether the West is to return to a sensible culture based on faith in the goodness of life or whether it is to descend further into violence and chaos.

Ultimately, *Let Us Now Praise Famous Men* is an important and remarkable book, but it is not a wise or mature one. Its central subject is James Agee himself, and this subject leads to a prose that is at times convoluted, meandering, and aimless, if also to passages of great beauty and precision. What is missing is the seriousness of a writer who understands much of life outside the self and who conveys that understanding with judgment and deliberation: a Dickens, a Conrad, a Dostoyevsky, a Proust, a Faulkner, a Thomas Mann, an Orwell, a Solzhenitsyn, a Lawrence even. Agee's name does not belong on this list, not because he lacked ability but because he had so little to say.

In *Let Us Now Praise Famous Men*, as in his other works, Agee is adrift, pitiful, and sad, searching but never arriving at answers. Agee inspired a cult-like following because a large and influential postwar generation shared his sense of cultural alienation and sought the same kind of authenticity and meaning in the repudiation of its cultural past. For most in the postwar generation, repudiation was soon abandoned as the responsibilities of work, family, and citizenship came to dominate their lives. James Agee's writing is important in the context of the culture of repudiation that strongly impacted Western civilization in the decades following World War II. Apart from the sheer genius of his writing, Agee's contribution to this cultural movement was significant, and he deserves to be remembered and read for the passion and dedication he brought to the task.

Notes

1. Caroline Blinder, "Introduction," *New Critical Essays on James Agee and Walker Evans: Perspectives on Let Us Now Praise Famous Men* (London: Palgrave McMillan, 2010), passim.

2. Bertrand Russell, *The Value of Philosophy*, chap. 15; qtd. in Roger Scruton, *An Intelligent Person's Guide to Philosophy* (New York: Penguin Books, 1997),13.

3. Paul Johnson, *Intellectuals* (New York: Harper & Row, 1988), 98.

4. Roger Scruton, *Modern Culture* (London: Continuum, 2000), 86.

5. James Agee, *Let Us Now Praise Famous Men: An Annotated Edition of the James Agee–Walker Evans Classic, with Supplementary Manuscripts* (*Collected Works of James Agee*), ed. Hugh Davis (Knoxville, TN: U of Tennessee P, 2015), 183. Further references in the text are to this edition.

6. Michael A. Lofaro and Hugh Davis, *James Agee Rediscovered: The Journals for 'Let Us Now Praise Famous Men' and Other New Manuscripts* (Knoxville, TN: U of Tennessee P, 2005), 40.

7. Ibid., 6.

8. Newsletter of the Federal Reserve Bank of St. Louis, online at https://fred.stlouisfed.org/series/A792RC0A052NBEA; retrieved 7-3-2019. See also Daniel Aaronson and Bhashkar Mazumder, "Intergenerational Economic Mobility in the United States, 1940 to 2000," *Journal of Human Resources* 43, no. 1 (Winter 2008): 139–72.

9. Alasdair MacIntyre, *Whose Justice? Which Rationality?* (South Bend, IN: U of Notre Dame P, 1988), 321.

10. An interesting example of the tenant attitude toward economic success can be found in the record of Florence Owens Thompson, the "Migrant Mother" depicted in the photographs of Dorothea Lange. In an interview conducted after her death, Thompson's children spoke of her strength, self-sacrifice, and desire to rise in the world. See Peter H. King, "One defiant family escapes poignant portraits of poverty," *Fresno Bee*, Section: Vision, F1, October 18, 1998.

FOUR

Confessions of Inadequacy

The Inescapable Influence of Let Us Now Praise Famous Men *on William T. Vollmann's* Poor People

ANDREW CROOKE

Elitist or Populist?

Among other disclaimers at the outset of *Poor People* (2007), William T. Vollmann remarks, "I certainly felt inadequate to sustain a meditation on any specific incarnation of poverty, as was so passionately attempted in *Let Us Now Praise Famous Men*."[1] This disavowal is doubly dubious. The collaboration between James Agee and Walker Evans is, ultimately, the closest model for Vollmann's wide-ranging photo-textual study. Moreover, his self-professed inadequacy may also seem suspect. After all, he is a prolific, erudite writer who has chronicled all sorts of exploited or marginalized characters. His fastidiously researched interdisciplinary books combine dollops of history, philosophy, geography, ethnography, social science, and investigative journalism with streaks of daredevil personal adventure, multimodal visual artwork, and radically experimental fictional techniques. Yet despite having won numerous literary awards and been called the most important living US author in a recent critical collection,[2] Vollmann remains something of a cult figure typically associated with the self-indulgent extremes of post-postmodernism.

At around three hundred pages of text, followed by 128 photographs, *Poor People* is a fairly short and accessible work for him. In its first sentence, he alludes understatedly to his "longish book about violence" (*PP* xi), *Rising Up and Rising Down* (2003), which runs to seven volumes in its original unabridged version. Likewise part travelogue and part treatise, his book about poverty has been referred to as volume eight.[3] Unlike Agee and Evans's deep exploration of Alabama tenant farmers, Vollmann does not concentrate on one impoverished group or place in *Poor People* but instead roams the planet assembling a patchwork of depressed, distressed, and dispossessed inhabitants. This broad inquiry, however, is a prelude to tighter focus on the disenchanted or disinherited. In Vollmann's next two projects, he narrows his scope to particular subcultures or communities: first American hobos and trainhoppers in his whimsical *Riding Toward Everywhere* (2008), then undocumented farmworkers and other downtrodden denizens of the California-Mexico borderlands in his monumental *Imperial* (2009).

Like all of his writing, *Poor People* grapples with various creative influences. In addition to adducing classic representations of poverty such as Jack London's *The People of the Abyss* (1903) and George Orwell's *Down and Out in Paris and London* (1933), Vollmann hails John Steinbeck's *The Grapes of Wrath* (1939) as "one of the best books about poor people" ever written and recognizes *Famous Men* (1941) as a deliberately doomed yet no less masterful enterprise, "a success because it fails" (*PP* xii). Vollmann reveals a great deal about his own approach to depicting poverty by cross-examining these two Depression-era inspirations, which he has linked to his work elsewhere as well. In an appeal to publishers when trying to place *Whores for Gloria* (1991), Vollmann claims it is of comparable merit to *The Grapes of Wrath* and *Famous Men* in that all three uphold "the dignity and beauty of being human even when a member of a despised or outcast class."[4] He again acknowledges his debt to both predecessors while wrestling with whether to cast *Imperial* as fiction or nonfiction. Defending Steinbeck against critical detractions (Agee's included) that he wrote simplistic or sententious novels, Vollmann declares him "the most American of us all," because by expressing outrage over the migrants' misfortunes he wasn't afraid to sound "un-American," to hector his compatriots so much that they would ban *The Grapes of Wrath*.[5] Protective not just of Steinbeck's literary reputation but of his left-leaning politics and anti-authoritative individualism—convictions that Agee also sprinkles throughout *Famous Men*—Vollmann admires above all what he rather fuzzily extols as the sincerity of both writers.

However, he notes a marked disparity in their tones, tied up with differing conceptions of audience, which troubles Vollmann's construction of a narrative voice in *Poor People*. Whereas Steinbeck's text is populist, Agee's is "an elitist expression of egalitarian longings" (*PP* xii). Any tenant farmers who happened on Agee's elaborate portrayal of them would surely have been perplexed, but Steinbeck did find some "Okies" among his multitude of readers.[6] Perhaps embittered by the fame of Steinbeck's book versus the flop of *Famous Men*, Agee's essay "Pseudo-Folk" (1944) savages *The Grapes of Wrath* for its inverted snobbery and mediocre artistry.[7] Vollmann disagrees, lauding Steinbeck for transforming "The Harvest Gypsies," his reportage on industrialized agriculture, into a heartfelt work of art about the Joad family. Yet Vollmann commends Agee and Evans, too, for transcending their own journalistic assignment in 1936. Bucking *Fortune* magazine's loftiness, Agee's fellow feeling flowed vulnerably toward the three tenant families. Hence "he fought with all his crafty, hopelessly unrequitable passion to make our hearts do the same" (*PP* xii). Nevertheless, according to Vollmann, reading *Famous Men* is like being "slapped in the face" (*PP* xiii). Agee himself sardonically avers that he wrote it "for all those who have a soft place in their hearts for the laughter and tears inherent in poverty viewed at a distance, and especially for those who can afford the retail price" (*FM* 12), thus reproaching his presumably privileged audience for smug self-satisfaction.

So which is Vollmann himself: elitist or populist? The answer may be a bit (or a glut) of both. As verbose as he is versatile, his kaleidoscopic tomes are in some ways inviting, in others intimidating, often due to sheer bulk.[8] Wondering who his readers might be, in *Poor People* he mentions receiving fan mail from prisoners, prostitutes, and other "impoverished ones," which flatters him "because I am rich and I want poor people to like me" (*PP* 287). On the other hand, granting that his books can be daunting, he realizes his subjects' lack of money and schooling makes it unlikely they will be able to appreciate his latest work. Echoing Agee's apprehension that his "Harvard education is by no means an unqualified advantage" (*FM* 251), Vollmann, who attended Cornell, allows of his style: "[W]hy *shouldn't* people who cannot afford my Ivy League education be discouraged by long sentences?" (*PP* 288). Indeed, *Poor People* is as dizzying a tour of his library as of the world. Citations from a host of sages augment Vollmann's dispatches from dozens of countries. Keeping up with him—with his far-flung travels and genre-flouting maneuvers—is no easy task. Redolent of Agee's standoffish preliminaries, peculiar appendices, contradictory footnotes, and chaotic organization in *Famous Men*, Vollmann's leapfrogging structure and recurring examples are supplemented by his half-scrupulous, half-facetious source notes, income table, and dictionary of salient terms, such as the caustically defined *normality*, *respect*, and *false consciousness*.[9] These meta-textual features, more restrained in *Poor People* than in his lengthier volumes, endow him with an intellectually elastic (if not elitist) apparatus around which to weave his and others' ideas about what it means to be poor.

Vollmann compares his methodology with Agee's to differentiate them, seemingly to obviate any "anxiety of influence." Nevertheless, the two texts share a fair amount, not least their compulsive confessions of inadequacy in representing the poor. "I might say," Agee announces cagily, "in short, but emphatically not in self-excuse, of which I wish entirely to disarm and disencumber myself, but for the sake of clear definition, and indication of limits, that I am only human" (*FM* 10). Similarly, Vollmann's efforts to anatomize poverty are, by his own admission, subjective, imprecise, and insufficient: characteristics for which Agee alternately indicts and defends himself. Moreover, even though Vollmann largely avoids Agee's self-loathing and maintains that he does not feel guilty but grateful about never experiencing poverty, no less agonizingly sincere are his endeavors to establish rapport with his subjects. While he does not strive for penetrating relationships, as Agee did in embedding himself with the cotton tenants, Vollmann's broodings on countless briefer encounters exhibit the same dual quality he critiques in the former's disposition: highbrow fury fused with naive love for destitute strangers. Obsessed with cataloging every detail of the farmers' lives, Agee berates himself for his shortcomings "in an abstruse gorgeousness of abasement that only the rich will have time to understand" (*PP* xiii). Vollmann's sometimes rarefied or longwinded prose likewise may put off many "poor" people, yet his compassionate conjectures about his interviewees and provocative asides to his readers—whom he assumes to be, like him, "rich"—turn his text, as with Agee's, into a self-reflexive, open-ended quest for communication across class lines.

Furthermore, as with Evans's photographs at the beginning of *Famous Men*, Vollmann's visual portfolio is a sobering counterweight to verbal idiosyncrasies. Also isolated from a torrent of words, the pictures concluding *Poor People* nonetheless play a pivotal role within his text, not only illustrating it but prodding him to mull over those he sought to connect with in person. Like Agee, for all his ink-spilling, Vollmann has misgivings about how abstract, indistinct, and biased writing can be. "Words cannot embody"; Agee recognizes, "they can only describe" (*FM* 192). Complaining about their density, inaccuracy, and lack of simultaneity, he rues that words resort to "a Rube Goldberg articulation of frauds, compromises, artful dodges and tenth removes" (*FM* 191). Consequently, the camera appears more trustworthy. By the same token, notes one critic, "Vollmann finds complexity of language morally suspect when describing poverty."[10] Just as he oxymoronically observes that "Evans escapes into the tell-all taciturnity of photography" (*PP* xiii), so too Vollmann relies on "the inhuman fidelity of the lens . . . to fix each object as it is."[11] Most of his photographs practice the self-effacing documentary mode—as if not consciously crafted by a human eye—that Evans refined during the mid-1930s.[12] As with Evans's portraits of the Gudger, Woods, and Ricketts families, Vollmann does not request special stances from his subjects.[13] Reflecting on why he usually solicits permission instead of snapping candids, he asserts, "I would rather fail to get a good photo than fail to be a good neighbor to others."[14]

In fact, Vollmann's success as a photographer offsets what he considers his literary as well as interpersonal failures. He prizes *Famous Men* not only for similar tensions between its representational tools but for its dissonance between intentions and performance. Evans's contribution counterbalances Agee's feverishness by recording the sharecroppers' adversities "calmly, undeniably, heartbreakingly, inescapably" (*PP* xii). Every turbulent emotion that Agee discerns in Mrs. Ricketts during the first photo shoot is substantiated by Evans's unflinching images of her cropped by herself and surrounded by her children, "the mother as before a firing squad, the children standing like columns of an exquisite temple" (*FM* 298). While not as self-assured behind the shutter or as aesthetically arresting across his archive, Vollmann's most memorable pictures are also frontal poses. For instance, his tightly framed portrait of Annah, an elderly Yemeni beggar (figure 4.1), resembles Evans's well-known composition of Annie Mae Gudger (figure 4.2). Annah's hand, clutching a flowery headscarf to her chin, rests just below the center of this image, right where the open collar of Annie Mae's patterned dress reveals her bare throat. Each woman, notwithstanding her deplorable circumstances, returns the camera's close scrutiny with a fiercely unsmiling gaze that rejects shallow pity, redirects inquisitiveness, and radiates individuality as intensely and delicately as any words that might be deployed. Therefore, in spite of positioning himself against Agee and Evans, both the verbal and visual components of Vollmann's *Poor People* bear the inescapable influence of *Famous Men*, bringing its amalgam of aesthetic ambition and ethical abashment along with him into the twenty-first century.

Obligatory Failures

Even if he disavows meditating for long on any single embodiment of poverty, Vollmann is intrinsically meditative. His reasoning, like Agee's, proceeds by induction, and he too presents not just the results of his thinking but the process,

FIGURE 4.1 Annah, beggar woman in Yemen, 2002. William T. Vollmann, *Poor People.*

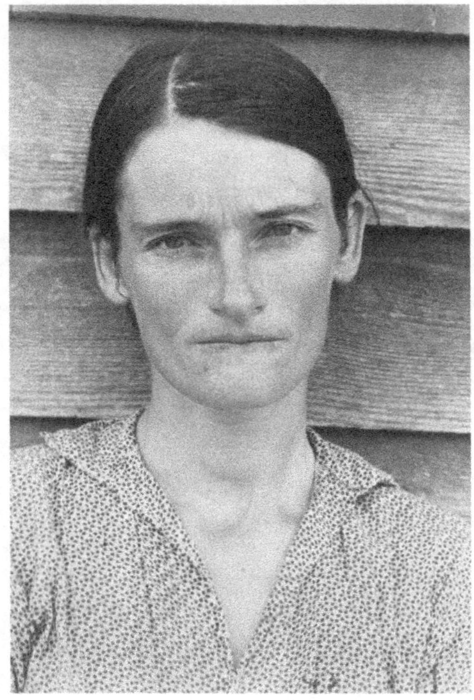

FIGURE 4.2 Annie Mae Gudger [Allie Mae Burroughs], Hale County, Alabama, 1936. Walker Evans, *Let Us Now Praise Famous Men.*

overlaid with all its ambivalences, ambiguities, and paradoxes. Analyzing the stories and portraits he collects in cities, villages, shantytowns, and refugee camps, Vollmann educes guarded generalizations. To his mind, "poverty is not mere deprivation; for people may possess fewer things than I and be richer; poverty is *wretchedness*" (*PP* 36). An emotional experience as much as an economic state, its dimensions, he theorizes, may comprise invisibility, deformity, unwantedness, dependence, accident-prone-ness, pain, numbness, and estrangement. When reviews of *Poor People* downplayed or frowned on such categorizing, they missed its intentionally speculative, scattershot nature.[15] Cautioning that the concept of *normality* varies so wildly from context to context as to be an arbitrary gauge of happiness, Vollmann's unconventional glossary defines *poor* as "unhappy in his or her own normality" and *rich* as "satisfied with one's normality, and reasonably able to apprehend it" (*PP* xxi). *Famous Men* sets itself up to fail, he says, insofar as it confronts the dilemmas of "two rich men observing the lives of the poor" (*PP* xii). Although Agee and Evans aim to collapse this gap—mainly through the writer's resolve to live with his subjects so that he could be with them "intimately and constantly" for several weeks (*FM* vii)—the tenants still remain so remote in their sense of normality that they cannot be readily grasped from a rich person's perspective. Accordingly, for all of Agee's paeans to an alert consciousness as the best instrument (aside, perhaps, from the camera) for capturing actuality, he must confess his myopia to circumvent condescension. A draft of his preface refers to *Famous Men* as "a record of blindness as well as of perception."[16] Instead of hiding his flaws, Agee exposes them, questioning his abilities to see the farmers and their environs clearly. Likewise chary of patronizingly facile observations, in *Poor People* Vollmann is careful to concede that his vision only extends so far.

There is a fine line, however, between confessing and trumpeting one's inadequacies. In *Famous Men,* Agee often crosses this line to indulge in reverse boastfulness. At the start of his "Work" chapter, "speaking of my verbal part of this book as a whole," he flaunts his unfulfilled effort to descend "devotedly into the depths of a subject, your respect for it increasing in every step and your whole heart weakening apart with shame upon yourself in your dealing with it . . . your unworthiness of it" (*FM* 259). Agee carries deficiencies proudly, as paradoxical proof that he is genuinely engaged with his subject. Cognizant that he will fall short of his unattainable goal to exalt reality without converting it into art, in a footnote to "*(On the Porch: 2*" he proclaims, "Failure, indeed, is almost as strongly an obligation as an inevitability, in such work" (*FM* 192). As a self-appointed mediator between the tenants and the wider world, in "Colon" he pledges to represent them "not lightly, not easily by any means: nor by any hope 'successfully'" (*FM* 81). But why should failure be obligatory for him? Why is he so obstinately opposed to success? Agee's next sentence, a rare third-person self-interrogation, elucidates the crux of his ethical conundrum: "For one who sets himself to look at all earnestly, at all in purpose toward truth, into the living eyes of a human life: what is it he there beholds that so freezes and abashes his ambitious heart?" (*FM* 81). Faced with an alien soul's inviolable vitality, he dares not transgress it in the vain or cocksure hope of divulging its essential character. Even as his heart melts upon befriending the three families, he despairs that words cannot do justice to their complexity and singularity. His ambition has been abashed. And yet Agee urges himself onward, with the foreknowledge of failure serving both to comfort his insecurities and wound his pride.

Vollmann is also impelled to broadcast his defects, in spite of his artistic ambitiousness and voluminous output. Relating his technical difficulties photographing in the desert for *Imperial*, he calls himself "a clumsy fellow with poor eyesight" and "a half-blind bumbler in sub-optimal conditions."[17] For his fictional series *Seven Dreams,* he adopts the authorial persona of William the Blind, a moniker not only made ironic because his hand-drawn maps were ostensibly "engraved on sight" but hinting at occlusions of insight as well.[18] *An Afghanistan Picture Show* (1992) parodies his altruistic ventures in support of that war-torn country and tenders a bizarre prayer "that this record of my failures may somehow in its negative way help somebody."[19] Expressing similar hopes for *Rising Up and Rising Down*, he portentously warns, "For its many failures I ask forgiveness from all."[20] Such apologies, in that massive study, come off, like Agee's, as false modesty. In *Poor People*, owing to its relatively scaled-back ambitions, Vollmann fesses up less ostentatiously. Albeit aware of his blind spots, he is just as bothered by his interviewees' limited foresight and eloquence. Clarifying why he cannot just compile but must gloss oral histories, Vollmann sadly comments, "Communication being . . . a skill of the rich, the poor people in this book sometimes failed to tell me what I longed to know" (*PP* 102). Yet while suggesting that they strain to articulate if not fathom the roots of their poverty, he averts a condescending tone by repeatedly confessing his own fallibility.

Hence Vollmann echoes Agee's repeated caveat that he can only write "a little" about all he absorbs. Agee uses this phrase as a charade of understatement, which seems to put him on the verge of forswearing his medium altogether but actually precedes lengthy sophisticated passages. After proposing to substitute found objects and body parts for words, his "Preamble" avows, "As it is, though, I'll do what little I can in writing. Only it will be very little" (*FM* 12). And as he remarks before embarking on a painstaking description, "I am hoping here only to tell a little, only so well as I may, about an ordinary house, in which I lived a little while" (*FM* 112–13). Bearing witness to daily existence on the farms, Agee misleadingly frets that he can set down a mere fraction of its minutiae, only to wear his pencil out scribbling incessantly. In practice, regardless of his modest pretenses, "a little" amounts to a lot in Agee's lexicon,[21] with which Vollmann is ineluctably familiar. As in *Famous Men*, the self-conscious first-person voice in *Poor People* is ever ready to point out "how little I know" (*PP* xv).

Each author therefore embeds overlapping failures in his book, creating paradoxical preconditions for success. For Agee, there are his failure to earn the farmers' unrestricted confidence, his failure to reproduce their lives adequately, and his readers' probable failure to take their lives seriously. For Vollmann, there are his subjects' failure to say profound things about their poverty and his failure to do anything uplifting about it. These are private failings of demeanor, discernment, representation, and illumination, in contrast to the public calamity Steinbeck decries by describing how the authorities destroy surplus food and let hungry people starve. "There is a failure here that topples all our success,"[22] Steinbeck deplores in a chapter Vollmann may have in mind when defending *The Grapes of Wrath* against charges that it is "mildewed" by such purposeful rhetoric and akin to works of socialist realism that "strive to be useful and fail in proportion to be beautiful."[23] Conversely, *Famous Men* may succeed in being beautiful at the cost of being useful, and perhaps at the cost of being sufficiently realistic. For some critics, Agee's determination to find virtue and beauty among the disadvantaged subverts either his characterization of or solidarity with them. Lionel Trilling praises both the book's photographs and text, yet identifies in the latter a blunder distinct from Agee's intentional failure to shape his material into a well-proportioned aesthetic form. While exonerating him of ever being "pious or sentimental, like Steinbeck and Hemingway," Trilling reproves Agee for the "failure of moral realism" resulting from his guilt-ridden refusal to see any blemishes of spirit or personality in the tenants.[24] Although Trilling later modified his judgment,[25] and although more recent commentators have quarreled with it productively,[26] others have extended its implications into forceful critiques of Agee's convoluted ethics as well as his compulsion to aestheticize the sharecroppers' privations.[27]

Like Steinbeck, however, Agee ultimately succeeded in pricking the complacency of his readership. Though *Famous Men* gained scant renown at first, after its 1960 republication it stimulated civil rights activists in the South.[28] Agee was no social reformer, but his insistence on loving the oppressed struck a radical chord during the War on Poverty and the movement to abolish racial inequalities. "He wanted to make people who were not poor feel what it was like to be up against it . . ." Evans reflected. "He was very angry about middle-class Americans, who buy security and take things for granted, while these people, who were human beings whom he loved, were shut out."[29] Agee's exhaustive inventories of the farmers' houses, clothes, chores—"with no detail, however trivial it may seem, left untouched, no relevancy avoided" (*FM* viii)—drive home socioeconomic disparities in a manner calculated to elicit awe and shame from more affluent readers. While class struggle may be a muted theme in *Famous Men*, its indictment of bourgeois values is even more searing than *The Grapes of Wrath*. As Linda Ray Pratt contrasts them, "Steinbeck's book teaches us the pathos which may inspire a New Deal, but Agee's book creates the consciousness that needs a revolution."[30] Similarly weighing the relative pragmatics of each writer, Vollmann esteems Steinbeck's political efficacy and ponders inconclusively on Agee's lasting impact: "What does more good, a generation of indignant college students or several million dollars' worth of beans, flour and powdered milk sent to this nation's poorest counties?"[31] Although Vollmann spurns the either/or quandary in some of his more youthful works, which brazenly undertook to "save the world" while simultaneously aspiring to literary greatness,[32] in *Poor People* he assumes a worldly-wise neutrality, neither crusading against social injustice nor hoping to make a concrete difference during his sojourns overseas.[33]

Mortal Insignificance

Vollmann's method seems quite simple: he crisscrosses continents, brashly yet sincerely asking people why they are poor while others are rich. But do his interviewees shed much light on their impoverishment? Do his musings on their replies provide productive ways to reconsider them? Vollmann candidly admits the limitations of his project. Rather than immerse himself firsthand in indigence, like Jack London and George Orwell, he is an unapologetic outsider curious about the causes and consequences of involuntary poverty. Those Vollmann interrogates are ordinary folks, on the whole less desperate or imperiled than the strung-out or violent ones depicted in his other books. As he explains of this selection process, "People who are poor but not in imminent danger of perishing have more of a chance of catching their breath and actually conceptualizing their poverty" (*PP* xv). His comprehension of them may be hindered, though, in that most differ from him not only in class status but also—as James Agee and John Steinbeck did not diverge from their subjects—in ethnicity, nationality, language, and religious background. *Poor People* is dedicated to Vollmann's interpreters, "without whom," he remarks self-deprecatingly, "I would have remained more deaf and ignorant than is already the case" (*PP* v). Moreover, he confesses that his brief meetings with respondents doubtless hamper his interpretations of their views. Yet Vollmann finds a redeeming quality in their passing acquaintance: "The impossibility of my gaining any dynamic understanding of these lives *over time,* my very lack of relevance to them, may enhance the truth of this presentation" (*PP* xv). In other words, he does not set out to prove anything definitive, or to perpetuate his ties with them, but to portray them as authentically as he can. Thus his mode is descriptive and comparative but neither comprehensive nor curative. By offering verbal and visual "snapshots of the ways in which certain poor people experienced their poverty at random moments" (*PP* xv), Vollmann is less overtly combative or polemical than Agee, who intended his book on "North American cotton tenantry" to be "a swindle, an insult, and a corrective" to typically shallow treatments of his "nominal subject" (*FM* viii).

Within and between chapters Vollmann hops freely about the globe, from Afghanistan to Colombia to the Philippines to the United States, but early on he introduces individuals from Thailand and Russia who serve as yardsticks for him. To compensate for the brevity of his other interactions, he dwells at length on Sunee, Wan, Natalia, and Oksana, regularly recalling their situations and attitudes. Likely an ex-bargirl abroad, Sunee is a moody alcoholic who despises her job cleaning offices and whose habitual gesture of flinging her arms outward symbolizes her suffocating existence in a Bangkok slum. As a Buddhist, she believes her poverty to be the result of bad karma from a previous life. Many others with whom Vollmann talks also suppose they were predestined to be poor, but an apparently poorer Thai woman, a sickly beggar named Wan (figure 4.3), astounds him when she claims to be rich. Albeit on guard against accusing anyone of false consciousness, since he strives to honor everyone's capacity for self-awareness, Vollmann nonetheless cannot agree with Wan, who like Sunee reappears throughout his text as a test case or touchstone for gauging other people's poverty. Natalia and Oksana, meanwhile, are rival beggars outside a St. Petersburg cathedral. They attribute their hardships less to destiny than to accidents: Oksana's son-in-law's radiation poisoning at Chernobyl, which leads to her family's displacement; Natalia's tick bite in infancy, which triggers her lifelong epilepsy. Even when his interpreter admonishes him, Vollmann persists in questioning Natalia (figure 4.4) as she accounts inconsistently for the fate of her children. "I was paying her to teach me, for my sake and yours, the particulars of her misery," he exculpates his nosiness (*PP* 60).

While the issue of payment complicates Vollmann's interviews, he never disguises these transactions but instead calls attention to them. "That's right!" he exclaims in a wryly defensive footnote. "I was paying for them; I was rich! Didn't that give my invasiveness carte blanche? In *Let Us Now Praise Famous Men*, Evans and Agee inspected every inch of their subjects' houses while the latter were away at church. Only you, the reader, can decide whether such knowledge as you gain from reading that long passage of the book justifies its means" (*PP* 16). This allusion is to "Shelter," in which Agee remorsefully confesses to rummaging through the Gudger house while the family was away—probably not at church, as Vollmann specifies—but there is no indication that Evans, who preferred staying at a hotel, likewise engaged in such snooping. In "Inductions," Agee relates how they negotiated with Bud Woods to pay room and board during their research. Eliding this arrangement, Vollmann dissociates his tactics in *Poor People* from their ethically dubious espionage. Yet in doing so he ignores the possibility that his subjects may distort their tales in hopes of getting more cash from him.[34] And who is to say they are poor in the first place? Vollmann's interpreter initially opines that Sunee's mother is not, for she owns assorted appliances (figure 4.5). Similarly, when he shows portraits of Oksana's family members (figure 4.6) to his "immigrant friends in America who worked in the so-called menial professions," they swear that "these people did not look poor at all!" (*PP* 67). Indeed, like Wan, Vollmann's interviewees often deny this label, finding contentment without material trappings, in kinship, spirituality, art, drugs, or another outlet that liberates them from economic anxieties. By contrast, those who do acknowledge their poverty variously blame the rich, the government, their hostile neighbors, or themselves. Whether furious or resigned, their responses do not always satisfy him. "In appropriate contradiction of this book's hopes and pretenses," he laments, "poor people's answers are frequently as impoverished as their lives" (*PP* 48). Despite eschewing intellectual elitism, such comments demonstrate that Vollmann is not immune to class prejudices.[35]

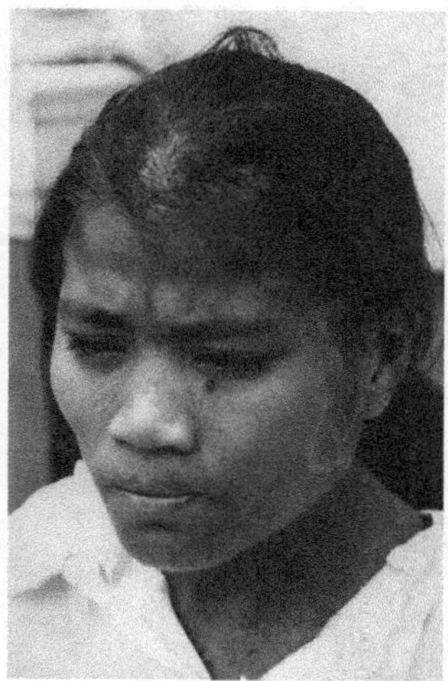

FIGURE 4.3 Wan, at Central Railroad Station, Bangkok, Thailand, 2001. William T. Vollmann, *Poor People*.

FIGURE 4.4 Natalia, [St.] Petersburg, Russia, 2005. William T. Vollmann, *Poor People*.

Although some of the information he gathers might be unreliable or unenlightening, Vollmann generally grants his subjects the benefit of the doubt and points his finger elsewhere. Nonhierarchical and nonjudgmental, he emphasizes, "Because I wish to respect poor people's perceptions and experiences, I refuse to say that I know their good better than they; accordingly, I further refuse to condescend to them with the pity that either pretends they have no choices at all, or else, worse yet, gilds their every choice with my benevolent approval" (*PP* 170). Instead, he echoes the dual challenge Agee poses in his "Preamble" by floating "the question: Who are you who will read these words and study these photographs, and through what cause, by what chance, and for what purpose, and by what right do you qualify to, and what will you do about it; and the question, Why we make this book, and set it at large, and by what right, and for what purpose, and to what good end, or none" (*FM* 8). Vollmann, in turn, addresses barrages of unanswerable questions to himself and his readers: "You are rich, so

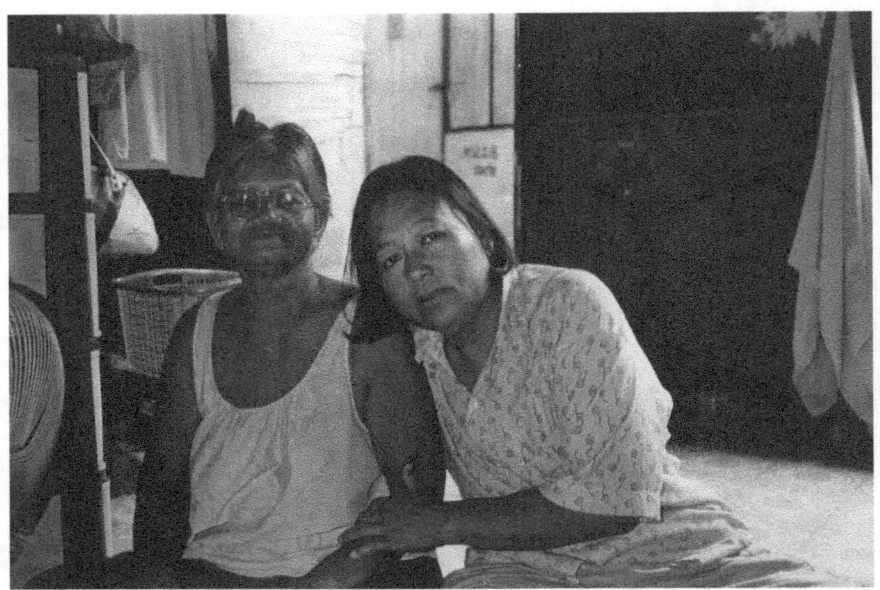

FIGURE 4.5 Sunee and her mother at the mother's home, Klong Toey slum, Bangkok, Thailand, 2001. William T. Vollmann, *Poor People*.

FIGURE 4.6 Oksana's family, [St.] Petersburg, Russia, 2005. William T. Vollmann, *Poor People*.

tell me: Who does that make you? What would *they* have been had poverty not diminished them? Would they be any happier?" (*PP* 289). One thought problem generates another, as he builds up chains of rhetorical vexations. Vollmann is frustrated, too, by his inability to bear full witness. In Muslim societies, for example, he rues not being able to reveal the countenances of burqa-clad women. He fails to supply evidence linking oil extraction in Kazakhstan to ill health and environmental degradation. While investigating snakeheads, the shadowy gangsters who smuggle illegal immigrants into Japan, he chides himself for neither meeting these criminals in the flesh (notwithstanding his reckless attempts) nor limning the toils in Fujian Province from which Chinese peasants risk so much to escape. Despite avowing that "unlike James Agee, I fear to give undue prominence to the joys of self-laceration," Vollmann postulates that his most successful chapter, "being the bluntest confession of inadequacy" (*PP* 203), is his sketch of "The Two Mountains," laid-off corporate employees who recycle cans and shelter in a tarp-roofed box under a Kyoto bridge. His outline of their circumstances must be truer than his more intricate ones, he reckons, "because it conveys and claims less" (*PP* 93), because he owns up to knowing nothing about them.

Beyond these failures of reportage, Vollmann regrets not doing more on behalf of his subjects. Admittedly impractical, like *Famous Men*, the book does not breathe a spirit of reform but merely pays "lip service to specific policy recommendations for improving poor people's lives" (*PP* 221). After asking how the United Nations measures the Human Poverty Index, Vollmann dismisses official calculations by adding flippantly: "Never mind. It won't make poor people any richer" (*PP* 237). Rather than laboring to eradicate poverty, he incites comfortable readers to rethink their conventional reactions—of pity, disgust, kindness, or wariness—toward penniless others. For instance, upon realizing that a deceptively armless beggar gripping a cup with his teeth has been outwitting passersby through a contortion of limbs (figure 4.7), Vollmann's annoyance is fleeting: "I thought he'd needed that money!—Immediately came the next thought: Of course he needs it!—Once that misunderstanding with myself had been cleared up (it lasted for less time than it took the man to rearrange his arms), I continued to pay his tithe, and with a cheerful heart" (*PP* 126). Such anecdotes operate as ethical interventions through which, either forthrightly or sarcastically, Vollmann spurs readers to reassess their own preconceptions and conduct.[36] He does not magnify his acts of charity, however. In fact, equating altruism with self-gratification, he criticizes the randomness of his procedure for bestowing alms: "If it amused

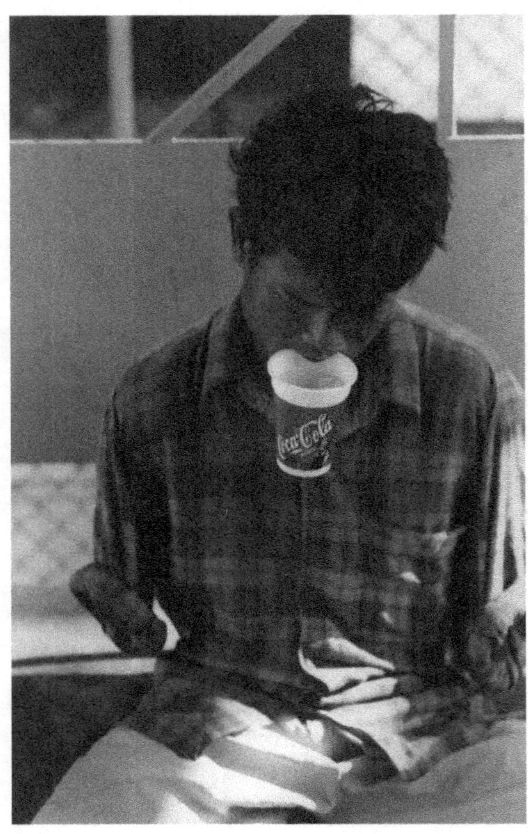

FIGURE 4.7 Beggar who pretended to be armless, Bangkok, Thailand, 2001. William T. Vollmann, *Poor People*.

me, I, a rich man, could choose a few poor people to be my pets, and then I could feed them in the most joyously self-congratulatory manner" (*PP* 93). Among squatters in Bogotá, he hands out "a little to the people I particularly pitied . . . while others equally poor or poorer I put off with excuses" (*PP* 253). His ideal encounter with a panhandler occurs in Belgrade, where a legless Serb thanks him for five dinars. Vollmann considers the exchange "nothing more or less than a handshake between two citizens of Earth . . . a transaction without egotism on either side," for "the significance was precisely in the insignificance. We saw each other; I gave; he accepted; we forgot each other" (*PP* 270). As for helping those he gets to know better, since Sunee confiscates and drinks up any cash Vollmann funnels to her daughter Vimonrat, he reaches this artistically inclined girl by buying her books and drawing supplies. With similar motives, he takes Oksana's granddaughter Elena, who also likes to draw, to a Chagall exhibition, before asserting that she was not poor when enthralled by art.

Seeking common ground across continents, cultures, and classes, Vollmann struggles to locate it. He notices that "poor countries are often richer than ours in time," that the division of labor is less rigid where people lead slower lives (*PP* 243). Pondering his rich acquaintances, he detects "the desperate burden of a leisured consciousness to those for whom survival comes easy; I enter their expensively barren houses, and I pity them. The ones who wrinkle their noses at the poor sometimes excite my anger" (*PP* 289). Yet whether through belligerence or ingratiation, the poor can get on his nerves as well. Outside his studio in Sacramento, he lets the homeless sleep in his parking lot, shakes their hands, chats with, and feeds them, but still establishes firm limits, protecting his "fortress" from vandalism and not permitting them inside. "I shut my door on them" becomes his unashamed refrain, echoed by his resentment that, at least socially, "didn't they shut their doors on me?" (*PP* 275). In spite of his trenchant "skepticism about the traditional divide between the 'deserving' and the 'undeserving' poor" (*PP* 274), Vollmann is distrustful or afraid of them at times. The enormity of human suffering, the alienation of class difference, and his instinct for self-preservation tempt him to isolate himself in his workshop, to adopt a course of inaction toward the poor,[37] a private policy by which "the only honest thing to do is remember them" (*PP* 286). More often, though, he is innately, actively empathetic. Less overwrought than Agee usually is—think of his fulsome spectrum of feelings when he first locks eyes with Sadie Ricketts and Louise Gudger—Vollmann nonetheless recounts occasions when his heart broke with love or sorrow for his subjects. He, too, scolds himself for emotional excesses: "These prattlings of my heart might be thrown away, like all the individuals, including you and me, that they concern. Poor people and rich people, we have in common our mortal insignificance" (*PP* 289). Thus death is the final leveler and reminder of shared humanity, laying to rest all the travails that Agee deems "normal predicaments of human divinity" (*FM* viii).

Whose Caption?

Yet nothing appears to transcend death, to confer a semblance of immortality, quite like a photograph. While Agee recognized that all people, rich and poor, would alike be drawn down into the earth, he was also fascinated by photographic reproductions of the more well-to-do dead on gravestones at Shady Grove.[38] On that note, in *The Book of Dolores* (2013), Vollmann quotes Beaumont Newhall: "'The fundamental belief in the authenticity of photographs explains why photography of people no longer living and of vanished architecture are so melancholy. Neither words nor the most detailed painting can evoke a moment of vanished time as completely as a good photograph.'"[39] Albeit ambivalent about this notion of authenticity, Vollmann reflects on his process and artifacts: "With landscapes, I took my time. But when I photographed people for *Imperial*, I plucked their vanishing moments more straightforwardly after Newhall's sense. . . . The longer I live, and the more *past* their portraits become, the more I will cherish them."[40] In *Poor People*, correspondingly, he mourns the decorative carvings on Kazakh houses slated for demolition, but consoles himself that they remain intact in his photographs. Yet the meaning of those (as of all) photos is necessarily a matter of interpretation. "A picture is worth a thousand words, no doubt, but which thousand?" he asks. "Is your caption the same as mine?" (*PP* xiii). Alluding to an uncaptioned Evans's picture, probably his portrait of George Gudger (figure 4.8), Vollmann underscores the riddle of photographic ambiguity: "A poor man stares out at you from a page. You will never meet him. Is he grim, threatening, sad, repulsive, determined, worn down, unbowed, proud, all of the above? What can you truly come to know about him from his face?" (*PP* xiii). While Vollmann denies that photographs can impart true knowledge, for that very reason he ruminates restlessly on the faces and places his camera preserves.

Not all of these lives and locales, however, are tied closely to his text. Several groupings of images in *Poor People* stand almost entirely apart from his otherwise thorough commentary. For example, his series on a homeless camp in Miami and a slumscape in Jamaica are concise photo essays, unmediated by words except for laconic captions on separate pages. As Evans accomplishes not only in *Famous Men* but also in *The Crime of Cuba* (1933) and *American Photographs* (1938), Vollmann constructs meaning through sequences of pictures. Five of his seven shots beneath the Miami freeway feature an African American woman named Ellen (figure 4.9), who is shown in her shack, beside the communal toilet, and at the fire hydrant where she obtains water. Viewers see her in two outfits, in sunshine and shade, with and without a cigarette. She displays three images of her own: sliding the ornamental lid off of a tin box, holding up her waterfall picture, and crossing herself before a Christ. Although unmentioned in the text, visually Ellen becomes one of the most prominent poor people in the

FIGURE 4.8
George Gudger [Floyd Burroughs], Hale County, Alabama, 1936. Walker Evans, *Let Us Now Praise Famous Men.*

book. In addition to discovering how she attends to basic needs in her makeshift abode, readers perceive how Ellen's meager belongings signify her inner world. Vollmann's half-dozen streetscapes from Jamaica likewise invite a narrative about life on the margins, with its garbage heaps, improvised dwellings, underground economy, and resilient inhabitants. Furthermore, creating thematic associations across geographical distances, he clusters photographs of workers pulling carts by hand, of victims who fell prey to robbers or civil wars or ethnic strife, of people at rest or play in diverse ramshackle settings, of individuals huddled over or gazing straight into his lens, of panhandlers' supplicating *wais* (peace signs). Thoughtful pairings and assemblages of pictures demonstrate that Vollmann conceives of and fashions his portfolio as an autonomous representational vehicle on par with his prose,[41] in accordance with Agee's declaration that the two mediums should be regarded as "coequal, mutually independent, and fully collaborative" (*FM* viii).

FIGURE 4.9 Ellen in her shack, Miami, 1994. William T. Vollmann, *Poor People*.

However, unlike Agee's somewhat disingenuous assertion that Evans's photographs do not illustrate the text in *Famous Men*, Vollmann's photos are in part illustrative. Not only does a list of captions precede them, but they are mostly arranged in order of their pertinence to his writing and cited therein, directing readers when to flip to the back of the book.[42] Beyond this function, moreover, pictures propel him to embellish imaginatively on his subjects, prolonging his engagement with them.[43] Vollmann details many exposures as meticulously as he retraces memories for which he has no photographic prompts.[44] A shot from Madagascar (figure 4.10), for instance, reveals "a baby's wool cap peeking like an onion-top from its swaddling-rags, which were nested in the rags of its beggar-mother who waited against a paint-scabbed wall by night, her eyes half-closed" (*PP* 95). At first glance, such ekphrastic exercises may seem formally redundant or merely corroborative, but his extensive descriptions spark telling frissons. Poring over his prints, even more than his notes, Vollmann arrives at ethical impasses, especially when he did not interview the photographed persons, when their sole contact was through his lens, either because they were unwilling to speak with him or because he kept his camera discreet due to cultural sensitivities.[45] Without having their words to confirm or belie their images, Vollmann can only tentatively contemplate why they are needy and how he might help them. "What is your *normality?*" he broods on the downcast subject of one photo. "I will never know. You are a Congolese beggar-girl staring down at her blanket-wrapped knees. Is your secret numbness, or estrangement, or simple pain? Do you tend toward acceptance, hope, escape, or none of the above? Whatever road I take, you exist unknowably beneath or above it; I cannot ever *see* you" (*PP* 246–47). As his italicization intimates, he is troubled less by the visible signs of poverty in this picture than by all that remains concealed within it.

Such incomplete identification with his subjects continually haunts him, and so, as Agee does, Vollmann compulsively enlarges on their beauty as well as their anguish.[46] By appealing to photography, he reappraises his initial impressions of the poor, and thereby rouses readers to do so too. In his chapter on deformity he recalls a Cambodian girl (figure 4.11) whose "nose baffled three doctors to whom I showed her portrait; the nostrils were still there, but then the bridge of the nose spread out beneath her eyes like clay carelessly molded by some child; . . . as if the potter who had made her simply needed one more moment to work her nose

FIGURE 4.10 Beggar woman, Antananarivo, Madagascar, 1994. William T. Vollmann, *Poor People*.

between his fingers, moisten it, and smooth it out to be as perfect as the rest of her" (*PP* 123). Vollmann cements this tender metaphor with a powerful statement followed by a sorrowful retraction of the intimacy he hankers after in peering at her face once more. "Were she my lover," he writes, "I could very easily find her beautiful. But why should I even imagine loving her? I never knew who she was" (*PP* 123). The next picture he refers to—described even more lavishly, a self-query interjected about whether he should mention certain details—is of an old Russian woman with scabs on her cheek who in person "seemed *unremarkable* because she stood shivering hopelessly in an icy doorway, ignored by all, with

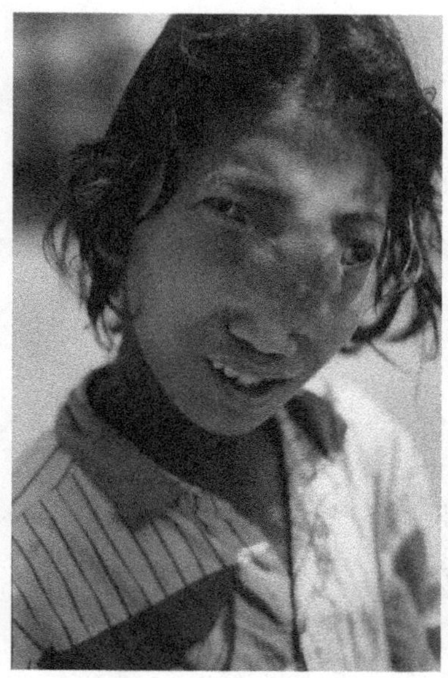

FIGURE 4.11 Beggar girl with deformed nose, Aranyaprathet, Thailand, 1996. William T. Vollmann, *Poor People.*

no money in her cup; she was invisible; but when I look at her image now, I'm appalled; her misery is monstrous" (*PP* 124).

Vollmann does a small part to alleviate such miseries, but he confesses that his gestures of generosity will be inadequate, just as the UN's "more aid, better directed" mandate will not vanquish the world's woes. Ultimately, his book's greatest success—like that of Agee and Evans—is not any sort of prescription to succor the poor but rather an incitement never to overlook their tangled pride, abjectness, tenacity, and frailty. In one of his finest and fiercest intercessions, implicitly linked to a photograph from Phnom Penh (figure 4.12), Vollmann asks, "The mother whose broad, firm, protective face tilts down like a sunflower toward the naked child she holds against her breast, what will she not do, if necessary to you or me, to enrich him with life?" (*PP* 291). The graceful simile in the first half of this sentence makes the threat tucked into its second half all the more unsettling. Behold, enjoins Vollmann, the poor can be as lovely and sturdy as a marvel of nature, but beware, in their will to endure they may stop at nothing, potentially harming "you or me," even if "we" intend to assist them. Again and again, he provokes his audience to this dual recognition through the use of both words and photographs. *Poor People* thus reads like a back-and-forth dialogue

FIGURE 4.12 Mother and child, Phnom Penh, Cambodia, 1994. William T. Vollmann, *Poor People*.

between Vollmann's verbal and visual documentation, an intense cooperation between his pen and his lens. In this way, despite standing in the shadow of *Let Us Now Praise Famous Men*, it also emerges into its own stark radiance of form and function.

Notes

1. William T. Vollmann, *Poor People* (New York: Ecco, 2007), xi; hereafter cited parenthetically in the text as *PP*. Vollmann refers to both the first and second editions: James Agee and Walker Evans, *Let Us Now Praise Famous Men* (Boston: Houghton Mifflin, 1941; 1960). My references, cited parenthetically in the text as *FM*, will be to the following edition: James Agee and Walker Evans, *Let Us Now Praise Famous Men: An Annotated Edition of the James Agee-Walker Evans Classic, with Supplementary Manuscripts*, ed. Hugh Davis, vol. 3 of *The Works of James Agee*, gen. eds.

Michael A. Lofaro and Hugh Davis (Knoxville: U of Tennessee P, 2015). Along with my focus on *Poor People,* this article will refer to these titles, from among many others by William T. Vollmann: *The Ice-Shirt* (New York: Viking, 1990); *An Afghanistan Picture Show; Or, How I Saved the World* (New York: Farrar, Straus and Giroux, 1992); *The Atlas* (New York: Viking, 1996); *Rising Up and Rising Down: Some Thoughts on Violence, Freedom and Urgent Means* (San Francisco: McSweeney's, 2003); *Riding Toward Everywhere* (New York: Ecco, 2008); *Imperial* (New York: Viking, 2009); *Imperial: Photographs* (Brooklyn: powerHouse Books, 2009); *The Book of Dolores* (Brooklyn: powerHouse Books, 2013). I am grateful to William Vollmann for permitting me to reproduce ten of his photographs in my essay and for sending me original flatbed scans of these images.

2. Christopher K. Coffman and Daniel Lukes, eds., *William T. Vollmann: A Critical Companion,* (Newark: U of Delaware P, 2015). For two essays especially germane to mine from this volume, see Aaron D. Chandler, "Egalitarian Longings: The Problem with Pity and the Search for Equality in *Poor People,*" 25–45; Françoise Palleau-Papin, "Imperial Photography," 295–315.

3. Michael Hemmingson, *William T. Vollmann: A Critical Study and Seven Interviews* (Jefferson, NC: McFarland & Company, 2009), 67.

4. William T. Vollmann, *Expelled from Eden: A William T. Vollmann Reader*, ed. Larry McCaffery and Michael Hemmingson (New York: Thunder's Mouth Press, 2004), 317.

5. Vollmann, *Imperial*, 178.

6. For the popular appeal of Steinbeck's novel, see Susan Shillinglaw's "This 'Middlebrow' Book" in her *On Reading* The Grapes of Wrath (New York: Penguin, 2014), 45–52.

7. See James Agee, "Pseudo-Folk," *Partisan Review* 11, no. 2 (Spring 1944): 219–23. Although he does not adduce Agee's article in *Imperial*'s "Bookscapes" section, Vollmann appears to have such criticisms in mind when protesting that Steinbeck gets pigeonholed as "a pseudo-common man who idealized the true common man" (176).

8. As incorrigible an ink-spiller as Agee, a few of Vollmann's impassioned and immodest defenses of his verbosity to publishers, editors, and agents include his "Letter Against Cuts," "Crabbed Cautions of a Bleeding-hearted Un-deleter—and Potential Nobel Prize Winner," and "My Life's Work," all in *Expelled from Eden*, 311–15, 319–23, 325–27.

9. Here is his definition of *false consciousness*: "A charge leveled against the perceptions and experiences of others whenever we wish to assert that we know their good better than they do" (*PP* xxi). While Vollmann thus critiques this cornerstone of Marxism, he does not utterly dismiss the standard definition but rather wrestles with it throughout his text.

10. Gayle Salamon, "Here Are the Dogs: Poverty in Theory," *Differences: A Journal of Feminist Cultural Studies* 21, no. 1 (Spring 2010): 170. Salamon contends that observers of the poor are often suspicious of rhetorical intricacy, and therefore put their "faith in unornamented description to offer the empirical truth of poverty" (171). Although she correctly identifies a "moralist anti-aesthetic" underpinning the approach of Vollmann and likeminded writers such as Orwell, Salamon overstates her case when charging them with "a derogation of the poor in the guise of a recognition" (171). On the contrary, in her call for a more rigorously theoretical discourse about poverty, rather than purely descriptive documentation, she misconstrues the deliberate friction between aims and means woven into works such as *Poor People* and *Famous Men.* As much as Vollmann does strive to simplify his language, he, like Agee, cannot avoid adorning it with

complex thoughts and imaginative connections while grappling with the privileges that prevent him from fully recognizing his subjects.

11. Vollmann, *Imperial: Photographs*, 212.

12. Despite working into the digital era, Vollmann also prefers to shoot either with 35-millimeter or 8x10–inch black-and-white film, when possible with a view camera mounted on a tripod, with the lens stopped down for maximum depth of field, as Evans often did to enhance the clarity of his photographs.

13. "I photographed them how and where they wanted," Vollmann says in *Imperial: Photographs* (217). The same rule applies to *Poor People*, in which the majority of his pictures are portraits taken wherever he crossed paths with impoverished individuals, whether or not he succeeded in soliciting their sentiments on poverty.

14. Vollmann, *Book of Dolores*, 19. Thus he seems even more ethically principled than Evans, whose subway photographs, collected as *Many Are Called* (1966; New Haven: Yale UP, 2004), were shot with a hidden camera. Nevertheless, in *The Book of Dolores*, after laying out his rules of "asking and thanking, paying those who need it, and refraining from making nonconsensual images," Vollmann then owns up to exceptions, such as when "a person is dead, unconscious, or otherwise a victim" (19). *Rising Up and Rising Down* includes pictures of this stripe as well as others that simulate acts of violence. Unlike Evans, Vollmann has risked his life numerous times to photograph war zones and other dangerous places.

15. Vollmann calls his categorizations in *Poor People* "capricious, not to mention at times mutually exclusive" as well as "sad and probably useless" (102). Nevertheless, he devotes a sizable portion of his text to them, which irritated or confused some reviewers. Walter Kirn, in "Show Me the Moneyless" for the *New York Times Book Review* (18 March 2007), complains about Vollmann's urge "to render lowercase realities as capitalized abstractions" (11). Preferring "passages of sustained description and pavement-level storytelling," Kirn disapproves of "philosophical interludes that undermine and dilute the stretches of portraiture" (11). Due to similar enthusiasm for the book's specificities, Michael J. Baxter, in "Always with Us" for *Commonweal* (21 November 2008), completely overlooks Vollmann's eight provisional categories. While Baxter is right that "*Poor People* issues no proclamations and provides no solutions" (28), he inaccurately claims that the book does not contain "big ideas about 'poverty' or sweeping generalizations concerning 'the poor'" (27). On the contrary, Vollmann frequently hypothesizes and generalizes, yet just as often qualifies if not contradicts his statements while exploring multifarious manifestations of poverty.

16. Michael A. Lofaro and Hugh Davis, eds., *James Agee Rediscovered: The Journals of* Let Us Now Praise Famous Men *and Other New Manuscripts* (Knoxville: U of Tennessee P, 2005), 149. In my interview with Vollmann on 18 August 2020, he reflected on this paradoxical quality of *Famous Men*, calling it "juvenile" and "irritating" as well as "incredible" and "inspiring."

17. Vollmann, *Imperial: Photographs*, 223, 216.

18. See the map preceding *The Ice-Shirt*, volume one of Vollmann's still-to-be-completed *Seven Dreams: A Book of North American Landscapes*, a series that reimagines encounters between Native Americans and their European invaders. In his preface to this volume, he issues a caveat typical for

him: "Readers are warned that the sketch-maps and boundaries here are provisional, approximate, unreliable and wrong. Nonetheless, I have furnished them, for as my text is no more than a pack of lies they can do no harm" (n.p.).

19. Vollmann, *An Afghanistan Picture Show*, xv. In a likeminded gesture, Vollmann dedicates his text "to all who try to help others, whether they succeed or fail" (v). For an incisive analysis of this book, see Michele L. Hardesty, "Looking for the Good Fight: William T. Vollmann's *An Afghanistan Picture Show*," *boundary 2* 36, no. 2 (Summer 2009): 99–124, in which she persuasively argues that it represents the well-intentioned failures of an archetypal American abroad. Along with linking this memoir's "Young Man" persona to the character of Robert Jordan in Ernest Hemingway's novel *For Whom the Bell Tolls* (1940), Hardesty traces tensions between failing to do good and failing to write well in several of Vollmann's other books, including *Poor People*. Identifying "this dialectic of failure" as a recurring feature of his work, she observes that "aside from the possible insignificance of the task of recording rather than acting, Vollmann has also admitted his continued failures to really understand his subjects" (123).

20. Vollmann, *Rising Up and Rising Down*, vol. 1, 28. Vollmann sounds less worried about any omissions in this somewhat ponderous, seven-volume, self-characterized "work of ornately descriptive ethics" than about potential flaws in the "moral calculus" he develops to evaluate excuses for violence (51). After enumerating his "methodological weaknesses," he again emphasizes, "*Although I have done my best to overcome these failings, I must sometimes have succumbed to them*" (52).

21. For other examples of "a little" description in *Famous Men*, see 5, 129, 215, 235, 242.

22. John Steinbeck, *The Grapes of Wrath* (New York: Viking, 1939), 363.

23. Vollmann, *Expelled from Eden*, ed. McCaffery and Hemmingson, 331.

24. Lionel Trilling, "Greatness with One Fault in It," *Kenyon Review* 4, no. 1 (Winter 1942): 102.

25. See "An American Classic," his reconsideration of the reissued *Let Us Now Praise Famous Men* for *The Mid-Century* (September 1960), which is reprinted in *Lionel Trilling: Speaking of Literature and Society*, ed. Diana Trilling (New York: Harcourt Brace Jovanovich, 1980), 374–80. Trilling reflects on his earlier review: "I think I have pointed to what is indeed a fault in Agee's moral vision, but I should now want to speak of it not as a 'failure' but as an example of what Gregory Bateson once called The Essential Error"—that is, the phenomenon that great writers often betray some systematically twisted insight which is inextricable from their overall perspicacity (379). As applied to Agee's willful "resistance to admitting that the bad mixed in with the good," Trilling propounds that "his brilliant intensities of perception and his superb rhetoric required him to affirm, if not actually to believe, that the human soul could exist in a state of radical innocence" (379).

26. For one such demurral to Trilling, see Jesse Graves, "A Blind Work of Nature: The Ethics of Representing Beauty in *Let Us Now Praise Famous Men*," in *Agee at 100: Centennial Essays on the Works of James Agee*, ed. Michael A. Lofaro (Knoxville: U of Tennessee P, 2012), 93–106. Graves proposes that "Trilling emerges guilty perhaps, exactly as Agee anticipated his audience of cultural elites would be, of the very sort of moral judgment from whose subjection Agee excuses the tenant farmers" (102).

27. Jeffrey J. Folks acutely analyzes "Agee's Angelic Ethics" in *Agee Agonistes: Essays on the Life, Legend, and Works of James Agee*, ed. Michael A. Lofaro (Knoxville: U of Tennessee P, 2007), 73–84. Folks argues that the writer felt instinctual yet duplicitous compassion for all those who suffer and whom he depicted in a sacred light, as with "the innocent vulnerability of the Gudger family in *Let Us Now Praise Famous Men*" (81). Gavin Jones also takes Agee to task for seeing only goodness and loveliness in the tenants' straitened conditions. As Jones contends in *American Hungers: The Problem of Poverty in U.S. Literature, 1840-1945* (Princeton: Princeton UP, 2007), "Agee's poor are blessed and beautiful not despite but because of their brutalization" (125), since "the poverty *itself* is attractive from a literary standpoint" (129).

28. For the book's impact on both white and black student activists in the South during the Civil Rights Movement, see Robert Coles's narrative in Ross Spears and Jude Cassidy, eds., *Agee: His Life Remembered* (New York: Holt, Rinehart and Winston, 1985), 96–100; and James A. Crank, "'In the Service of an Anger': *Let Us Now Praise Famous Men* and the American Civil Rights Movement," in Let Us Now Praise Famous Men *at 75: Anniversary Essays*, ed. Michael A. Lofaro (Knoxville: U of Tennessee P, 2017), 211–26.

29. Evans qtd. in William Ferris, *The Storied South: Voices of Writers and Artists* (Chapel Hill: U of North Carolina P, 2013), 181.

30. Linda Ray Pratt, "Imagining Existence: Form and History in Steinbeck and Agee," *The Southern Review* 11 (January 1975): 97. Agee does not call explicitly for political revolution, however, but rather expresses considerable skepticism if not contempt toward revolutionists. Nevertheless, *Let Us Now Praise Famous Men* does attempt to instill a revolution in social consciousness, as T. V. Reed demonstrates in "Aesthetics and the Overprivileged: The Politics and Ethics of Representation in *Let Us Now Praise Famous Men*," in his *Fifteen Jugglers, Five Believers: Literary Politics and the Poetics of American Social Movements* (Berkeley: U of California P, 1992), 22–57. For another judicious deliberation—albeit one that conflates too readily the discrete contributions of Agee and Evans—on the book's "pragmatist aesthetic," its surmounting of "sentimental identification" with the tenant farmers through "intertextual irony," see Jeanne Follansbee Quinn, "The Work of Art: Irony and Identification in *Let Us Now Praise Famous Men*," *NOVEL: A Forum on Fiction* 34, no. 3 (Summer 2001): 338–68.

31. Vollmann, *Imperial*, 173.

32. Lampooning his ardent but ineffectual impulses of foreign aid and goodwill, which propelled him on a 1982 trip that served as the basis for *An Afghanistan Picture Show*, Vollmann subtitled the book "How I Saved the World."

33. In the same vein as *Poor People*, Vollmann explains in vol. 5 of *Rising Up and Rising Down* how he has compromised as both a writer and a crusader for the sake of advancing his career: "Some years ago, I sold my soul to the magazines. The price I got was excellent: money enough to buy whatever I wanted (my wants, perhaps, are small), adventures in exotic countries, and more liberty of expression and behavior than my friends get accorded. In exchange I laid down my illusions about painting The Big Picture, not to mention 'making a difference'" (551).

34. In a footnote to vol. 5 of *Rising Up and Rising Down*, as a matter of practical ethics, Vollmann encourages journalists to spread their funds liberally: "Always pay for information as

generously as you can; always help the needy when you can. It is their misery, after all, which makes news, and thereby pays your bills" (601). My students, however, tend to find his approach problematic, as many of them have wondered whether financial inducements led Vollmann's interviewees to embellish their poverty or otherwise fabricate their life stories. Vollmann estimates having spent $100,000 to research *Poor People*, which then earned him back only about $30,000. Throughout the book he refers to himself as *rich*, though Vollmann defines this adjective in terms of personal contentment rather than economic status. By the way, I appreciate his generosity in allowing me to reprint his photographs free of charge, a gesture prompted by his innate friendliness but made ironic (for me at least) by his supposition that I myself am "not a rich man." William Vollmann, personal interview, 18 Aug. 2020.

35. According to Salamon, Vollmann betrays bad faith by writing off the meaningfulness of people's responses to his basic query: *Why are you poor?* In "Here Are the Dogs: Poverty in Theory," Salamon alleges, "He poses a theoretical question, but in practice, Vollmann is not quite asking after their self-understanding, for he believes that the poor can have neither self nor understanding, that both of these are luxuries of the rich. This transforms his question into a formal organizing device rather than an adjuration for meaning" (174). Although Salamon's argument is compelling, she overstresses it when claiming that "Vollmann's rendering of poverty offers it, and poor people themselves, as merely squalid and blank" (171), and that "Vollmann is transformed into the passive recipient of knowledge by the narrative labor of his subjects" (175). On the contrary, by richly describing those he meets and showing himself in dialogue with them, Vollmann becomes actively (if ephemerally) involved in their lives. Hence, despite his disclaimers about the doubtful significance of the answers he records, Vollmann nonetheless professes that they "bear meaning of inexpressible value to me; I've been able to pore over them long after my interviewees forgot me" (*PP* xv).

36. For an example that blends forthright and sarcastic tones, "Crime without Criminals" begins: "I'm going to tell you an ugly little story now, a story which sickens and shames me in my heart; but fortunately it takes place in a country most of us have never heard of, and, moreover, the saddest parts are all secondhand, without 'hard evidence,' so we might as well pretend that they're untrue" (*PP* 173). Later in the chapter, Vollmann writes, "All over the world I have heard the cry: *But what else can we do?* from opium growers, street prostitutes, terrorists, and others whose actions might be considered controversial. If you believe, as I do, that everybody, even a condemned prisoner in his death cell, retains some degree of moral freedom, then the people of Sarykamys who express loyalty to that oil money (and I never heard a single soul in Kazakhstan explicitly reject it) become complicit in their own destruction. Of course, you and I are more guilty than they. We create the demand for TCO's product [crude oil refined by Tengizchevroil, a multinational consortium], we pollute the atmosphere with it, and about Sarykamys we don't give a rat's ass. And if you disagree with me about your own responsibility, read this story to the end and then decide whether you would be willing to forgo your petroleum addiction for a single day" (*PP* 190–91). Thus Vollmann shifts from blaming his subjects for their passivity about the health risks of fossil fuels to holding himself and his geographically illiterate readers accountable for their consumerist apathy. Incidentally, after having read *Famous Men* in bits and pieces over the years,

Vollmann first absorbed it straight through during this trip to Kazakhstan in the winter of 2000, which he said made for a strange contrast, due to the cold, with Alabama in the summer of 1936. William Vollmann, personal interview, 18 Aug. 2020.

37. In *The Book of Dolores* Vollmann asserts this fatalistic credo: "My task as a literary writer is to describe the interplay of life and death as beautifully and accurately as I can. . . . My despair about the general category of unmerited suffering has become resignation. I see no justice in the natural order, and so I seek to present the struggle, if that is what it is, between life and death, as equivalent to the dancing of a flower in the wind" (48).

38. Not only detailing these photographs but also reflecting on the continuum between life and death, Agee recalls one of "a fifteen-year-old boy in sunday pants and a plaid pullover sweater, his hair combed, his cap in his hand, sitting against a piece of farm machinery and grinning. His eyes are squinted against the light and his nose makes a deep shadow down one side of his chin. Somebody's arm, with the sleeve rolled up, is against him; somebody who is almost certainly still alive: they could not cut him entirely out of the picture" (*FM* 353–54).

39. Newhall qtd. in Vollmann, *The Book of Dolores*, 12.

40. Vollmann, *The Book of Dolores*, 14.

41. Vollmann's volumes frequently incorporate a medley of visual elements (maps and drawings as well as photographs). Sixteen uncaptioned photos bookend his palindromic travel tales in *The Atlas*. The unabridged edition of *Rising Up and Rising Down* contains twenty-five portfolios with captions, totaling more than 300 photographs, a dozen of which are reprinted in *Poor People*. Following the latter's form of arranging pictures in a separate section at the back, *Riding Toward Everywhere* includes sixty-five snapshots from his excursions on freight trains. For his colossal borderlands project, Vollmann prepared companion volumes, each titled *Imperial*: one with illustrations interspersed amidst his lengthy small-font text, the other with some 200 large-scale silver and duotone plates preceding an essay on his photographic practices and motivations in the documentary mode. As for his self-portraits dressed up as a woman, *The Book of Dolores*, with its mélange of image-making techniques, is a more subjectively arty construction.

42. In an inversion of this cross-referencing system, Vollmann's *Imperial: Photographs* brackets boldfaced numbers after certain captions so as to tie these images to chapters in the companion text volume.

43. Regarding his use of photography as a tool for extended scrutiny of the people and places he encountered while researching the Imperial Valley, Vollmann remarks in *Imperial: Photographs*, "I wanted to store them all in my mind's compartments, so that I could bring them out whenever I desired them. . . . I hoped that the lens would see as much as possible, so that I could later improve my education" (217).

44. Vollmann performs a similar maneuver in *An Afghanistan Picture Show*, which in spite of its title does not include any photographs from the slideshow he originally put together to chronicle his trip. Rather, as Hardesty perceptively points out in "Looking for the Good Fight," Vollmann substitutes lengthy descriptions of the images for actual reproductions of them. These passages emphasize his vexed role as a photographer, reevaluating "moments of incomprehension and miscommunication" while "trading the work of documenting suffering and rebellion for recognizing his subjects and telling their stories" (112).

45. For instance, Vollmann ruefully notes in his "Invisibility" chapter: "To show you how Afghan women look, I sometimes paid poor ladies to take their portraits, which felt to them and to me like the most sordid kind of prostitution, and sometimes from behind or from a distance, so that I'd not be seen, photographed burqa'd ladies walking down the street. In Afghanistan, to take a photograph of a woman was as illegal as photographing a secret defense installation. In Pakistan, it merely brought crowds of disgusted and enraged men" (*PP* 121).

46. Near the end of *Poor People*, for example, he puzzles over why "Natalia's face is to me of all the people's in this book the most beautiful?" (289). Earlier, he describes her thus: "The sea-green eyes in that pale, doughy Russian face, that blue-green coat one shade darker than her eyes, the way one always found her sitting on cardboard on the sidewalk with her legs tucked under her and the Cathedral of the Spilled Blood diminishing her beneath its candy-colored grandeur—these were the facts concerning Natalia" (51–52). Vollmann also rhapsodizes over the elusive, aesthetically conflicting details in photograph 1, captioned "Woman of the Burned Land, Madagascar, 1994," which portrays, as he broods, a "beautiful, dirty young woman" who "gazes at me in patience and the gentle hope that I might do something for her," since her "life for no reason that I could see was so much harder than mine" (287–88).

FIVE

"In Every Detail It Has Edge"

James Agee Reviews the South (1927–1948)

MICHAEL A. LOFARO

To plumb Agee's book and film reviews to survey his thoughts on the South (the "it" that he cites in the title above), one question is immediate: does he provide his readers an insider's view of these works, or does their Southernness and his sense of identity have somewhat less effect on his columns that appear as early as from his days at Phillips Exeter through his professional career as a critic for *Time*, *The Nation*, and other publications? Given his birthplace in Knoxville, Tennessee, and its use as the locale for his *A Death in the Family* (1957) and his attending St. Andrew's School in Sewanee, Tennessee, his setting for *The Morning Watch* (1950/51), one might also question Agee as to whether Appalachia is the South or a distinct region? The answer will likely differ for many readers because of their own birthplace, their area of approach (history, literature, geography, politics, etc.), or informed or uninformed suppositions and inclinations. Interestingly, James Rufus Agee never really decided. Born in Knoxville, Tennessee, he calls himself a Southerner; but also, reared in the foothills of the Great Smoky Mountains, he states that his people were mountain people, to differentiate and stress the cultural uniqueness that that geographical/topological features help to create.[1]

Counting Appalachia as the South, most of Agee's formative years take place there. In Tennessee from his birth through his freshman year in high school, he returns, however, only for assignments from *Fortune*. Two are for articles on the Tennessee Valley Authority,[2] and another, his eight-week venture into the deep South of central Alabama, results in an article that *Fortune* declines to publish, but eventually becomes *Let Us Now Praise Famous Men* (1941). On leave from *Fortune* from November 1935 to May 1936, he spends six months on Anna Maria Island off the west coast of Florida, then visits New Orleans in April, and then Sewanee to see his mentor, Father Flye, before returning to New York City. Although little of his mature life is spent in the South, the bulk of his public and personal writing demonstrates that his relationship to it as a region is clearly a most meaningful one.

His journals for *Famous Men* set the stage for his mindset in writing that work, which topically and geographically is the most Southern that work Agee produces, but also foreshadow many of his future opinions on the South and what it represents.[3] And while clearly his entries are not intended as reviews, it is in his journals that he explains most clearly his relationship to the region, at least in 1936. Agee says that he is overjoyed to get the assignment for *Fortune* to do "a family piece on sharecroppers" because such travel seeing "new cities and new country and people or things and places . . . is likely to open up your brain and your senses, your sense of pleasure, your sense of 'reality', as wide as they ever get." He goes on to examine his particular connection to the South:

> I was born in the south. I spent my first fifteen years about equally divided between a Tennessee city and Tennessee mountains, and since then I had lived north and had seen the south very little, not at all until two years before. In a limited, entirely unstudied way I knew a good deal about the south in terms of some of its parts, and I a great deal more than loved this country.
>
> My father was of mountain people who were tenant farmers. My mother was Michigan born, raised in the south; she was of middle-class, somewhat cultivated, small capitalists. My father died when I was six and though I spent some lucky years in a mountain school most of my life had been middle-class. I have always more resented this fact than not, and have to a degree felt cheated and irreparably crippled of half or more than half of what I am.
>
> I am not quite such a fool as to think anything can ever really be "done" about this sort of thing; but here was about the most that could be done. . . .
>
> Also, though I knew the south, the Tennessee mountain-city-valley aspects of it, I knew little or nothing about the cotton country, beyond a rough idea of the look of it and an even sketchier idea of just what the situation was there, beyond what I had got out of Tobacco Road, some passages in Faulkner, and a few meetings of the Committee for the Defense of Southern Workers, the purpose of which, raising money, was all right enough, but which leaned pretty tiresomely on such words as terrorism and fascism and which by the cheap uses of the word had already made

me unable to hear, say or think "sharecropper" without a certain amount of nausea. (12–13)

Added to this somewhat perplexed sense of self at a time that is the near mid-point of the present chronological scope of Agee's reviews, is another obvious issue: any analysis of his critical comments is, of necessity, at least one remove from his own opinions.[4] In reviewing books and films about the South, most of which are fictive, Agee feels obliged to identify and portray the author's or creator's point of view about the region and how it is conveyed. He most often keeps each book and film as the focal point of the review, rather than using them as a platform for expounding his beliefs. Nonetheless, in several reviews he does seem to indicate some personal evaluation and preference as to the nature of the South and its depictions, both in his comments and in his choice of what to review and at what length.

Treating these reviews yields a portrayal of the South that reached Agee's widest audience by far during the critical years of the Depression and World War II. *Famous Men* (1941) was the only significant piece of his prose published during this period, and it sold only six hundred copies before its reissuing in 1960, after which it remained continually in print. Agee's articles for *Fortune* (1932–1937) contained a few brief glimpses of the South, but generally centered with great precision upon the business aspects of the subject at hand, as was expected of him, and at $1.00 per copy, the audience for *Fortune* was elite and narrow.[5]

The premise of this investigation, therefore, is that by evaluating all of Agee's reviews that have a Southern connection over his entire career as a reviewer, it is possible to discern some sense of "his" South, or at least how he constructs it from his experiences and memories, and to help readers to understand his vision of what constitutes its "accurate" depiction(s). These materials have previously received little attention. His book reviews suffered near total neglect and, while rightfully famous for his film reviews and essays, those centered on the South are among the least well known. Agee's South, as here presented, is extracted from repeated themes and emphases in his reviews of these books and films, texts in which he examines and often entertains readers with his well-written, insightful, and occasionally audacious responses.

An overview of his comments on the South that are of significant length, those not just of a one- or two-line comment, reveals thirteen book reviews in the *Philips Exeter Monthly, New Masses,* and *Time* that range from May 1927 to August 10, 1942. Similarly included are thirteen film reviews in *The Nation* and *Time* from January 23, 1943 to August 9, 1948, with one additional manuscript film review of *The Grapes of Wrath* (c. 1940) recorded in his journals for *Famous Men* (140–43). Two film reviews ostensibly dealing with the South are excluded because of a lack of relevant comment on anything Southern. Fortunately, they are among the five films that Agee reviewed twice in different publications and his subsequent reviews of those same films do qualify.[6] Although the chronological division of the book and film reviews suggests two relatively different periods of his professional life, Agee's interest in both genres was longstanding, as witnessed by significant passages in many of his early letters to Father Flye and in Agee's own work.[7] For convenience, the reviews are treated below by genre and chronologically.

Since an interpretation of Agee's views of the South would likely add yet another layer to the understanding of his depictions, sizeable quotation of his book and film reviews is a major part of this survey. These primary sources reveals his opinions as well as the praise and critical barbs for which he is famous, a temperament evident even in his juvenilia.

James Agee's first review of things Southern is published in Phillips Exeter Academy's *Monthly* magazine for July 1927. He evaluates Sinclair Lewis's new book *Elmer Gantry,* a work included here since its Midwest, over-the-top, ecstatic, evangelical, fundamentalist preacher-con man titular figure has a Southern tinge for many readers. Agee is encouraged by Lewis's treatment of the large subject of religion and revival, but sees the novel as one of the author's lesser works because of its obvious, overdone, and heavy-handed molding of characters and prejudice: "Where Lewis should have used a black snake whip he has substituted a slapstick, and into the slapstick he has driven twenty-penny nails" (407). And in his almost joyful critical damnation of the work, the rising high school senior notes that "Lewis' mouth had shriveled in a mummy-like smile; he dipped his pen not in ink, but alternatively in vitriol and T.N.T." (406).

Nine years later, in treating Herbert Asbury's *The French Quarter* ("Sins and Synonyms,"*New Masses*, 11/17/36), Agee rejects what he sees as a middlebrow approach to the underbelly of Southern culture a la New Orleans as as heavy-handed an exploitation of stereotypes as Lewis's:

> Mr. Asbury must have put a great deal of work into it; doubtless he has to make a living; and doubtless he enjoyed a lot of the work. Doubtless also, a good many other people will enjoy it, and they will include people to whom "slums" mean "low-life," and to whom "slums" and "low-life," particularly of the past (which somehow is always more "picturesque" and "colorful" than the present) are "amusing" or even "fascinating"; who relish synonyms like bagnio, bordello, etc.; and such wordage as "a troupe of ten exquisite strumpets." They will get vicarious pleasure out of accounts of brawls and murders and "case-histories" of prostitutes who happened to be especially "colorful." They will enjoy the feeling of being in the know as they read in some detail of the intimate relationships between vice and municipal politics. They will enjoy the feeling of getting a little ahead on their "Americana." All right, let them. In the course of adolescent revolt most middle-class boys of any intelligence, and some girls, go through such a phase, but those capable of maturity outgrow it young. (515)

Agee's sexism aside, he sees some redemption for the book from the hard-earned facts that Asbury presents: "since such detail furnishes some light against which to candle the social egg, and since there is some usefulness in realizing in what essential ways the past was like, and unlike, the present, it is a book on which the head can be used" (516). Also worthy of note is Agee's own use of specific details in his prose and imagery that supports the development of his long-term contention that books and films benefit from great specificity and accuracy.

His next review, which encompasses two books, strikes close to home for Agee. "Sharecropper Novels," appears in *New Masses* on June 8, 1937, only ten months after his trip with Walker Evans to Mills Hill, Alabama, on assignment for *Fortune*, likewise to produce a work on sharecroppers. After the article's rejection, Agee begins the transformation of his text and Evans's photographs into *Famous Men*, and his opinions of *Black Earth* and *River George* are seemingly framed by the same desire for realistic representation of the situations of the white and black sharecroppers who are the respective protagonists of each work. Of *Black Earth*, after noting some violence and class struggles between generations of sharecroppers and between them and the class of owners above them, Agee writes: "There is one great strength in his book, and that is the painful conviction which grows on you that nearly everything he writes of has actually happened. Once that conviction becomes established, the whole account takes on a new and really large value; you sit in on the trouble, and a whole year's life, of a family you would probably care to know all you can about. It is no longer just an unsuccessful novel" (519). As for *River George*, which Agee views as even less successful, he still finds worth in its realism, saying of both works: "the writing is clear and unpretentious enough to make it possible to see through it, as into a lighted home, the true country and society and the individuals he writes of" (520). Agee's evaluations capture much of his hope for *Famous Men* in its intended co-equal interplay of photographs and text.

Agee's view of James Still's first novel, *River of Earth* (*Time*, 2/5/40), set in Hardin County, Kentucky, shows a connection between the heart of Appalachia and the deep South as a region: "The problem it [*River of Earth*] fairly solves is that faced by many Southern novelists: how to be sectional without being affected" (424). He loves Still's treatment of poverty and applauds his realism and use of understatement, reversals, and irony. For example, besieged by free-loading kinfolk after the mine shuts down, food is running short; the simple solution—Mother moves her children, stove, and a bit of furniture into their small smokehouse, and then burns down her bigger shack so the sponging relatives will have to leave.

On another standard Southern theme, Agee notes that Still's treatment of rural religion is what Lewis's is not—subtle. Still's story is told "in a clear, dry style as unsentimental as his seven-year-old's [narrator's] eyes." Given the eccentricity of the characters, "He might easily have overdone it." But even when his jackleg preacher soars to wild rhetorical heights in dialect, he is no Elmer Gantry. Agee approvingly comments that "Author Still restrains even this. His boy hero goes to sleep; another begins inattentively to whittle" (425).

Agee again stands as a Southern analyst in regard to Erskine Caldwell's *Trouble in July* (*Time*, 3/11/40), a reworking of a standard tale of "how a colored boy named Sonny Clark is hunted down and lynched for a rape [of a sluttish white women] he did not commit." After examining Caldwell's intertwining of racism, sex, and violence, as the members of the mob "break into Negro cabins, strip a Negro couple, whip the husband, turpentine's his wife's belly, rape a mulatto girl," kill Sonny, and stone his accuser to death, Agee evaluates the perceptions and realities of the South as the knowledgeable insider/outsider: "Standpat southerners deny such stories with heat and hatred; non-Southerners know too little to have any right to an opinion. Author Caldwell's taste for close crowding of extremes of cruelty, pity, irony, inconsistency and comedy; his occasional tendency to stack his cards, still further obscure these important facts: that the South is a country of extremes; that for all his faults Caldwell is one of the best and fairest recorders of them" (431). Realism trumps sensationalism; the accuracy of the depiction is more important to Agee than Caldwell's "close crowding of extremes," because racism, sex, the threat of miscegenation, and violence are part of the story of the South, whether stereotypical or not.

In a review that he entitles "Genius-a-la-King" (*Time*, 4/1/40), Agee praises the novel *The Hamlet*, Faulkner's tale of Reconstruction and the first part of the saga of the Snopes family, for its precision in developing a legion of memorable Southern characters, many of whom echo those of Caldwell and the nineteenth-century humorists of the Old Southwest. Sharpsters, conmen, and suckers abound; "Eula Varner is a semi-superhuman embodiment of unmitigated sex, already embarrassingly female at the age of eight"; "Mink Snopes murders a widower named Houston"; and to fulfil the grotesque, Mink is in turn gruesomely attacked by Houston's hound; and the "idiot" Ike Snopes, whose true love is a cow, receives a bizarre antidote: "The villagers, to cure the idiot of 'stock-diddling,' slaughter the cow and require him to eat of her" (434–35).

Agee's admiration for Faulkner mirrors his own emphasis upon the realism and detail that he believes is necessary to good writing; likewise, he believes that, at their best, as in novels like *Black Earth* and *River George*, and in his own uncategorizable *Famous Men*, such depictions can be transcendant and approach the visual:

> Through his people, both normal and daemonic, through his animals, through his fascination in the mysteries of gesture, tones of speech, stature of objects, phases of weather, and through his magical ability to isolate them in words, William Faulkner records the much-investigated South more subtly and truly than any dozen more simple reporters on it.
>
> If an anthology were made of it, this novel would contain perhaps 100 each of almost incredibly beautiful poems, lyric paintings, scenes from motion pictures. Faulkner has learned more from films, and could give them more, than any other writer. (435)[10]

Carson McCullers's *The Heart is a Lonely Hunter* (*Time*, 6/10/40) reunites quirky characters and religion as Southern topics for Agee. While not enthusiastic about this author's first novel, he still likes the odd central characters of the deep Southern mill town: "a half-mad anarchist, a Negro doctor desperate to free his race, a girl who loves music, and a quiet, watchful café owner [who] all come to share a mystical admiration for deaf-mute John Singer." Agee notes as well the need for a Messiah for these "human Christs and semi-Christs" in a "suffering world" (438), thus reinforcing the grotesque and religion as two standard themes in the portrayal of the South.

In one of his few nonfiction book reviews featuring the South, Agee follows much the same formula that he applies when analyzing fiction. While not stepping out of his role of reviewer to comment directly on the South, Agee's summary of W. J. Cash's *The Mind of the South* (*Time* 2/24/41) features the light Cash shines upon some of Agee's favorite qualities of the region—an "enigma," and "ancient riddle"—to explain it more "than any other book before it" (450). Cash's emphasis upon the "'backcountry pioneer farmer'" rather than the aristocrat pleased Agee, who had just finished *Famous Men*, as did the "Southern traits" Cash presented: "individualism, puerility, a tendency to violence, romanticism, hedonism, piety, a passionate love of rhetoric and politics" (450–51). Agee then expands upon Cash's treatment of class, both by wealth and race (though he avoids a "head-on" examination of the "fascinating complex of problems surrounding the Negro"), paternalism, the merging of religion and politics in which "pure hedonism and iron puritanism could lie down together without fighting over the blankets," of "rural individualism [that] was sharpened into a violent sense of personal honor," and of women placed upon a pedestal of "'downright gyneolatry.'" Agee definitely approves of the "honest, temperate, eloquent and kind" way that Cash treats his subject (452), a description that one might also apply to the reviewer's own literary works.

In his review of Thomas Wolfe's *The Hills Beyond* (*Time*, 10/20/41), Agee centers in upon another of the traditional themes associated with the South: the enthralling lure of immersion in the past. Agee, who also obsessed over his ancestors and planned to build upon his three books of personally based, creative nonfiction prose to produce a Proustian saga of his family from its beginnings in America to the present day, is clearly most fascinated with the title-piece of this posthumous collection, the "ten propitious chapters of the novel Wolfe was working on when he died. *The Hills Beyond* was to be the story of the ancestors of George Webber. In these chapters, Wolfe laid out a brilliant panorama of nineteenth-century Southern society, its law, war, murder, and myth. Somewhere past midstream in his transition from wild lyric romanticism to humanism, this prose here lost in effusive splendor, but gained in wit, firmness, and control" (455). Agee balances his analysis of Wolfe's style with the subject the author treats, and his "brilliant panorama of 19th-Century Southern society, its law, war, murder and myth," is a list that contains some of the subjects central to the Agee's work, his fascination with the South, and its people.

Agee concentrates upon the same themes and their variants in his review of Faulkner's *Go Down, Moses* (*Time*, 5/11/42), the last of the Yoknapatawpha novels. According to Agee, Faulkner evinces a kind of geographical determinism in which the South's people and land are inextricably linked and cursed, as well as notes the treatment of race and the sense of an Edenic primitive past as a myth destroyed by corporate greed. The review is worth quoting at length:

> The book is made up of seven stories. They are about the same set of people: Mississippi planters and Negroes and their descendants; and have a common theme: the land. A linked theme is that of blood and its heritage. Negro-white miscegenation pads through the pages like a housecat, and the presence of Indians makes a sort of bottomless pit into the past. Sub-themes, which have more interest for Faulkner than for his readers, are money (one 100-page story centers on his old theme of buried treasure) and what he calls the "curse" which is laid on the South. . . .
>
> On the pre-cotton Southern wilderness he is superb. Nearest thing to a central character is old Ike McCaslin, who has retained, throughout his life, the born huntsman's anarchic feeling for the wilderness. . . .
>
> In *The Bear*, the wilderness is epitomized in Old Ben, an almost immortal bear; Ike, now 16, is in at his death, at the death of the dog who was fierce enough to hold him, at the death and primeval funeral of Ike's Indian mentor. Not many years later Ike sees the beginning of the wilderness' end. The forest is sold to a Memphis lumber company, and Faulkner's description of the sinister little locomotive prodding in the wilderness is one of the best passages he has written. (461–62)

Agee clearly values the detailed realism of Faulkner's portrayal of the South's underclasses, who in turn provide the gritty fodder for his pen. In a passage that could easily be inserted into Agee's *Famous Men*, published the year before this review, Agee praises Faulkner's prose as a historical mirror:

> Faulkner knows his own country as few men do. His details of farming, hunting and folkways are as tangible as rusty nails and as tough as legal writ. There are magnificent flashes of a dirt lane which runs "pale and dim beneath the moonless sky of corn-planting time"; of a godforsaken Arkansas farmhouse in which an ex-slave sits in a frock coat, reading through lensless spectacles; of a blow across the "hard hollow-sounding face" of a mule; of a rattlesnake's "thin sick smell of rotting cucumbers"; of some moving, semi-literate pages from an old plantation ledger. . . . (462)

Agee's final comments on Faulkner's work extends beyond the regional to regard the South as a metaphor for the United States as a whole, and perhaps best sums up the critic's view of the South as well. Agee states that the book's "special value is its evocative (though local) exploration of the U.S. national source and dawn. In it is a sometimes merely yeasty, sometimes 100-proof sense of those powers and mysteries of land and the people on it which make a nation" (463). The past dominates both Faulkner's and Agee's South.

Eight months into the second World War, Agee's review of Howard Fast's *The Unvanquished* (*Time*, 7/13/42) focuses on the author's chronicling the dark early days of the American Revolution and how he explores George Washington's character and growth from his "retreat across Manhattan's East River" to his "recrossing of the Delaware" (468), and then draws parallels to the initial period of the WWII conflict. Agee highlights Fast's conclusion that the Revolution helped change Washington from a Southerner, a rich Virginia farmer who rode to the hounds, to a national figure and beyond, to "'a man of incredible stature, a human being in some ways more godly and more wonderful than any other who has walked on this earth.'" Similarly, Agee hones in on Fast's portrayal of the other side of Washington that casts him as a paradox and, in fact, as a Southern grotesque somewhat akin to Poe's Roderick Usher:

> He was also a very simple man, a foxhunting Virginia plantation squire, "slow and awkward at introspection, which he regarded as something slightly sordid." He was a man of colossal dignity. He had thin red hair, outsize hands, feet, nose, jaw, and his outsize body was "skin wound on bones, with broad shoulders and broader hips." His face was deeply pockmarked. When he could not sleep, he used to reassure himself by stroking the scars. He was "a sickly man, and he had the sickly man's intimate knowledge of death." He had "a physical abhorrence of physical fear." (469)

Moving a century or so ahead in his last book review dealing with the South, Agee treats two novels respectively set during Reconstruction and the later nineteenth century. In commenting on *I Can Lick Seven* by Robert Richards and *River Rogue* by Brainard Cheney (*Time*, 8/10/42), Agee continues the themes that seem for him to form continuity for the South—the past, violence, race, class, greed, the rape of a former Eden, and the grotesque. After quoting or paraphrasing Richards's details of the New South as a "heartbroken half-wilderness" of deflowering, savage dog packs, marauders, murders, deserters, castrations, the Klan, and con men, Agee states that

> The New South was, in sum, violence, cruelty, humiliation, poverty, despair, sorrow, murder, a confusion between self-interest and selfless patriotism, of which Author Richards can write like a blow between the eyes, and which sometimes he overdoes. If corpses dropped less often than ripe plums, in less tricky postures of amazement at death, and if fingers moved less automatically to triggers, this would have been a better novel. (474)

In scrutinizing Cheney's novel, Agee adopts the opposite view of the main character, Snake Sutton, praising him as the center "of some superb fights, crooked and raw deals, and river adventures" (474). Agee evidently has in mind some correct level of violence that is true to the South, or his evaluation may have something to do with the class of the novels' protagonists. Melancthon Fowinkle is a "baldish intellectual" plantation owner (473) in Richards's tale, and Cheney's Snake is part-grotesque, part-failed American Dream:

> Snake Sutton is a hard-muscled, sensitive, moral dimwit who climbs, tooth & nail, from social dereliction (a childhood among swamp Negroes) to the throat-cutting peak of local business and society (a timber firm of his own, a blueblood marriage). Then he goes back again. On the way up, he has an affair with a bordello keeper (part real, part Hollywood) and a fascinating raftsman's apprenticeship to a gigantic veteran of the rivers. (474)

In moving from his treatments of books to Agee's film reviews involving the South, the reader sees unity in his vision. He expands upon many of the same themes noted in his book reviews, but exhibits a somewhat greater directness in criticism. To wit, in an unpublished 1940 review of *The Grapes of Wrath*, he lambasts the film as phony documentary, one

> so successfully disguised as "reality," that it has deceived even its creators. I suggest that it is virtually worthless in any direct way, but endlessly interesting as an encyclopedia of flaws, substandards, inadequacies, self-deceptions, deceptions of the public, opportunities impaired for the future, and, at very best, of painful disappointments. (Journal 6.2, 141)

The film's depiction of the American Dream is as false as Snake Sutton's "success" proves in *River Rogue*. It is "an elaborate, flawlessly false and logical and vulgar, collective dream: general America's dream of a lot of things about itself" that bears so little resemblance to the plight of dust-bowl farmers that "as a moving picture of what it is supposed to be about, it is to say it most kindly, inadequate. And if one is severe in proportion to the nobility of the attempt—and I certainly think one must be—it touches the threshold of goodness about three instants. The rest of it merely stinks" (Journal 6.2, 142).

Agee is somewhat kinder in his treatment of *Tennessee Johnson* in *The Nation* (2/23/43), which he regards as a not-all-that-bad bio-pic set during the Civil War. He applauds realism where he finds it, underscoring that for him it is a prerequisite for true art in book and film, and then goes on to present an impassioned plea for how to make a "good historical film."

> Within the limits of its nearsighted traditions it does its very best; but anyone who wants a measure for the inadequacy of that should watch Morris Ankrum, as Jefferson Davis, announcing the secession of Mississippi.
>
> It is unimportant whether Ankrum is perfect, or anywhere near it. The important thing is that he works in a world apart from the rest of the company; a world where good historical films have a chance to exist. He looks like a daguerreotype, not an impersonation. He bears himself like a man of 1860, not like a studious actor in a costume picture. He talks like a half-crazy devil. He supplies, in fact, the two primal requirements of the camera, in whose neglect or dilution you might better not use a camera at all: living—rather than imitative—visual, aural, and psychological authenticity, and the paralyzing electric energy of the present tense as against the rest of the show's glossy, comfortably researched reenactment at eighty years' remove. . . .
>
> Here by some accident is this actor, dead right in every essential, showing up the bumbling of the rest. If all that he means had been realized, and studied, the following suggestions would be unnecessary. . . .
>
> Since Americans of the nineteenth and twentieth centuries differ in face, bearing, speech, and spirit as deeply as the men of different races, scour the country for the atavisms and actors who can at least suggest the difference, and preserve us from any more of these affable masquerades.
>
> The historical events or inventions must look like newsreels made under ideal conditions, or poor ones if that edges the illusion of veracity.
>
> The "private-life" scenes must attempt a related kind of realism which so far has only been dabbled at, stagily, in Lubitsch's earliest films, and innocently, through transcendent chromos, in *The Birth of a Nation*.
>
> If you can give this realism poetic clarity without blurring its naturalistic clarity, you will have the beginnings, at least, of a good historical film. . . (550).

In reinforcing his views, Agee reveals a bit of why he is always named as one of the top film critics of all time. He is entertaining as well as serious. "Those who think that I am quibbling over detail instead of deploring an ignorance of basic obligations should logically think the same if I objected to a performance of a

Mozart quartet on a bass ocharina, a kazoo, and a team of Hickman whistles, or pointed out inadequacies in a production of *Coriolanus* which was staged by a particularly art-minded group of fox terriers" (551).

The following year, Agee begins his film column in *Time* (12/11/44) with a quick inflation-deflation hook typical of his reviews: "*Dark Waters* (United Artists) has all the makings of a first-class thriller and now & then seems likely to become one. But the grade-A eggs it breaks never quite make an omelet" (196). Agee loves the Southern Gothic brought to the upstate old Louisiana sugar plantation. Given the "terror of groaning shutters and sudden extinctions of the lights, or [when the heroine] follows the beckoning of inchoate voices into the swamp, it is as impossible for the audience as for the victim to know what is plain fact, what is the hallucination of a crumbling mind, who if anybody is to be trusted" (196). Adding excitement is a version of a "witches' Sabbath," and the "fustily ornate interiors of the mansion, with their finely caught gloom even in bright daylight," but nonetheless the film is still inadequate as art: "In this kind of melodrama, which depends strongly on atmosphere and psychological overtones, absolute belief is indispensable. Sample oversight: the failure effectively to suggest the peculiarly oppressive, damp heat of the locale" (196–97).

The Southerner is another film that Agee reviewed twice.[9] In *Time* (5/21/45), the author of *Famous Men* proves a tough audience for a film detailing one year in the life of Texas cotton farmers, "the strenuous, upward year after they have climbed the rung from migratory labor to tenant farming" (258). Agee regards this depiction of their struggle with the land and the seasons as "cinema's first wholehearted attempt since *The Grapes of Wrath* to portray in stirring fiction the lives of real people, in a real world, using their courage against real difficulties" (258). The devil for him, however, is still in the realistic details: "People who know the South well will sometimes wince; even people who do not know the South may find the picture not wholly convincing" (259). But for him, the film's achievement lies in its capturing of the simplicity and beauty of lives lived on and from the land: "Very few American moving pictures have understood so poetically such matters as the beauty and meaning of lighting the first fire in a new home; of using all your strength and sense in hard work and watching the tangible result; of cooking and eating the meat you have hunted and killed; or the anguish of watching all your hopes struck flat by one spasm of the sky" (259).

In *The Nation* (6/9/45), Agee continues to delight in the Thoreauvian simplicity of the *Southerner*'s treatment of the year's natural cycle as well as in the beauty of the film's depiction of setting, with his last comment perhaps reflecting his admiration for Walker Evans's documentary photography. The film is

> one of the most sensitive and beautiful American-made pictures I have seen. There is a solemnly eager, smoky, foggy 'possum hunt which may have been studio-faked for all I know; it gets perfectly the mournful, hungry mysteriousness of a Southern country winter. There is an equally good small-town street; I have seldom, in a movie, seen the corner of a brick building look at once so lonely and so highly charged with sadness and fear. (694)

His plaudits are countered by an evisceration of character portrayal that echoes his impassioned plea for realism in his review of *Tennessee Johnson* two and one-half years earlier: "most of the people were screechingly, unbearably wrong. They didn't walk right, stand right, eat right, sound right, or look right, and, as bad or worse, behind the work of each it was clear that the basic understanding and the basic emotional and mental—or merely human—attitudes were wrong, to the point of unintentional insult" (695). Following up on the unconscious patronizing that is all too prevalent in depictions of the Southern poor as a rural underclass, Agee ends his comments in sheer frustration:

> I don't want to *go on.* I am afraid that in my objection to this kind of inaccuracy there are streaks of parochial pedantry and snobbery. But mainly, so far as I know, my objection comes out of a respect for people. If you are going to try to show real people, in a real place, I think that you have to know how their posture and speech and facial structure can alter even within the width of one county; that you have to communicate the exact beauty of those minute particulars without their ever becoming more pointed to the audience than to the people portrayed, and without a single false tone; that if you don't you are in grave danger of unconscious patronage, you don't see or appreciate or understand your subjects as well as you think you do, you stand likely therefore to be swamped by your mere affection or respect, and so perhaps should give up the whole idea. (696)

Impaling stereotypes extends even to Disney animated films for Agee. In *Make Mine Music* (*The Nation*, 4/27/46) he notes of some of the depictions of ruralness that "The best I can muster is a polite but nauseated smile . . . . There is an infinitely insulting animation of a hill-billy ballad [*The Martins and the Coys*] which I cannot doubt that many hill-billys will love, a fact which grieves me all the more because I have hill-billy blood myself." (727) In a subsequent review of the film for *Time* (5/6/46), Agee adds that it will "offend those who think such caricature as insulting as the hush-mah-mouf kind of comic contempt for Negroes." (309) While he likes some of the other episodes, Agee notes that "my affection for the tacky is highly ambivalent" (727) and also displays his sometimes bludgeoning wit: "There is a friendly number about adolescent lovers of corrupted jazz which forces me to suspect that, next to a really thorough chain reaction [Agee wrote the cover story for *Time* (August 20, 1945) on the dropping of the first atomic bomb], the best hope of the human race lies in segregation of the sexes up to the age of perhaps ninety." (727)

In Agee's positing of the urban-rural divide in the reviews, the rural is nearly always identified with the South. Even though the locale of *The Egg and I* is rural Washington state, Agee at first likes much of this story of the city couple who retreat to the country to try to run a poultry farm: "the show is rife with sure-fire laughs." (*Time* 4/28/47, 359) However, "The picture is, indeed, just a little bit too sure-fire for its own good. It has some faint hints of realistic rustic meanness and kindliness. It also has moments of innocently ribald energy which may not be wholly authentic to the backwoods, but are pretty good as lively, half-demented comedy" (359). He also applauds the rustic portrayals of "decayed neighbors" (359) by Percy Kilbride, but in *The Nation* (5/10/47) acidly notes that "Marjorie Main, in an occasional fit of fine, wild comedy, picks the show up and brandishes it as if she were wringing its neck. I wish to God she had" (783-84). Main did receive a nomination for best supporting actress for her performance. Supporting the stereotype of rural = South = hillbillies is the fact that this film's spin-off is the series of Ma and Pa Kettle movies, starring Kilgore and Main in the title roles. Later, *The Egg and I* also serves as the inspiration for the *Green Acres* television series (1965-1971), in which Eddie Albert and Eva Gabor move from New York City to a run-down farm in the conspicuously odd rural community of Hooterville, a town mentioned as well in the first year of TV's *The Beverly Hillbillies.*

New Orleans (*Time*, 7/14/47) is a film through which Agee enjoys the performances of great black jazz artists, such as Louis Armstrong and Billie Holiday, but he cannot abide the lack of reality: "An elementary history of the cellar art, *New Orleans* barely hints at the fascinating redolence and toughness of New Orleans' red-lighted Storyville, where jazz was born, and little of it is imaginatively filmed . . . . At the end, regrettably, jazz becomes 'respectable'—probably the worst break it could get" (388-89).

Unfortunately similar stereotypes are commonplace for Agee in *The Romance of Rosy Ridge.* (*Time*, 9/27/47) Set in the Missouri Ozarks immediately after the

Civil War, the film stars "Van Johnson as a plumpish Barefoot Boy" (420) who wanders in to help a family named MacBean with the harvest. Irritated by the formulaic nature of the film, Agee unleashes some light satire: "Besides being useful around the house and barnyard, Van is quite a man with the mouth organ, the banjo, his larynx, and the ladies" (420). The North-South conflict surfaces as barn-burning and "Old Man MacBean, a 100% Rebel, has a burning question: Are the stranger's britches blue or gray? The stranger, who feels that the war is over now and that people should be sociable again, irritatingly insists on wearing enigmatic checkered pants. At last his hideous secret comes out: he was not only a Union soldier, but a schoolmaster to boot. Ultimately, of course, he unmasks the barn-burners, pacifies MacBean, and gets the girl" (421). Realistic detail is also generally absent: "there are some rather pretty bits of deep-country detail (e.g., hustling the hay in ahead of a storm). But *Rosy Ridge* attempts to base its romance on authentic and charming Americana. The job requires more than prettiness and benevolent patriotism. Faces, hands, clothes and postures need to suggest hard work, real life and a certain tension of character, rather than mere magazine illustration" (421).

Echoing too much of the framework of *Gone with the Wind* for Agee, *The Foxes of Harrow* (*Time*, 10/13/47) features Rex Harrison as a riverboat gambler who becomes a Louisiana plantation owner before the Civil War and imports a fiery vixen, Maureen O'Hara, from New Orleans to be his wife. Their tumultuous relationship yields a club-footed son, whom Harrison tries too hard to harden. Agee retrains any fulminations of his own against the obvious parallels, and undercuts the key scene with relative ease: "Eventually the little boy, hearing his parents quarrel, falls downstairs and dies. The stock market does the same" (424). Agee also regrets the lost opportunity to treat race in the South: "Probably because the author of the original bestseller, Frank Yerby, is a Negro, the best thing in the picture is a more than ordinary interest in slaves and their lives; but even this feature is drowned in ornateness and theatricality" (425).

It is perhaps unusual to treat a foreign film such as Luigi Zampa's *To Live in Peace* (*The Nation*,12/13/47) in a treatment of Agee's view of the South, but the review does yield a commentary on race in the South. A WWII black soldier concealed in the basement of a peasant's house makes free with the wine cellar and his noise alerts a German soldier searching the upstairs of the house. Agee delights in the belief that the film's simplicity of portrayal is free from prejudice—What would any soldier do in a wine cellar?—and notes that

> the whole thing is done and passed over, without any psychological or moral elaboration. As a native of this country, with more than enough experience both of the South and of non-Southerners who think they mean well by Negroes, I am like many other Americans particularly impressed by the whole treatment of the Negro; it is the only pure presentation of a man of his race that I have seen in a movie. As a human being, who would rather be a citizen of the world than of the United States, I am as deeply impressed by the treatment of the German. . . . (816)[10]

Agee also likes the apparent "newness" of *Tap Roots* (*Time*, 8/9/48), at least for the "average ex-student of U. S. history," because it runs against Hollywood's normal grain in depicting the South: "it is the story of Mississippians who refused to secede from the Union, holed up in a valley, and stuck by their guns until the guns were shot out of their hands. Another angle fully as novel to moviegoers is the Handsome Confederate Officer (Whitfield Connor). Not only is he not the soul of gallantry & honuh; he has the soul of a razorback" (520). These reversals do not, however, compensate for the lack of detail and subsequent lack of depth: "it would have been interesting to know, in a little more detail, just why these Southerners felt so contrary; what their neighbors thought of them (and vice versa); what their relations were with the Yankees; and how they managed to survive as long as they did. However, all such questions are swamped in slick-fiction formula" (520).

While his early life may or may not have had a profound impact upon his critical perspective, it is at least clear from his work as a reviewer that Agee identifies with the South, that he believes that the South had a distinct identity, and that he views the South from both the position of an inside and an outside observer. Through this theoretical lens, he appropriates a unique agency to apply to his book and film reviews to produce not summaries, as had formerly been the case, but to make judgments that reveal his standard of art, both fictive and documentary, with the ultimate goal of supporting accurate and affective representations of character and place. These reviews reflect Agee's consistency; they reveal the self-same agency, standard, and goal evident in *Famous Men* and in *The Morning Watch* and reach fruition in his posthumously published Pulitzer Prize–winning work of creative nonfiction set in Knoxville, Tennessee, *A Death in the Family.*[11]

In sum, over a period of twenty-one years, Agee's reviews allow him to present and analyze the South as a multifaceted combination of realism and romanticism and potential,[12] an approach that rejects many stereotypes, holds fast to others, craves exactitude and detailed descriptions, yet fosters emotive moods of reflection, and even perhaps meditations, on a long list of subjects: class, violence, murder, oppression, prejudice, the grotesque, sex, rape, religion, law, politics, loyalty, ancestor worship, Edenic nature, corruption, loss, poverty, greed, heroes, con men, intelligence, race, and society as a whole, in a South that is both of and not of its time.

The seedbed of this extensive catalog is again found in Agee's journals for *Famous Men*, as he ponders part of his automobile trip to Alabama with Walker Evans. In this passage, the South that he professes to know from his early years is a reality that also inspires the imagination and, as such, is perhaps an anticipation of his book and film reviews. His South is a complex intersection of worlds, one that he knows is elusive, that he and Evans experience as they cross a bridge that for Agee is both real and symbolic, within and outside of time. His journey brings him to a place whose past lives on in the present in a unique and ever-changing vitalism that, as he concludes below, has and maintains its "edge."

> This bridge was entirely of the city and of the twentieth century, and so were we and our way of moving and our will to speed. We cut through country that was a certain, poor, kind of twentieth century South and yet that was of no century but was the misused property of the sun and sky. This was not just obvious contrast, though: it had the quality and taste that happens when in your body[,] two recalls of entirely disparate parts of your past experience intersect.
>
> Negroes and white men who were of such country drove these trucks, casually and efficiently enough, too. Others had built this bridge and this road. And yet that only made it still more strange. For these people and this country, though they are of our century, and represent a great and ill-recognized weight not only in human existence but in history, do not belong to time as most cities and city people do. It would be no more correct to call them primitive, a [*sic* or] medieval, or old-fashioned, than to call them modern: they simply do not belong to time, though they must take part in it; they belong to some other order of existence: just as animals, or uninhabited parts of the earth, do not belong to time in the sense of the word.
>
> Moreover this is not just true of any part of the country: it is much stronger in the South and has a special quality there. The South is generic, basic, primal, like my idea of what China must be or of what Czarist Russia must have been. And yet in every detail it has edge, and participation and involvement in what we think of as the present. (60)

Notes

1. For *Death*, see *A Death in the Family: A Restoration of the Author's Text*, ed. Michael A. Lofaro, a CSE/MLA Approved edition (Knoxville, TN: U of Tennessee P, 2007). It is volume 1 of The Works of James Agee, General Editor, Michael A. Lofaro, Associate General Editor, Hugh Davis. Agee's *The Morning Watch* first appeared in the Rome-based literary journal *Botteghe Oscure* in 1950, and was subsequently published in the United States by Houghton Mifflin the following year. For more on Agee's Appalachian-ness, see the present author's "Progress Priced Too Dear: Appalachia and Appalachian Pastoral in the Work of James Agee," *Journal of Appalachian Studies* 17 (Spring/Fall 2011): 85–107, and "James Agee's *A Death in the Family:* Personal Identity and Conflict in an Emerging Appalachia," in *Agee at 100: Centennial Essays on the Works of James Agee*, ed. Michael A. Lofaro. (Knoxville: U of Tennessee P, 2012), [107]–133.

2. *Complete Journalism, Articles, Book Reviews, and Manuscripts*, ed. Paul Ashdown, which is volume 2 of The Works of James Agee, General Editor, Michael A. Lofaro, Associate General Editor, Hugh Davis (Knoxville: U of Tennessee P, 2013). For "Tennessee Valley Authority," *Fortune*, October, 1933, and "T.V.A.: Work in the Valley," *Fortune*, May 1935, see pages 77–90 and 197–222, respectively.

3. *James Agee Rediscovered: The Journals of* Let Us Now Praise Famous Men *and Other New Manuscripts*, ed. Michael A. Lofaro and Hugh Davis (Knoxville: U of Tennessee P, 2005), 12–13. Henceforth cited parenthetically in the body of the paper.

4. Agee's search for self or for identity is a major theme in the critical studies written about him and his work. Among book-length studies, see, for example, Hugh Davis, *The Making of James Agee* (Knoxville: U of Tennessee P, 2008); Laurence Bergreen, *James Agee: A Life* (New York: Dutton, 1984); Kenneth Seib, *James Agee: Promise and Fulfillment* (Pittsburgh: U of Pittsburgh P, 1969); Genevieve Moreau, *The Restless Journey of James Agee* (New York: Morrow, 1977); James Lowe, *The Creative Process of James Agee* (Baton Rouge: Louisiana State UP, 1994); Alfred T. Barson, *A Way of Seeing: A Critical Study of James Agee* (Amherst: U of Massachusetts P, 1972); Alan Spiegel, *James Agee and the Legend of Himself: A Critical Study* (Columbia: U of Missouri P, 1998); and Mark Doty, *Tell Me Who I Am: James Agee's Search for Selfhood* (Baton Rouge: Louisiana State UP, 1981).

5. In addition to Agee's TVA articles (see note 2 above), his piece on "Cockfighting" for *Fortune* (March 1934) contains some focus upon the South. See Ashdown, *Complete Journalism*, 114–22. See also "Cock and Bull Stories: Luce's *Fortune* Magazine Features Hemingway and Agee on the Business of Bloodsport" in this volume for Henry Luce's vision for his magazine.

6. Agee's book reviews are, unless otherwise noted, taken from the Ashdown, *Complete Journalism*. Page numbers are cited parenthetically in the body of the text.

Elmer Gantry, by Sinclair Lewis, *Phillips Exeter Monthly*, May 1927, 405–7.

"Sins and Synonyms," Review of *The French Quarter*, by Herbert Asbury, *New Masses*, November 17, 1936, 515–16.

"Sharecropper Novels," Review of *Black Earth* by Louis Cochrane [sic. Cochran], and *River George*, by George W. Lee, *New Masses*, June 8, 1937, 519–20.

"Mountain People," Review of *River of Earth*, by James Still, *Time*, February 5, 1940, 424–25.

"Recent & Readable," Review of *An American Exodus*, by Dorothea Lang and Paul Schuster Taylor, *Time*, February 12, 1940, 427.

"Lynching Comedy," Review of *Trouble in July*, by Erskine Caldwell, *Time*, March 11, 1940, 431.

"Genius-a-la-King," Review of *The Hamlet*, by William Faulkner, *Time*, April 1, 1940, 434–36.

"Messiahs," Review of *The Heart is a Lonely Hunter*, by Carson McCullers, *Time*, June 10, 1940, 438.

"Psychoanalysis of a Nation," Review of *The Mind of the South*, by W. J. Cash, *Time*, February 24, 1941, 450–52.

"Last Words," Review of *The Hills Beyond*, by Thomas Wolfe, *Time*, October 20, 1941, 455.

"Dark-Ride Through Dawn," Review of *Go Down, Moses*, by William Faulkner, *Time*, May 11, 1942, 461-63.

"How to Go to War in a Hammock," Review of *The Unvanquished*, by Howard Fast, *Time*, July 13, 1942, 468–69.

"Men From the South," Review of *I Can Lick Seven*, by Robert Richards, and *River Rogues*, by Brainard Cheney, *Time*, August 10, 1942, 473–74.

Agee's film reviews are taken from the *Complete Film Criticism and Essays*, ed. Charles Maland, volume 5 of The Works of James Agee, General Editor, Michael A. Lofaro, Associate General Editor, Hugh Davis (Knoxville: U of Tennessee P, 2017). Page numbers are listed parenthetically in the body of the text. Although it does not deal with the South, for a fine general overview of Agee's film aesthetics and the methodology of his film reviews, see Maland's "Historical Introduction," xxiv–xxxix.

"On a Number of Things about *The Grapes of Wrath*" (c. 1940), in Lofaro and Davis, eds., *James Agee Rediscovered*, Manuscript journal 6.2, 140–43.

Tennessee Johnson, *The Nation*, January 23, 1943, 549–52.

Dark Waters, *The Nation*, December 9, 1944 (nothing Southern), 656.

Dark Waters, *Time*, December 11, 1944, 196–97.

The Southerner, *Time*, May 21, 1945, 258–59.

The Southerner, *The Nation*, June 9, 1945, 694–96.

Make Mine Music, *The Nation*, April 27, 1946, 726–27.

Make Mine Music, *Time*, May 6, 1946, 309–10.

The Egg and I, *Time*, April 28, 1947, 359.

The Egg and I, *The Nation*, May 10, 1947, 783–84.

New Orleans, *Time*, July 14, 1947, 388–89.

New Orleans, *The Nation*, August 2, 1947 (nothing Southern), 803.

The Romance of Rosy Ridge, *Time*, September 27, 1947, 420–21.

The Foxes of Harrow, *Time*, October 13, 1947, 424–25.

To Live in Peace, *The Nation*, December 13, 1947, 815–17.

Tap Roots, *Time*, August 9, 1948, 520.

7. *Letters of James Agee to Father Flye*, ed. Father James Harold Flye (New York: George Braziller, 1962). It is difficult to find, for example, a letter from Agee during his time at Phillips Exeter or Harvard that does not mention and comment on literature. His well-known love of films and Charlie Chaplin has its first mention before Agee is old enough to attend elementary school in *A Death in the Family*. See Lofaro, ed., *A Death in the Family: A Restoration of the Author's Text*, 145–47.

8. Among the many treatments of Faulkner's career in Hollywood, see Peter Lurie and Ann J. Abadie, *Faulkner and Film* (Jackson: U of Mississippi P, 2014).

9. See note 5 above for those films reviewed twice by Agee.

10. Agee's views on race never appear as a major topic in his own work. For example, when he converted the proposed manuscript for his *Fortune* article, "Cotton Tenants," into print in *Famous Men*, he dropped a significant section devoted to African American sharecroppers. See Let Us Now Praise Famous Men: *An Annotated Edition of the James Agee–Walker Evans Classic, with Supplementary Manuscripts*, ed. Hugh Davis, volume 3 of The Works of James Agee, General Editor, Michael A. Lofaro, Associate General Editor, Hugh Davis (Knoxville: U of Tennessee P, 2015), 565–646. For the magnitude of the shift, see Michael A. Lofaro, "*Famous Men* By the Numbers: An Analysis of Agee's Changes from *Cotton Tenants* to *Let Us Now Praise Famous Men*," in Michael A. Lofaro, ed. Let Us Now Praise Famous Men *at 75: Anniversary Essays* (Knoxville: U of Tennessee P, 2017), 245–56. See also James A. Crank, "Racial Violence, Receding Bodies: James Agee's Anatomy of Guilt," in Lofaro, ed., *Agee at 100*, 53–74. Perhaps Agee's most compelling statement on race appeared in a previously unpublished piece in reaction to the Detroit race riots of 1943. See James Agee, "America Look at your Shame!," Michael A. Lofaro and Hugh Davis, eds., *The Oxford American* 43 (Jan.-Feb. 2003): 35–39.

11. Published in 1957, two years after Agee's death, *A Death in the Family* received the Pulitzer Prize in 1958.

12. For a Freudian example of how Agee describes the potential of the South, see Davis, *The Making of James Agee*, 124. *Famous Men* itself is perhaps the prime evidence for how Agee uses the potentiality of the South. It also demonstrates his love of photography and his fascination with its interplay with text as co-equal forms of representation. For some additional information, see several of the essays in *New Critical Essays on James Agee and Walker Evans: Perspectives on* Let Us Now Praise Famous Men, ed. Caroline Blinder (NY: Palgrave Macmillan, 2010), and Lofaro, Let Us Now Praise Famous Men *at 75*.

SIX

Stephen Crane through the Admiring Lens of James Agee

JEFFREY COUCHMAN

Between 1950 and 1954, James Agee wrote four adapted screenplays. Two of those scripts, *The Blue Hotel* and *The Bride Comes to Yellow Sky*, were based on stories by Stephen Crane (1871–1900), who inspired Agee to do some of his best work for the big screen.[1] Not that the other two adaptations were hackwork. One was *The African Queen*, based on a novel by C. S. Forester, and the other was *The Night of the Hunter*, adapted from Davis Grubb's best-selling novel. The film version of *The African Queen* was an immediate hit on its release in 1951, and *The Night of the Hunter*, although it did little business when it premiered in 1955, is now a recognized classic. Agee, however, shared credit for those feature-length screenplays. On *The African Queen,* he collaborated with director John Huston, though he suffered a heart attack shortly after beginning work on the film. Huston, with an assist from Peter Viertel, completed the script during Agee's hospitalization. While recuperating, Agee submitted scenes and notes on plot and characterization, but the final screenplay was not the complex love story he had envisioned. Agee's first draft for *The Night of the Hunter*, though it intelligently restructured Grubb's novel for the screen, was long and unwieldy. The film's director, Charles Laughton, stepped in as an uncredited collaborator and helped Agee craft a spare, elegant script.[2] The Crane adaptations, which were commissioned by producer Huntington Hartford, are solo flights; Agee worked alone to create carefully structured screenplays that are superb realizations of Crane's stories.[3] Unfortunately, the feature-length *Blue Hotel* was not filmed in Agee's lifetime. Although the initial script would have required cutting to be ready for the screen—and notes from Hartford and his associate George W. Tobin point the way toward a revision[4]—the draft overall is a solid foundation for a final production script. A forty-two-minute version of Agee's screenplay was produced for the television series *Omnibus* in 1956, the year after Agee died. Joseph Hurley's revision condenses Agee's dialogue and action for live broadcast, but it retains the shape of the original script and proves that Agee's first draft is a compelling dramatization of Crane's story.[5] In contrast to his work on *The Blue Hotel*, Agee's script for the forty-minute *Bride Comes to Yellow Sky* required little alteration when it went into production in 1952. The film, well directed by Bretaigne Windust, shows how effectively Agee captures the comedy and the underlying melancholy of the original story.[6] Taken together, *The Blue Hotel* and *The Bride Comes to Yellow Sky* provide a clear picture of Agee's skill at transforming prose into cinema.

Agee might never have teamed up with Crane if not for Huntington Hartford, heir to the fortune of the Great Atlantic & Pacific Tea Company. In 1949 Hartford was dabbling in film, producing the crime movie *Tough Assignment* (dir. William Beaudine) to provide a role for Marjorie Steele, the woman he married that same year.[7] Another pet project, a film version of "The Blue Hotel," focused on disparate groups of men. Crane's story, first published in 1898, is about travelers—an Easterner, a cowboy, and a Swede (a tailor from New York)—who spend a snowy night at a hotel in Fort Rompers, Nebraska, owned by a jovial host named Scully. The frightened Swede, harboring a troubled conception of Nebraska as the Wild West depicted in violent dime novels, assumes that many men have been killed in the hotel and believes that he himself will be killed that night. Despite his fears, he accuses Johnnie, the hotelkeeper's son, of cheating at cards. To defend his honor, Johnnie fights the Swede while the other men watch and the cowboy cries to Johnnie, "Kill him! Kill him!"[8] Johnnie, however, is defeated. The Swede leaves the hotel and walks through a snowstorm to a saloon, where a professional gambler is playing cards with two businessmen and a district attorney. Fresh from his triumph over Johnnie, the Swede tries to get the men to drink with him, has a confrontation with the gambler, and, as if it were predetermined, is killed by the gambler's knife. A coda jumps ahead several months to a meeting at a ranch near the Dakota line between the cowboy and the Easterner, who reveals that he saw Johnnie cheat but said nothing about it. "We are all in it!" he says. "Every sin is the result of a collaboration. We, five of us, have collaborated in the murder of this Swede" (170). John Huston suggested to Hartford that James Agee write the adaptation of Crane's dark tale. Agee had spent time with Huston while researching an article about the director for *Life* magazine, and he had told Huston that he wanted to become a screenwriter.[9] (After finishing the script, Agee sent a copy to Huston, evidently hoping that he would direct the film. Huston's response to the script is not on record.[10])

Although *The Blue Hotel* was never produced, in 1952—the year after Agee and Huston had collaborated on the script for *The African Queen*—Hartford again turned to Agee to adapt another Stephen Crane story. "The Bride Comes to Yellow Sky," likewise published in 1898, opens with Jack Potter on a train from San Antonio, heading with his bride back to Yellow Sky, where he is the marshal. Potter has not told anyone about the marriage, and he worries how the town will receive his wife. Meanwhile, in Yellow Sky, a drunken roustabout named Scratchy Wilson wanders the town with a pair of revolvers, terrorizing a group in a saloon, spoiling for a shootout with his old antagonist, Jack Potter. When Potter and his bride arrive in Yellow Sky, Scratchy confronts the marshal. When he discovers that Potter is unarmed and, worse, that he is married, Scratchy gives up the fight and trudges off, his feet making "funnel-shaped tracks in the heavy sand."[11] The amusing story had a perfect role for Marjorie Steele, who is appealing onscreen as the titular bride, holding her own with Robert Preston, who has a good time portraying the fumbling embarrassment of a new husband. (Minor Watson also thoroughly enjoys himself as the bellowing braggart Scratchy Wilson.)

In many respects Agee and Crane are different writers, but in other ways they are a perfect fit. James R. Fultz succinctly sums up fundamental differences: "Crane's prose is swift, abrupt, nervous; Agee's is lyrical and richly cadenced. The one tends toward concentration; the other tends toward augmentation." Yet as Fultz goes on to say, "For all their differences, both use a particularized, visual language."[12] Here, for example, is Crane's description out the window of a moving train in "The Bride Comes to Yellow Sky," followed by Agee's description of train yards out the window of Jay Follet's car in his novel *A Death in the Family*:

> Vast flats of green grass, dull-hued spaces of mesquite and cactus, little groups of frame houses, woods of light and tender trees, all were sweeping into the east, sweeping over the horizon, a precipice. (109)

> The L&N yards lay along his left, faint skeins of steel, blocked shadows, little spumes of steam. . . . Along his right were dark vacant lots, pale billboards, the darker blocks of small sleeping buildings, an occasional light.[13]

The two passages, with their straightforward prose and similar rhythms, seem almost to be by the same author. Both writers also look squarely into the darkness and the light of existence. Crane's doom-laden "Blue Hotel" is a sharp contrast to his comic story of violence defused in "Bride." Agee's *Death in the Family* is a novel about loss and family conflict that is laced with a quiet, amused understanding of human foibles. Then, too, because Agee was born and raised in Tennessee but went to Harvard and settled in New York City, he was attuned to Crane's fascination with the clash of Western and Eastern cultures. Agee's admiration for Crane's writing is clearly on display in his two adaptations. Agee has a fine ear, and he knows good dialogue when he hears it; he uses much of Crane's dialogue verbatim or with only minor changes. Lines from Crane's narrative turn up in stage directions, sometimes in quotation marks, sometimes unquoted. When Agee creates his own dialogue or actions, his aim, for the most part, is to develop the character relationships and plot points delineated by Crane. If here and there he deviates from his source, he does so to reshape the written text for its new life on the big screen, not to erase what Crane has done.

Driven by his strong feeling for Crane's work, Agee plunged obsessively into adapting "The Blue Hotel." Biographer Laurence Bergreen reports, "In three days and nights of ceaseless writing he released a torrent of pent-up creative energy," producing more than a hundred pages.[14] "Pent-up creative energy" is an apt phrase. Agee had been fascinated with film all his life. In the late thirties, he published two film treatments replete with lighting and editing effects and an imaginative use of sound.[15] Several years later, he helped photographer Helen Levitt film her short documentary *In the Streets* (1948). Between 1941 and 1948, Agee wrote film reviews for *Time* and the *Nation*, all the while harboring a desire to write and perhaps direct his own films. In his *Blue Hotel* script, Agee details, to list a few of his filmic touches, lighting effects, sound effects, complicated camera moves, and dramatic cuts between characters to exhibit tensions and underlying threats. Liberated to play with film at last, Agee is a forerunner to members of the French New Wave. Like François Truffaut and Jean-Luc Godard, who also moved from writing about movies to creating films, Agee revels in the possibilities of cinema.

Crane opens "The Blue Hotel" with a long paragraph that describes the blue Palace Hotel and its effect on people who see it. The hotel, with its distinctive color, "was always screaming and howling in a way that made the dazzling winter landscape of Nebraska seem only a gray swampish hush. It stood alone on the prairie, and when the snow was falling the town two hundred yards away was not visible. . . . It was not to be thought that any traveler could pass the Palace Hotel without looking at it" (142). To match Crane's careful descriptions, Agee uses two long action paragraphs (i.e., stage directions that describe settings, characters, and events) to depict specific images on the screen, even suggesting infrared cinematography to capture the contrast between an overcast night sky and snow on the ground. He delights in turning the camera lens into the eye of the viewer: "As our eyes become accustomed to the darkness, we see an immense perspective of snowed land, and a very distant horizon against a black sky which holds two thirds of the screen." Like an experimental filmmaker willing to take his time for a photographic effect, Agee specifies "a maximum thirty seconds" for a transition from darkness to "the light of late morning" and follows that direction with a series of instructions for subtle alterations of "shading and detail"—a "coal-black" train station, a hotel that gives off "an always more and more sinister and unearthly fish-belly glare."[16] In emphasizing the sinister aspect of the hotel, Agee differs from Crane, who initially stresses the "opulence and splendor" of the Palace Hotel (142). Agee chooses from the very start to immerse the audience in the perspective of the Swede, who comes to think of the hotel as a threatening place.

Eventually, Crane himself describes lighting in a way that reveals the inner turmoil of the Swede. When innkeeper Scully appears in a doorway, for example, the Swede sees his grim face and eyes in "mysterious shadow" and thinks of him as a murderer (149). Agee understands the cinematic possibilities for such an expressionistic use of lighting and asks for "scare-lights" on Scully's face in the doorway to "startle even the audience" (420). Later, when the Swede thinks that Scully is about to poison him, Agee specifies "witch-like lamplight" to convey Swede's distorted view of Scully and his surroundings (424).

Agee uses light for a different effect at a key moment in the script. In the course of a card game, Crane writes, "During a lull caused by a new deal, the Swede suddenly addressed Johnnie: 'I suppose there have been a good many men killed in this room'" (145–46). Agee expands the lull and concentrates on lamplight that is "tender and magical in the fading day." The lighting creates a "mysterious yet peaceful mood" that intensifies the shock of the Swede's sudden statement (414).

In the story, the Swede's words prompt tense dialogue between the men, which culminates with the Swede's anguished cry, "I suppose I am going to be killed before I can leave this house!" At this climactic moment, Crane says, "The wind tore at the house and some loose thing beat regularly against the clap-boards like a spirit tapping" (146–47).

The sound is perfect for the film medium, and Agee dramatically develops the offscreen noise. He moves the sound forward to a point midway through the conversation between the men. The mysterious tapping begins quietly and then grows louder as the men talk, reaching its loudest pitch at the moment the Swede says, "I suppose I am going to be killed before I can leave this house!" (416–17). Lighting, dialogue, and sound combine to amplify the tensions in the room.

At another dramatic high point, Agee fastens on an aural effect in Crane's narrative. When the Swede accuses Johnnie of cheating, the men all begin yelling at once. "In this tumult," writes Crane, "no complete sentences were clear. 'Cheat'—'Quit'—'He says'—These fragments pierced the uproar and rang out sharply" (157). Agee dramatizes the moment, even providing a graphic representation of the voices on the script page:

> The players meanwhile are all simultaneously repeating their lines . . . with only very close ad lib variations: out of the din of their voices only key words ring out sharply. The weave of salients is roughly:
>
> *Stop* n . . .
> *Wait* a mom . . .
> *Quit* now . . .
> He says . . .
> He *did!* . . .
> *What's the good* . . .
> *Fight* . . .[17] (440)

Along with lighting and sound, Agee uses the camera in inventive ways to replicate the atmosphere that Crane establishes in his story. On the page, by describing men in close contact in a small room, Crane generates a sense of claustrophobia and potential violence. To play a game of High Five close to a stove, the men "pulled their chairs forward until their knees were bunched under the board." The cowboy, a "board-whacker" who "whanged" his winning cards down upon the table, "sent thrills of indignation into the hearts of his opponents" (145). Once Johnnie has been accused of cheating, the "little den" becomes "hideous as a torture-chamber" (156).

To visualize the claustrophobic tensions in the hotel, Agee employs a moving camera that roams among the men, peering into their faces as they eat or play cards, framing them clustered together in cramped spaces. The intrusive camera becomes yet another character in an already crowded space, a point that Agee makes explicit when, during the fight sequence, the Swede makes a "sudden drive toward the CAMERA, the fighters all but knock it over, and the CAMERA has to 'step' quickly aside, mindful for a moment only of its footing, as the fighters pass in a blur" (448–49). Shortly before the fight, when the men are in an uproar over the Swede's accusation that Johnnie cheated, the camera closes in on the men and "makes, fairly fast and accelerating, steadily tighter and faster and closer, the circling movement by which a tethered heifer winds herself up short around a post. . . . As the CAMERA thus ropes them in they all close tighter and tighter against one center as if it were literally a rope around them: they come as close as five people can get" (440). No doubt that image was inspired by Crane's succinct description of the men rushing forward in the aftermath of Swede's accusation: "The five had projected themselves headlong toward a common point" (156). The swift, dizzying movement of the camera, accompanied by the cacophonous shouts of the men, makes this a dazzling cinematic moment that matches the high drama of the scene in the story, where Crane spends a page and a half depicting the chaos in the room.

Agee may be enamored of long, continuous takes, but he does not neglect the power of editing. Crane tells us that the Swede, sitting beside a stove at the hotel, "seemed to be occupied in making furtive estimates of each man in the room. . . . He resembled a badly frightened man" (144). Agee captures that fear in a series of cuts from the Swede's worried looks to faces of the others, who appear sly and secretive (402). After the Swede has accused Johnnie of cheating at cards, Agee provides the following sequence of shots:

> COWBOY—HIS EYES TO JOHNNIE
> (His look means: Boy, will he back down on a man that accuses him of cheating?)
> JOHNNIE—HIS EYES TO SWEDE
> (His look means: You lying son of a bitch, take that back or fight.)
> SWEDE—LOOKING STRAIGHT BACK AT JOHNNIE
> (His look means: You know damn well you cheated.)
> SCULLY—HIS EYES TO JOHNNIE
> (His look means: How about it, son?)
> EASTERNER—HIS EYES AT JOHNNIE
> (His look means: For God's sake let's not have a fight.) (441–42)

Throughout his script, as he specifies lighting and sound effects or lays out camera moves and editing plans, Agee writes from the perspective of a director. In his dramatic intercutting from eye to eye, he shares with a director like Martin Scorsese an appreciation of silent looks rhythmically edited. *New York Times* writer Mekado Murphy reports a conversation with Scorsese "about how much tension can be created through an actor's expression and subtle cues, rather than spoken lines." Scorsese explains to Murphy that the structure of a sequence honoring Frank Sheeran (Robert De Niro) in *The Irishman* "is all about the looks."[18]

And the looks are all about the characters. Even when Agee adds his own details to portray the people onscreen, he generally serves the characters created by Stephen Crane. He watches the way Scully and his guests walk to the hotel, and he describes in great detail the way the men eat. When it comes to fleshing out the characters in these scenes, Agee drops the role of screenwriter and becomes a novelist, delighting in words that picture the men. He devotes half a dozen lines to Scully's eating habits, for example, including these observations: "a business-like but rather frugal and finicky eater, even a touch of old-maidishness; an old fashioned and rather cute old guy; . . . he's just an aging pappy at home, re-loading" (400). Yet his descriptions preserve the original characterizations. For instance, Crane's cowboy is uncouth and boisterous, and his Easterner is reserved. In Agee's script, the cowboy "walks like a horseman" and shovels in globs of food; the Easterner is "neat-footed along the icy boards" and fastidious when he eats (395, 401).

Agee does, however, give the Easterner an occupation: journalist for a Philadelphia newspaper. Roberta Madden points out that in Crane's story, "each of the other characters states his line of business; the fact that the Easterner does *not* seems calculated. . . . The script replaces intentional colorlessness with depth and detail in order to engage the viewer."[19] Her observations are sound. Yet if Agee differs from Crane in his initial presentation of the Easterner, he goes on to provide the reporter with a motivation that bolsters an important theme at the heart of Crane's story: lack of understanding between the American West and East. Agee's Easterner tells Scully, "Back east we're all so ignorant of the rest of the country. . . . I just want to learn what things are really like, if I can, and tell others who don't know" (399). His words link to the scene in the story where Scully, to counteract the Swede's notion that the West is wild and murderous, tells him, "Why, man, we're goin' to have a line of ilictric street-cars in this town next spring. . . . Why, in two years Romper'll be a met-tro-*pol*-is" (149–50). Agee uses those exact words in his screen version of the scene, right down to an emphasis in "metro*po*lis"—though he chooses not to italicize the *l* (421).

Because the Swede is the main character, it is natural that Agee expands upon his portrayal the most. Sometimes he invents dialogue and behaviors in order to flesh out Crane's characterization; at other times he subtly alters the original rendering of the Swede.

During a scene at supper, Crane says that "the Swede fizzed like a fire-wheel" and "seemed on the point of bursting into riotous song." He "domineered the whole feast, and he gave it the appearance of a cruel bacchanal" (154). Agee fills in Crane's general view, providing some five pages of fizzing actions and words. Before he sits down to supper, the Swede cranks a machine that plays a disc of mechanical music ("some potpourri of Waldteufel waltzes or of early honky-tonk ragtime"), imitates a "rasping" violin, "smacks his hands together loudly and does a peasant dance step." Touching on the theme of East versus West, he jabbers on about the joys of New York and the loutishness of these supposed Western "tough guys." He mocks Scully's unmarried daughter and needles Johnnie ("gonna make a *man* of him someday hah Johnnieboy? . . . If he can eat *enough*"). In Crane's story, the Swede is loud and belligerent, hardly a likable character. But in Agee's script, the Swede's rambling, boorish speeches, punctuated with odd spoonerisms ("Oh, *marr*don me paddum") and "a slow tremendous growling belch," make the Swede even less appealing (428–33).

Agee takes evident pleasure in heightening the Swede's obnoxious behavior, but then he invents other details to balance the picture and create sympathy for the man. In the script, for example, the Swede tells Scully, "Don't never trust *no*body. Be ready for *any*thing. . . . My father beat *that* into me" (420). At the moment of his death, Agee builds on this statement with imagery from the Swede's point of view. His shift to the Swede's mind is all the more surprising, given the omniscient perspective maintained by Crane, who describes the death with a mixture of passive and active voices: "There was a great tumult, and then was seen a long blade in the hand of the gambler. It shot forward, and a human body, this citadel of virtue, wisdom, power, was pierced as easily as if it had been a melon. The Swede fell with a cry of supreme astonishment" (168–69). The Swede's sudden death in Crane's story becomes a protracted, operatic demise in Agee's script. After the Swede has been stabbed, he steps back slowly and then sinks even more slowly. As he goes down, Agee cuts to a montage of the Swede's dreamlike fantasies and memories. The long sequence of shots, accompanied by a rising "supersonic tone" of "unbearable intensity," includes sad wish fulfillment (the men congratulating him after his fight, and Johnnie lifting the Swede's hand "as the victor's") and painful violence (the Swede's father whipping his crying son; a little boy, presumably the Swede, crying as he is beaten in the face by another boy). Agee comes out of the montage to watch the Swede stumble backwards and finally sink to the floor (481–83). The images in the Swede's mind have no source in Crane; the only connection to the story at the instant of the Swede's death is the sense of compassion and loss that Agee shares with Crane.

In his notes on Agee's script, associate producer George W. Tobin says this about the death sequence: "The flashback idea is brilliant and should be seriously considered in attempt to weave it into the story effectively. If impractical can be dropped."[20] Those words neatly sum up Agee's montage. Fascinating, highly cinematic, it is not essential to the story. The imagery even subverts the character presented by Crane. In the story, the Swede's odd behavior throughout is mysterious; we never understand what drives either his fears or his aggressions. Because he is so different from the other characters, all of whom are familiar types, the Swede takes on a larger-than-life quality. Agee's backstory of childhood beatings, meant to help explain what shaped the Swede, makes the character less enigmatic, reduces him to the more commonplace size of the others in the film.

The montage works against scenes in the script where Agee himself enlarges the Swede's portrayal. One such scene occurs two pages after the montage, when the viewer sees the final seconds of the Swede's life. Agee specifies "orthochromatic film," which does not see the full spectrum of light, for a series of shots: the saloon, "modeled on postcards of 1890–1910," an extreme close-up of the Swede's left eye, which "if technically possible, is glazing as we watch," and a cash register sign that reads, "This registers the amount of your purchase"—a symbolic image from Crane's story (485–86). The sudden shift to the look of another time raises the Swede to a mythic dimension removed from the sordid events of a small Midwestern town in the dead of winter.

Even before the fateful scenes in the saloon, Agee elevates the Swede while assigning him bizarre behavior. After the man has defeated Johnnie and walked out into a snowstorm, Agee pictures in his face "a hunger for enormity, violence, bragging, love, glory, something, anything so long as it is huge enough to meet him half-way." If all that seems impossible for an actor to convey, Agee provides actions to express "desperation and joy." The Swede hits the air with his fists and then, "grinning and weeping and moaning," drops his suitcase and kicks it, and finally, "with his right fist, he hits himself as hard as he is able on the joint of the jaw." To help lift the Swede even higher into a realm beyond the other characters, Agee envisions a choppy, fast-motion film technique in which "we use only every third frame; then every second; . . . meanwhile slurring the CAMERA speed a little, fewer frames per second, so that his speed of approach is at all times superhuman and grotesque." After all these convulsions onscreen, Agee describes the Swede as a kind of Everyman proceeding "with a strange peacefulness and hope and sweetness—a tired Pilgrim on the homestretch to Paradise" (463–64).

These moments in the film appear to be Agee's way of visualizing a striking passage in which Crane reflects on the Swede's progress through the storm: "One viewed the existence of man then as a marvel, and conceded a glamour of wonder to these lice which were caused to cling to a whirling, fire-smote, ice-locked, disease-stricken, space-lost bulb. The conceit of man was explained by this storm to be the very engine of life. One was a coxcomb not to die in it. However, the Swede found a saloon" (165). Human beings may be no more than "lice," but they conceive themselves to be as grand as the elements themselves, capable of battling a storm—even, as in Agee's script, punching back at the air. That "conceit" is at once ironic and glorious. In both the story and the film, if the Swede were to die in the storm, he would die at the height of his imagined triumph and exaltation. But he finds a saloon and meets a miserable death. Agee heightens the irony of the Swede's finding shelter from the storm by having him wash his bloody face and hands with snow and then walk toward the saloon, "his face alight with anticipation and new hope" (472).

Agee finds another way to set the Swede above the other characters and thereby generate sympathy for him: he makes a significant change in the structure of the story. In Crane's text, the Swede's erratic behavior makes it seem at first that Johnnie did not cheat and is being wrongly accused. The Swede's sense of victory in the saloon—as though he had defeated Johnnie in a righteous battle—looks like the conceit of a deluded braggart. His angry determination to make the gambler have a celebratory drink with him seems merely a continuation of his bellicose behavior at the hotel. It is not until Crane jumps ahead several months to the meeting of the cowboy and the Easterner near the Dakota line that we discover the Swede was right: Johnnie had cheated at cards. At that point, we have to revisit the story and re-evaluate our response to the Swede. Learning after the fact that he stood alone against men who either knew or did not care that Johnnie cheated makes the Swede's lonely death more poignant and makes him look more heroic. Learning the truth also changes our role in the story. "We are all in it!" says the Easterner (169–70). Any reader who thought the Swede was paranoid and unhinged becomes complicit with the men at the hotel in their antagonism toward the outsider.

Crane's abrupt leap into the future, which makes us return to the past, is an effective literary device. On film, a flash-forward to a new location, where the Easterner just happens to meet up with the cowboy, would be a jarring finish. Agee wisely stays in present time right down to the end. Between the Swede's walk through the snowstorm and his arrival at the saloon, Agee inserts a scene at the hotel in which the Easterner states that Johnnie cheated. Agee expands upon Crane's final scene near the Dakota line by bringing in Scully and Johnnie, who, clearly lying, denies that he cheated and is backed up by his father and the cowboy. As James Fultz says, "Agee's adaptation gives more emphasis to Crane's theme of human responsibility."[21] Unfortunately, to emphasize that theme, Agee adds to the Easterner's moralizing with explicit dialogue: "[The Swede] was the only brave man here tonight. . . . My bet is, he's been sick all his life, with cowardice. . . . He stood up to it tonight. . . . *We're* the ones who've put him in danger! . . . Any man is in danger who has spent a lifetime in fear and humiliation, and then suddenly finds his right to be alive" (469). Near the end of the scene, to drive home the way in which Crane implicates the reader in the guilt of the men, the Easterner looks "from man to man and, at one moment, directly into the lens," and then says about the Swede, "He's my conscience. Yours too, if you only knew it" (471).

Cutting the didactic dialogue from the script would still leave the viewer with the all-important knowledge that the Swede was right, that he stood his ground against men who banded together to crush him. Thanks to Agee's rearrangement of Crane's story, when the Swede enters the script's saloon he at first moves on a moral plane above the others back at the Blue Hotel. We appreciate his solitary victory over Johnnie—and over his own fears—and understand his desire for celebration and companionship. We then watch helplessly as a man who had justice on his side becomes overbearing and violent until he fulfills his own prophecy that he would be killed on this night.

Agee crafts a resonant conclusion for his screenplay by bringing the Easterner and the other men back into the story for a final confrontation in the saloon. The Easterner has been out looking for the Swede, and Scully, Johnnie, and the cowboy have trailed after the Easterner to make sure that he does not write up what they consider false stories about Johnnie and the town. Agee's decision to make the Easterner a journalist pays off well in this scene. The men's lack of concern over the Swede's death ("You ask me, that feller was *lookin'* for trouble," says the cowboy) and their deep concern about their reputations place these characters in a moral sphere below that of the Swede. Contemptuous of the trio, the Easterner says, "Tell whatever story you please," and goes on to echo words from Crane's story: "Every sin is a collaboration." Agee adds a final line that expands on Crane's idea: "Everybody is responsible for everything" (486–87).[22]

The men leave the saloon, and Agee rounds his script off in a way that is more satisfying than Crane's abrupt ending, in which the cowboy says, "Well, I didn't do anythin', did I?" (170). Agee returns to the shot of the Palace Hotel that opens the film and watches "three tiny figures" enter. "After a few seconds, light appears in the upstairs windows. After a few more seconds, the downstairs light goes out. Then one upstairs light. Then the other. The sky is emblazoned with a freezing virulence of patterned stars . . . and very slowly, like a prodigious wheel, the whole sky begins to turn" (488). The screenwriter has orchestrated his final images to vivify the fiction writer's wondering picture of human beings clinging to "a whirling, . . . ice-locked, . . . space-lost bulb" (165).[23]

It is a loss that Agee never had a chance to revise his script and try to move *The Blue Hotel* into production. Yet under any circumstances, the bleak tale would have faced obstacles getting made in Hollywood. It must have been an appealing prospect for Agee when, a year later, Huntington Hartford gave him another opportunity to team up with Stephen Crane on a story that had a brighter chance of reaching the screen. "The Bride Comes to Yellow Sky" shares certain elements with "The Blue Hotel." The Swede imagines an Old West that no longer exists (if it ever did), and Scratchy, the aging gunfighter in Yellow Sky, clings to his Western ways in the face of encroaching civilization. Both characters are volatile misfits at odds with a tight-knit community, and each story is charged with an underlying threat of violence. "Bride," however, treats the threat lightly and resolves its tensions in a comic finale. Agee, fresh off his work with John Huston on the tightly structured *African Queen*, met Crane on his own lighthearted terms and wrote a lean adaptation of "The Bride Comes to Yellow Sky." For example, instead of using several sentences to describe lighting effects and the placement of characters, Agee opens *Bride* with a simple picture of Yellow Sky's main street: "Late summer dusk; SOUND of church bell O.S. [offscreen]. PULL DOWN onto Potter's little home."[24] Other camera movements in the script are kept to a minimum: a dolly here, a pan there. To bring Crane's story to cinematic life, Agee rejects the experimental techniques of *The Blue Hotel* and concentrates on developing characters and revising Crane's structure.

Crane provides little detail for his secondary characters. Agee moves into the void and creates lively, sharply defined people. One important change is to transform Crane's nameless barkeeper into a tough-talking widow named Laura Lee. Adding another woman to the script allows Agee to paint a contrast between the rough frontierswoman who runs the saloon and the naive, refined bride whom Jack Potter brings into town. Agee even adds a suggestion that Laura Lee is attracted to Potter. Although she denies being "sweet on Jack," she admits that "if I was, that's the only one *man* enough" since her husband died ten years ago (362). When she meets the bride, Laura Lee's eyes "fall, tragic and defiant" (389). The two women become a living image of an idea central to the story: the rough-and-tumble life of the Old West is dying, giving way to a new world of civilizing manners.

Agee also dramatizes that clash of cultures by pitting Laura Lee against a "nattily dressed Drummer" (367). Unlike Crane, Agee lets the viewer know what product the drummer is selling: stockings. "'Ex*quis*ite' stockings," he says. "Paris to your doorstep, that's our slogan" (369). He tries to interest Laura Lee in a pair, but discovers the difference between this country woman and his usual clientele:[25]

> DRUMMER (*soft and almost lascivious*): . . . Sheer as twilight air. . . . Nothing like it ever contrived before, by the most inspired continental designers, to give style to the ankle and moulding (*sic*) to the calf. . . . And they run all the way up—opera length. . . .
>
> LAURA LEE (*across him*): Save yer breath young feller. Why, if my husband had caught me in a pair o' them things, he'd 'a' broke my jaw. You're in the *wrong territory*, son. 'Cause this is a man's country. It's a hard country. (374)

Neither Crane nor Agee identifies the drummer as an Easterner, though Crane refers to him as a "foreigner" (115). Yet this stranger, clearly out of his element in a small Texas town, seems like a traveler from the East—or from an urban area influenced by Eastern mores. (The film accentuates the drummer's Eastern qualities by casting the decidedly non-Texan Dan Seymour and costuming him in a checkered three-piece suit, which sets him apart from everyone around him.) In Crane's story, the drummer exists solely to help with exposition. He is new to the town, so the barkeeper and others in the saloon have to explain to him (and therefore to the reader) that Scratchy periodically goes on a drunken tear with his guns and that he and Jack Potter, the marshal, are likely to have a fight. Agee retains much of Crane's explanatory dialogue, but he fleshes out the drummer thematically to let us see the man's fears of these Western events alongside his smooth, Eastern salesmanship.

Agee uses the scene between Laura Lee and the drummer to sharpen another dramatic idea, one that is merely hinted at in the original story. While Scratchy is on his rampage, Crane's barkeeper says, "I wish Jack Potter was back from San Anton'. . . . He would sail in and pull out the kinks in this thing" (116). His language is colorful but mild. Agee's Laura Lee states dramatically how dependent the town is on the marshal and points to an impending showdown between Potter and Scratchy: "Comes to shootin', he's the only one in town can go up agin him" (376).

Because Scratchy, as Potter's antagonist, is central to the story, Crane provides significant details to draw his portrait. According to the barkeeper, Scratchy is "a wonder with a gun" and "a terror when he's drunk." He also says that Scratchy is a holdover from a more lawless time, "about the last one of the old gang that used to hang out along the river here." As Scratchy stalks the town, he holds in each hand "a long, heavy, blue-black revolver," but he wears "a maroon-colored flannel shirt . . . made, principally, by some Jewish women on the east side of New York" and boots that "had red tops with gilded imprints, of the kind beloved in winter by little sledding boys on the hillsides of New England." He is a man clinging to the West even as he is overtaken by the East. And he still enjoys having power over the people of Yellow Sky. Crane says that Scratchy "was playing with this town. It was a toy for him." His face "flamed in a rage begot of whisky. His eyes, rolling and yet keen for ambush, hunted the still door-ways and windows. He walked with the creeping movement of the midnight cat." He shoots at a dog, not intending to hit it but only to terrorize the animal, fires on the windows of his best friend's house, and ends up at Potter's house, where he howls "challenges, mingling with them wonderful epithets." But the house is empty, regarding him "as might a great stone god." Crane ends Scratchy's prowl of the streets with an unsettling image of frustrated fury: "the spectacle of a man churning himself into the deepest rage over the immobility of a house" (116–18).

Agee retains Scratchy's past, though he turns the gunslinger into more of an anachronism by making him not merely "one of the old gang," as in Crane's story (116), but the *last* of the gang that hung out by the river (376). He keeps Scratchy in "pseudowestern" clothes (372) and sends him into the streets of Yellow Sky on a shooting spree. Yet he delights in developing Scratchy in even more detail. Although at one point Agee asks for a close-up to show the drunkard's "mad, frightening" eyes and mentions that "he is eaten up with some kind of interior bitter wildness" (377), he is chiefly interested in bringing out the comic aspects of

Scratchy's behavior. Fultz remarks on the way that Agee, a devotee of silent film comedy, concentrates throughout *Bride* on "vivid, silent" humor that the writer "missed in contemporary films."[26] Thus Agee adds a scene in Scratchy's house, where the man guzzles whiskey while he cleans his pistols. The script, in keeping with silent film technique, indicates a single shot that concentrates on Scratchy's hands. The framing helps turn what might otherwise be sinister imagery into a parody of a familiar scene in Western movies: the gunfighter's preparation for a showdown. Agee describes hands that move "lovingly" and "delicately" as they wipe down revolvers with a rag, point a gun at Indians on a calendar, pick up a whiskey bottle, and move out of the shot so that Scratchy can take an offscreen drink. The precisely choreographed visuals are accompanied by offscreen sounds that punctuate or play against the images: the sound of Scratchy's drinking or his voice "tranquilly drunk, humming as much as singing, 'Brighten the Corner'"[27] (366).

In another added scene at Scratchy's house, Agee, as he did in *The Blue Hotel*, turns a moving camera into a character. This time, however, the camera takes over the viewpoint of someone in the story; we see a room through Scratchy's eyes. In the world of *Bride*, the camera moves not to intensify the drama but to create comic effects. Having loaded a cartridge belt, Scratchy stands up, and to convey his drunken state "the CAMERA . . . goes into a short SPINNING BLUR IN AND OUT OF FOCUS" and "proceeds into a slow, wobbly DOLLYING PAN, past window and bureau to pegs where Scratchy's hand fumbles among his few clothes" (372). Agee's rollicking camera would be right at home in a silent comedy like Buster Keaton's *One Week*, in which the camera, swiftly revolving 360 degrees, sends the viewer spinning alongside Buster in a house whirling round and round during a windstorm.[28]

With an eye on the comic possibilities of Scratchy's walk through town, Agee does not let the gunman shoot at a dog. Scratchy does, however, shoot unerringly (left-handed) at a whiskey bottle he tosses into the air, and he fires on Jack Potter's house. Instead of ending at Potter's house in impotent rage, Scratchy begins his walk at the house in a scene that becomes a kind of vaudeville routine. For the house is not empty. The second floor is a jail, and a prisoner by the name of Frank Gudger is inside.[29] The character is Agee's invention, and the writer was so enamored of the role that he ended up playing the part himself and doing a fine job as the amiable prisoner. Although a minor character, Frank fits neatly into the theme of the fading West. In a later scene, he tells Laura Lee that he is tired of reading his collection of Western magazines: "Done read 'em four or five times. Git tired of it, all that bang-bang stuff" (368). During his scene with Scratchy, Frank also exhibits his opposition to "that bang-bang stuff." He tells Scratchy to stop shooting. "Hit's dangersome," he says, to which Scratchy fires another shot. "Ye done busted my lamp chimbley," cries Frank (378–79). The humorous scene also exists for another purpose: to give Scratchy an objective and a clear motivation for wandering through the town. Frank and Scratchy have a comic colloquy about the whereabouts of Potter that leads Scratchy to believe his enemy is at the saloon. With that goal in mind, he sets out on his journey.

During his walk, Scratchy shoots the deacon's electric doorbell so that it rings continuously and fires "stinging" shots at a church bell. In a slapstick prelude to his irreligious blasts, he shoots at a hanging potted fern and sends it crashing "with a foomp" to the porch floor of Jasper Morgan's house. Morgan had hired Scratchy to clean out his cess-pool. Scratchy calls out to Morgan's empty house, "Git yerself a lot o' fancy plumbing, an' ye ain't man enough to clean out yer own cess-pool. 'Let Scratchy do it.' Ain't nuthin' so low but Scratchy'll do it for the price of a pint" (379–80). Scratchy's history in the town, new to the script, creates sympathy for the man. Laura Lee is certainly sympathetic when she, too, tells Jasper in the saloon that cleaning a cess-pool is "a job ye do yourself—and nobody ought to have to do it for him. . . . If I had to do a job like that fer you, I might tie on a few myself" (369).

Laura Lee provides another perspective on Scratchy in dialogue with the drummer. She tells him that she will not shoot at Scratchy because she's a poor shot and might kill him.

> DRUMMER: Well, it'd be pure self-defense if you did. . . . Good riddance *too, I'd* say. . . .
> LAURA LEE (*low*): Mister, Scratchy Wilson's an old friend. Nobody'd harm a hair of his head if they's any way out—let alone kill him. (376)

For Laura Lee's speech, Agee adapts lines from the barkeeper in Crane's story, who says that when Scratchy is sober "he's all right—kind of simple—wouldn't hurt a fly—nicest fellow in town" (116). Agee, however, offers a more comprehensive view of Scratchy's complicated relationship with the town.

Scratchy himself might be surprised to hear that the town has friendly feelings for him. He expands on his sense of degradation in a monologue shouted to the townsfolk hiding in their houses. He boasts of himself as "*boss* in *this* town" even as he laments having to cut a "purty lawn . . . if ye can't get a Mex cheap enough.

. . . I could wipe every one of ye offen the face o' the earth, a-hidin' behind yore women's skirts, ever' respectable last one of ye!" (381). Fultz relates Scratchy's "adolescent exhibitionism" to "the tradition of the tall tale" and cites a pertinent comment by Mody C. Boatright in *Folk Laughter on the American Frontier* about "the frontiersman's contempt for the values of comfortable gentility, of mere law-abiding respectability."[30] Scratchy, with a voice that Agee calls "preternaturally powerful" (377)—his version of Crane's declaration that Scratchy's yelling had "no relation to the ordinary vocal strength of a man" (116–17)—is the descendant of a frontier legend like Mike Fink, "the great roarer of the Mississippi," who could, among other feats, battle a wolf to the death with his bare hands.[31] When Scratchy reaches the saloon, Agee even puts the renegade's final call to the marshal in capital letters: "JACK POTTER?"

It is the sympathetic Laura Lee who persuades Scratchy that Potter is not in the saloon.

> SCRATCHY (*uncertainly*): You wouldn't fool me, would ye, Laura Lee?
> LAURA LEE (O.S): I never did, did I? (383)

From this point on, Scratchy is more or less tamed. And when at last he confronts Potter for the gunfight that never happens, the roarer is silenced.

Agee gives Scratchy a fully dimensioned life onscreen simply by adding to the character that Crane pictures. To develop Jack Potter, Agee borrows an approach from his adaptation of *The Blue Hotel*: he alters Crane's structure to reinterpret a character.

Crane lays out his tale in four parts. Part I begins with Potter and his bride on a train, returning from San Antonio and arriving at Yellow Sky. Part II goes back in time—twenty-one minutes before the arrival of Potter's train—to the Weary Gentleman saloon, where characters talk about Scratchy Wilson on a rampage. Part III depicts Scratchy's drunken, violent walk through the town. Part IV returns to the moment of Potter's arrival with his bride and concludes with an anticlimactic showdown between Potter and Scratchy, who is left without an enemy, without a purpose in life.

Agee creates a chronological narrative that begins with Jack Potter in scenes unique to the screenplay. In a carefully crafted opening, Agee sets up Potter's relationship with several characters and reveals plot threads that he will weave together throughout the script. Agee's new organization begins with Potter leaving Yellow Sky for San Antonio. During his departure, we meet Potter's prisoner,

Frank, who calls to the marshal from the second-floor prison, and we learn that Frank is allowed to let himself out of jail for mealtimes, under the watchful eye of the marshal's surrogate, Laura Lee. Potter is established as a firm, though trusting and genial, officer of the law. Then Potter runs into Deacon Smeed, who is not happy about Potter's friendly relationship with his prisoner. "Do you think that—ah—looks right?" asks the deacon, to which Potter replies, "Afraid I ain't worryin' *how* it looks, Deacon." Potter also does not care how it looks that he never comes to church. "I ain't got nothin' against church-goin'," he tells the scolding deacon, "I just don't hold with it fer myself" (357–58). As a man of freethinking independence, Potter stands apart from the community he watches over.

In his new opening, Agee also enunciates a central theme of the story. He does this in a subtler way than the film itself, which opens with words from a narrator. Referring to Kipling's "Ballad of East and West," the narrator intones, "Yes, East is East and West is West, in the words of the ballad, and the setting of our second story is indeed the West—the Wild West of the Texas plains, just dying out at the turn of the century." It seems unlikely that Agee wrote those explanatory words. He prefers to work the East-West theme into natural dialogue, as in the following exchange between Potter and Laura Lee at the saloon, just before the marshal leaves for San Antonio:

> LAURA LEE : . . . I tell you, Jack, when you waded in here and cleaned the town up, it wasn't just a favor you done us. Everything's gettin' too blame respectable. . . . If things get too tame around here, you'll up and quit town fer good.
>
> POTTER: Uh, uh. I aim to be buried here. Besides, long as ole Scratchy busts loose now and then, things won't never get too tame. (359–60)

Agee thus elaborates on Crane's theme of the Old West versus Civilization by creating a backstory for Potter as the lawman who tamed the wild town. He also artfully brings in Scratchy, whose name evokes the past and looks ahead to events in the present-day story. When Scratchy comes into the bar, we learn the details of his history with Potter. Crane has his barkeeper mention that Potter "shot Wilson up once—in the leg" (116). From that single comment, Agee devises dialogue about their earlier gunfight:

> SCRATCHY: You're a fine one to talk about gunplay. Mean sneakin' skunk!
> POTTER: Sneakin'? It was fair and above board, like it always is.
> LAURA LEE : He just beat ye to the draw, an' you know it.
> SCRATCHY: That don't make my leg no happier. (361)

Potter and Scratchy also talk about potential gunfights ahead: "One o' these days," says the marshal, "you're gonna shoot to kill, an' swing fer it, an' then all of us'll be sorry." Potter, touching once more on the Old West theme, tells Scratchy that his gunplay in the past "was all right, agin the kind o' varmints that used to be around here in the old days—You come in right handy. . . . But you can't go shootin' up law-abidin' citizens an' git away with it" (361).

Potter leaves the saloon, where we linger long enough to hear Laura Lee's comment about Jack Potter as the only "one *man* enough" for her to marry. Her line prompts a cut to Potter on a train, looking out the window into the night, which is followed by a splendid cinematic transition:

> CAMERA SLOWLY PANS, losing his face, then his reflected face, squaring on the dark land flooding past.
>
> FADE OUT
>
> FADE IN
>
> INT. PARLOR CAR
>
> CAMERA LOOKS SQUARELY through window at fast-moving daylit land, reversing direction of previous shot; then in a SLOW PAN picks up the reflection of Bride's face in window. (362)

With that scene, the script picks up where Crane's story begins. Agee then continues the story by cutting between Potter and his bride on the train and events in the town. Crane's flashback structure works well on the page. It creates suspense. The reader anticipates the impending showdown once Scratchy and the other characters catch up to the time of the train's arrival. Agee has a shrewd understanding that for a narrative film, the tale will benefit from a chronological flow. He maintains suspense in his own way as he moves back and forth between train and town. Here, for example, are two clever transitions:

> 1. While seated in the dining car and reaching for his wallet, Potter "makes the odd, helpless gesture of putting aside a holster which isn't there." (Agee's detail shows that Potter's Western ways are being tamed and also looks toward the moment when the unarmed marshal comes up against Scratchy and a pair of pistols.) Potter tells his bride, "Fust time in years I ain't totin' a gun." A dissolve brings in a shot of Scratchy's loaded cartridge belt "heavy and lethal across his knees" (371–72).
>
> 2. When Scratchy pulls "a real shocker of a necktie" off a hook, the film irises out (circles down on an image until the screen goes black) and then irises in on Potter's "more conservative tie," which he nervously adjusts (372).

The smooth intercutting maintains a forward narrative drive: Scratchy makes steady progress on his hunt for Potter while the train hurtles toward Yellow Sky. The two plot lines eventually converge at the moment Potter and his bride round a corner in town and are confronted by Scratchy.

In the scenes devoted to Potter and his wife on the train, Agee adheres to the general outlines of Crane's couple—two bashful, inexperienced adults who seem like children on an excursion at once thrilling and frightening—even as he expands on Crane's ideas and alters the pair as he sees fit. Potter in the story "sat with a hand on each knee, like a man waiting in a barber's shop." The bride "continually twisted her head to regard her puff sleeves. . . . They were evidently very happy" (109). From those simple descriptions, Agee, after setting up an imaginative two-shot that looks like "a provincial wedding portrait of the period," forms a tableau in which a concentration on hands and faces conveys emotions in a witty, economical way:

> His large, spread hands englobe his knees; hers are discreet in her lap. He stares straight ahead, his eyes a little unfocused. She keeps looking around. With almost the manner of a little girl, she draws a deep breath and utters a quiet sigh of joy, at the same time slightly raising, then relaxing, the hands on her lap. . . . He lifts his own hands from his knees; decides they were where they belong; carefully replaces them. (362–63)

Crane never gives the bride a name, and Agee strangely maintains her anonymity, but at times he does shade in new aspects of his "Bride." She, for example, looks forward to moving from a big town to a place "where ever'body *knows* ever'body else" (364). In a follow-up to Potter's conversation with Deacon Smeed, she expresses wonder that Jack never goes to church. "I don't know what I'd do, for lonesomeness, without no church to go to," she says (370).

Potter's actions and words in the dining car also change in Agee's hands. In the story, Crane says that the couple are steered through their meal by a waiter who views them "with the manner of a fatherly pilot" (111). In the script, Potter asserts his independence by rejecting the table that the waiter first offers them and then, after the waiter suggests the ham, orders chicken. Even though he is surprised to discover that the price of the meal has gone up to a dollar and a quarter, he insists on ordering it, in opposition to the waiter's assurance that he can "'commodate folks of more moderate means" (366–67). Agee's marshal is a man accustomed to being in charge and will not be led even in unfamiliar circumstances.

Some of Agee's additions touch on a subject that Crane never even hints at: the sexual fears of the newlyweds. Potter innocently says, "One of these days we'll go on a trip overnight," but that makes each of them "quietly aghast with embarrassment" (365). In the dining car, they both reach for a napkin that has fallen to the floor. "Their hands touch accidentally and fly apart as if they had struck a spark." Potter then "bumps the table making a clatter and the Bride slops a little of the coffee from the pot . . . onto their clothes." The mild slapstick of this moment makes the couple all the more endearing. It also brings them physically closer: "He with his handkerchief, she with his napkin, they gently dab coffee off each other; they are embarrassed but not at all at odds" (371).

Once in the town, they draw closer still. Crane sets the couple in Yellow Sky, has them turn one corner, and come face to face with Scratchy. Agee prolongs the situation. Potter, who has already expressed concern that he did not let the town know he was getting married, tells his bride, "I just can't face 'em if we can help it. . . . What I want, I want to sorta *sneak* in, . . . an' make home without nobody seein' us." The bride is at her most engaging in response:

> BRIDE (*fervent*): Oh gee, if only they don't ketch us!
> POTTER (*incredulously grateful*): You don't hate me fer it?
> BRIDE (*with all her heart*): *Hate* you?
> They look at each other with entirely new love. (384)

Agee constructs a sequence perfectly suited to film: Potter and his bride, thoroughly enjoying the game, sneak through the streets. At one point, Agee calls for a classic comic shot when, "between the rear of two buildings . . . Potter's head comes CLOSE INTO SHOT, then the Bride's" (385). Sadly, the film does not include this image.

When finally they turn a corner and find Scratchy, their happiness turns to terror. In the story, Potter has a vision of the luxurious Pullman car, gleaming with "all the glory of the marriage, the environment of the new estate" (119). The flashback generates suspense—will he die at this moment of glory?—but it also emphasizes the divide between the gun-wielding Scratchy and the unarmed, domesticated marshal. If Agee had still been in his *Blue Hotel* vein, he would no doubt have used Crane's flashback and even elaborated on it. For this script, however, Agee remains in the present and keeps the focus on Scratchy and Potter. With very little change, he uses Crane's excellent dialogue, in which Scratchy is bewildered to find that Potter has no gun and is still more disconcerted to find that his nemesis is now married.

SCRATCHY: Well, I 'spose it's all off now.
POTTER: It's all off if you say so, Scratchy. You know I didn't make the trouble. . . .
SCRATCHY: Well, I 'low it's off, Jack. (*he shakes his head*) *Married*!
He looks up with infinite reproach, sadness and solitude. (388)

The final descriptive words do not come from Crane. They illustrate Agee's profound compassion for Scratchy at this moment of loss, however comic he might have been in the course of the film. In the draft of the script published in *Agee on Film*, Scratchy, as in the story, puts his guns in his holsters and walks away. Agee then adds his own denouement to round off the tale of Potter and his bride. The characters we have met, including Laura Lee, the drummer, and Deacon Smeed, come out onto the street. Potter looks sadly at the departing Scratchy even as he carries his bride over the threshold of his house. From the second story, Frank "slams down handfuls of improvised confetti," which has been made from "the torn pictures of the murderous faces and weapons of early western fiction." This farewell to the Old West is balanced by Frank's greeting to the new order: "Proud to know ye Miz Potter!" In the final image, the rom-com ending gives way to Crane's story. In a close shot, we see the "funnel-shaped tracks of [Scratchy's] feet in heavy sand" (389–90). They are the tracks of a dinosaur, a creature on the verge of extinction.

Agee, however, revised the ending. The new version is not in the script published in *Agee on Film*, but it is, with minor changes, the ending used on the screen.[32] The revision eliminates the romantic comedy elements, gives obsequious dialogue to Deacon Smeed ("Thank God you're back, Marshall!"), and ends with Potter gazing at Scratchy far down the street. Scratchy takes his revolvers from his holsters, "hefts them, looking at them; then opens both hands and lets them fall to the ground, and, without looking back, walks slowly around the corner out of sight." The final shot remains the "funnel-shaped tracks." Scratchy's dropping his beloved guns is a powerful image of desolation and defeat. Without the homecoming and confetti, the ending is more autumnal. It is suffused with a deeper sorrow than Crane's poignant summation of Scratchy's life: "in the presence of this foreign condition he was a simple child of the earlier plains" (120).

Agee's sensitive readings of "The Bride Comes to Yellow Sky" and "The Blue Hotel" led in each case to a screenplay that is, to use Agee's own words in connection with the art of adaptation, a "transfiguration rather than a translation."[33] Crane's "Bride," elliptical, with characters lightly brushed in, has the feel of a sketch. Agee transfigures the work by making it a fully developed story. He builds a complete world: a town of interconnected characters who look back to a rich past and look ahead to changing times. He transfigures "The Blue Hotel" by finding a style that is, to use Agee's words once more, "subjective" and "visually expressive."[34] Agee employs a wide range of cinematic techniques to create a visual extravaganza and to develop both the main character's inner life and his mythic image.

Yet for all his departures from and additions to the original stories, Agee is intent on remaining true to the essence of Crane's works. He retains and amplifies such themes as individual courage, collective cowardice, and the tension between savagery and civility. He crafts dialogue and action to match the tone established by Crane. The very form of each script supports the mood of each story. In *The Blue Hotel*, Agee's dense descriptions of cinematic devices and the actions of his characters contribute to the suffocating atmosphere of Crane's story. His restrained approach in *The Bride Comes to Yellow Sky* suits the light, swiftly moving piece that Crane wrote.

Agee was able to balance translation and transfiguration in his adaptations because he himself juggled different forms. As a fiction writer, he respected Crane's prose. As a screenwriter, he knew how to turn Crane's striking imagery and aural effects on the page into vivid sights and sounds on film. Beyond those technical considerations, Agee seems to have found something of a kindred spirit in Stephen Crane, an artist who shared his keen sense of the mingled sorrow and comedy of life. Before Huntington Hartford would let Agee work with Crane, however, he insisted that Agee submit a sample of his handwriting. Hartford believed that "a man's penmanship was the key to his character."[35] We can be grateful that Hartford, peering through his microscope at Agee's cramped, nearly illegible scrawl, liked what he saw and brought the two writers together to engage in their remarkable collaboration across time.

Notes

1. *The Blue Hotel* and *The Bride Comes to Yellow Sky* are published in James Agee, *Agee on Film*, vol. 2, *Five Film Scripts by James Agee* (New York: McDowell, Obolensky, 1960). The two scripts, along with variants and annotations, will be republished in a forthcoming volume of Agee's solo-produced screenplays and narrations in the University of Tennessee Press series *The Works of James Agee*. (See next note for further details about the series.)

2. For more information about Agee's work with Huston and Laughton, see James Agee, *"The African Queen" and "The Night of the Hunter": First and Final Screenplays*, ed. Jeffrey Couchman, vol. 4 of *The Works of James Agee*, gen. eds. Michael A. Lofaro and Hugh Davis (Knoxville: U of Tennessee P, 2017).

3. An earlier adaptation of "The Bride Comes to Yellow Sky" was written for Huntington Hartford by David Dortort. The script has vanished, so it is impossible to know if Agee used any elements from Dortort's version. Letters in the files of the Motion Picture Association of America suggest, however, that the two scripts were entirely different. For one thing, the Dortort version was for a television production, and Agee was writing for film. When George W. Tobin, a producer at Hartford's company, submitted the Dortort script to Joseph I. Breen at the Production Code Administration, he said in a letter dated November 23, 1951, that the Dortort version "will go into production in December 1951 at KTTV Studios." That production never materialized. A year later, on January 7, 1952, Tobin submitted Agee's script and wrote to Geoffrey Shurlock at the Breen Office, "This is a complete re-write of the David Dortort script which was previously submitted" (*Face to Face*, Motion Picture Association of America [MPAA], Production Code Administration Records, Margaret Herrick Library, Academy of Motion Picture Arts and Sciences, Beverly Hills, CA).

4. "The Blue Hotel," by Stephen Crane, screenplay, notes, 1948, 6pp. [should be "1950, 5pp."], box 2, folder 5, James Agee Collection, Harry Ransom Center, The University of Texas at Austin. Hartford's page and a half of notes are dated "10/23/50." Tobin's two and a half pages are not dated. Each set of notes includes the term "critical analysis" at the top of the first page. Hartford is particularly concerned with cutting repetitive dialogue. Tobin suggests trimming dialogue, condensing action, and cutting out specific shots, including the inventive image of a mechanical-music disc that casts an ironic halo on the troubled main character.

5. "Blue Hotel," revised 11/15/56, *Omnibus* Production Book, season 5, vol. 8, Nov. 25, 1956, box 4, folder 152, Saudek-*Omnibus* Collection, Wesleyan Cinema Archives, Middletown, CT. The live *Omnibus* production aired on ABC, Nov. 25, 1956. It was directed by Fred Carney and starred Arthur O'Connell as the Swede. Rip Torn played Johnnie in what is, according to the Internet Movie Database (IMDb), his screen debut.

6. *The Bride Comes to Yellow Sky* was paired with another short film, *The Secret Sharer* (written by Aeneas MacKenzie, based on a story by Joseph Conrad, directed by John Brahm), and released as *Face to Face* (RKO, 1952). The title comes from Rudyard Kipling's poem "The Ballad of East and West." A narrator at the start of the film explains that in each story "two strong men stand opposed," and he quotes lines from Kipling's ballad: "But there is neither East nor West, Border nor Breed, nor Birth, / When two strong men stand face to face, tho' they come from the ends of the earth!"

7. Lisa Rebecca Gubernick, *Squandered Fortune: The Life and Times of Huntington Hartford* (New York: G. P. Putnam's Sons, 1991), 78–80. In 1949 Hartford also produced *Hello Out There*, based on a play by William Saroyan. George W. Tobin adapted the play, and the short film was directed by James Whale. Marjorie Steele played a cook who befriends a convict. Hartford was not happy with the result, and the film was never released. See Gubernick, *Squandered Fortune*, 82, and *Hello Out There*, IMDb.

8. Stephen Crane, "The Blue Hotel," in *The Works of Stephen Crane*, ed. Fredson Bowers, vol. 5, *Tales of Adventure* (Charlottesville: UP of Virginia, 1970), 160. Both "The Blue Hotel" and "The Bride Comes to Yellow Sky" are readily available in *The Portable Stephen Crane*, ed. Joseph Katz (1969; New York: Penguin Books, 1977). "The Blue Hotel" was originally published serially in two issues of *Collier's Weekly*, November 26 and December 3, 1898, and then included in *"The Monster" and Other Stories* (New York: Harper & Brothers, 1899). Subsequent references to the story will be noted parenthetically in the text.

9. Laurence Bergreen, *James Agee: A Life* (New York: Dutton, 1984), 321; John Huston, *An Open Book* (1980; New York: Ballantine Books, 1981), 212–13. Agee's article about Huston, "Undirectable Director," appeared in *Life* on September 18, 1950. It is also available in James Agee, *Complete Film Criticism: Reviews, Essays, and Manuscripts*, ed. Charles Maland, vol. 5 of *The Works of James Agee* (Knoxville: U of Tennessee P, 2017), 898–910.

10. In a letter to Huston dated September 19, 1950,.Agee says in reference to *The Blue Hotel*, "I'm sending out the first draft today, to George Tobin. . . . On the whole I feel good about it and about some things in it I feel very good. I only hope you will, and that they will" (John Huston papers, Margaret Herrick Library). On Huston as a possible director for *The Blue Hotel*, see Alex Madsen, *John Huston* (Garden City: Doubleday, 1978), 150, and Bergreen, *James Agee*, 322.

11. Stephen Crane, "The Bride Comes to Yellow Sky," in *Works of Stephen Crane*, 5:120. The story was originally published in *McClure's Magazine*, February 1, 1898, and republished in *"The Open Boat" and Other Tales of Adventure* (New York: Doubleday & McClure, 1898). Subsequent references to the story will be noted parenthetically in the text.

12. James R. Fultz, "High Jinks at Yellow Sky: James Agee and Stephen Crane," *Literature Film Quarterly* 11, no. 1 (1983): 47.

13. James Agee, *A Death in the Family: A Restoration of the Author's Text*, ed. Michael A. Lofaro, vol. 1 of *The Works of James Agee* (Knoxville: U of Tennessee P, 2007), 171.

14. Bergreen, *James Agee*, 321–22. The information comes from an interview with Agee's wife, Mia Fritsch Agee.

15. James Agee, "Notes for a Moving Picture: The House," *New Letters in America*, ed. Horace Gregory (New York: Norton, 1937), 37–55, rpt. in *The Collected Short Prose of James Agee*, ed. Robert Fitzgerald (Boston: Houghton Mifflin, 1968), 149–73; James Agee, "Man's Fate," *Film: A Quarterly of Discussion and Analysis* 1, no. 1 (November 1939): 51–60, rpt. in *The Collected Short Prose*, 203–17. "Notes for a Moving Picture" is a series of surrealistic images. "Man's Fate" adapts a section of André Malraux's 1934 novel *La condition humaine* in which Chinese prisoners await execution.

16. *The Blue Hotel* in *Agee on Film*, 2:394. Subsequent references to the script will be noted parenthetically in the text.

17. This was not the first time Agee used a diagonal layout to enhance a sound effect. In his novel *A Death in the Family*, written for the most part in 1947–1948, and published posthumously in 1957, Jay Follet drives off down an alley behind his house, while his wife Laura stands on the porch, listening to the sounds of the departing Model T:

Cutta wawwwwk:
Craaawwrk?
Chiquawkwawh.
Wrrawkuhkuhkuh.
Craarrawwk.
rrrrrwrk?
qrk.
rk:

Whereas the diagonal flow of words in *The Blue Hotel* conveys a reverberating din, here, Agee's formatting, along with the gradual shortening of his onomatopoeic inventions, sends the car fading away in the distance. Agee, *A Death in the Family: A Restoration*, xxxi, 169.

18. Mekado Murphy, "Behind the Camera with Oscar," *New York Times*, Febuary 6, 2020, Arts.

19. Roberta Madden, "'The Blue Hotel': An Examination of Story and Film Script," *Film Heritage* 3, no. 1 (Fall 1967): 23.

20. "The Blue Hotel," by Stephen Crane, James Agee Collection, Ransom Center, 2.

21. James R. Fultz, "Heartbreak at the Blue Hotel: James Agee's Scenario of Stephen Crane's Story," *Literature Film Quarterly* 21, no. 4 (1980): 428.

22. In his notes, George W. Tobin has a decidedly different view of this final confrontation between the Easterner and the others. He says, "Scene as written is long, anti-climax [*sic*] and pedantic. Will weaken picture to have long post-mortem." Tobin suggests replacing the scene with one between the Easterner and the Gambler from a section of the script he calls the "Tag," though he believes that the dialogue can be tightened: "The summing up scene between Easterner and Gambler should be the simple Crane scene, short and clear" ("The Blue Hotel," by Stephen Crane, Ransom Center, 2). The "summing up scene" he mentions is not in the screenplay published in *Agee on Film*. Tobin is reading a typescript that has been lost. Letters in the Wesleyan Cinema Archives explain the unfortunate disappearance. On April 26, 1957, Robert Saudek, creator of *Omnibus*, sent Agee's *Blue Hotel* typescript to Professor Wilbur Frohock for an unspecified reason. In a cover letter he writes, "The 'Blue Hotel' script is, as you see, badly pencilled. Disregard this editing. Jim's work is the typewritten text. Editing was done this year in adapting it for 'live' television." (See n. 5 for information about the *Omnibus* production.) In a letter to Saudek dated August 27, 1959, Frohock, evidently responding to Saudek's inquiry about the whereabouts of Agee's script, explains that while he was abroad in France, the script had been sent to David McDowell, head of the James Agee Trust. No doubt McDowell needed the script for his volume of five Agee screenplays, which was published the following year. The trail of the original *Blue Hotel* typescript ends with McDowell. Saudek evidently never saw the screenplay again. It has yet to turn up in any archive (Robert Saudek and Wilbur Frohock correspondence, *Omnibus* Production Records, Season 5: 1956–57, Scripts and Production Material, series 6, box 4, folder 146, Wesleyan Cinema Archives).

23. On the last page of his notes, Tobin says, "I do not favor the alternate (court room scene) ending," and Hartford in his very first note concurs: "Picture should end at conclusion of scene

in bar, after murder of the Swede" ("The Blue Hotel," by Stephen Crane, Ransom Center). Agee evidently wrote a scene that showed at least part of the trial of the Gambler. His alternate ending in the courtroom, part of the lost typescript of *The Blue Hotel* (see previous note), would be fascinating to read, though surely Tobin and Hartford were right to feel that the scene would be extraneous and that Agee's organic conclusion is the way to end the film.

24. *The Bride Comes to Yellow Sky* in *Agee on Film*, 2:357. Subsequent references to the script will be noted parenthetically in the text.

25. Subsequent block quotations are formatted in the style of scripts published in the University of Tennessee Press series *The Works of James Agee* (see n. 2).

26. Fultz, "High Jinks at Yellow Sky," 52. Agee's essay "Comedy's Greatest Era" (*Life*, Sept. 5, 1949) reveals just how much he missed silent comedy in contemporary films. As Charles Maland says in an introductory note to his reprint of the piece, "Agee was able in this essay to help resuscitate interest in film comedy of the 1910s and 1920s through one of his most inspired writings about the movies" (Agee, *Complete Film Criticism,* 874; "Comedy's Greatest Era" appears on 875–93).

27. The full title of the hymn is "Brighten the Corner Where You Are," published in 1913 with words by Ina D. Ogdon and music by Charles H. Gabriel. See https://hymnary.org/text/do_not_wait_until_some_deed_of_greatness.

Although anachronistic, the hymn is amusingly ironic as Scratchy prepares his weapons for action:

Do not wait until some deed of greatness you may do,
Do not wait to shed your light afar;
To the many duties ever near you now be true,
Brighten the corner where you are.

The film, however, uses a hymn that Scratchy would have known. He sings a verse from "Bringing in the Sheaves," lyrics by Knowles Shaw (1874) and music by George A. Minor (1880). See https://hymnary.org/text/sowing_in_the_morning_sowing_seeds. Agee also wanted to use "Brighten the Corner" for a community sing in *The Night of the Hunter*, but it was once again replaced by "Bringing in the Sheaves." See Agee, "*The African Queen" and "The Night of the Hunter*," 761, 848n.

28. *One Week*, dir. Buster Keaton and Eddie Cline (Metro, 1920). In his first draft for *The Night of the Hunter* (1954), Agee outlines several sight gags for a scene in which the film's villain tries to prevent two children from escaping a basement, though he says that ultimately the scene "is to be designed by a comedy expert—ideally Buster Keaton" (Agee, "*The African Queen" and "The Night of the Hunter*," 612–13). By the time Agee wrote those words, Keaton was dividing his time between lucrative stage appearances in Europe and guest shots on such American television programs as Ed Sullivan's *Toast of the Town* and *The Gary Moore Show*. The great silent clown had been rescued from "at least partial oblivion" by Agee's high tribute in his 1949 essay "Comedy's Greatest Era" (see n. 26), which "marked the real beginning of the enormous revival of interest in Keaton's work" (Tom Dardis, *Keaton: The Man Who Wouldn't Lie Down* [1979; New York: Limelight, 1996], 110, 258–61). Although Keaton never worked on *The Night of the Hunter*, he paid his own tribute to

Agee at the start of his autobiography: "That kindly critic, the late James Agee, described my face as ranking 'almost with Lincoln's as an early American archetype; it was haunting, handsome, almost beautiful.' I can't imagine what the great rail splitter's reaction would have been to this though I sure was pleased" (Buster Keaton with Charles Samuels, *My Wonderful World of Slapstick* [1960; New York: Da Capo, 1982], 11).

29. Agee was fond of the name Gudger. In *Let Us Now Praise Famous Men* (1941), Agee used the name George Gudger for Floyd Burroughs, in whose house he lived while doing research in Alabama with photographer Walker Evans. In his first draft of *The Night of the Hunter* (1954), Agee used the name Jim Gudger (see Agee, "*The African Queen" and "The Night of the Hunter*," 495).

30. Fultz, "High Jinks at Yellow Sky," 52; Mody C. Boatright, *Folk Laughter on the American Frontier* (New York: Macmillan, 1949), 22. Boatright and Fultz both use the term "adolescent exhibitionism."

31. Walter Blair and Franklin J. Meine, eds., *Half Horse Half Alligator: The Growth of the Mike Fink Legend* (1956; Lincoln: U of Nebraska P, 1981), 213–14. Such a tall-tale character is typical of the humor of the Old Southwest. For a series of lively narratives about Mike Fink, Davy Crockett, and others, see Walter Blair, *Tall Tale America: A Legendary History of Our Humorous Heroes* (1944; Chicago: U of Chicago P, 1987) and relevant chapters in Walter Blair, *Native American Humor: 1800–1900* (1937; San Francisco: Chandler, 1960). See also Hennig Cohen and William B. Dillingham, eds., *Humor of the Old Southwest*, 3rd ed. (1964; Athens: U of Georgia P, 1994).

32. Agee's revised ending is in a copy of the script at the University of Iowa (*The Bride Comes to Yellow Sky*: Screenplay by James Agee from the story by Stephen Crane, 45 p., Albert Zugsmith Papers, The University of Iowa Libraries, Iowa City, Iowa, 43–45). Apart from the ending and the elimination of scene numbers, the script in *Agee on Film* matches the Iowa draft. It is not clear why the revised ending was not published.

33. James Agee, review of *Great Expectations*, dir. David Lean, in Agee, *Complete Film Criticism*, 800. Originally published in the *Nation*, July 19, 1947.

34. Ibid., 799.

35. Gubernick, *Squandered Fortune*, 84.

SEVEN

"This Lyrical Image"

James Agee on the Photography and Film of Helen Levitt

CAROLINE BLINDER

James Agee's role as a proponent of a distinctly visual aesthetic in the 1930s shifted from that of photography into something more cinematic in the postwar era. While Agee's film reviews for the *Nation* and *Time* magazines (1942–1948) and his screenwriting for John Huston and Charles Laughton during the 1950s are relatively well-known, his collaboration with the photographer and cinematographer Helen Levitt on the short film *In The Street* tends to be overlooked.[1] This is a shame, for Agee's writing on Levitt is crucial for an understanding of both his own and her practice. It allows us a rare insight into how a prewar documentary aesthetic in photographic terms was transformed into a postwar cinematic aesthetic, one in which Agee sought to redefine the visual through the still *and* the moving image. By taking an idea of lyricism as his starting point, Agee used the filmic qualities of Levitt's photography to illuminate an aesthetic in which the streets of New York became the staging areas for a distinctly urban and lyrical form of documentary practice.[2]

Simultaneous to working on *In The Street*, Agee was writing on *A Way of Seeing*, an introduction to Levitt's first monograph of street photography.[3] In it, Agee sets out to move from a definition of photography in still terms to something much more fluid and temporal, a form of photography, he argues, "so filled with movement, so fluid and so transient . . . that the undeveloped eye is too slow and too generalized to foresee and to isolate its most illuminating moment."[4] For Agee, a particular sense of motion can be discerned by the photographer who is able to "isolate" what is most illuminating about the scene before them. It is here—according to Agee—that the lyrical image finds its apotheosis as the most "volatile, the richest in emotion . . . and the most nearly related to the elastic, casual and subjective way in which we ordinarily look around us."[5] The ability to mimic how we "ordinarily look around us" does not mean, however, that the most realistic photograph is the most lyrical, nor that the camera's ability to capture things that move rapidly proves its synchronicity with the human eye. Rather than defined in terms of its fidelity to realism, the lyrical image represents the possible synthesis of our subjective emotional way of looking at things and the objective world around us. What Agee wants in effect is a collapse between the physical world and the experiential nature of vision, and between the mechanical abilities of the camera and the intuitive ability of the photographer.

In order to define this lyrical image Agee distinguishes between two forms of documentary photography: the static, meditative gaze versus the lyrical, emotional gaze. In large part, the aim is to establish the lyrical gaze as a form of photography capable of capturing the durational aspects of the cinematic, or rather, a form of photography capable of capturing a continuum of lived life by focusing on particular instances in time. To do so, Agee compares it with the meditative gaze, a more measured and static look at things in their proper place at the proper moment. In the meditative gaze "the static work is generally the richest in meditativeness, in mentality, in attentiveness to the wonder of materials and of objects." Opposite this lies, then, the lyrical image in which a photographer—such as Levitt—is able "to foresee and to isolate the most illuminating moment" by imaging how things happen in time rather than "after the fact."[6]

For Agee, Levitt's mastery of the lyrical image meant that she was able to take the durational aspect of cinema into the photographic image and vice versa, something that Agee had seen already in Levitt's still photography from the 1930s. Nonetheless, it is Levitt's move from photography into film projects during the 1940s that enables Agee to really consolidate these ideas. As two artists moving increasingly into film—Levitt as an editor and cinematographer and Agee as a critic and writer—the decision to actually collaborate on a filmic project must have seemed a natural move. In attempting to cross the boundaries between a nominal notion of photographic realism and a more cinematic form of lyricism, *In The Street* also presents itself in generic terms as a suitably neutral topic for a collaboration designed, above all, to illustrate the lyrical image. As a short experimental film—with no linear plot or conventional narrative to detract from the imagery—*In The Street* synthesizes Levitt's visuals and Agee's ruminations on urban life. Running at only fourteen minutes, it shows what appears to be a meandering camera on the streets of East Harlem following local residents as they casually stand in front of their apartments and shops, children play on the street, faces look out of windows, and housewives and grandparents talk and gesticulate seemingly unaware of the camera. It shows a cross-section of the ethnic and social demographic in postwar New York as well as a sense of the everyday life of people loitering and observing and—above all—the vigor of New York streets in summer with children playing and running around unsupervised. The subjects are not unfamiliar to documentary film work of the period but they are usually presented in more overtly sociological terms, such as an informational film about a particular neighborhood or an assessment of the growing metropolis and its problems.[7] *In The Street*, on the other hand, appears to follow Levitt's thematic interest in children already established in her street photography of the 1930s, in particular as they dress up, play-fight, and anarchically run around. At first glance, *In The Street* appears therefore to simply be an animated version of Levitt's earlier photographs, were it not for the short paragraph of writing by Agee that introduces the film: "The streets of the poor quarters of great cities are, above all, a theatre and a battleground. There, unaware and unnoticed every human being is a poet, a masker, a warrior, a dancer, and in his innocent artistry he projects, against the turmoil of the streets, an image of human existence."[8] Agee focuses on the "streets of the poor quarters" and its "human beings" as the territory of the lyrical image; an image that is not quite a photograph but something like it "filled with movement, fluid and so transient" it can capture "the irrefutably actual as perceived by the poetic imagination."[9] Here, the beauty of the "ordinary metropolitan soil" enables the streets to be both a "theatre" and a "battleground" for a particular form of human interaction, a place where the power of "reality" in all of "its unmasked vigor and grace" shows how the "actual world constantly brings to the surface its own signals, and mysteries."[10] In both *A Way of Seeing* and *In The Street*—according to Agee—Levitt's use of realism transcends the mundane nature of her subject matter, instead proving how "the irrefutably actual" can become a pathway into those urban "signals and mysteries" otherwise hidden to the naked eye.

While Agee's fascination with the city becomes a way to reestablish both how the lyrical and the urban operates, it is also very much part of a longer, ongoing fascination with childhood itself. Much can be said about Agee's constant return throughout his writerly career to his own childhood and how he uses the perspective of the child as an indicator of various liminal stages, from puberty into adulthood, incomprehension into understanding, and a way to reconnect with his own subliminal desires and fears.[11] Without a doubt, Agee's collaboration with Levitt while working on autobiographical material must have influenced his perspective on and interest in childhood. More crucially, in the context of *In The Street*, it brings an additional layer to the issue of temporality within the process of filming and writing in general.

For all of its lack of design and apparent delight in the random nature of public interactions, *In the Street* is thus far more than a series of emotionally charged vignettes, just as Levitt's photographs are more than simply snapshots of working-class people on the streets of New York.[12] As a response to changing patterns of urbanization in the immediate postwar era, the film also looks backwards, perhaps even in a nostalgic way, to a prewar version of avant-garde film-making in which the politics of working life comingle with a more poetic take on realist aesthetics. Again, connections could be made between Agee's compulsion to return to his own childhood and his tendency to see childhood metaphorically as a state of heightened intensity; an emotional landscape as well as a more communal one. Both Agee and Levitt were enthralled by European and Russian art cinema of the 1930s and in particular by Jean Vigo's French versions of poetic realism in his early documentary *A Propos de Nice* (1930), which also features footage shot by Boris Kaufmann of children playing games in the street, and the feature film *Zéro de Conduite* (1933), shown for the first time in the United States during the summer of 1947 at the Fifth Avenue Playhouse, New York. It is likely that while filming *In The Street*, Agee reviewed *Zéro de Conduite* across two weeks, June 28 and July 5, 1947 (*The Nation)*.[13] Agee defended his use of two weeks of column space because *Zéro* de Conduite was "in its own unprecedented world from start to finish" one of the "few great movie poems" and, as such, worthy of adulation.[14]

The fact that Agee was working on *In the Street* with Loeb and Levitt while reviewing *Zéro de Conduite and* writing the introduction to Levitt's book of photographs is crucial. The combination not only facilitated the use of Levitt as a litmus test for Agee's version of the lyrical image, but also made him rethink the boundaries and capabilities of still photography and cinema and hence the difference between the temporal flow of still and moving images.[15] In this respect, interlinking the still and moving camera is crucial for Agee's attempt to define the lyrical image. However, while Agee uses Levitt to conjure a realism that is more poetic than informative, the remnants of his previous, more famous collaboration with the photographer Walker Evans in *Let Us Now Praise Famous Men* (1942) are still in evidence.

In *Famous Men*, Agee insists on describing all objects animate and inanimate that present themselves to his gaze, the insignificant and the everyday, the beautiful and the base, as equally important.[16] It is in fact the indexical nature of Evans's camera and its ability to patiently wait for the moment when the landscape and its inhabitants cohere that Agee wants to emulate throughout the book. In *Famous Men* the supremacy of Walker Evans's meditative gaze is precisely what affords him the gravitas and stature that Agee deems necessary for the sharecroppers to be more than simply sociological subjects. The meditative gaze—in this respect—is well suited for the act of "choosing details whose insignificance shows they were not invented," the knick-knacks and meagre belongings of the sharecroppers in Alabama and the dilapidated structures in which they live.[17]

In The Street, on the other hand, focuses on the activities of children rather than the stiffly posed sharecroppers of the previous decade. Here, the larger-than-life gestures and mimicry overtake the presence of external objects and other people. Children are not only central to the film, but also epitomize the transition from Levitt's still photography of children in similar situations to that of moving images. Children are perfect because they are by nature so uncontainable and partly because Levitt often choses to photograph them mid-movement. When asked about the difference between photographing children and adults, Levitt's response: "One is a picture of people who are moving, the other is of people who are still" indicates that for her the temporal aspects of photography supersede any sociological intent.[18] Children are thus both exemplary of how bodies move in space and useful emblems of the way in which time functions pictorially. In other words, they are more than simply available subjects, as their presence denotes a performative as well as temporal quality.

The fact that children are nearly always present either in the margins or centrally in *In the Street* is one of the reasons that Levitt's role as a photographer is often gendered, made more empathetic, and by implication feminine. This image of her as a female flaneur traversing the urban landscape adds to a reading in which events seem to just happen in front of her lens, downplaying the idea that a deliberate aesthetic is at play.[19] Defining her photographs as "non-pictorial and non-documentary" in a 1941 Guggenheim application, Levitt wanted to avoid conventional definitions of pictorialism or documentary applied to her work. While the focus on children playing and running around *In The Street* may appear relatively "easy," the images are nonetheless replete with various social, political, and economic meanings. As Alan Trachtenberg points out, "the

FIGURE 7.1 Children Playing in East Harlem, 1942. Helen Levitt.

unqualified visibility of poor people" is a consistent and crucial component of Levitt's photographs.[20] Nonetheless, Agee insists on the children *In The Street* as agents within an environment that is above all performative rather than socioeconomic. The streets of East Harlem are overwhelmingly working class, but for Agee, their value is first and foremost as staging grounds for the release of a certain unconscious energy, that "innocent artistry"—he claims—that surpasses even the "turmoil of the streets." The language implies that the children represent a form of spontaneity only found in those liberated from rational conventions, a form of unconscious exuberance matched only by the fact that the environment they occupy can be seen as the whole of consciousness, a world onto itself. In this way, the city becomes an extension of the artist's psyche, as well as an emanation of something potentially larger than the artist him- or herself. According to Rancière:

> This way is precisely, says Agee, the only serious attitude, the attitude of the gaze not grounded on any authority . . . ; the entire state of consciousness that refuses any specialization for itself and must also refuse every right to select what suites its point of view in the surrounding . . . , to concentrate instead on the essential fact that each one of these things is part of an existence that is entirely actual, inevitable, and unrepeatable.[21]

According to Rancière, the attraction to certain moments is due to their unrepeatability. It is a domain that, in cinematic terms, is capable of incorporating space without being hampered by narrative restrictions; a space in which Agee can draw a connection between the arrested moment of still photography and the fluidity of cinema. Once again, children are important, not because they emblematize all of life in East Harlem, but because they are momentarily liberated from it through play and movement. They facilitate—in other words—a vision of the city as a metaphor for our consciousness made expansive, made panoramic, and hence filmic.

The move into a more panoramic version of Levitt's previous photographs of New York are liberating for Agee. In both *In The Street* and Levitt's photographs, thresholds, vacant lots, gutters, and city stoops exist throughout as free spaces liberated from the routine of work and school, liminal areas situated between the public and the domestic spaces of the city. *In The Street* punctuates the filmic equivalent of a stroll within such locations, as though they constitute visual cuts in an otherwise fluid scenario. They act as spaces for intercommunicative activity, for the inhabitants of the neighborhood to stop and chat and to register the rhythm of the neighborhood. In this sense, there is a language of mediation, communication, and togetherness at play here–even without the presence of actual dialogue or speech.

Agee's previous attempts to get as closely as possible to the thing or things rendered in his collaboration with Walker Evans in *Famous Men* could be seen as a form of mediation as well, albeit a mediation that is much more respectful, even painfully cautious at times. In *In the Street*, a different sense of freedom is at play—one facilitated by Agee allowing his own voice to be taken over by the authority of Levitt's movable eye. While Agee's deliberate circling around the constituent parts of the sharecroppers' lives in *Famous Men* constituted both a methodology and a subject in its own right, Levitt's circling of East Harlem in cinematic terms appears more relaxed, less organized and archival by nature. Without a chronological narrative, the events appear almost arbitrary, something that has prompted the critic Sanchez to argue for Levitt's form of realism in *In the Street* as essentially surreal: "These features give the film a slightly hallucinatory air, which does not come from manipulating the light or lenses, or from a subjective consciousness . . . the film's oddness comes instead from the disconnected quality of its subjects; from the obtrusive materiality; and from a certain unruly quality in the objectual world."[22] Sanchez argues that it is "not the real, but the surreal" that best describes the intangible and disconnected qualities of *In The Street*. However, Agee's use of the term "fantastical" to define the lyrical image is not about the juxtaposition of the surreal and the real but about the juxtaposition between the lyrical and the ordinary. In fact, it is when the lyrical and the ordinary coincide that things connect rather than disconnect in *In The Street*. Events may appear random, and in some ways "surreal," but the camera's ability to capture them as a continuous flow of urban life makes it a more romantic - in a connective sense - rather than radically surrealist exercise. Here is a version of the city that can incorporate the liberating aspects of the unconscious without succumbing to its supremacy in surrealist terms. Again, it is about a vision of the urban landscape as one unified consciousness. For Agee, I would argue, this is not so much a take on European Surrealism as it is a lyrical interpretation of a form of realism that extends from a more utopian, romantic version of American modernism, one founded upon the ideals of nineteenth-century transcendentalism as much as of European avant-garde practice. Like his American precursors, Thoreau not the least, Agee's participation in the production of the documentary process is a way to directly immerse himself in the documented environment. This desire for a sense of immersion and proximity within the documentary process was explicit in Agee's insistence on living with the sharecroppers during the writing of *Famous Men*; but here another form of visual alignment and immersion takes place. In both cases, Agee wants the process of documentation in itself to be an extension of the artist's camera—for him, an immersive process in the first place.

For Agee, Levitt's aesthetic—although it carries the vestiges of something surrealist—is therefore first and foremost another form of realism:

> it is worth noticing that in much of her [Levitt's] feeling for streets, strange details, and spaces, her vocabulary is often suggestive of and sometimes identical with that of the Surrealists. . . . But I think that in Miss Levitt's photographs the general feeling is rather that the Surrealism is that of the ordinary metropolitan soil which breeds these remarkable juxtapositions and moments and that what we call "fantasy" is, instead, reality in all of its unmasked vigor and grace.[23]

Levitt's urban "soil" may be suggestive of a surrealist turn toward the unexpected, but it is still representative of a realism attuned to a version of the "fantastical" as a variant *within* realism rather than as its opposite. It is the "ordinary metropolitan soil" that facilitates the metropolis as a territory that is extraordinary rather than mundane. The camera, in this regard, is the apparatus that facilitates the "unmasking" of reality. For Agee, then, it is not about a radical rewriting of urban life. Instead, it is a more reflective consideration of how various "remarkable juxtapositions and moments" can cohere through the lyrical image.

In one of the first pieces of critical writing on Levitt, "The Art of Poetic Accident: The Photographs of Henri Cartier Bresson and Helen Levitt" (1943), James Thrall Soby defines Levitt's and Cartier-Bresson's photography as representative of that "decisive moment" in which "gestures, persons and narrative congeal in a quantum of time virtually without temporal extension."[24] For Soby, the decisive moment is, above all, about stopping time in order to visualize those instances–a man jumping across a puddle, a child grimacing at his own reflection—that have no imaginable temporal extension. For Agee, however, the issue of temporal extension is crucial in the context of the lyrical image—it proves that photography can be about an ongoing lyrical continuum rather than a brief moment intercepted. The transaction between the photographer and the spectator may be crystalized in one spectacular "decisive" moment photographically speaking, but the movement of film *In The Street* proves that images *are* always just one moment in time, that things have occurred before the film begins and will continue to do so after the film "ends." Because *In The Street* uses so many of the same subjects and places as Levitt's still photography, the temporal quality of her previous photographs of children becomes more apparent as well. We recognize the subject matter as Levitt's domain but we also see the subjects come to life in ways that were previously impossible. In a roundabout manner, the durational aspects of the film *In The Street* shows how the photographs can never entirely be duplicated, while at the same time, giving them a new lease on life.

Levitt's focus on childhood is one element that distances her from a more European-inspired, prewar surrealist aesthetic. In this respect, Levitt looks forward to the postwar sensibility of the Nouvelle Vague rather than the anarchical fervor of prewar surrealism.[25] Like Truffaut's films about street kids, the innocence and vulnerability of childhood allows for an emotive view of the city writ large; a city that operates as the staging area for a particular type of realist melodrama and where children offer living proof of the adaptability of the human body to the rigors of city life. This is why, as Trachtenberg notes, the "children scattering the wreckage of vacant lots or installing themselves as living statuary on crumbling building facades" are able to bring "the inanimate infrastructure and its saturated messages of class distinction to . . . life."[26] For Trachtenberg, then, the children are harbingers of an oblique form of politics, one that combines the physical and the architectural aspects of the city.[27]

If Levitt's politics are oblique compared to other documentary efforts from the 1930s and 40s, it is partly because she (and Agee) take their cue from an almost celebratory approach to class distinction and to its potential as an energizing force within the arts. To return to Jean Vigo's homage to childhood anarchy, *Zéro de Conduite*—the film Agee was reviewing while working on *In The Street*—it becomes obvious how influential it was on Agee's attitude toward film and toward the politics of cinema.[23] In Agee's review of *Zéro*, the selfsame qualities of childhood anarchy and exuberance provide a clue to his fascination with Levitt's work: "the spirit of this film, its fierceness and gaiety, the total absence of well-constructed "constructive" diagnosis and prescription, the enormous liberating force of its quasi-nihilism, its humor, directness, kindliness, criminality, and guile, for me as satisfying a revolutionary expression as I know."[29] At first glance, Agee's review seems—above all—to praise *Zéro de Conduite* for its theme of liberation in the face of bourgeois oppression. The plot—a revolt against school authorities by a gang of disenfranchised students at a boarding school—is more joyfully anarchical than nihilistic. But underneath the anarchical behavior of Vigo's child-warriors, it is Vigo's (and Levitt's) ability to move fluidly between a form of observation and a sense of direct immersion that most impresses Agee: "As I see it, the trick is simply that Vigo gets deeper inside his characters than most people, is not worried about transitions between objective, subjective, fantastic, and subconscious reality . . . in order to insist that these several levels of reality are equal in value and inter penetrative."[30]

For Agee, the "inter penetrative" nature of what he deems "objective, subjective and fantastic reality" in *Zéro* paradoxically verifies the film's realist credentials. Vigo's ability to get inside his characters proves that he can be true to their actual lived lives, and at the same time, prove his lyrical abilities as a filmmaker. And again, children are the characters that guarantee the authenticity of what is shown, the refusal to abide by school rules a sign of their refusing to enter into a utilitarian sphere of work and adulthood. Above all, however, it is *Zéro*'s aesthetic use of the camera that is duplicated in *In The Street*, specifically the use of locations as props for children to overpower, mount and climb, as seen in figure 7.2.

Agee's appreciation of Vigo's use of a boarding school as the setting for a juvenile revolution is, as in Levitt's photography, linked to various spaces that act as transitions between play and work. In *Zéro*, the dormitories and playgrounds of the school represent the unexpected link between joyfulness and escape; a feeling not dissimilar to Levitt's photographs, in which the unfinished, broken down, and evolving nature of the city provides the space for children to play unsupervised. In Levitt's work, it is noticeable how much of New York is marked by its gaps and architectural voids as it is by its thoroughfares and shops. Because of this, the critic Max Kozloff defines Levitt's children as "small explosive parenthesis on weary and alien streets"—as though their status is always a bit precarious and uncertain. For Agee, however, they appear just as much as agents on a stage designed by themselves and for themselves.[31]

If the vacant lots and streets are stages for play, it is in the actual unstoppable upward movements of the children that the qualities of the filmic are most visible in *In The Street* and *Zéro de Conduite*. The urge to overcome gravity can be seen in *Zéro*'s final pillow fight, a famous lyrical interlude in slow motion that accentuates the graceful flight of the feathers rushing from the broken pillows and bedding used as makeshift weaponry, as seen in figure 7.3. Partly it is the slow sense of choreography and the potential for sudden movement that stands out,

FIGURE 7.2 Vintage print gifted by Helen Levitt to James Agee, circa 1942.

FIGURE 7.3 The pillow fight in *Zéro de Conduite.*

FIGURE 7.4 Chalk fight in *In the Street.*

but it is also the camera's acceptance of the materials at play here. In other words, as in Levitt's photographs, it is the acceptance of the children entirely taking over the frame in front of us that is paramount.

Going back to Agee's original distinction between the meditative photography of Walker Evans and Levitt's "lyrical image," the shots here appear to be the antithesis of Evans's thoughtful framing of stationary objects and people. On the contrary, these "lyrical images" seem to catch an energy that is barely contained by the frame of the film. What sets it apart though is not just the constant movement. Figures are caught in medias in poses that often obscure rather than illuminate exactly what is taking place.

This fascination with movement is present even in Levitt's more "meditative" subjects that punctuate the incessant movement of life on the streets of East Harlem—more specifically, shots of street graffiti. Unlike Brassaï's photos of Parisian graffiti that look like miniature artworks, Levitt's come across as the active scribbles of a collective unconscious. Here we have a visible trace of how humanity inscribes itself into the city's architecture through vernacular slurs, messages and drawings as seen in the example of two little girls whose serious demeanors are characteristically incongruent given what they are drawing.

It is no coincidence, then, that the chalky street fight in *In The Street*—in which a group of boys swing socks full of chalk at each other, as seen in figure 7.4—is eerily similar to the pillow fight at the end of *Zéro de Conduite*. Not only does the chalk heighten the cinematic effect of the children running toward and away from each other but their attempts to literally mark each other with the white chalk—like the feathers in Vigo's pillow fight—show a similar upward movement. In both instances, the material moving and flying around operates as an escape from the forces of gravity, turning something mundane upside down. Chalk and feathers may be intangible objects within the larger framework of a concrete city and, in *Zéro*'s case, an institutionalized boarding school; nonetheless, it is precisely the "flighty" nature of the material in comparison to the gravitas of the environment that makes it lyrical.

In Levitt's case, what was previously used to inscribe meaning into the walls and sidewalks of East Harlem in the form of graffiti is unleashed in the chalky fight that marks the climax of *In the Street*. Chalk—both in its more obvious presence and its potential as a marker—emblematizes the intransient nature of graffiti and the explosive but graceful movements of the children fighting. It is also a marker for a collective idea of cinema as a genuinely democratic and anonymous

FIGURE 7.5 Image from *A Way of Seeing.* Helen Levitt.

form of communication accessible to all. As Agee writes in *A Way of Seeing*: "the intuitions of a child with chalk" can "command every disparate element within the frame of the photographs into a grandly unified, cryptic significance . . . untouched by any interposition of consciousness between the hand and the source of fullest knowledge."[32] Agee's "grandly unified cryptic significance" bears some similarity to how he writes about the torn and tattered remnants of advertising in the sharecroppers' homes in *Famous Men*. In *Famous Men*, he likens the beautiful handprint of a child on a makeshift wall to a larger cosmic message, elevating the inscriptions of the family so that these, too, however mundane, can carry them into a higher plane. They become, in other words, objects that transcend their initial purpose just as the graffiti *In The Street* becomes much more than simply another vernacular inscription. By re-establishing the graffiti within a wider animated environment, Levitt also allows it to become form of caption or voiceover to the images. In "Children as Visionaries" (1987), Robert Coles's introduction to a reprint of Levitt's photographs, graffiti is also described as the surest sign of the illusory, temporary nature of certain unmistakably urban marks: "We'll never be able to return to those streets, meet those children, view their chalky efforts, ask about them directly or indirectly . . . through the medium of chalk applied to asphalt–what vulnerable but quite immediate and assertive reality there is."[33]

For Cole, this "vulnerable but quite immediate and assertive reality" is a way to define the intersection between childhood and photography and the temporal nature of Levitt's overall practice. It establishes an immediacy that is encrypted and yet vulnerable to change, not unlike the camera's ability to make the past feel present and yet irrevocably gone at the same time. According to Roy Arden, "Whereas her photographs appear as poetic compositions made in a timeless limbo, the film is a series of roughly cut passages from historical time's relentless progress."[34] This paradox—one might argue—the attempt to render a sense of timelessness through the continuous movement of people through time is, to a large extent, written into the cinematic process itself. But in Agee's case, the desire for immediacy and timelessness is absolutely tied to his vision of childhood as both transcendent and unmistakably real, and—as mentioned previously—it oftentimes renders his language more romantic than "documentary." By turning the children into conduits for an unconscious and universal language, the city becomes "the image of human existence" that Agee promises in the introductory blurb to the film. In *Famous Men*, Agee's tendency to romanticize the sharecroppers is used to show that despite their poverty, they too can be redeemed. In some ways, the urban landscape in Levitt's work contains a similar impetus, which can be problematic. By side-stepping various socioeconomic realities Levitt's children remain—for Agee—" innocently delicious creatures at large and unconquerable in a less than delicious world."[35] Circumventing the issue of racial and economic disparity in East Harlem, Agee's rhetoric is ill-equipped to deal with the wider structures of power and control that also permeate the city. To enable the city—and, more specifically, East Harlem—to act as a site of daily resistance as well as a particularly lyrical gaze is not easy. The anarchical chalk fight toward the end of *In The Street* has certain social connotations because it shows an awareness of the latent hostility and anger that crisscrosses the city's poorest neighborhoods; but ultimately, the aesthetic nature of the chalk flying through the air is what arrests the viewer's eye. To some extent, then, we are dazzled by the very chalk that obscures our view of the children themselves, a perhaps too easy metaphor for how Levitt's documentary gaze risks glossing over the social landscape around her. For Agee, such social ramifications are not always on his radar. More importantly for Agee, these children are as effective as agents of change as Jean Vigo's unleashed children of the bourgeoisie in *Zéro.* A certain rashness and aggression may be present in *In The Street* and in *Zéro,* but it is always under the surface of what appears to be merely lighthearted play. It is never, in this respect, the precursor for something more violent or uncomfortable.

It is curious, then, given that Agee so often signals his socialist concern for the plight of the working people, that so little is made of socioeconomic issues in his essay on Levitt *A Way of Seeing*. For Alison Dean in "The Invisible Helen Levitt," Agee—like many subsequent critics—often inadvertently ends up downplaying the complexity of Levitt's work for precisely this reason. As Dean puts it:

> But if Levitt is connected with some privileged depiction of humanity, as critics such as . . . James Agee suggest, then in the discourse of her contemporary moment she is also connected with complicated perceptions of race, dance, poetry, and grace; with the fantasy of democracy her modern walking seems to embody; with the infantilization of women . . . and with the complicated views about what makes a "true American" in New York's diverse neighbourhoods."[36]

As Dean rightly notes, national identity, gender, and a host of other issues invariably come into play in Agee's attempts to divest Levitt from the usual strictures of documentary practice—not least the fact that Agee downplays the social deprivations of East Harlem because he wants the lyrical image to be firmly situated there. In Agee's case, the city is romanticized in order to accommodate the lyrical image and because he seeks to depict an idea of neighborhood as a safe haven of sorts rather than as a competitive space of labor and capital. Dean's point about the infantilization of Levitt—in turn—touches on some important differences in how Agee deals with Walker Evans and Levitt comparatively speaking. But, in this instance, it is a difference based less on innate sexism and more on Agee's intense desire to write Levitt into the very city that he and she documents. In wanting to establish her photography and cinematography as a genuinely immersive practice, Agee positions Levitt as an emotionally engaged observer and, in the process, inevitably romanticizes the environment in which she works. In James Thrall Soby's reading of Levitt, the children are also conduits for something romantic and more transcendent; a transcendence that partly depends on the authenticity of the working-class environment that they occupy:

> Her preference is for the children of Harlem, where the relationship of child to city is more acute and real than in prosperous sections of New York, where the pavement is the nurse of the young, a blackboard for their fantasy. She photographs children at the weird climax of their activities, recording their daring, the ruthless energy of their dreams, . . . In doing so she furnishes a document on childhood which should be of great value.[37]

Soby's vision of children as natural, more instinctual, and less self-conscious beings is not only similar to Agee's later reading, but also exemplifies to some extent the new type of humanist postwar ethos that will culminate in Edward Steichen's 1955 *The Family of Man*, another photographic project in which children are often sentimentalized as innocents above all. For Soby, the children are transformative beings performing for both posterity and an audience of adults, a sentiment that echoes Agee's on multiple levels. In similar tones, the writer on photography and curator Newhall Nancy Newhall also affirmed Levitt's attraction to both primitivism and the unconscious sphere in an early catalogue introduction to Levitt's work: "The children of the poor are not starched and supervised. Roaming in tribes through the streets and empty lots, they inherit to the full the magic and terror of the inscrutable world. Joyous, vicious, remote, or sad, these photographs arouse in adults a swift and poignant succession of emotions."[38]

In both cases, children are useful because they exemplify ordinary working-class people in moments of collective interaction. Writing in *A Way of Seeing*, Levitt's "leverage upon the materials of existence"—as Agee puts it—rests on her ability to capture those micro-relations and gestures that speak to our common humanity across class and ethnic lines. In other words, a touch or a glance has currency because it is more than a series of unintentional albeit beautiful moments. The editing of these gestures and movements may not create an overt narrative that explains what life was truly like in *In The Street* but they nonetheless "record" that "movement of creativeness" in which the observer and subject come together.

Agee's verbal posturing can be hard to stomach for contemporary audiences. And yet, his gushing sense of the images' transcendent qualities is a part of a wider American postwar modernism in which the desire to marry the instinctual with the artistic is an intrinsic part of documentary work. As Agee puts it:

> I would not for a moment want to try to persuade any reader who mistrusts the irrational, to suspend this mistrust, and look further into these pictures. I am nevertheless convinced that these photographs cannot be fully enjoyed, or adequately discussed on a purely naturalistic or rational basis. Many of them prove, rather, that the actual world constantly brings to the surface its own signals, and mysteries. . . . it is remarkable that so little of this lyrical work has been done, . . . for it is after all, the simplest and most direct way of seeing the everyday world, the most nearly related to the elastic, casual and subjective way in which we ordinarily look around us.[39]

The "signals and mysteries" that Levitt brings to the surface are—like the graffiti in *In the Street*—another way to scan the city for legibility. According to Trachtenberg, Levitt's forte lies, among other things, in being able to acknowledge the American metropolis as a city of potential "of bottomless obscurities, inscriptions upon inscriptions."[40] For Agee, it is the "uncanny relation among surfaces" that makes the city transcendent; a place where "we all powerfully interdepend upon and enhance one another, reverberating like mirrors locked face to face the illimitable energies set up in the paradox formed in the irrefutably actual as perceived by the poetic imagination."[41] In his usual convoluted fashion, Agee describes how the camera acts as both a reflective and creative device. It relies on the presence of the "irrefutably actual," and yet its power emanates ultimately from the lyrical charge it brings to its subject, a charge accentuated by the mimetic qualities of the camera "reverberating like mirrors locked face to face." As Agee argues: "I suspect that only the reader who recognizes this, in his own terms, will thoroughly understand and agree with what I mean by a photograph as a good work of art; or by a lyrical photograph."[42]

The belief that a particular form of visual lyricism is inherent within the urban also carries some risk. For Agee, the transient and fleeting nature of the gestures of play are proof of a lyricism that depends on community and an affirmative view of mutual support in the face of economic deprivation. Agee's desire to link his definition of a visual form of lyricism to the ontological nature of the photograph itself oftentimes strains at the seams. That there is something arresting in the inconsequential actions of children does not mean that the act of recording them is necessarily beautiful or lyrical. For Agee, it is clearly crucial that the viewer is implicated in the process of looking through the camera's ability to give us a sense of proximity to the subjects shown, something that the lyrical image can do because it is the "most nearly related to the elastic, casual and subjective way in which we ordinarily look around us."[43]

In Levitt's world, children epitomize the lyrical image precisely because they refuse to be entirely captured in their still form and because they interact so fearlessly with the camera. The refusal to stand still, to stop moving guarantees their usefulness as, at once, innocent and insistent. As Agee writes: "The overall preoccupation, is, it seems to me, with innocence, not as the word has come to be misunderstood and debased, but in its full original wildness, fierceness, and instinct for grace and form . . . what Yeats's phrase calls 'the ceremony of innocence.'"[44]

By using Yeats's phrase "the ceremony of innocence," Agee turns photography into a deliberate and ritualized set of actions rather than something ordinary. A tightrope is navigated in this respect, as Levitt's images seek to both align the viewer with the subjects shown and still present them as extraordinary—the same dilemma that Rancière outlined in Agee's attempt to be both journalistically faithful to and adoring of the sharecroppers in *Famous Men*. In *In The Street*, the tactile qualities of the gestures, the touching and fighting that takes place there, may give us a sense that the "ceremony of innocence" is real. Nonetheless, this does not guarantee that it speaks to us of much more than the aesthetics of "grace and form" rather than lives genuinely lived.

In drawing a line, at times almost seamless and at others more visible between Levitt's still and movable aesthetic, film comes out as the most immersive. *In The Street*'s version of East Harlem is more present in some ways than Levitt's photographs but also more transient and fleeting, which is perhaps one of the reasons that it has been overlooked within her larger oeuvre. It is not coincidental that Agee never mentions the fact that *In The Street* contains a decidedly "unrealistic" soundtrack—a piano piece written for the film rather than recorded sound. With its improvisatory jazz score, the silent nature of the film accentuates the broad physicality of the action taking place, continuously reminding us of its distinctly cinematic qualities. Jazz urbanizes the environment and adds a distinct flavor to the film's more vernacular roots in different lyrical terms as well. Without the noise of kids screaming, of trucks, traffic, and other urban disturbances, the lyrical aspects of the film's movement are accentuated differently, and the editing becomes more noticeably tied to the soundtrack. It is, as Agee would have appreciated, both reminiscent of silent cinema and yet discernibly modern.

More curious about the processes of visual flux than in specific actions, the non-narrative element of *In The Street* must have felt like a rare freedom for Agee. Levitt's ability to conjure the filmic in her photography and vice versa is proof of the "lyrical" image's ability to dissolve the boundaries between the still and the moving camera. Nonetheless, the cinematic qualities of *In The Street* do more than re-enact a visual flux of her still images; they also trace Agee's desire to create a concurrence between his own vision and that of Helen Levitt. It allows him to take an idea of the camera already established through his writing in *Famous Men* and on Walker Evans and re-position the camera as an apparatus able to animate and not simply capture the world around him. I propose, then, that Agee did not fully articulate what could rightly be called a photographic ethos until the concurrence of his own vision with that of Helen Levitt. Agee's collaboration with her on several movie projects after *In The Street* (he also wrote the voiceover for /commentary for *The Quiet One* [1948]) allowed him to take an idea of the camera already established through his writing on Evans and re-position it as an apparatus able to animate and not simply capture the world around him.[45] Levitt gave up photography in 1948, possibly to dedicate herself to film projects, returning again to still photography in 1959, when she received the first of three Guggenheim fellowships; but, in many ways, the seamless move from one medium into another is consistent with the vision outlined by Agee.

What Agee recognized was that the gestures and movements in Levitt's cinematography could bring to life the continuum of something already present in her photographs. It could make photography both still and moving collide with something beneath the surface. In this sense, it was as though Levitt's photographs could attach an unseen value to the interior life of her subjects something only achievable—according to Agee—somewhere between photography and film. If the people we see *In the Street* still carry an emphatic charge, it is not because Agee wanted them to epitomize his definition of the lyrical image, but because in their still *and* movable form they remain so unmistakably alive.

Notes

1. *In the Street* was initially screened in 1948 and then re-released in 1952. James Agee wrote parts of the screenplays of for John Huston's *The African Queen* (1951) and Charles Laughton's The *Night of the Hunter* (1955).

2. Agee coins the phrase "the lyrical image" in his introduction published posthumously to Levitt's first monograph *A Way of Seeing* (New York: Viking Press, 1965). Only recently has Charles Maland's edition of the complete film reviews and essays by James Agee on film included "A Way of Seeing." For more on this, see: Charles Maland, *The Works of James Agee*, Vol.5., *Complete Film Criticism—Reviews, Essays, and Manuscripts*, (Knoxville: U of Tennessee P, 2017).

3. Originally written around 1946, *A Way of Seeing* was not published until 1965.

4. Charles Maland, *Complete Film Criticism–Reviews, Essays, and Manuscripts*, (Knoxville: U of Tennessee P, 2017), 864. Volume 5 in *The Works of James Agee*, General Editor, Michael A. Lofaro; Associate General Editor, Hugh Davis.

5. Ibid., 866.

6. Agee, *Complete Film Criticism*, 865.

7. Helen Levitt's more famous filmic collaboration is precisely a more traditional exposé of the consequences of urban ills. Levitt edited Sidney Meyers' s *The Quiet One*, a 1948 documentary that chronicles the rehabilitation of a young disenfranchised African American boy in New York. The film was nominated for an academy award for best documentary film and the voice-over commentary for the film was written by James Agee.

8. *In the Street*, 1948 (re-released 1952), 14 mins,. Dir. Helen Levitt, cinematography by Helen Levitt, Janice Loeb, and James Agee. Music by Arthur Kleiner.

9. Agee, *Complete Film Criticism*, 867.

10. Ibid., 868.

11. Two particular projects were instigated roughly around the same time that Agee worked with Levitt on *In The Street*: *The Morning Watch* (1950), a short autobiographical novel written between 1947 and 1950 about Agee's life at an Episcopal Boarding school following the death of his father, and *A Death In The Family*—completed in 1948 but published posthumously in 1957—also an autobiographical account of Agee's upbringing in Knoxville, Tennessee. *A Death in The Family* was awarded the Pulitzer Prize for fiction in 1958.

12. See Max Kozloff's essay on Levitt: "A Way of Seeing and The Act of Touching: Helen Levitt's photographs of the 40s," *The Privileged Eye* (Albuquerque: U of New Mexico P, 1987), 29–43.

13. Agee, *Complete Film Reviews*, 794.

14. Ibid., 796.

15. For more on the connection between cinema and photography, see: Caroline Blinder, "Animating the Gudgers: On the Problems of a Cinematic Aesthetic in *Let Us Now Praise Famous Men*," *New Critical Essays on James Agee and Walker Evans: Perspectives on* Let Us Now Praise Famous Men, (New York: Palgrave Macmillan), 145–164.

16. For more on the connections between Emerson's "transparent eyeball" and documentary photography, see Caroline Blinder, " 'The Transparent Eyeball': On Emerson and Walker Evans," *Mosaic* 37, no. 4 (2004): 149–63.

17. Jacques Rancière, "The Cruel Radiance of What Is: Hale County, 1936–New York, 1941," *Aisthesis–Scenes from the Aesthetic Regime of Art*, (London: Verso, 2013), 245–63.

18. As quoted in Elizabeth Margaret Gand, "The Poetics and Politics of Children's Play: Helen Levitt's Early Work." *UC Berkeley*. 2011. ProQuest ID: Gand_berkeley_0028E_11263. Merritt ID: ark:/13030/m54f1vq7. Retrieved from https://escholarship.org/uc/item/2sf6765x. According to Gand, "by 1943 upwards of fifty of Helen Levitt's photographs of children had merited inclusion in the Museum of Modern Art."

19. The recent discovery and marketing of the photography of Vivian Mayer is another instance of how attractive this concept of the female flaneur is. Much more could be said about how Mayer's reputation rests on a longer lineage and discourse surrounding female photographers in the 20th century.

20. Alan Trachtenberg, "Seeing What You See: Photographs by Helen Levitt," *Raritan* 31 (Spring 2012): 1.

21. Rancière, "The Cruel Radiance of What Is," 250.

22. Juan Antonio Suarez Sanchez, "Avant-garde Cinema, Surrealism and Agee and Levitt's *In The Street,*" *Atlantis* 18 (1996): 390–406, 396.

23. Agee, *Complete Film Criticism*, 870. For a more detailed analysis of the use of surrealism in the work of Agee, see: Hugh Davis, *The Making of James Agee* (Knoxville: U of Tennessee P, 2008).

24. James Thrall Soby, "The Art of Poetic Accident: The Photographs of Cartier-Bresson and Helen Levitt," *Minicam* 6 (March 1943): 29–30.

25. Much could be said about possible alignments between Levitt's use of children and the French Nouvelle Vague (Truffeaut's *400 Coups* etc.) to the Italian Neorealist school (Rossellini's *Germany Year Zero*, 1948).

26. Trachtenberg, "Seeing What You See," 4.

27. Agee's voiceover and input into his other cinematic collaboration with Levitt, *The Quiet One* is discussed in Chuck Maland's *Complete Film Criticism*.

28. *Zéro de Conduite* was released in France 1933, then banned and for legal reasons not released until 1947 in the U.S. Much could be said of her filmic influences, that she saw Alexander Dovzhenco's 1935 film *Aerograd* four or five times at the Photo League in New York and that she was well acquainted with both Jean Cocteau's *Le Sang d'un Poète* as well as Jean Vigo's *Zéro de Conduite*.

29. Agee, *Complete Film Criticism*, 797.

30. Ibid., 795.

31. Max Kozloff, "A Way of Seeing and the Act of Touching: Helen Levitt's Photographs of the Forties," in *The Privileged Eye: Essays on Photography* (Albuquerque: U of New Mexico P, 1987), 29–40, 30.

32. Agee, *Complete Film Criticism*, 872.

33. Robert Coles, Introduction to *In The Street* (Durham: Duke UP, 1987), 5.

34. Roy Arden, "Useless Reportage: Notes on Helen Levitt's *In The Street,*" *Afterall: A Journal of Art, Context, Inquiry* 6 (2002): 101.

35. Agee, *Complete Film Criticism*, 873.

36. Alison Dean, "The Invisible Helen Levitt," *Performance Matters* 2 (2016): 36.

37. James Thrall Soby, "The Art of Poetic Accident: Photographs of Cartier-Bresson and Helen Levitt," *Minicam* (March 1943): 28–33, 95.

38. As cited in "Helen Levitt: Childhood as Performance, City as Theater," *The Lion and the Unicorn* 25 (April 2001): 213.

39. Agee, *Complete Film Criticism*, 869.

40. Trachtenberg, "Seeing What You See," 7.

41. Agee, *Complete Film Criticism*, 870.

42. Ibid.

43. Ibid., 869.

44. Ibid., 890.

45. As mentioned earlier, *The Quiet One* is a 1948 American documentary directed by Sidney Meyers with camera work by Helen Levitt and Janice Loeb. James Agee wrote the voiceover commentary in this documentary about a disturbed inner-city African American boy.

EIGHT

Cock and Bull Stories

Luce's Fortune *Magazine Features Hemingway and Agee on the Business of Bloodsport*

MICHAEL A. LOFARO

This is the tale of three men: Henry Luce, the publisher of *Fortune*, and Ernest Hemingway and James Agee, who wrote for his magazine. In creating *Fortune* magazine at the age of thirty-one, Henry Luce was a self-made millionaire hoping to build upon his success with *Time* magazine, which he founded in 1923. Inauspiciously, the prospectus that he sent out to solicit advertisers on September 1, 1929, just preceded the Wall Street October stock market crash and the magazine missed its scheduled launch on New Year's Day by one month. The project aimed, according to Luce, to answer "the need of Big Business for a distinguished and de luxe monthly magazine, vividly portraying, interpreting and recording the Industrial Civilization." He intended to market it to the "most wealthy people [who] find the large civilization-moulding operations of industry and finance of fascinating and vital concern to them." Luce was quite clear about the status of his readers; his "Ideal Super-Class Magazine's price ($10 [per year or $1/issue]) will be a barrier so high that only the reader both enthusiastic and well-to-do will vault it."[1] That year the price of one issue was twenty times that of a loaf of common bread.

To justify *Fortune*'s price, it was revolutionary. It was oversized at 11 x 14 inches, contained 150 to over two hundred pages, and was printed on heavy cream-colored paper in multiple colors. Compared to competing business magazines that printed their numbers and statistics in black and white, *Fortune* was nearly a coffee-table book. Luce said that it would be "surpassingly beautiful," "richly illustrated," "a distinct expression of American genius," and its editorial content would be known for its "arresting vitality," characteristics that all proved true.[2] Reviewing the first issue, the *New York Times* (February 2, 1930) called it "sumptuous to the point of rivaling the pearly gates"[3] The last of Luce's touted traits—prose of "arresting vitality"—led him, through his editors-in-chief, to hire such gifted writers as Dwight Macdonald, Archibald MacLeish, Alfred Kazin, John Kenneth Galbraith, and James Agee, because he believed it was easier to teach great writers the business world rather than to teach business and financial writers how to make their prose literate and interesting.[4]

Hemingway was a guest writer; Agee was on *Fortune*'s staff and uncredited for his articles. Both men's journalism had a very discernable impact upon their literary ventures, but in obviously different ways. Hemingway seemingly incorporated a good deal of that style in his fiction, even though he himself viewed journalism as separate from the literature he produced. Agee, soon to engage in an ongoing philosophical debate over journalism's ethical nature, purpose and use, utilized an often-florid style in *Let Us Now Praise Famous Men*, and as well later developed differing styles widely divergent from it in his journalism to come, such as his mastery of *Time*-ese in writing for that magazine.[5] Neither man knew each other, but Agee was an enthusiastic admirer of Hemingway's writing, praising him in two letters. On November 13, 1927, he asked Father Flye: "Did you read, in (I think) the July issue of the Atlantic [Monthly], a prize-fighting story called Fifty Grand? The author, Ernest Hemingway, published a rather sensational novel, The Sun Also Rises, last year and this fall a book of short stories, Men Without Women. They're terrific, and fine—all I've read of them."[6] And in a letter to Dwight Macdonald in March 1930, he noted that he had "done very little reading,—beyond re-reading most of Hemingway."[7]

Ernest Hemingway was thirty-one when his "Bullfighting, Sport and Industry" appeared in *Fortune*'s second issue in March 1930.[8] A veteran newspaper man, he had also already published *In Our Time* (1925), in which six of the eighteen sketches dealt with bullfighting, and featured the sport in his novel, *The Sun Also Rises* (1926), and in the first and longest story in *Men Without Women* (1927), "The Undefeated." All of these works displayed his fascination with bullfighting, and his fame rated a by-line in *Fortune* as a contributor.[9] The sport's early centrality was similarly noted in Hemingway's humorous aside in a June 24, 1923, letter to Isabel Simmons: "We are going down to Pamplona in Spain for the great bull fighting f[i]esta. Wish you were going along. Bull fighting ought to have a stalwart pre-natal influence don't you think?"[10] His first wife, Elizabeth Hadley Richardson, was pregnant with their child (John) at the time.

Hemingway, it seems, was also quite interested in cockfighting. In "Hemingway's Earliest Piece of Fiction Discovered," the author, Jason Daley, stated that cockfighting tickets were discovered in the Bruce archive of Hemingway materials.[11] Additional testimony that Hemingway was an aficionado of cockfighting as well as bullfighting was apparent from the cockfighting pits installed on the grounds of his estate, now museum, in Cuba.[12]

James Agee, who graduated from Harvard in 1932, was only twenty-four when his "Cockfighting" article appeared in *Fortune's* March 1934 issue.[13] He was beginning his career and grateful to have a job in the Great Depression that involved writing. A further point of interest was that he was hired upon graduation in part because of his senior year creation of a parody of *Time* magazine, Luce's first publishing venture. Like many other of the early journalists in Luce's stable of literate business writers, Agee's world view was often at odds with the conservative nature of the financial magazine.

Hemingway and Agee both took on the subject of the business of bloodsport for *Fortune* in the Depression but did so in rather different ways. Already a proven author of fiction, nonfiction, and journalism, Hemingway treated his assignment as a factual piece, playing up *Fortune's* business nature. Where his fine prose is a significant part of his earlier journalism on the bullfights from 1923, in his *Fortune* article such passages mainly appear only as the first sentence or two of each of the initial three major sections. Perhaps best was Hemingway's opening of the second section, entitled "Fighting Bulls." "The Spanish fighting bull is as different from any domestic bull as the wolf is from the dog. He is not merely a vicious form of the same animal, he is a separate and wild strain directly descended from the wild bulls that roamed the Iberian peninsula, and he is closer kin to the Cape Buffalo, supposedly the most deadly of African big game, than to the Hereford, Jersey or Durham."[14]

In the main, however, his article was factual, explanatory, and dominantly economic. The fourth section "Horses and Tips" was a turning point, and little artistry followed in two subsequent sections. It appeared that Hemingway, a far more experienced professional reporter than Agee, gave Luce and *Fortune* exactly what he believed a business publication should have, rather than following Luce's more literate vision. The magazine's editor introduced the text of the article as "dealing with the economics of the bullfight business in Spain . . . ," and its extracted headnote, which separates the title from the text and is in a far larger typeface, emphasized money: "Marcial Lalanda made over $150,000 last year. But the bull breeding sons of Don Eduardo Miura took in only $33,000. Then there is the matter of the *propina* [a gratuity or tip, in this case from the matador to his employees for the fight]."[15]

FIGURE 8.1 Manet's "The Toreador," from a private collection (original in color).

FIGURE 8.2 *Bullfight* by Goya (original in color). From the author's collection.

According to Carlos Baker, despite its business focus, Hemingway's "Bullfighting" article for *Fortune* did serve an important purpose in his literary work. It inspired him to return to a dormant project that became *Death in the Afternoon* (1932), a work termed by Lawrence Broer "his spiritual autobiography and . . . the critical turning point of his life and career." Baker, states that "The book he now turned to was not fiction at all, but the fulfilment of a five-year-old dream. . . . He had made a small start on it with the article, 'Bullfighting, Sport and Industry,' completed in Paris shortly before he sailed in January, and just published in the March number of *Fortune*." It seems likely that his bullfighting articles for the *Toronto Weekly Star* on October 20 and 27, 1923, were a seedbed for the book as well. The *Fortune* article had evidently turned Hemingway's attention back to the future tome that he had earlier described to Maxwell Perkins in a letter of April 15, 1925, as a work on Spanish bullfighting, as "a sort of Doughty's Arabia Deserta of the Bull Ring, a very big book with some wonderful pictures."[16] Intriguingly, Agee, in a letter postmarked October 14, 1932, to "Goofy" (Christopher V. Gerould), restated his ongoing praise of and engagement with the author's works: "*Death in the Afternoon*—Hemingway's best book and I stick to it."[17] While still a subject lacking scholarly investigation, Agee's opinion of the work may have influenced his own creative work as well. In certain ways, *Death in the Afternoon* was a possible forerunner of the experimental journalism that was a core part of *Let Us Now Praise Famous Men*. Did Hemingway's use of minute, at times excruciatingly intense detail in *Death in the Afternoon* find a reflection in *Famous Men*? And did his "spiritual autobiography" on bullfighting serve to inspire Agee's creative autobiography and his later focus on death in *The Morning Watch* (1950/51) and *A Death in the Family* (1957)?[18]

Although Agee's piece is named "Cockfighting" in the table of "Contents" of the issue,[19] the editor omitted that word in the interior title and printed one instead that mimicked Agee's more romantic overall approach. The article was entitled "Not to Eat, Not for Love"; and then the separated headnote continued: ". . . but for the sheer delight of battle, the gamecock fights. And a forbidden sport persists, its ancient technique intact."[20] Agee, writing four years later than Hemingway, was a quick study at business writing, but with just two years as a professional journalist, perhaps was not as focused or as in control of his prose in presenting the business of cockfighting as Hemingway was with bullfighting, or perhaps played to his creative strengths, or simply paid more attention to Luce's vision for the magazine.

No matter what their respective histories or motivations, a comparison of the introductions of both contributions demonstrated their divergence. Hemingway opened by declaring: "Formal bullfighting is an art, a tragedy, and a business. To what extent it is an art depends upon the bulls and the men who are hired to kill them, but it is always a tragedy and it is always a business."[21] After this point Hemingway chose, however, not to develop the themes of art and tragedy, only that of business, and devoted the remainder of his introductory paragraph to statistics estimating earnings from the fights.

The first paragraph of Agee's "Cockfighting" struck a far different note, one that provided a stark contrast to even the more appealing nonbusiness prose of Hemingway's previous newspaper columns and other literary efforts on bullfighting.

> You are a gentleman. You have a taste for sport (most likely horses), leisure to indulge it, and an estate. One quiet morning you walk down to your stables. As you come around the side of the barn, you hear a soft, but violent fluttering of wings, an agitated hissing, a passionate exclaiming of low voices. You look down, and there are your Negroes (if you happen to be a southern gentleman) crouched in a wide circle on the ground, leaning on bent knuckles, peering into the center of the ring. They are watching two birds, large and brightly colored, that cling together beak to beak with arched necks, dancing up and down, while their wings whir and they slash at each other viciously, rapidly, with their spurs. The birds are gamecocks, most ferocious of all domestic creatures, and their dance is fatal—it can end only in death. And you are present at one of the many new births of man's most ancient sport, legally extinct in at least forty of the United States, frowned on in all, minor and surreptitious pleasure of the rich, secret passion of the poor, purpose of the Heel Tap Club,[22] most exclusive in the world: cockfighting.[23]

Agee also included a bit of Babbitt-bashing in his piece, both ridiculing the A.S.P.C.A. and noting that the upper crust said that "It is the timid, weak spirited bourgeoisie . . . who take away cockfighting from both their inferiors and their betters."[24]

Hemingway's earlier columns on and incorporation of the business of bullfighting, however, demonstrated more artistry and the same spirit of the romance of bloodsport noted in Agee's first paragraph, far more than did the article that he produced for *Fortune*. His two newspaper articles on the subject for the *Toronto Weekly Star*, for example, reflected this difference in Hemingway's engagement and clearly served in part as sources for the descriptions and ideas for his assignment in *Fortune*. In the first, "Bull Fighting a Tragedy," he described the "three absolute acts of the tragedy" as performance and ritual.[25] But even when addressing the topic of business in the article for the *Weekly Star*, he incorporates allusion, a device found nowhere in his article for *Fortune*.

> Bull fighting is an exceedingly dangerous occupation. In sixteen fights I saw there were only two in which there was no one badly hurt. On the other hand it is very remunerative. A popular espada [matador][26] gets $5,000 for his afternoon's work. An unpopular espada though may not get $500. Both run the same risks. It is a good deal like Grand Opera for the really great matadors except they run the chance of being killed every time they cannot hit high C.[27]

And in his follow-up piece, "Pamplona in July," Hemingway opened by calling the two-week festival "the World Series of bull fighting," and then launched into a captivating description of his arrival. He saw,

> Really beautiful girls, gorgeous, bright shawls over their shoulders, dark, dark-eyed, black-lace mantillas over their hair. . . . All day and all night there is dancing in the streets. Bands of blue-shirted peasants whirl and lift and swing behind a drum, fife and reed instruments in the ancient Basque Riau-Riau dances. . . .[28]
>
> All the carnivals I had ever seen paled down in comparison. A rocket exploded over our heads with a blinding burst and the stick came swirling and whishing down. Dancers, snapping their fingers and whirling in perfect time through the crowd, bumped into us before we could get our bags down from the top of the station bus.[29]

By comparison, Hemingway's writing in *Fortune* is dry, factual, relatively flat, and substantively not in accord with Luce's premise for the magazine. A brief sample of this type of his prose dealt with Marcial Lalanda, whom Hemingway termed "the best, the most skillful, the most consistent and the highest paid matador in Spain." In it, Hemingway merely expanded upon the financial tone of the article's headnote: "Marcial Lalanda this year gave eighty-six fights at an average price of well over 12,000 pesetas. This would gross him over a million pesetas. The price of the fights varied slightly and the exchange on the peseta also varied during the summer, but it is accurate enough and no exaggeration to say that Marcial Lalanda gave eighty-six fights at an average of $2,000 apiece."[30] It was in a letter to Maxwell Perkins on December 15, 1929, that Hemingway supplied perhaps the best reason for the more mundane nature of his prose for *Fortune*. He completely disagreed with the idea of Luce's new venture:

> —Am trying to write an article on bull fighting as an industry for "Fortune[.]" Archy Mac Leish asked me for it—written in journalese full of statistics—It's a romance of business magazine—there's no romance in the article—They probably won't take it—Am keeping it as dull as possible—Every aspect I touch on if I could go on and write about would make a long chapter in a book—They wanted something between 5,000 and 20,000 words and I told them it would cost $2500—So they want something over 2500 words for $1000.00 instead—Their magazine came out just at the time of the Crash which was hard luck—But if ever a magazine sounded like useless balls this one does—Am doing it for Archy—how he got mixed up with them God knows—[31]

Hemingway's attitude led to an unwavering economic focus in the article, which was certainly filled with "journalese full of statistics" and "no romance." He chose not to describe even one of Lalanda's bullfights or that of any other matador, and consequently did make the piece "as dull as possible" for the reader hoping for more. A reasonable comparison to his other early journalism on bull fighting, like that quoted previously, underscored the strong contrast.

His decision on the focus of "Bullfighting" was perhaps all the more odd, if one takes into account American matador Sidney Franklin's description in his autobiography of his first encounter with Hemingway in Spain in August 1929, only eight months before the *Fortune* piece appeared. While Franklin stated in his work that at the time he had "never heard of Hemingway," the author soon fascinated him:

> As we chatted, I realized that this fellow had a choice selection of English terms for bullfighting which up until then I had been at a loss to translate. And he used them very casually, as though it were old stuff with him. Besides, he was the first person who spoke to me in American English who appeared to have a deep understanding of the business. . . . I drew our conversation into channels which would show me just how much he knew about bullfighting. And, little by little, he amazed me. He was familiar with events and instances which only a deep sincere student of the subject could know about.[32]

Franklin was so taken with Hemingway that, after a five and one-half hour lunch, he happily had the author accompany him on his next matches. He asked Hemingway if he would stand behind the inner wall of the rings, the *barrera*, "if you're not afraid to see them that close" and later, after finding out how much Hemingway knew of the maneuvers of the great matadors of the past, "worked out a system of signals" through which the author would read the crowd and coach Franklin on when to incorporate those homages. The matador concluded by stating that "This direction from him was the cause of my meteoric rise." They eventually spent four months together.[33]

Agee never overtly resisted or indicted Luce's original vision for *Fortune* during his tenure there in that manner Hemingway did, despite what some might term the magazine's contradictory premise. In fact, six months before the publication of his article, Agee wrote to Father Flye that although he understood "business very poorly," he was really "interested in doing well with this job: in making it a part of my career.—" As time passed, however, he did believe that his position at *Fortune* stifled his progress and art as a writer.[34]

Whatever their differences, both works also provided fertile fields for incorporating the artwork that Luce wished to distinguish *Fortune* from all other magazines in the field. Hemingway's article was graced by reproductions of paintings in full color: one, for example, was a full page picture of Manet's "The Toreador" from a private collection (see figure 8.1); and another, a two-thirds page scene, of the *Bullfight* by Goya from the Metropolitan Museum of Art (see figure 8.2). Also featured were ten black-and-white etchings by Goya of bullfighting scenes from the same museum.[35] On the other hand, Agee's "Cockfighting" was less lavish, and illustrated mainly by commercially available photographs from Gosden Head, Ltd., and from two private individuals. Even though it contained six color illustrations, four half-page ones that were reduced in size by sidebars of explanatory text, and three of 2 x 3 inches, the layout was far less sumptuous than that of Hemingway's article. It had, in addition, however, four circular photographs of a cockfight, each two inches in diameter as a visual lead-in to the piece (see figure 8.3), and an in-house black-and-white sketch (4 x 4 inches), and a color Currier & Ives picture (4 x 5 inches).[36]

The difference in illustration may be due both to Hemingway's status as a writer and Agee's as an employee, and also to the fact that, by 1934, *Fortune* was successfully established and, in 1930, Hemingway's "Bullfighting" was in its second issue, a time when Luce was trying to recruit readership. All but two illustrations in Agee's "Cockfighting" featured only cocks; however, these two others were significant more for their content than the quality of illustration. One was the color reproduction of Currier& Ives's 1882 "De Boss Rooster,"[37] (see figure 8.4) which depicts near–minstrel show caricatures of African Americans surrounding the two combatants, with one cock dead. While both bloodsports were described in

FIGURE 8.3 Visual lead-in to James Agee's "Cockfighting" (originally arranged vertically to border the left side of the page). From the author's collection.

the texts as having popularity across class lines, of the two articles, Agee's tended to focus a bit more on the poor and on race, although he began with "gentlemen" as perhaps a tip of the hat to the status of *Fortune*'s readers, before mentioning "your Negroes (if you happen to be a southern gentleman)." In these instances, the article echoed the racial bias of the times. The other Agee illustration, the in-house black-and-white line drawing, linked the two sports with its caption "Like a Miniature Bull Ring: The Cockpit"[38] (see figure 8.5) and appeared as well, though perhaps not definitively so, to reinforce gender, racial, and class divides. It shows a male audience, almost exclusively white, sitting in the covered bleachers observing the fight, and two black trainer-handlers of the fighting cocks in the ring. Thus Agee and/or his editor seemed to reflect the discriminatory attitudes of America in the 1930s, a fact far less the case in the author's later works. "Cotton Tenants" [1936], which was the seedbed for his *Let Us Now Praise Famous Men* (1941), and "America, Look at your Shame!," his posthumously published piece on the Detroit race riots of 1943, progressively revealed far less stereotypical views.[39] No class or racial bias was evident in Hemingway's article. Writing of Spain, he seemed to value the Gypsy bullfighters as much as the Spanish, a fact dramatically highlighted by another near full-page color reproduction in *Fortune*, that of "The Family of the Gipsy [alternative spelling] Bullfighter" by Ignacio Zuloaga,[40] included courtesy of the Hispanic Society of America.

In the final analysis of the texts, it was regrettable that Hemingway, with so much enthusiasm and knowledge in hand about bullfighting, chose not to indulge some of the "romance" of the literary that Luce hoped would distinguish his business magazine and justify its price. Incorporating some of his material from *The Sun also Rises*, or perhaps his description of Pedro Romero, the young matador, or a historical vignette from his 1923 columns, would likely have broadened the appeal of his *Fortune* article and brought it more in line with Luce's wishes.[41] Perhaps a corroborating partial judgment, William White chose not to include "Bullfighting" in his standard anthology of Hemingway's journalistic work.

Agee, never the great sportsman or bloodsport enthusiast that Hemingway was, did fulfill Luce's concept for *Fortune*, likely both because of his position as an employee and his literary inclination. He provided a primer for cockfighting and the facts and figures about its business and peppered his writing throughout with interesting allusions, anecdotes, and vignettes. The readers learned more and more as the article progressed, no matter what their view on the mayhem of the sport,[42] or on its conflicting reflections of class struggle and broad egalitarianism,

FIGURE 8.4 Currier & Ives's 1882 "De Boss Rooster" (original in color). From the author's collection.

FIGURE 8.5 "Like a Miniature Bull Ring: The Cockpit." From the author's collection.

or on its appeal to American individualism. They understood after reaching its conclusion why some people felt so strongly about their participation and the sport's continuance. As Agee wrote:

> Those who love the sport are not discouraged by its clandestine nature. With the fanatic fervor of all enthusiasts, they gather covertly in dark, deserted places, from Christmas until Independence Day, to see their birds win a main [event] or two, then die. . . . Like some members of a sinister secret order, they meet silently on the appointed day: Gentlemen, breeders, yokels, gangsters—society's highest and its lowest, seldom those in between who comprise the Public. . . . Like members of a secret order, too, these sportsmen have their unwritten code of honor. Nothing unites them but their common passion and the peril of the Law. . . . The cocking clan has also its High Moral Purpose: its value of the gamecock as an example of ideal courage. They love to quote the speech Themistocles made to his Athenian army in 480 B. C., on the way to Salamis: "These animals fight not for the gods of their country, nor for the monuments of their ancestors, nor for glory, nor for freedom, nor for their progeny, but for the sake of victory, and that one may not yield to the other." Rugged individualists are these rooster worshipers, and they will remind you that the eagle was chosen to symbolize the U. S. by only two votes over the cock.[43]

Clearly, Agee reveled in the "romance" that Luce wished to infuse into *Fortune* in "Cockfighting," perhaps more than in several of his other assignments for the magazine, and certainly more than most of the staff writers. Part of his authorial achievement in this article was that he incorporated the history, folklore, and culture of the sport and portrayed it as well as a form of sacred ritual, echoing many of Hemingway's sentiments about bullfighting in his pre-*Fortune* work.[44] Or, as Genevieve Moreau says, in Agee's article cockfighting is portrayed as "not merely an entertainment, it was a sacrament, the cock itself the symbol of a mortal though triumphant individualism."[45] Hemingway, one is tempted to say, despite writing on one of his favorite topics and his article's opulent illustrations, simply gave Luce the business.

Notes

1. "Fortune Prospectus, September 1929, Volume One, Number Zero," *Fortune*, http://fortune.com/1929/09/01/fortune-prospectus-september-1929-volume-one-number-zero, accessed January 22, 2019. Note that square brackets in the text of the present article indicate editorial clarifications/insertions.

2. Ibid.

3. *New York Times*, http://search.proquest.com/hnpnewyorktimes/docview/99062813/E08D0CCB5EB04F11PQ/26?accountid=14766, accessed January 22, 2019.

4. For more information on Henry Luce, see Alan Brinkley, *The Publisher: Henry Luce and His American Century* (New York: Alfred A. Knopf, 2010); Ralph G. Martin, *Henry and Claire: An Intimate Portrait of the Luces* (New York: Putnam's, 1991); James L. Baughman, *Henry R. Luce and the Rise of the American News Media* (Boston: Twayne Publishers, 1987); J. W. Swanberg, *Luce and His Empire* (New York: Scribner's, 1972); and John Kobler, *Luce: His Time, Life, and Fortune* (New York: Doubleday, 1968).

5. See, for example, Paul Ashdown, ed., *James Agee: Selected Journalism* (Knoxville: U of Tennessee P, 1985), xxix. My thanks to Professor Ashdown for first pointing out to me the existence of the Hemingway article and suggesting its comparison to Agee's as well as for a valuable commentary on the present investigation. See Paul Ashdown, ed., *James Agee: Selected Journalism*, xvii. There he also gives a general comparison of their journalism (xiv–xvii), but does not analyze the two pieces. And, although it does not mention the two works treated in this article, for a broader sense of the impact of Hemingway's and Agee's journalism upon their literature, see David T. Humphries, *Different Dispatches: Journalism in American Modernist Prose* (New York: Routledge, 2006), 107–24, for *The Sun also Rises* (1926), and 125–69, for *Let Us Now Praise Famous Men* (1941) treated comparatively with Zora Neale Hurston's *Mules and Men* (1935). See also Michael Jacobs, "From Cotton Pickin' to Acid Droppin': James Agee and the New Journalism," in Let Us Now Praise Famous Men *at 75: Anniversary Essays*, ed. Michael A. Lofaro (Knoxville: U of Tennessee P, 2017), 343–65, and for Hemingway, see Robert O. Stephens, *Hemingway's Nonfiction: The Public Voice* (Chapel Hill: U of North Carolina P, 1968), 3–40. On the language of *TIME*, see Alan Brinkley, "The *TIME* of their Lives," *Vanity Fair* (May 2010), online at https://www.vanityfair.com/news/2010/05/time-magazine-henry-luce. Some hallmarks of *TIME*-ese were condensed articles (usually limited to four hundred words), inversion of the elements of a sentence, and the creation of new words and hyphenated compound words. For more on the context of *Fortune* in the 1930s, its divided treatment of wealthy versus non-elite people and businesses, and Agee, see EL's (Erling Larsen's) "*Let Us Not Now Praise Ourselves*," his review of the 1960 reissue of *Let Us Now Praise Famous Men*, in *The Carleton Miscellany* 2 (Winter 1961): 86–97. My thanks to David Madden for sending me his copy of the journal.

6. James Agee, *Letters of James Agee to Father Flye*, ed. James H. Flye (New York: George Braziller, 1962), 31. In a November 18, 1929, letter to his friend Christopher V. (Goofy) Gerould, Agee's praise continued: "A Farewell to Arms is the balls." In James Agee Papers, University of Tennessee Special Collections, MSS 3824, box 1, folder 4.

7. James Agee to Dwight Macdonald, undated (March 1930). Dwight Macdonald Papers, Yale University Manuscripts and Archives, box 5, folder 64. In a July 8, 1930, letter to "Goofy" (Christopher V. Gerould), is a satiric section in which Agee parodies the Paris artists and American ex-patriots of The Lost Generation and chats about he and "Hem" being great friends (James Agee Papers, University of Tennessee Special Collections, MSS 3824, box 1, folder 5). A bit earlier, Agee's enthusiasm for Hemingway's writing was made clear in a critical paper on *A Farewell to Arms* on February 26, 1930, when he was a sophomore at Harvard. See the University of Tennessee Special

Collections, MS 2730 box 8, folder 14. As part of his introduction, Agee says that "I think he [Hemingway] comes nearer greatness than any other living American author. . . ."

8. The Hemingway article appeared on pages 83–88, 139–40, 142, 144, 146, and 150 (notes). The original twenty-one-page typescript is in the Hemingway Papers at the John F. Kennedy Presidential Library and Museum. Cited in Sandra Spanier and Miriam B. Mandel, et al., eds., *The Letters of Ernest Hemingway* (Cambridge: Cambridge UP, 2018), 4 (1929–1931), 208n2. For *Fortune's* treatment of the typescript and notes, see the editors' explanatory note on page 251. Hemingway's interest in the notes not used by *Fortune* is later mentioned in his letter to John Herrmann (c. May 12–17, 1930), 4, 290.

9. Hemingway published *A Farewell to Arms* in 1929. On bullfighting and Hemingway, see several of the essays in Carl P. Eby and Mark Cirino, eds., *Hemingway's Spain: Imagining the Spanish World* (Kent, Ohio: Kent State UP, 2016). See also Michael Reynolds, *Hemingway: The 1930s* (New York: W. W. Norton, 1997), and Keneth Kinnamon, "Hemingway, the Corrida, and Spain," in *Ernest Hemingway's The Sun Also Rises: A Casebook*, ed. Linda Wagner-Martin (New York: Oxford UP, 2002), 125–38.

10. Sandra Spanier, Albert J. DeFazio III, and Robert W. Trogdon, eds., *The Letters of Ernest Hemingway* (Cambridge: Cambridge UP, 2013), 2 (1923–1925), 30. See also, Carlos Baker, ed., *Ernest Hemingway: Selected Letters*, 1917–1961 (New York: Scribner's, 1981), 84.

11. Smithsonian.com, October 4, 2017, Smithsonian, https://www.smithsonianmag.com/smart-news/hemingways-earliest-piece-fiction-discovered-180965098/, accessed January 22, 2019.

12. See, among several references, *Lonely Planet*, https://www.lonelyplanet.com/cuba/havana/attractions/museo-hemingway/a/poi-sig/370285/358014, accessed January 22, 2019.

13. The Agee article appeared on pages 90–95 and 146.

14. Hemingway, "Bullfighting," 83. That Hemingway later went back to his article (or remembered his own phrasing) is clear, since he expands upon these same thoughts in his magnum opus on bullfighting *Death in the Afternoon* (New York: Charles Scribner's Sons, 1932), 105.

15. Ibid.

16. Carlos Baker, *Ernest Hemingway: A Life Story* (New York: Charles Scribner's Sons, 1969), 209; and Spanier, et al., eds., *The Letters of Ernest Hemingway* 2, 318, or Baker, *Ernest Hemingway: Selected Letters*, 156. Hemingway expands his thoughts on how he will create his bullfighting magnum opus as a personal testament in a subsequent letter to Maxwell Perkins on December 6, 1926. Ruth Sanderson, Sandra Spanier, and Robert W. Trogdon, eds., *The Letters of Ernest Hemingway* (Cambridge: Cambridge UP, 2015), 3 (1926–1928), 176, and Baker, *Ernest Hemingway: Selected Letters*, 236–37). See also, of course, Hemingway's own text for *Death in the Afternoon*. For the newspaper articles, see William White, ed., *By-Line: Ernest Hemingway* (New York: Charles Scribner's Sons, 1967), 90–108. Hemingway's reference to "Arabia Deserta" is to Charles M. Doughty's *Travels in Arabia*, 2 vols. (Cambridge: Cambridge UP, 1888). Hemingway mostly likely had access to its reissue in 1921 by Jonathan Cape (or a subsequent reprinting of this new edition), with new introductions by the author and an extremely laudatory introduction on its accuracy and encyclopedic nature by T. E. Lawrence. See also, Edward F. Stanton's insightful chapter on *Death in the Afternoon* in his *Hemingway and Spain: A Pursuit* (Seattle: U of Washington P, 1989), 91–125;

and Lawrence R. Broer, "Bulls and Bells: Their Toll on Robert Jordan," in *Hemingway's Spain: Imagining the Spanish World*, ed. Carl P. Eby and Mark Cirino (Kent, OH: Kent State UP, 2016), 196. For a brief chronology of Hemingway's time in Spain before his article for *Fortune*, see José Luis Castillo-Puche, *Hemingway in Spain: A Personal Reminiscence of Hemingway's Years in Spain by his Friend* (Garden City, NY: Doubleday & Co., 1974), 371–74.

17. In James Agee Papers, University of Tennessee Special Collections, MSS 3824, box 1, folder 6.

18. Some of the overt parallels to—or perhaps influences upon—*Let Us Now Praise Famous Men* can be seen in Hemingway's incredibly detailed descriptions of the people and places, the sense of ritual and mystique in bullfighting, and in specifics such as both texts' ties to religion. In terms of method, Agee's Preface to *Famous Men* could as equally apply to Hemingway's meticulous approach to *Death in the Afternoon*: "Ultimately, it is intended that this record and analysis be exhaustive, with no detail, however trivial it may seem, left untouched, no relevancy avoided, which lies within the power of remembrance to maintain, of the intelligence to perceive, and of the spirit to persist in" (Hugh Davis, ed., Let Us Now Praise Famous Men: *An Annotated Edition of the James Agee-Walker Evans Classic, with Supplementary Manuscripts* [Knoxville: U of Tennessee P, 2015], viii). Also of course worthy of mention is the extensive use of photographs in both works.

Ritualistic behavior likewise plays a prominent part in the books. In *Famous Men*, note Agee's description of the sharecroppers' last stage in their traditional pattern in tending young cotton plants: "The fourth sweeping is so light a scraping that it is scarcely more than a ritual, like a barber's last delicate moments with his muse before he holds the mirror up to the dark side of your skull. The cotton has to be treated very carefully. By this last sweeping it is making. Break roots, or lack rain, and it is stopped dead as a hammer." And much of *Death in the Afternoon* is devoted to the adherence—or failure to adhere—to the pre-Christian and Christian aspects of what Hemingway calls "the ritual of the bullfight" (24 and ff.).

On the sacredness of life, Agee says "So that how it can be that a stone, a plant, a star, can take on the burden of being; and how is it that a child can take on the burden of breathing; and how through so long a continuation and cumulation of the burden of each moment one on another, does any creature bear to exist, and not break utterly to fragments of nothing: these are matters too dreadful and fortitudes too gigantic to meditate long and not forever to worship" (Davis, *Famous Men*, 271, 49). This religious or sacred nature of *Famous Men* has often been explored. For example, see James S. Miller's interesting take on how Agee "sacralize[s]" objects in *Famous Men* in "Inventing the 'Found' Object: Artifactuality, Folk History, and the Rise of Capitalist Ethnography in 1930s America," *Journal of American Folklore*, 117 (Fall 2004): 385–89. Also, when dealing with the religious or sacred in *Death in the Afternoon*, Hemingway notes that a matador's passes with the cape are called "veronicas" and explains the derivation of the term as a homage to St. Veronica as matadors seek to replicate the manner in which she is depicted holding the cloth to wipe the face of Christ. The same general sense of religion and the sacred is evident in the matadors' prayers in church to the Blessed Virgin, and later in Hemingway's stating that the matadors' experience a feeling in the bull ring "as profound as any religious ecstasy" (*Death in the Afternoon*, 65–66, 90, 206–7, respectively).

Similar rough parallels to *Famous Men* are in Hemingway's occasional direct address to his readers (see, for example, 203–5) and particularly in his statement that the nature of a book is an inadequate medium through which to communicate bullfighting fully. Note the beginning of a long paragraph on the organic experiential mode that his book lacks: "It should have the smell of burnt powder and the smoke and the flash and the noise of the traca [a string of firecrackers] going off through the green leaves of the trees and it should have the taste of horchata [likely tiger nut "milk," mixed with sugar and water], ice-cold horchata, and the new-washed streets in the sun, and the melons and beads of cool on the outside of the pitchers of beer; the storks on the houses in the Barco de Avila and wheeling in the sky and the red-mud color of the ring; and at night dancing to the pipes and the drum with lights through the green leaves and the portrait of Garibaldi framed in leaves . . ." (271). And Hemingway's conclusion may also have made an impact on Agee: "Let those who want to save the world if you can get to see it clear and as a whole. Then any part you make will represent the whole if it's truly made. The thing to do is work and learn to make it. No. It is not enough of a book, but still there were a few things to be said. There were a few practical things to be said" (278). Compare both Hemingway's statements above to Agee's: "If I could do it, I'd do no writing at all here. It would be photographs; the rest would be fragments of cloth, bits of cotton, lumps of earth, records of speech, pieces of wood and iron, phials of odors, plates of food and excrement. . . . A piece of body torn out by the roots might be more to the point. . . . As a matter of fact, nothing I might write could make any difference whatever. It would only be a "book" at the best" (*Famous Men* 11–12). Both authors were certainly a part of the experimentation with the documentary form that marked the 1930s.

Obvious large differences exist between the authors' works as well, not the least of which is Agee's emphasis, however diversely formulated, upon social justice, a theme that is not a part of Hemingway's plan for *Death*. Likewise, Agee's *Famous Men* has nothing comparable to Hemingway's ongoing device of episodically trying to explain bullfighting to an "old lady" in a dialog, because she was the only person in the group who had viewed a bullfight and stated that she likes a part of it (*Death* 64–182). Significant other influences upon Agee's work have also been explored. See, for example, Davis, *The Making of James Agee*, 105–98, for the influence of surrealism on *Famous Men*. See also several essays in Lofaro, Let Us Now Praise Famous Men *at 75: Anniversary Essays*, 95–210. On Hemingway, see Miriam Mandel, ed., *A Companion to Hemingway's* Death in the Afternoon (Rochester, NY: Camden House, 2004). Mandel's *Hemingway's* Death in the Afternoon: *The Complete Annotations* (Lanham, MD: Scarecrow Press, 2002) is also quite useful. Again, thanks to Paul Ashdown for suggesting this future line of inquiry briefly illustrated above.

19. Agee, "Cockfighting," 51.

20. Ibid., 90.

21. Hemingway, "Bullfighting," 83. In *Death in the Afternoon*, Hemingway states that "Bullfighting is the only art in which the artist is in danger of death and in which the degree of brilliance in the performance is left to the fighter's honor." He then proceeds to explain that "In Spain honor is a very real thing" and expands upon honor's implications (91–92).

22. A "Heel Tap" is originally a peg placed in a shoe's heel for stability while it is being crafted and is removed when the shoe is finished. Also, however, "A person leaving any liquor in his

glass, is frequently called upon by the toast master to take off [drink] his heel tap." See *A Classical Dictionary of the Vulgar Tongue*, 2nd ed. (London: S. Hooper, 1788), 124. In this case, Agee may also reaching for a partial pun, since the metal gaff for a fighting bird, which replaces the natural spurs, is fastened to the cock's heel. But, as he makes clear in the text, the "Heel Tap Club" is a "small, secretive society of cockers" of "eight members" and their friends, with its "roving headquarters about Boston and New York" ("Cockfighting" 95).

23. Agee, "Cockfighting," 90. For a reprinting of "Cockfighting," see Paul Ashdown's volume 2 in The Works of James Agee, *Complete Journalism: Articles, Book Reviews, and Manuscripts* (Knoxville: U of Tennessee P, 2013), 114–22. For a very early work on cockfighting whose title argues favorably for the sport, see R. H. [Robert Howlett], *The Royal Pastime of Cock-fighting, or The Art of Breeding, Feeding, Fighting, and Curing Cocks of the Game. Published purely for the good, and benefit of all such as take Delight in that Royal, and Warlike Sport. To which is Prefixed, A short treatise, wherein Cocking is proved not only Ancient and Honourable, but also Useful, and Profitable* (London: D. Brown, 1709).

24. Agee, "Cockfighting," 146.

25. White, *By-Line*, 96–97. The October 27, 1923, article is also reprinted in the Hemingway Library Edition of *The Sun Also Rises* (New York: Scribner, 2014), 199–207 as Appendix I. Other material bearing on bullfighting in the novel appears in Appendix II, which conveys Hemingway's early drafts of the novel.

26. Although "espada" literally means sword, it is also means matador.

27. White, *By-Line*, 96.

28. The Riau-Riau dance began in 1914 and was a sanctioned part of "The Running of the Bulls," the summer San Fermin Festival.

29. White, *By-Line*, 99–100. See Hemingway's letter to his friend William D. Horne on July 17–18, 1923, for another version of his excitement over the bullfighting festival. In part, he says: "It's a great tragedy—and the most beautiful thing I've ever seen and takes more guts and skill and guts again than anything possibly could. It's just like having a ringside seat at the war with nothing going to happen to you." (Spanier, et al., eds., *The Letters of Ernest Hemingway* 2, 36, and Baker, *Ernest Hemingway* 88). In a subsequent letter to Sylvia Beach, on November 6, 1923, he notes that he and wife Hadley named their first son John Hadley Nicanor and explained its inspiration as "Nicanor Villalta the bull fighter" (Spanier, et al., eds., *The Letters of Ernest Hemingway* 2, 68, and Baker, *Ernest Hemingway* 97). Hemingway's first trip to Spain was in May of 1923. A later article for *Esquire* (January 1934) revealed a change in Hemingway's opinion of and disappointment with bullfighting in Spain (White, *By-Line* 147–51).

30. Hemingway, "Bullfighting," 142.

31. Spanier, et al., eds., *The Letters of Ernest Hemingway*, 4, 203–4. See also Baker, *Ernest Hemingway*, 317. Also reprinted in Matthew J. Bruccoli, ed., *The Only Thing that Counts: The Ernest Hemingway / Maxwell Perkins Correspondence, 1925–1947* (New York: Scribner, 1996), 136. In an earlier letter to MacLeish, Hemingway said he "would write the article for $2000.00" (December 1, 1929; Spanier et al., eds., *The Letters of Ernest Hemingway* 4, 176). In a letter of August 28, 1929, from Santiago de Compostela, Spain, Hemingway told Perkins that "We leave here day after

tomorrow—for Madrid—want to see Sidney Franklin of Brooklyn—They say he's good—[.] Spanier et al, eds., *The Letters of Ernest Hemingway*, 4, 76. Also in Baker, *Ernest Hemingway*, 116.

32. Sidney Franklin, *Bullfighter from Brooklyn: An Autobiography of Sidney Franklin* (Upper Saddle River, NJ: Prentice-Hall, 1952), 172–73.

33. Ibid., 176–81. See also Kinnamon, "Hemingway, the Corrida, and Spain," 132–33. It was not Franklin's last encounter with Hemingway. In his autobiography, Franklin notes that they went together to Cuba to try to introduce bullfighting (213–15) and that the matador later went to Spain with him as an "assistant" war correspondent (215–35), but the latter material focuses very little on Hemingway. For some of Hemingway's thoughts on the matador, see the appendix to the autobiography entitled "Sidney Franklin as a Matador" that was taken from his *Death in the Afternoon*, 241–45. Hemingway's "A Short Estimate of the American, Sidney Franklin, as a Matador" is perhaps more readily available in that work on his unnumbered pages (503–6).

34. *Letters of James Agee to Father Flye*, 66. In the same letter, Agee also describes his "misgivings" about his job as detrimental to his writing, that "its prison walls [were] distinctly thickening" (67). On other "misgivings" and on combining his job and artistry, see *Letters of James Agee to Father Flye*, 77, 81–82, and his letter to Goofy of August 21, 1933 (James Agee Papers, University of Tennessee Special Collections, MSS 3824, box 1, folder 7). For his evaluation of the same conflict, likely at the end of his tenure at *Fortune*, see Agee's undated typed letter "Dear Tom." In it he describes his taking up journalism "because I, or others depending on me, had to eat. But I've had the humbling pleasure of learning a great deal to respect and to honor about journalism and journalists, quite as seriously as the best kind of work I might ever hope to do" (James Agee Papers, University of Tennessee Special Collections, MSS 3824, box 1, folder 12). For Agee's delight in getting the *Fortune* assignment that would ultimately become *Let Us Now Praise Famous Men*, see *Letters of James Agee to Father Flye*, 92, and his letter of June 17, 1936 (James Agee Papers, University of Tennessee Special Collections, MSS 3824, box 1, folder 8). For a brief, enlightening commentary on Agee's work at *Fortune*, see the introduction ("A Matter of Beauty") of Paul Ashdown's *Complete Journalism*, xvii–xxii. An untitled, unpublished eight-page typescript by Agee that he intended to expand gives a very interesting, lightly satiric view of the magazine, its audience, and its staff. From internal evidence, it likely dates from 1937 or a bit later. See University of Tennessee, Knoxville, Special Collections, MSS 3824, box 7, folder 3.

35. Hemingway, "Bullfighting," 85, 84, and 86–87.

36. Agee, "Cockfighting," 92–93, 91, 94, 90, 95, and 94.

37. Ibid., 94.

38. Ibid., 95.

39. For "Cotton Tenants," see Davis, *Let Us Now Praise Famous Men*, 565–646. For an analysis of the change of focus, especially on race, between the two works, see Michael A. Lofaro, "Famous Men By the Numbers: An Analysis of Agee's Changes from "Cotton Tenants" to *Let Us Now Praise Famous Men*," in Michael A. Lofaro, ed., Let Us Now Praise Famous Men *at 75: Anniversary Essays*, 245–56. "'America, Look at your Shame!': A Previously Unpublished Essay by James Agee," is edited and introduced by Michael A. Lofaro and Hugh Davis, in the *Oxford American: The Southern Magazine of Good Writing* (January/February 2003), 35–39. Also published

as "James Agee, 'After the Riots,'" *Harper's* 306 (June 2003): 27–31, and in Louis Menand, ed. *The Best American Essays 2004* (Boston: Houghton Mifflin, 2004). For more on the Detroit riots, see: Harvard Sitkoff, *Toward Freedom Land: The Long Struggle for Racial Equality in America* (Lexington: UP of Kentucky, 2010), 43–64; Alfred M. Lee and Norman D. Humphrey, *Race Riot (Detroit, 1943)* (New York: Octagon Books, 1968); and Dominic J Capeci, Jr. and Martha Wilkerson, *Layered Violence: The Detroit Rioters of 1943* (Jackson: U of Mississippi P, 1991).

40. Hemingway, "Bullfighting," 88.

41. For perhaps Hemingway's best primer on bullfighting for non-Spanish and non-specialist readers, see his *Death in the Afternoon.* The December 6, 1926, letter to Maxwell Perkins, cited in note 16, likewise reveals more excitement on Hemingway's part, even in regard to business. In it, for example, Hemingway states that bullfighting "really is terribly interesting—being a matter of life and death—and anything that a young peasant or bootblack can make 80,000 dollars a year in before he is twenty three does something to people" (Sanderson, et al., eds., *The Letters of Ernest Hemingway* 3, 176, and Bruccoli, *The Only Thing that Counts*, 52–53.)

42. Agee, "Cockfighting," 146.

43. Ibid., 91.

44. In his article "Bull Fighting a Tragedy," Hemingway never proposes that bullfighting has the "High Moral Purpose" that Agee notes for cockfighting. Instead he says "I am not going to apologize for bull fighting. . . . Bull fighting is not a sport. It never was supposed to be. . . . It is a tragedy, and it symbolizes the struggle between man and beasts" (White, *By-Line* 95–96).

45. Genevieve Moreau, *The Restless Journey of James Agee* (New York: William Morrow and Co., 1977), 118.

NINE

You Cruise, You Lose

A Panoramic View of Agee's "Havana Cruise"

PAUL ASHDOWN

James Agee boarded the turbo-electric ocean liner *Oriente* on Saturday afternoon, June 5, 1937, but the ship's departure on its 1,168-mile voyage to Havana was delayed due to a strike that had begun at 9:30 a.m. Labor trouble was common on the Ward Line, and the *Oriente* was held up for the second time in eight days. Stevedores, in sympathy with striking steamfitters, refused to work. The crews stopped unloading seventeen thousand boxes filled with Cuban pineapples shipped to New York on the last return voyage, while machinery, "sporting goods," possibly weapons, automobiles, and mail bound for Cuba remained on the dock. The *Oriente* did not leave its rustic berth on the East River at the end of Wall Street until 2:00 a.m. Sunday.[1]

With engines thrumming, the workhorse harbor tugs *Walter L. Meseck* and *William F. Meseck* withdrew the *Oriente* "from all intimacy with the intricate and tenderly lighted stone of the city and let her loose on the river," Agee wrote in his journal. "She squared the stern upon that lifted harp which forms Brooklyn with Manhattan, and, with an almost noiseless sheathing of water, sank with the gap of the river through a complication of islands and out upon the dark coastal sea, and, training her energies upon Havana, bored along with the solid steadiness of a truck on a highway." As the *Oriente* churned past Sandy Hook under clear skies and headed into the moderate southerly winds blowing up along the Atlantic coast, most of the 132 passengers were in their cabins. Agee and photographer Walker Evans, acquaintances since 1935 and friends from a *Fortune* magazine assignment in Alabama the previous summer, talked before retiring. Also aboard, and ostensibly traveling separately, was Agee's wife, Olivia "Via" Saunders Agee. *Fortune* wanted Agee to write about passengers on a low-budget excursion to

FIGURE 9.1 From a 1939 publicity brochure. Courtesy of the Björn Larsson Collection.

Cuba to conclude an entire issue of *Fortune* devoted to shipping. Evans was to take photographs to accompany the article.[2]

On the evening of June 4, Agee had attended the Second Congress of American Writers at Carnegie Hall on 7th Avenue with Robert Fitzgerald. The League of American Writers was supporting the Loyalist side in the Spanish Civil War. Among those attending were Archibald MacLeish, Thornton Wilder, Martha Gellhorn, Earl Browder, secretary of the Communist Party USA, and a special guest who had flown in from Bimini to give the keynote address. Ernest Hemingway was late, however, and a delegation had been sent out to look for the often crapulous author in hotels, bars, and airports.[3]

About 10:00 p.m. Hemingway, perspiring in a heavy dark blue suit, arrived and was heard to bellow "Why the hell am I making a speech?" Hemingway was there to promote Joris Ivens's propaganda film in support of the Republic, *The Spanish Earth*, written by Hemingway and John Dos Passos. MacLeish introduced Hemingway, who leaned awkwardly on the lectern with an elbow. Given a boisterous welcome by the 3,500 writers in attendance, Hemingway, recently returned from Spain, spoke of the difficulty of writing truly in wartime. "There is only one form of government that cannot produce good writers," he warned, "and that system is fascism. For fascism is a lie told by bullies. A writer who will not lie cannot live or work under fascism." In a time of war, "the rewards for writers are all suspended. Certainly it is more comfortable . . . to discuss and to maintain positions—skillfully chosen positions with no risk involved in holding them, positions to be held by the typewriter and consolidated with the fountain pen."[4]

Earlier in the year, Agee had praised another pro-Loyalist propaganda documentary, *Spain in Flames*, also with commentary by Hemingway. Agee's notebooks expressed his increasing concern with fascist demagogues in the United States. Fitzgerald recalled that while Agee supported the Republic, "I don't think he ever saluted anyone with a raised fist or took up Spanish . . . . He had joined battle on another ground." That ground was Alabama, not Spain, and Agee was struggling with early drafts of what, with Evans's photographs, would become *Let Us Now Praise Famous Men*. Six years later, he would write critically in the *Nation* of the film version of Hemingway's novel of the Spanish Civil War, *For Whom the Bell Tolls*, noting that Hollywood extracted offending references to fascism. On the day after seeing Hemingway and *The Spanish Earth*, however, Agee was going on a cruise. If Hemingway's call to arms resonated with Agee, he first was going to have to fight fascism on an ocean liner or in Havana. But Hemingway also had warned writers not to let politics get in the way of truth. In an *Esquire* article published in December 1934, he had attacked critics who urged writers to focus only on social issues. He advised writers not to "let them suck you in to start writing about the proletariat if you don't come from the proletariat just to please the recently politically enlightened critics. . . ." Agee would measure such words carefully.[5]

II

Evans had first seen Hemingway in Paris in 1926. He had not met Hemingway until he arrived in Cuba on May 19, 1933, at the behest of publisher J.B. Lippincott to take photographs for journalist Carleton Beals's book *The Crime of Cuba*, an unsparing investigation of the bloody eight-year reign of President Gerardo Machado, an admirer of Mussolini's fascist Italy. Hemingway had come to Havana in April and was staying at the Hotel Ambos Mundos. He was introduced to Evans and invited him to supper. Hemingway was angry about Max Eastman's nasty review of *Death in the Afternoon* in *The New Republic*, and Evans commiserated over libations. Hemingway remembered Evans as a "nice kid" and said they were "both working against Machado at the time." Evans had written in his diary that the political situation was then critical. The 442 photographs Evans took during his month-long stay in Cuba, including the thirty-one published in the book, did nothing to cast Machado in a favorable light, nor did the stories that became the first chapters of the novel *To Have and Have Not* that Hemingway would publish in 1937. But neither was trying to topple the regime in 1933. Evans had "a wonderful time with Hemingway. Drinking every night." Evans sensed "a very instinctive bond between him and me, and he knew it. But I was very wary of him. He was . . . a very hard man to come close to. But in one way I did. I really thought he was a great artist at that time and he loved that recognition. He could see that I knew what he was about." Evans later told Agee he had been mugged on his way to a house of ill repute during this first visit to Cuba and had been relieved of most of his money. When he arrived, "he could not meet the price. The girls were terribly concerned and didn't want to take any money at all. This is a very crooked city, though." Short of funds, Evans accepted Hemingway's loan of $25 so he could stay another week, and then neglected to pay him back. [6]

Worried that his photographs might be confiscated by Machado's police, Evans asked Hemingway to hold on to some of them for safekeeping. When he didn't hear from Evans, Hemingway placed the prints and negatives in a storeroom in the back of Sloppy Joe's bar in Key West, where they remained until after the writer's death. The photographs were displayed in Key West's Custom House in 2004 and put up for auction in 2017. Hemingway's son, Patrick, and others have speculated that Hemingway drew upon Evans's Cuban photographs in writing *To Have and Have Not*. Some of the street images Evans photographed do seem to correspond to passages in the novel and Hemingway's Harry Morgan stories. Evans and Hemingway each may have recognized in the other's work a spare style and there may have been a reciprocal influence. Evans was attracted to the documentary style of French photographer Eugène Atget and the American photographers Ralph Steiner and Berenice Abbott, and profoundly influenced Agee's work, especially in *Let Us Now Praise Famous Men*. "Hemingway went to Spain to learn to write; for Evans it was on the streets of Havana that his style and subject meshed and he found his own way as a photographer," said Judith Keller, an art historian and photographic curator at the J. Paul Getty Museum. "Havana was Spain for Evans."[7]

Agee's first biographer, Geneviève Moreau, asked Via Agee and Evans what they remembered about the cruise twenty-five years later.

> [Agee's] immediate task was to investigate the opportunities open to the tourist and to find out which social classes tended to select the cruise in preference to other forms of travel, and for what reasons. Therefore, in addition to looking up the statistics, he needed to speak to as many cruise passengers as possible. In order to avoid arousing suspicion, the three decided to separate and to conceal their relationship from the other passengers, but they tried often to meet secretly in order to share impressions. When they met in public they occasionally spoke to each other with an intimacy that would have betrayed them had they not been able to quickly and cleverly restore the illusion. By the end of the voyage, however, their connivance had become apparent to many of the tourists.[8]

Agee biographer Laurence Bergreen has the three deciding to "hide their true identities from the other passengers for the duration of the voyage. They would not reveal even that they knew one another and would meet only in secret to compare notes and impressions. While Agee walked the decks and ate the over-generous meals, Via and Evans broke the pledge long enough to establish a rapport." Bergreen offered no source, but drew on Moreau.[9]

Evans biographer Belinda Rathbone, who interviewed Via Saunders Agee Wood in 1991, added additional detail and speculation.

> Agee had begun to think of himself and Evans as spies. Their experience in Alabama had made them feel most acutely the subversive nature of their craft; from now on they would operate as undercover agents in the field of journalism. . . . The idea of the spy helped to make the Havana cruise more bearable. On board the *Oriente*, in a mood of playful but pointed irony, Jim, Walker, and Via agreed to conceal their personal relationships to one another from the other passengers. By posing as strangers rather than as the friends, partners, and allies that they were, they hoped to convey an air of critical indifference. As an ultimate act of disguise, Via removed her wedding ring.[10]

The spy theme is an important element of *Let Us Now Praise Famous Men* due to Agee's *King Lear*–inspired verse in the volume with its "Spies, moving delicately among the enemy . . . ," but the trope owed more to Evans than it did to Agee. Evans had been obsessed with spies during his 1933 Havana assignment. Riding a bus, for example, he noted in his diary that the vehicle was "full of spys [*sic*], counter spys, plain clothes men, secret agents and ordinary thieves." He took photographs from sites of concealment and was so concerned about security that he left some photographs with Hemingway rather than risk having them confiscated by Machado's police. In 1938, Evans shot his famous New York subway photographs with a camera concealed beneath his topcoat and a shutter release running down his sleeve and into his palm. His unobtrusive style made him famous.[11]

The mood of "playful but pointed irony," as Rathbone put it, must have resembled a Molière drawing room comedy at sea with spies at play. There was, curiously, no Olivia Saunders Agee on the passenger list. There was a Saunders, but the passenger was Mr. Irving Saunders. There was no "O." or "V." listed as a first initial for any of the female cruise passengers. The passenger list identified fourteen women who appeared to be traveling alone, but none named Saunders or Agee. She would have needed identification to board the ship. In his journals, Agee does mention "V.," so she was aboard. He noted that when a Miss Russell took "V." to tea, the men flirted, making Miss Goss jealous.

At the time, the Agee marriage was in deep trouble. Bergreen characterized the couple's relationship in the early months of 1937 as "cold, abrasive, lifeless" and "doomed." Agee was romancing Alma Mailman, who would become his second wife. The "rapport" between Walker and Via blossomed into an affair. In November, Evans made twenty-one nude studies of Via with a 35-mm camera. The negatives are in the Walker Evans Archives at the Metropolitan Museum of Art in New York. The Agees' marital dissolution, according to Moreau and then Bergreen, was all explained in an unpublished film script, *Bigger Than We Are: A Love Story*, written by Agee not long before his death. Bergreen assumed the cruise article was an attack on Via and her family. Agee's "running feud with Via informed every satirical jibe. In castigating the passengers, he flaunted his contempt for her haut bourgeois upbringing and tastes. . . . By the time he finished the article he had become so angry with the Saunders' world that he considered himself a Communist 'by sympathy and conviction.'" Bergreen got ahead of himself by quoting Agee because his specific words did not appear, along with other comments about communism, until the publication of *Let Us Now Praise Famous Men* in 1941. In a February 17, 1936, letter he wrote to Father James Flye from Anna Maria Island in Florida, however, Agee did say of communism that "an awful lot of things do seem somewhere near and right from that, or essentially that, point of view."[12]

The entire scenario, especially Bergreen's conflation of marital discord with Agee's general attack on the passengers, is far-fetched. The ménage à trois spy conspiracy with its eavesdropping, trysts, secret rendezvous, feigned indifference, voyeuristic notetaking, and hidden wedding ring, strains credulity. Agee did not need his quarrel with Via to ridicule the passengers, whom he described as "representatives of the lower to middle brackets of the American urban middle class," hardly the high society she supposedly represented. That class favored voyages to Europe. "It wasn't a very expensive outing they were taking . . . $70 was enough to cover every expense except tips for six days, including two conducted tours of Havana," Agee wrote. In his notes, he observed that "none of them were at all wealthy; none were desperately poor; none would be described as 'smart'; none even particularly cultivated." They seemed little different from the families who lived on Highland Avenue, the street where he grew up in Knoxville, Tennessee, which he remembered as a "little bit mixed sort of block, fairly solidly lower middle class, with one or two juts apiece on either side of that." Fitzgerald confirmed that in 1937 Agee "had become grimmer about American middle-class ways and destinies," but it is not clear what he made of the passengers on the *Oriente* when he had the tenant farmers in Alabama on his mind as well.[13]

III

The *Oriente,* named for Cuba's unruly eastern province, hotbed of revolutions, was launched May 15, 1930, at Newport News, Virginia, one of the first ships financed by protectionist construction subsidies from the United States Shipping Board to private companies to rebuild the U.S. Merchant Marine. Like its sister ship, the *Morro Castle*, the *Oriente* was 508 feet long, 70.9 feet at the beam, and weighed 11,520 gross register tons. Each ship met specifications for troopship conversion in the event of war. Each had 335,000 cubic feet of cargo space, making them the largest ships built for traffic along the East Coast. Each featured five passenger decks and could accommodate almost five-hundred passengers. All decks were made of steel, laid with teak. Dining, writing and smoking rooms, saloons and formal salons featured styles inspired by the Italian Renaissance, the French Empire, and the Palace of the Doges. Above the smoking room was an arched, semi-circular skylight in two-toned amber glass. Below this carapace, shop girls and Agee's band of spies could mingle for drinks and conversation with commercial travelers, Cuban nationals, retirees and perhaps a few communists as the ships approached Cuba.[14]

FIGURE 9.2
Passengers gather in the *Oriente*'s lounge for drinks and conversation. Courtesy of the Björn Larsson Collection

The Ward Line's troubles with the sisters started when the *Morro Castle* was caught in a hurricane while en route to New York during its September 13, 1933, run up the coast from Havana. By September 16, the liner was fighting 100-mile-per-hour winds off Cape Hatteras, and had lost its radio antenna and all communication. It safely reached New York two days late on September 18, thanks to the seamanship of its master, Captain Robert Renison Willmott, an English-born sailor who had been aboard a Ward Line vessel in New York Harbor when the *Carpathia* arrived in 1912 with survivors from the *Titanic*. On November 11, the *Morro Castle* had to leave Havana two hours early when the ship was raked by machine-gun fire during fighting between communists and government forces. Such confrontations were always possible in Havana, nor were the *Morro Castle* and the *Oriente* disinterested parties, as they routinely trafficked in arms shipments. Stories about agitators, saboteurs, smuggling rings, out-of-favor Cuban generals, and stowaways fleeing the dictatorships had burdened the Ward Line

FIGURE 9.3
Food service on the *Oriente.* Courtesy of the Björn Larsson Collection.

from the beginning. There also had been reports that Chinese emigrants, unwelcome in the United States since the passage of the Chinese Exclusion Act of 1882, had made their way in large numbers to Cuba, and then were smuggled aboard Ward Line ships and other carriers to American shores.[15]

The singular event that was to haunt the Ward Line and the *Oriente* occurred in the early morning hours of September 8, 1934, when the *Morro Castle* caught fire six miles off Sea Girt, New Jersey, in a squall and drifted ashore at Asbury Park, New Jersey, taking the lives of 134 people. The sibling ship had left Havana on its return trip to New York on September 5. Hemingway passed the ill-fated liner in the harbor as he left the city that afternoon on the Key West ferry. Later investigations showed that Captain Willmott had appeared worried throughout the voyage. In Havana, Willmott had been warned by the port's chief of police that a communist agent might be aboard the ship, intending to set a fire and murder the captain. Willmott's concern seemed well founded when he was found dead in his cabin on the evening of September 7. Neither the cause of Willmott's death nor the reason for the fire was ever officially determined, and the ship's destruction was put down to negligence. Suspicion later fell upon the *Morro Castle's* radioman, George White Rogers, an arsonist who died in prison after being convicted of murders unrelated to the *Morro Castle.*[16]

The *Oriente* continued the Havana run after the sinking of the *Morro Castle*, and the Ward Line did what it could to affirm the safety of the passengers. The *Oriente* arrived in New York on September 11 with 311 passengers, and the company allowed journalists to inspect the ship and conduct interviews. The *New York Times* reporter called attention to the *Oriente's* sister ship. "It required little imagination to reconstruct the scene that took place on the blazing ship early Saturday morning. The contrast between the orderly appearance of the *Oriente* and the skeleton-like hulk of her sister ship, aground off Asbury Park, made the picture all the clearer." The *Oriente* left for Havana on September 15 with 149 passengers, which the company pointed out was an increase of fifty passengers over the sailing a year before.[17]

The *Oriente* had its own moment of notoriety when the ship arrived in Havana on July 2, 1935, with a delegation of fifteen American liberals intending to investigate Cuban labor and social conditions. Headed by the playwright Clifford Odets, the delegation, plus two hapless schoolteachers not part of the group, was detained by submachine gun–wielding Cuban police, "seized, menaced, insulted," and taken to a naval prison for interrogation. Some two hundred police and soldiers swarmed the docks to prevent agitation by communists. The Americans were returned to the ship and told to leave Cuba. Odets later wrote that neither U.S. Ambassador Jefferson Caffery nor the ship's officers offered any aid. He mocked the *Oriente's* Swedish-American captain, Oscar L. Seastrom, as exclaiming: "By golly, I never seen nothing much like this before." Odets insisted that investigating "a military dictatorship of high finance was no joke. Night was coming on when we sighted the low warm hills of the island. If one might only be able to relax to enjoy this fertile, scene, as, for example, the ordinary cruise passengers were doing, most of them loaded with rum and rich food." Among the books seized in the luggage of committee members was *The Crime of Cuba*, with photographs by Evans. Despite the Odets incident, and the earlier sinking of another Ward Line ship, the *Mohawk*, on January 25, 1935, off the New Jersey coast, the line claimed on July 21, 1935, that it had escaped the jinx of the *Morro Castle* disaster. It noted the success of the *Oriente*, which had sailed with more than three hundred passengers. But labor unrest, much of it prompted by conditions revealed during the *Morro Castle* investigation, caused delays for the *Oriente* through 1937. On June 14, 1941, four years after the publication of Agee's "Havana Cruise," the *Oriente* was purchased by the army as a troopship and rechristened the *Thomas H. Barry*. The ship saw service in both the Pacific and the

Atlantic. On October 12, 1945, the *Barry* rammed and sunk a trawler east of New Bedford, Massachusetts.[18]

The *Morro Castle* and the *Oriente* had entered service in the midst of the great age of travel writing. British and American writers found travel between the wars a release from the encumbrances of the Great War, a time of reflection and self-discovery, an opportunity to write elegies for dying civilizations and a mandate to seek out undiscovered outposts with a new urgency. Paul Fussell cited as examples Hemingway's *Death in the Afternoon* (1932) and *Green Hills of Africa* (1935), and D. H. Lawrence's American journeys. The great ocean liners attracted literary vagabonds such as Alec Waugh, who found sea travel "one of the cheapest ways of living, certainly for a freelance writer who carried his office with him and could work in his cabin or in a saloon." In New York, Waugh recalled, "you were always conscious of the liners that you saw from your office and apartment windows. There was a feeling, in consequence, that you had very little time, that you had to make the most of every contact quickly." The liners gave writers the freedom and opportunity to mingle with the rich at a bargain price and revel in their own eccentricities. Fussell distinguished between travel and what came before—exploration—and what came later—tourism—which Fussell deplored. Mass tourism "attracted the class-contempt of killjoys who conceived themselves independent travelers and thus superior by reason of intellect, education, curiosity, and spirit." Tourism, being egalitarian, made it "difficult to be a snob and a tourist at the same time." With war looming, many of the literary travelers became spies and sleuths and then correspondents reporting from war zones, ending travel as excursion and escape. The East Coast and Gulf Stream waters through which the *Oriente* sailed would soon be home to German U-Boat wolfpacks as the cruise industry drifted toward irrelevance.[19]

Agee's travel had been limited to ocean voyages in the summer of 1925 that took him to Boulogne in France and back with Father Flye when he was fifteen, just before he began his studies at Phillips Exeter Academy. The two took a bicycle tour through Picardy, where they saw the landscape ravaged by the Great War, and also visited England. In the summer of 1929, following his freshman year at Harvard, Agee worked as a migrant laborer in Oklahoma, Kansas, and Nebraska, hitchhiked to California and Mexico, then bummed his way back to his mother's home in Maine via Arizona, New Mexico, and the Midwest with a stopover in Pennsylvania to visit a roommate. This journey was the likely source for Agee's story "Death in the Desert," published in the *Harvard Advocate* in 1930. In 1934, he wrote "The Great American Roadside," a *Fortune* article about automobile travel, and another about the dark side of the horse racing industry in Saratoga Springs, New York, in 1935. He spent the winter on Anna Maria Island in Florida where he began writing "Knoxville: Summer 1915." Besides the Alabama project in 1936, Agee had not done much literary travel writing before "Havana Cruise." Although more castaway than mariner, Agee kept a catboat at City Island, New York, for Sunday sailing during the summer. He was a good swimmer, eager to plunge into the waters of the Sand Cut behind St. Andrew's School in Tennessee or compete on the swim team at Exeter, but was more at home on land than on the water. His voyage on the *Oriente* was a deadline assignment to study the tourist, not the traveler. "Havana Cruise" was neither leisurely literary travel nor documentary immersion. Agee was not Hemingway at war or chasing tarpon in the Gulf Stream or hunting big game in Africa, and only briefly did he resemble D. H. Lawrence in the New Mexico desert.[20]

IV

Agee wrote through most of the first night at sea, but at some point he found his bunk and slept until first light. "Just now they lay beneath light sheets in the curious postures of sleep," he scribbled in his journal, while "slowly, darkness drained westward on their nation; the clear Atlantic daylight intensified. It lifted them into the levels just beneath consciousness: they stirred, eyes tightening; they burrowed in their bunks; one woke, and awoke his wife; their cruise had begun." He wasted no time before observing the passengers. A woman he saw "leaned against the rail hand-in-hand with an amateur photographer and said how much she was fascinated by people who really lived, and that Ernest Hemingway must have lived very intensively if he knew what she meant, and didn't he feel the same about people who really lived?" Agee described her in his notes: "Dumb; a mine of clichés. Does some writing; loves reading, is chiefly fascinated by people who live . . . . Somewhat class conscious. A friend bought her a copy of the *Daily Worker* and told her to give it to a sailor." The juxtaposition of a photographer and Hemingway in the same sentence suggests the "amateur" might have been Evans.[21]

Next he saw an elderly couple, identified in the article as Mr. and Mrs. B., strolling the decks at 7:30 a.m., having awakened early by "force of habit." The couple might have been, according to corresponding names beginning with the letter "B" on the passenger list, the Basches, the Boyds, or the Brandenburgers. Other passengers were introduced as character types. Mrs. C. (Campbell?) and her "feeble" sister "helped each other up the stairs, their lungs laboring." A Miss Cox, "in severely informal new sports attire," and her "frugal and sweet-smiling spinster aunt," Miss Russell, made their appearance. Miss Cox was, like other young women aboard, among those "low-salaried office workers upon whom the self-sufficiency, the independence of city work and city living had narrowed their inestimable pressures of loneliness and of spiritual fear," and thus "desperate" predators "who searched among the men as for steamer smoke from an uncharted atoll." In fact, many of the single female passengers were probably teachers. Next, "an aging Jew in a light flannel suit gazed sorrowfully at the Atlantic Ocean." A handsome young man "who resembled an airedale sufficiently intelligent to count to ten . . . and graduate from a gentleman's university came briskly to the dining room in sharply pressed slacks and a navy blue sports shirt, read the sign, dashed away, and soon reappeared plus a checkered coat and a plaid tie." The headwaiter, "a prim Arthur Treacher type," convoyed his guests to their tables with the gestures of an Eton-trained sand-hill crane in flight."[22]

Agee assumed this derision and misogyny reflected the same criteria used by the passengers to size one another up at breakfast. "The appraisals of clothes, of class, of race, of temperament, and of the opposed sexes met and crossed and flickered in a texture of glances as swift and keen as the leaping closures of electric arcs, and essentially as irrelevant to mercy." As fiction, this might have unspooled a lively shipboard satire. As personal journalism, ostensibly based on fact, Agee's literary license drifted into the sea of speculation. Why surmise that Mr. and Mrs. B. were habitually early risers? Could he be sure Miss Russell was frugal or Miss Cox earned a poor wage, was lonely and looking for male companionship because she had turned out in new clothes? Were women of similar age also looking for romance, perhaps with the not-too-bright "airedale?" Was the "aging Jew" Jewish? Agee estimated thirty-seven Jews were aboard the ship, about one-third of the non-Cuban passengers, so the odds were reasonable, if irrelevant. Perhaps the man's countenance was not sorrowful at all as he inhaled the morning sea vapors. [23]

Agee interviewed some passengers and learned their names, occupations, ages, places of residence, and other details. He added physical descriptions and sometimes gave passengers and crew descriptive names such as Thin Man, Wallflower, Narrow Face, Vanity Fair, and Red. He and Via leaned in on conversations.

FIGURE 9.4
Passengers enjoy the smoking room on a Havana Cruise. Courtesy of the Björn Larsson Collection.

Evans's observations are not much in evidence in Agee's notes. Agee deduced that his subjects were mostly from New York and Eastern Seaboard cities. About one-third were middle-aged, one-third married (the actual percentage, according to the manifest, was closer to 44 percent), and most of the rest were aboard "for a hell of a big time." He guessed that unattached women exceeded unattached men by a ratio of four-to-one going to Havana, and six-to-one returning to New York. Moreover, the passengers were unaccustomed to leisure, and were "of that vast race whose freedom falls in summer and is short." Sadly delusional owing to lack of experience and opportunity, and hungry for heroic adventure and romance, they were limited by "their strongest and most sorrowful trait: their talent for self-deceit." Of the *Oriente* herself, Agee thought the ship "fashioned in the image of her clientele: a sound, young, pleasant, and somehow invincibly comic vessel, the seafaring analogy to a second-string summer resort, a low-priced sedan, or the newest and best hotel in a provincial city." Agee quoted an officer on the *Oriente* as anticipating "a better class of people" during the winter months, when the "good average crowd" of philistines presumably was back at their low-salaried office jobs, replaced by well-heeled dandies on their way to southern climes.[24]

But the conspicuously prosperous were not aboard the *Oriente* on this cruise, as Agee continued drubbing the passengers and crew with sarcasm. Crew members awoke "like rain-chilled insects that fair weather warms." Seastrom, the captain ridiculed by Odets, was to Agee a bloviating "dickensian-built Swede." Earle M. Wilkens, the cruise director, failed to prod reticent passengers to mingle, seemed to be at odds with the assistant purser, and organized a minstrel show. The chief steward, Charles Hart, "a professionally Cute Character whose popularity [was] significant of the whole nature of the cruise," entertained passengers with his "modest account" of the *Morro Castle* disaster. At least one crewman claimed to have been aboard the doomed ship. It would have been instructive to learn what he said. A fire drill later elicited "a few cracks about the *Morro Castle* and for that sinking feeling travel on the Ward Line . . . ." Jokes about fires would have been in poor taste after the *Oriente* passed the Lakehurst Naval Air Station in New Jersey, where the *Hindenburg* had burst into flames just a month earlier.[25]

The passengers' choice of reading matter, such as *I Can Get It For You Wholesale*, a 1937 novel by Jerome Weidman, was decidedly lowbrow. Agee described *Lost Ecstasy*, a 1937 novel by Mary Roberts Rinehart, as "a piece of housewives' problem fiction about the troubles of a sophisticated deb who marries a big clean cowboy." Miss Russell found it "too serious." Mrs. C. read *News-Week* and thought it was "awful cute." A "torpid husband sat under five fathom of the Sunday *Times* and stuffed in the state of the world without appetite while wife caught a beauty sleep with her nostrils inverted, her goggles cockeyed, and her mouth open." The 1937 Paramount feature film *John Meade's Woman* was shown after dinner to a "packed house that received it with polite apathy." The foppish airedale "and a duplicate appeared in naughty trunks, laid towels aside from their pretty shoulders, oiled themselves, and, after a brief warm-up, began to play deck tennis furiously before the gradually assembling girls." Agee tossed in bits of conversational eavesdropping to ridicule shipboard courtship rituals that seemed to go embarrassingly awry, and singled out passengers for gratuitous scorn. "The wow of the evening was a blonde who was born out of her time: her glad and perpetually surprised face was that which appears in eighteenth-century pornographic engravings wherein the chore boy tumbles the milkmaid in an explosion of hens and alfalfa."[26]

As the *Oriente* rounded the Florida coast and turned toward Cuba, however, Agee looked ahead with an airy wistfulness as the pleasure cruise became a more mythic voyage into the Gulf Stream:

> Far out to starboard, small, frail, and infrequent, lights walked past. They denominated the low and bone-white coast of pre-Columbian unimagined Florida . . . ; the remote lights thickened and were Miami; and Miami spread, and sank into the north; and the lights thinned, and just at this time there was a new feeling through the body of the ship. . . . The ship had left the shelf of the continent behind and had directed herself upon the world's deep water. Not very far ahead now, beyond a bulge and world shape of this water, tumescent beneath the shade of the summer planet, her whole sleep stirred and streamed in music such as this, Havana lay.

Detached momentarily from his preoccupation with the passengers, Agee seemed under the spell of Hemingway, his fellow magazine journalist whose more lapidary homage to the Gulf Stream, "the last wild country there is left," had appeared in *Esquire* magazine little more than a year earlier. Once out of sight of Havana, Hemingway had written, the mariner was alone and the sea eternal.[27]

V

Commencing well before Agee's article, the long-standing American romance with Cuba flourished in the decades after the Spanish-American War in 1898 and Cuban independence in 1902. The Platt Amendment, passed in 1901, stated the terms for U.S. intervention and occupation. American settlements spread across the island. Cuba's appeal as a resort and tourist destination was based on its proximity, its familiarity, and its salubrious climate, especially after the passage of the 18th Amendment establishing Prohibition in the United States in 1920. The expansion of steamship service and air travel gave Cuba the same sort of resort status as Florida with the added appeal of being foreign and exotic. Aeromarine Airways launched the first scheduled U.S. international passenger service, from Key West to Havana, on November 1, 1920.[28]

More than two million U.S. tourists visited Cuba between 1920 and 1940. Some ninety thousand tourists arrived in 1928, the number almost doubling by 1937, the year Agee arrived, despite the Depression. Cuban tourism had always appealed to rich and famous Americans, such as Hemingway, yet the island was notable for its broad appeal to working-class and middle-income visitors, such as those aboard the *Oriente*. Many came to attend conferences sponsored by trade groups and professional associations. Havana tourism was linked to Miami tourism, and those visiting the "Magic City" were offered side trips aboard the Havana-America Steamship Corporation and other carriers. Nightclubs, casinos, and sporting events, including boxing matches, horse races, golf tournaments, and jai alai games, added to the island's lure. Then there was the popularity of Cuban dance music and Hollywood films including *The Girl from Havana* (1929), *Cuban Love Song* (1931), and *Havana Widows* (1933) as well as popular songs such as Irving Berlin's *I'll See You in Cuba*. Many came to the island just to make a fast buck. American novelist James Gould Cozzens described Havana as full of "adventurers, misinformed idiots, knaves, murderers, thieving contractors, corrupt officials, lease hunters—every form of rogue and rascal. It was then the last and worst American frontier, with the ethics and atmosphere of all frontiers; life, depraved and violent; honor, non-existent; and fabulous money loose for the stealing."[29]

Machado fled Cuba August 12, 1933, after Sumner Welles, appointed U.S. ambassador to protect U.S. interests and prevent revolution, failed to mediate an insurrection crisis. Welles influenced the appointment of Carlos Manuel de Céspedes to the presidency, but he was ousted after a few weeks in a coup d'état that saw the emergence of Fulgencio Batista, who ran the country intermittently until he was deposed by Fidel Castro in 1959. Batista was on the cover of *Time* magazine on April 26, 1937, and if Agee read the sister Luce publication before departing he would have learned that "Boss Batista commands the biggest army in Cuba's history (12,000 regulars, 20,000 reserves and a national police force of 4,000)."[30]

Not much about the island's alleged magic impressed Agee or the passengers, however. Seen at a distance, Havana, "riding the close horizon with an illusion of magical buoyancy which the ship's tender motion gave it, steadily and magnificently expanded like an opening flower." Up close, it was a different matter. About 4:00 p.m. on Tuesday, June 8, the *Oriente* docked, only to be greeted by an ominous welcoming party. Agee noted in his journal that the "soldiers in tan and members of Batista's other army, the police, in blue, stiffly strolled, or stood stiffly among them, with nightsticks and fire irons." He observed the studied plumage of the passengers who planned to go ashore: "Men in white linen and in Panamas and in fresh white shoes and new foulard ties, tinted handkerchiefs drooping from their pockets, the women in white hats and white sharkskin coats, in white silk dresses, in new prints, in new pink or blue pastels, in spiked heeled white shoes, in sandals, which exposed, or set off at its most irresistible, the brutal nail of the great toe." Once the passengers disembarked in Havana for the first of two tours, they were handed over to a "spectacled brown-uniformed hog with a loud retching voice who stuffed them into a noisy flotilla of cars." Agee left out of the article, but not his notes, his sense of how the passengers were perceived as the cars plowed through narrow streets, horns blaring, pedestrians scrambling, some tossing advertisements into the vehicles and jumping up on the running boards to sell trinkets. Evans tossed one a coin. "Cool, dressed-up, clean, looking around them, ten carloads strong of bastards. Every eye you catch in the streets is full of contempt and hatred." Elsewhere in his journal he softened and expanded this impression:

> The cars were now brimming with shy, gay, sheeplike people who waved . . . . One senses among the tourists a collective surprise which was an amalgam of embarrassment, pleasure, amusement, pride and plain dumbness as they were conveyed so loudly through the crooked city and looked mildly and not unkindly at these ragged, ignorant foreigners and the awful streets they lived in. There were many flickering meetings of eyes between the tourists and the Cubans and invariably the Cuban eyes, however they might differ, had in common their measure of scorn and of hatred.[31]

As Evans took photographs, a priest led them through the eighteenth-century Church of Our Lady of Mercy, where they saw a garish selection of "bruiselike Italianate paintings, an assortment of wax martyrs under glass among shriveled real and fresh wax flowers, and the high altar with all the electric lights on." Cathedral pilgrimages had been an exotic feature of American mass tourism in Europe for seventy years, so the visit added international authenticity to the Havana excursion. "Catholic art and ritual embodied a feast of color and incense and music unknown in meeting houses" in the United States, according to cultural historian Jackson Lears. Agee, raised an Anglo-Catholic and leaning left, thought the passengers skipped the more earthy art that dealt with working conditions, capital, and labor. From the church, they next were guided through a small cigar factory, where Agee observed in his journal that workers had been kept rolling cigars long after their shift was to end because the tour had been delayed. The tourists gawked at the workers "as if they were in a zoo. None of the men looked up." From the factory, they passed through a cemetery and then approached the Maine Monument, where "the hog reminded his little charges how the U.S. gave Cuba Hobson's (not by any chance Iscariot's) Kiss and made our little brown boy friend safe for the canebrake, the sugar mill, and the riding boss, and his island a safe place for decent citizens to do business in." At some point, Agee broke away from the tour to sketch his own impressions of Havana. This led to lyrical descriptions, such as: "Colonades and tall thin windows in all; each very fancy in same way, no two houses quite alike; an infinitely varied uniformity like that of water. Buff and pink and brown and yellow and blue and white." At the dock, he talked with crew members and deck officers when he could find them, attending to the sailors' grumblings, vulgar boasts, and concupiscent dreams.[32]

Between the tours, "a goose dinner was served aboard the *Oriente* for those who mistrusted the dirty foreign food." On the night tour, the tourists watched a jai alai game, visited Sloppy Joe's Bar, and the classier Sans Souci, two of Hemingway's hangouts, although the author was not in town. At Sloppy Joe's, "the Grant's Tomb of bars, at which no self-respecting Cuban would be caught dead, the tourists themselves seemed a little embarrassed." The tourists straggled back to the *Oriente* in the early morning hours, and, according to Agee, were glad to be leaving Havana when the ship departed about noon. "Of those who liked Havana there were two schools: those who spoke of it as quaint, and those who spoke of it as cute. Most of the passengers detested it and were glad to see the last of it. . . . A middle aged man in glasses said to the group: 'When you see the Statue of Liberty you're going to say, this is the country for me.'" The return trip was a disappointment as the passengers realized the cruise was coming to an end with their expectations mostly dashed. "Friday was worst of all. The Gulf Stream was gone, the water was cold and gray, the weather was cold and gray and rather windy, and by afternoon the ship was traveling very slowly in a deathening absence of engine pulsation, for it had been decided to delay docking until Saturday morning. The passengers were depressed beyond even appetite, and a majority of them stayed below." He added in the notes that "a lot of the girls began to stay out of sight; it was bad for them to be seen too much without men." On deck, he talked to a "thin Englishman who ran a Cuban sugar mill and abhorred Batista's nationalism." Those passengers who congregated in the lounge "sat in the hotel-lobby furniture and tried to read, or talked in the voices used when a dear aunt is passing out upstairs." After the "last supper, with its tasseled menus, its signal flags, hats, and noisemakers, things picked up." There was heavy drinking in the bar and dining room as passengers danced to the music of the ship's band, quarreled and shattered glassware until admonished to behave. By 2:30 a.m., the last of the passengers repaired to their bunks as the *Oriente* glided along the coast where the *Morro Castle* had burned.[33]

At 4:00 a.m. a cornetist appeared in the corridors playing "The Sidewalks of New York." Presently, a steward rapped on Agee's cabin door and called his attention to the Statue of Liberty coming into view. Agee, the unnamed "passenger" at the end of his article, looked out as the *Oriente* passed Bedloe Island, then pondered the lights of the city beyond. He concluded his article with a prose-poem in the manner of Whitman and Hart Crane.

> The water lifted and relaxed in one slow floor of glass. The city lifted, it seemed, a mile above it, and very near; and smokeless behind the city, morning, the mutilation of honey. The city stood appareled in the sober purple and silver of supreme glory, no foal of nature, nor intention of man, but one sublime organism, singular and uncreated; and it stretched upward from its stone roots in the water as if it were lifted on a dream. Nor yet was it soft, nor immaterial. Every window, every wheatlike stone, was distinct in the eye as a razor and serenely, lost, somnambulists, the buildings turned one past another upon the bias of the ship's ghostly movement, not unlike those apostolic figures who parade with the clock's noon in Strasbourg.

In his notes, he had indicated the apostolic figures were in Cologne. An alert copy editor made the correction and saved *Fortune's* staff the chore of reading hundreds of letters pointing out the error.

VI

Fortune's September 1937 issue, in which Agee's article appeared, was entirely devoted to shipping, an industry, the magazine stated, "about on a par with the soft-drink business, but the latter makes a tidy profit while shipping operates at a horrible (and apparently perpetual) loss." The shipping business was a doubtful subject for a magazine celebrating success. *Fortune* intended to question an industry receiving a "direct subsidy" by the New Deal through the 1936 Merchant Marine Act, which had provided operating subsidies to U.S. flag ships tied to specific international trade routes. The act called for more American-owned and built ships and American crews. *Fortune* claimed a subsidized business turned a democratic economy into an "economy of statism, in which business exists, not by virtue of its inherent profits, but because a powerful central government wills it to." *Fortune* lamented that there was an absence of data about the shipping industry. "And from the standpoint of intelligent statistics and/or analyses, the shipping business is a shambles." An article in *American Shipper* in September 1991 took a look back at the *Fortune* maritime issue and concluded that most of the problems remained, but said nothing about the passenger cruise industry, which was booming.[34]

Advertisements in the *Fortune* issue plugged shipping companies, hotels, alcohol, and cruising. The table of contents promised articles about Joseph P. Kennedy, the head of the U.S. Maritime Commission; marine subsidies; the Bethlehem Shipbuilding Corporation; the Merchant Marine Act of 1936; the U.S. Merchant Marine; ports; the Hog Island Shipyard in Philadelphia; foreign trade; unions, exports, and other topics. Although the passenger business was up in the first half of 1937, it was only a "minor appendage" of the shipping industry, according to *Fortune*, and little more than a sideline to freight services. "From the standpoint of a subsidized merchant marine the passenger is, if not inconsequential, at most a byproduct." Except for the "behaviorism of a Havana Cruise," as interpreted by Agee, *Fortune* dismissed the passenger as a factor of interest. "Havana Cruise" appeared on the last editorial page with an editorial preface: "Have you ever taken a cruise? If so, this is what you may have looked like and here are some of the things you may have done. FORTUNE sent an anonymous reporter on a cruise, and he came back with this human document that has little to do with the profound economic problems of the merchant marine." Agee's assignment did not fit well with the issue. Wealthy *Fortune* readers prospering in the Depression were asked if they had taken a cruise. If they had, and were gulled into reading the article, they found passengers on the *Oriente* portrayed as dopes, decidedly *not* the sort of people they imagined they encountered on a cruise to the Mediterranean, prompting class snobbery and condescension. It would be an odd strategy for any business, especially a business magazine, to insult its customers, especially when the magazine featured shipping industry advertisements.[35]

Additionally, Evans's work did not mesh with Agee's text. Mellow thought the photographs lacked "the searching, starker enquiry of the photographs made for *The Crime of Cuba*." Evans photographed the tourists "in a motorcade stopping traffic while standing in their touring cars to take in the sights, or herded like well-dressed sheep along avenues much tidier than those he had photographed a few years earlier." His photograph of the tourists in Sloppy Joe's Bar revealed them "glasses raised aloft, and convivial enough," not as miserable as Agee made them out to be. They looked curious, eager, engaged and for the most part having a fine time. Nothing indicates they were being "herded" anywhere, and if they looked like sheep it was only because they were comfortably dressed in summer whites.[36]

VII

"Havana Cruise," the last of the thirty articles Agee wrote for *Fortune* between 1932 and 1937 to be published in the magazine, has received the most critical attention, but little context. Richard Oulahan, writing for *Life* in 1963, called the "esteemed story" an "acid scrutiny of the passengers aboard a cruise ship" and a "departure in style for the usually gentle Agee." Fitzgerald recalled seeing an earlier draft of the "excruciating Caribbean 'vacation cruise,'" an even more potent "masterpiece of ferocity, or would have been if it had been printed uncut," reflecting Agee's increasing pessimism about "American middle-class ways and destinies . . . ." Moreau said "Havana Cruise" read like great fiction achieving "profound social criticism when he describes the tourist as the helpless, anonymous, middle-class victim of the unscrupulous tourist industry, whose main motive, of course, is profit." Thomas Connery, editor of a reference volume on American literary journalism, thought Agee had transformed a routine assignment into a "bitter tale of American middle-class types behaving boorishly as they chase false dreams." Mellow considered the article "a minor masterpiece of travel writing, a sardonic, racy account," and from the beginning "definitely seriocomic."[37]

William Dow considered "Havana Cruise" an inversion of what Agee did in *Let Us Now Praise Famous Men.* By focusing on "self-contented upper- and middle-class ideals, self-indulgence on a mass scale, and the selling of consumption," Agee had reproached the parvenu rather than praised the pitiful. "Havana Cruise" mocked those Agee called self-deceived aspirants to the more affluent life of the ocean voyager, certain this modest excursion would meet their expectations and their budget. Dow said the article took "a devastating look at the mass-mediated American culture of the 1930s," an obsession of the decade. For Dow, the final images reinforced a mood of "locked-in uncontrollability and the impossibility of change." The ship drifted toward its berth, its "ghostly movement" repetitive like the workings of a clock juxtaposed against the fixed spires of the organic city. The passengers languished, "unable to comprehend their meanness and sterility." They could not distance themselves from their class identities any more than the tenant farmers could escape their own constraints or the passengers of the Morro Castle could exit their burning ship.[38]

Stephen M. Park placed Agee and Evans among those anxious 1930s liberals desperate to avoid a "radical paternalism" by assuming a "posture of innocence," especially in writing about Cuba and Latin America, but also Alabama. The documentarians of the era faced "anxiety and constant need to prove the veracity" of their account. Through his work with Beals and Agee, Evans subconsciously paired images from *The Crime of Cuba* with the Alabama photographs, "finding similar faces and similar conditions of poverty in these regions separated by a mere eight hundred miles." This paternalism, for Park, "conflated representations of Latin America and the American South" in condescending terms.[39]

Agee saw the irony of the Spanish-American War's Maine Monument "capstoned by the quaint word Liberty" in Batista's Cuba, a protected sanctuary for Americans to do business, and yet it was not Cuba, but the passengers who were the target. Agee and Evans insisted they were not tourists. They were imposters—journalists as spies. *Let Us Now Praise Famous Men* would take up the moral quandary of false representation and exploitation, the humanity of the tenant farmers as opposed to the inanity of the tourists. Some lingering memory of Havana may have carried over into *Let Us Now Praise Famous Men* when Agee brooded in the Alabama book about how "the gulf lies dreaming, and beneath, dreaming, that woman, that id, the lower American continent, lies before heaven in her wealth. The parks of her cities are iron, loam, silent, the sweet fountains shut, and the pure façades, embroiled, limelike in street light are sharp, are still."[40]

Joshua Roiland, who teaches literary journalism at the University of Maine, considered "Havana Cruise" a "bitter, at times misogynistic, take on a middle-class cruise filled with unhappy couples and desperate singles. The cultural commentary reads, today, as obvious and easy: materialism and sexual gratification do not lead to happiness. . . . Agee's [voice] is beautiful: elliptical, snide, and ultimately sad."[41]

Jack Neely, a journalist and historian writing in Agee's home town, thought "Havana Cruise" showed the empathetic writer of *Let Us Now Praise Famous Men* and *A Death in the Family* "could also be, given sufficient provocation, a smartass. . . . Especially when cooped up on the same ship with more than 100 frantic, silly tourists. . . . People with a little money and no clear idea of what to do with it." For *New York Times* book reviewer and future Agee biographer Dwight Garner, "Havana Cruise" was "savage reportage" and a "cooly cynical account of traveling to Havana by commercial cruise liner. . . ." Canadian novelist and journalist Stephen Henighan, writing in the *Times Literary Supplement*, thought Agee "savaged the vapidity of the first cruise holidays" with "bracing sarcasm and an original style."[42]

These assessments of "Havana Cruise" acknowledged the wit and the nastiness of Agee's attack while neglecting the larger story Agee might have written. Agee said as much in a November 26, 1937, letter to Father Flye. "I'm glad you liked the Cruise article for I feel sure you know its cruelty was used to inspire pity in readers who never feel it when it is asked in another's behalf directly." Perhaps he was seeking absolution for the article. "I would like to do the same article over more fully, and better." In his Plans for Work, submitted with his application for a Guggenheim Fellowship in 1937, Agee proposed a project that would expand on the technique he said he developed in "Havana Cruise." "I should like to apply this to the behavior of a wealthier class of people on, say, a Mediterranean cruise." Was he feeling remorse for his cruelty—by his own admission—in "Havana Cruise?" In fact, he intended to write more about Havana. In a late night journal entry on Wednesday, January 12, 1938, in New York, he said he put aside a new start on the "Alabama book" to find "what might be publishable, needing money. Nothing looked so. Sat down to start something that might be. Havana." On January 27, 1938, he wrote: "I am at a point with the Havana thing that would require what I can't now possibly give it: 'orchestration', and a big development." He complained of exhaustion, guilt, and depression, then indicated that work was "the only way out, and the only thing which can give any integrity and vitality to anything else in my life. I guess I will try to write more of Havana." He did not, but he dreamed about it. In a December 1, 1938, entry in his notebooks, he mentioned a "long dream the other night of Havana and its waterfront. Alma, I, Jorge, Walker I think others." When he wrote about Havana, a Hale Country, Alabama, crossroads town in *Let Us Now Praise Famous Men,* he called it Madrid, a city in the hands of a fascist dictator.[43]

Robert Coles, the James Agee Professor of Social Ethics at Harvard, wrote that when he first read *Let Us Now Praise Famous Men,* he was put off by "page after page of anger directed at nameless others, including the reader . . . constantly taking swipes at his own kind, writers and intellectuals. . . ." He and his students realized, however, that Agee's sarcasm, "near hysteria," and self-flagellation were what made Agee's "sustained exhortation so powerfully instructive." Agee was conceptualizing his Alabama book as he wrote "Havana Cruise." The wrath of the sea voyage, in which he was not much interested, spilled over into the splenetic outrage of the Alabama project, but with a shift to first-person in the documentary style. Agee changed targets, upped the intensity, shifted from mockery to moral scrutiny and confession, and turned his guns on himself.[44]

VIII

Putting "Havana Cruise" in context requires a panoramic sweep of the political, cultural, historical, journalistic, and literary horizon, an inventory of facts and impressions revealing more of Agee's and *Fortune's* purposes amid the desultory events that all but submerged the project. For this reason, placing the article agreeably within Agee's oeuvre has been problematic. It seems to bob about at sea like a cask of fine Cuban rum that has tumbled overboard from the deck of a cruise ship in a tropical storm.

Many American and British writers and photographers have found literary material in Cuba and on the sea routes to the island. In addition to Evans, these included Hemingway; Cozzens; Beals; Stephen Crane, who covered Cuba for the *New York World* and the *New York Journal*; Richard Henry Dana; Winston Churchill, who, as a foreign correspondent, wrote for the *Daily Graphic* in Cuba in 1895; Richard Harding Davis, who covered Cuba for the *New York Journal*; Lawrence S. Haas with United Press; James Doyle Phillips, Ruby Hart Phillips, and Herbert Matthews, all with the *New York Times*; Jules Dubois with the *Chicago Tribune*; photographer Dickey Chapelle; Robert Taber with CBS News; Graham Greene and even Errol Flynn, a journalist-turned-actor-turned-journalist who wrote features for the *New York Journal American*. Agee was singular and predictably idiosyncratic.

Nothing in "Havana Cruise" suggests that Agee the reporter was on a voyage of personal discovery on the *Oriente* or in Havana, a tenderfoot traveler from an advanced culture who entered the primitive as the "tourist-intruder . . . the schlemiel-reporter from New York," as Alan Spiegel described the perennial plotline of so many romantic tales of adventure and exploration. That was more the self-referential Agee of *Let Us Now Praise Famous Men*. In "Havana Cruise," he did not try to make contact with the natives or his shipmates in situ in order to understand them. Agee came to observe, ridicule, and exploit them (for their own good, according to his disclaimer to Father Flye) until he could return to the dreaming spires of New York, where he truly felt something. Of Havana he could say, "The passengers saw their best of Havana before they set foot in it." He described Havana as "one of the whoriest cites of the Western Hemisphere." So much for the romance of the tropics. As a traveler, Agee was never equivocal. Eight years earlier, while traveling as a vagabond bindlestiff in the West, he wrote a friend that "Kansas is the most utterly lousy state I've ever seen." To that point, he had not seen many.[45]

It is surprising that Agee wrote so little of the *Morro Castle*, considering that the *Oriente's* ill-fated sister ship received massive news coverage that continued long after the fire and prompted shipping reform and safety regulations, none of which he mentioned. Many of the passengers must have been apprehensive or at least curious to be reprising the *Morro Castle's* last sea voyage in a duplicate ship. Had they no reaction, that indeed would have been a triumph of public relations for the Ward Line. Their lack of curiosity about Havana is also puzzling. Cuba was in turmoil, an island in the news. Did the story accurately reflect their indifference or Agee's? Hemingway's *To Have and Have Not* was published October 15, 1937, just a month after Agee's article was in the hands of subscribers. By early November, Hemingway's novel was fourth on national bestseller lists and probably on more than a few of the *Oriente* passengers' nightstands. The story added a bit of swagger to their otherwise tame experiences in Cuba, and could be read safely in a New York apartment. Hemingway targeted some of the same tourist types Agee found so amusing in "Havana Cruise." *To Have and Have Not* had some of the bite promised by Hemingway's talk at the writers' congress in New York. If Agee was paying attention to what Hemingway said, it came out more in *Let Us Now Praise Famous Men*, not "Havana Cruise." He tried to write that book "truly." "Havana Cruise" struck a false note despite some fine passages.[46]

An extensive literature about the passengers and crew aboard the *Morro Castle* is available. Authors compiled their stories based on interviews, newspaper, and magazine articles and court testimony. The passengers and crew were demographically similar to those Agee met aboard the *Oriente*. Many behaved heroically during the *Morro Castle* ordeal, saving the lives of others. How they experienced the cruise is well documented because their fate exposed them to the press and later historians. The political situation in Cuba had changed somewhat in three years, but was approximately the same. Agee, of course, had no ready access to this information, and no time to collect it if he did, and so relied on observation alone to write a profile. A fuller impression of the passengers on the sister ships emerges, however, if the *Morro Castle* literature is compared to "Havana Cruise," emphasizing their humanity and character as well as their foolishness in unguarded moments.[47]

Agee came up against the limits of magazine journalism in "Havana Cruise," as evidenced by the condescending "little brown boy friend" phrase slipped in without elaboration. The assignment was odd from the beginning, perhaps an editorial afterthought to showcase one of *Fortune's* star writers. A writer other than Agee might have looked at the assignment as an innocuous one-week paid vacation. Agee was incapable of turning in a perfunctory response even when he did not have much editorial space to work with. He had, after all, a growing reputation to maintain. Fitzgerald said an earlier version of the article had been cut. Perhaps Agee had intended to say more about Cuba, and only the single skewering sentence survived the copy pencil. Whatever version Fitzgerald saw may have included some of the angry material in Agee's journals that was excised from the published article. His more limited attempts at a poetry of introspection, evident in the brief transitional passages about the ship, the sea, the Statue of Liberty and New York, were better realized in the 1939 "Brooklyn Is" piece he wrote for *Fortune*, but which *Fortune* rejected. Its block-by-block inventory captured the "physique and whole tone and metres of the city itself. You have only to cross a bridge to know it: how behind you the whole of living is drawn up straining into verticals, tightened and badgered in nearly every face of man and child and building. . . ." By the time he wrote "Brooklyn Is," he was deeper into *Let Us Now Praise Famous Men*. "Brooklyn Is" is more lyrical than "Havana Cruise," and not as sarcastic.[48]

A recently discovered and as yet unpublished project offers evidence that Agee may have been more affected by the "Havana Cruise" than he let on (see Appendix 2). In early 1939, Agee lived for two months at 179 St. James Place in the Clinton Hill area of Brooklyn not far from the Brooklyn Navy Yard and the Buttermilk Channel, where he could observe nautical traffic and ship building. Five years earlier, Hemingway had purchased his yacht *Pilar* from the Wheeler Shipyard at the end of Cropsey Avenue. Evans became entranced by the same Brooklyn docks in 1959 and produced a portfolio of photographs he titled "On the Waterfront." Agee wrote a sea story he titled "Freighter's Sailing Day" about a cargo ship, the S.S. *Typicus*, tethered to Pier 34 across from Governors Island and late for departure south to Rio de Janeiro with a storm rising. Replete with gusty nautical jargon and brash dialect, the story feels authentic with rich detail and vivid if somewhat stereotypical characters. Agee's descriptive powers and smart similes (the "blade beats upon the water with a noise like the slow hooves of a tired drayhorse walking through a covered bridge") propel the story although nothing much happens. The departure alone is of sufficient interest, "awesome magic concocted out of a witches' broth of wind and snow, blocks and ropes, snarling winches, unintelligible shoutings, and impenetrable darkness." A harbor pilot makes the "whole operation appear deceivingly easy," and so does the author. The story confirms he could have done more with the *Fortune* article.[49]

"Havana Cruise" was included in the Library of America's American sea writing anthology in 2000. Washington Irving, James Fenimore Cooper, Edgar Allan Poe, Herman Melville, Mark Twain, Jack London, Hemingway, and John Steinbeck were among the other writers included. The editor insisted that, after more than sixty years, it was unlikely that anyone would "ever capture as well as Agee the melancholy nexus between the pursuit of pleasure at sea and the 'inestimable pressures of loneliness and spiritual fear' experienced in modern life ashore." Even so, "Havana Cruise" was not much of a sea story, less appealing than "Freighter's Sailing Day." The great, salty literature of sea writing shows the organic interaction of wave, wind, and water, crew and passengers, marine life, myth and history, fire, fog, and fury on the wine-dark sea and grey-dawn breaking. David Foster Wallace wrote a better account of the experience of cruising fifty-nine years after "Havana Cruise." Wallace's "Shipping Out—on the (nearly lethal) comforts of a luxury cruise," published in *Harper's* in 1996, was not a great sea story either, however. Dwight Garner thought the earlier "Havana Cruise" read "like a protean, footnote-free version" of Wallace's story. He judged them similar to the extent that both writers suggested, "You cruise . . . and fundamentally you lose." Wallace made explicit what Agee implied: "There is something about a mass-market Luxury Cruise that's unbearably sad."[50]

Another popular article about cruising, "The Casual Ark," had appeared in the *Saturday Evening Post* on April 7, 1934, five months before the *Morro Castle* disaster. The author, novelist Joseph Hergesheimer, had written a travelogue about Havana in 1920. He described the passengers aboard an unnamed liner that visited Martinique, Venezuela, Curaçao, Jamaica, and Panama. They were the wealthier class of passengers who read *Fortune*, a richer target for Agee, and those he proposed writing about in his Plans for Work. Hergesheimer wrote about the vacuity of the upper middle class in a grandiloquent style lacking the wit of Agee's later prose. He commented on the sameness of the male lawyers, bankers, undertakers, clergymen, manufacturers, merchants, and doctors aboard, and the blandness of the women, even "less variously engaged." The passengers' clothing showed no originality, as if they reveled in uniformity. Their judgments of other people followed the lines of social importance. Unlike the *Oriente* passengers, as Agee saw them, Hergesheimer's passengers "liked the ship, the food, all the sights, and said the weather was miraculous." While the *Oriente* passengers looked for romance, according to Agee, Hergesheimer said he "could not see that romance, in its conventional, approved form, existed at all. The moon, the nights, were magnificent, but no couples appeared to be intoxicated by the moonlight and the promise of a common ecstatic future." It was "a very-well-behaved and moral shipload." No less misogynistic than Agee, Hergesheimer judged that the women "had the appearance of commitment to an existence without the need of responsibility or thought." There was less of the apparent class, gender, and cultural insecurity that Agee observed aboard the *Oriente*. The passengers Hergesheimer wrote about "never fundamentally entertained the remote chance of any end to their order. . . . They were engaged by luxury, pleasure and the present; the abstract future was fainter in their minds than the island of Martinique, rapidly vanishing in a tender, blue haze of evening." Agee's article was more interesting. Hergesheimer's may be the more accurate, if no less sad. *Fortune* was more comfortable mocking the déclassé than holding up a mirror to the audience it was trying to reach.[51]

Postscript

Agee never went on another cruise. He died May 16, 1955. The *Thomas H. Barry*, née *Oriente*, remained in reserve service and was tethered to a pier on the James River in Virginia until removed by the Bethlehem Shipbuilding Corporation on November 4, 1957, and scrapped. Hemingway died July 2, 1961. Evans said of him in 1971: "Photography is reporting. I am interested in reporting. . . . Hemingway was a hell of a good reporter, did it to begin with, and was always grounded in that." Evans died April 10, 1975, almost twenty years after Agee. On May 10, 1941, Oscar L. Seastrom, sixty-two, still captain of the *Oriente*, was honored by his employers on the fiftieth anniversary of his going to sea at the age of twelve in his native Sweden. The *New York Times* ran an article accompanied by a photo identified as Captain Seastrom. A week later, the *Times* ran a correction, indicating the photo of Captain Seastrom was in fact a photo of the late Robert R. Willmott, captain of the *Morro Castle*. Captain Seastrom died on February 5, 1954, in Hawaii. Hergesheimer died on April 25, 1954. The Ward Line and Cuba Mail Steamship Company stopped using American flag ships in 1954, was sold to a Cuban company on June 30, 1956, and liquidated soon after. [52]

The cruise line industry itself almost died after the *Yarmouth Castle* caught fire at sea on November 13, 1965, and sank about 110 miles east of Miami. Ninety passengers and crew died in the tragedy. Edwin Stephan, the general manager of Yarmouth Cruise Lines, a small firm that operated the *Yarmouth Castle*, knew how to save the industry. He founded Royal Caribbean Cruises in 1969, now one of the world's largest cruise operators along with Carnival Corporation and Norwegian Cruise Line. The firms acquired new and larger ships to attract more middle-class passengers, the same demographic Agee chose to parody. The popularity of an ABC network television romantic comedy, *The Love Boat*, which ran for 249 episodes from 1977 to 1987 plus several specials, did the rest. The series was inspired by Jeraldine Saunders's 1974 book *The Love Boats*, based on the author's experiences as a cruise director. The original 550-foot cruise line "Love Boat" used as the backdrop for the series was scrapped in 2012. Agee had called the *Oriente* a "somehow invincibly comic vessel." He was prescient in 1937, but could not have anticipated what cruising would become forty years later. Had the passengers' flirtations been more comic than tragic, and the ship less haunted by the *Morro Castle* disaster, gunrunning, and revolutionary conditions in Cuba, the *Oriente* might have been seen in retrospect as the prototype for *The Love Boat* and its era. Had Agee lived to the age of seventy, he might have been encouraged to write "Havana Cruise Revisited" in 1979 or 1980 to assess what had become of the cruise ship industry. It was not to be. Nevertheless, by 2017, a record 25.8 million passengers cruised globally with some twelve million passengers sourced from U.S. ports. Wallace, Agee's successor in lampooning the ocean cruise, died September 12, 2008, a suicide. Cruise ship travel to Cuba ended after the 1959 revolution and resumed only in 2016. In 2019, however, the United States again suspended cruises to Havana or elsewhere in Cuba indefinitely. Beginning in 2020, the Covid-19 virus torpedoed the entire cruise line industry for several seasons.[53]

Notes

1. The date of the cruise has been omitted or misreported in the Agee literature. Agee biographer Laurence Bergreen said, without citing a source, that the *Oriente* departed on "a bright August morning. . . ." Agee biographer Geneviève Moreau gave no date but said the article was submitted to the magazine "in the early part of July 1937." Evans biographer Belinda Rathbone also gave no date. James R. Mellow, another Evans biographer, said the Agees and Evans boarded "on a bright early summer morning," but cited no source. Agee said in the "Havana Cruise" article that the trip occurred "in early summer," but in his journals he listed the correct date in late spring. "Oriente Delayed 2d Time in 8 Days," *New York Times*, June 6, 1937; Laurence Bergreen,

James Agee: A Life (New York: E.P. Dutton, 1984), 192; Geneviève Moreau, *The Restless Journey of James Agee* (New York: William Morrow, 1977), 157–58, 305; Belinda Rathbone, *Walker Evans: A Biography* (New York: Houghton Mifflin, 1995), 149–51, 320; James R. Mellow, *Walker Evans* (New York: Basic Books, 1999), 360. James Agee Collection, MS 1998, box 1, folders 1 and 2, Special Collections, University of Tennessee Library, Knoxville. Subsequent references to these folders will appear as "James Agee Collection."

2. "Havana Cruise," *Fortune* 16, no. 3 (September 1937): 117–20, 210–20; James Agee, "Havana Cruise," *Complete Journalism: Articles, Book Reviews, and Manuscripts*, ed. Paul Ashdown, *The Works of James Agee,* vol. 2 (Knoxville: U of Tennessee P, 2013), 292–306. "Havana Cruise" is referenced in some sources as "Six Days at Sea." An article's title in the magazine's table of contents is sometimes different from the headline above the article within the publication. The New York and Cuba Mail Steamship Company, popularly known by its earlier name, the Ward Line, published a list of passengers for the *Oriente.* Passengers received an eight-page, 5 ½ x 7 ½" booklet on Sunday, June 6, 1937. The first passenger listed is Mr. J. Agee; the twenty-fourth listed is W. Evans. The passenger list identifies sixty-eight passengers aboard for the six-day cruise. An additional sixty-four passengers are listed as "For Havana," meaning that they would either stay in Havana or stay an extra week. For the article, Agee counted the names on the passenger list for the six-day cruise, identified about twenty names, "mostly Cubans," as those returning to Havana, leaving forty for the thirteen-day cruise. A few no-shows may have accounted for any difference. The *New York Times* reported that the liner had booked 127 passengers, which might be the more accurate figure. Bergreen, *James Agee*, 192; Moreau, *Restless Journey*, 157–58, 305; Rathbone, *Walker Evans*, 149–51, 320. Mellow, *Walker Evans*, 360; Agee, "Havana Cruise"; James Agee Collection.

3. Robert Fitzgerald, "A Memoir," in *James Agee: The Collected Short Prose*, ed. Robert Fitzgerald (New York: Houghton Mifflin, 1968), 66; "Creators' Congress," *Time* 29, no. 25 (June 21, 1937): 101–02; "Fight on Fascism Urged: Writers Call on Members of Craft to Combat War Spirit," *New York Times*, June 5, 1937.

4. "Creators' Congress"; "Fight on Fascism Urged"; Ernest Hemingway, "Fascism Is a Lie," *New Masses* 23, no. 13 (June 22, 1937): 4; Carlos Baker, *Hemingway: A Life* (New York: Charles Scribner's Sons, 1969), 313.

5. Fitzgerald, 66; *James Agee Rediscovered: The Journals of Let Us Now Praise Famous Men and Other New Manuscripts*, ed. Michael A. Lofaro and Hugh Davis (Knoxville: U of Tennessee P, 2005), xxix, 45; *Complete Film Criticism: Reviews, Essays, Manuscripts,* ed. Charles Maland, *The Works of James Agee*, vol. 5 (2017), 571–74; Ernest Hemingway, "Old Newsman Writes: A Letter from Cuba," in *By-Line: Ernest Hemingway: Selected Articles and Dispatches of Four Decades,* ed. William White (New York: Scribner's, 1967), 184.

6. Mellow, *Walker Evans*, 180–81, 199; Rathbone, *Walker Evans*, 80–81; Baker, *Hemingway*, 241–42. See, for example, Ernest Hemingway, "One Trip Across," *Cosmopolitan* 96 (April 1934): 20–23, 108–122; Maria Morris Hambourg, Jeff L. Rosenheim, Douglas Eklund, and Mia Fineman, *Walker Evans*, (Princeton, NJ: Princeton UP, 2000), 52–53.

7. Clara Buckley, "Forgotten Photos Recall Havana Friendship," *Miami Herald*, January 15, 2004, https://www.cubanet.org/htdocs/CNews/y04/jan04/15e9.htm, accessed December 16, 2019;

David Gonzalez, "Walker Evans's Cuba, via Ernest Hemingway," *New York Times*, November 7, 2017; Rathbone, *Walker Evans*, 46–47; Michael Brown, "Walker Evans Ernest Hemingway, Havana 1933," Catalog 50, Michael Brown Rare Books, Philadelphia, Pennsylvania, 2017, https://www.abaa.org/images/blog/evansbest1.pdf, accessed December 16, 2019; Judith Keller, *Walker Evans*, The Getty Museum Collection (Malibu, CA: The J. Paul Getty Museum, 1995), 62–63; Walker Evans, *Walker Evans: Havana 1933*, ed. Gilles Mora (New York: Random House, 1989).

8. Moreau, *Restless Journey*, 11, 157–58.

9. Bergreen, *James Agee*, 192.

10. Rathbone, *Walker Evans*, 149, 151.

11. *Let Us Now Praise Famous Men: An Annotated Edition of the James Agee-Walker Evans Classic, with Supplementary Manuscripts*, ed. Hugh Davis *The Works of James Agee*, vol. 3 (2015), 5; Douglas Eklund, "Exile's Return: The Early Work, 1928–34," in Hambourg et al., *Walker Evans*, 45, 53; Alfredo José Estrada, *Havana: Autobiography of a City* (New York: Palgrave Macmillan, 2007), 193–95; Mia Fineman, "Notes from Underground: The Subway Portraits," in Hambourg et al., *Walker Evans*, 107–8.

12. Moreau, *Restless Journey*, 158–61; Bergreen, *James Agee*, 183–90, 202–203, 220, 428; Rathbone, *Walker Evans*, 153; "Bigger Than We Are: A Love Story" draft, notes, general outline, undated, box 4 folders 21 and 22 James Agee Collection, University of Tennessee Library, Knoxville; "Thirty-two 35 mm Film Frames on Uncut Roll: 1 of Dance Class, 21 Nude Studies of Olivia Saunders Agee and 10 Portraits of Ursula Bitter, 1937," Metropolitan Museum of Art, New York; *Letters of James Agee to Father Flye*, 2nd ed. (Dunwoody, GA: Norman S. Berg, 1978, orig. pub. 1962), 87.

13. "Havana Cruise," 294; James Agee, "Knoxville: Summer 1915," *Partisan Review* 5 (August–September 1938): 22–25; Fitzgerald, "A Memoir," 64.

14. Peter C. Kobler, "Triumph and Tragedy, T.E.L. Morro Castle and Oriente," *Steamboat Bill: Journal of the Steamship Historical Society of America* 46, no. 2 (Summer 1989): 106–27; William McFee, "The Peculiar Fate of the Morro Castle," *The Aspirin Age, 1919–1941*, ed. Isabel Leighton (New York: Simon and Schuster, 1949), 321.

15. "Liner Docks Here After Cuba Fight," *New York Times*, November 12, 1933; Gordon Thomas and Max Morgan Witts, *Shipwreck: The Strange Fate of the Morro Castle* (New York: Dell, 1973, orig. pub. 1972), 14, 17, 135; Brian Hicks, *When the Dancing Stopped: The Real Story of the Morro Castle Disaster and Its Deadly Wake* (New York: Free Press, 2006), 14, 42; Hal Burton, *The Morro Castle* (New York: Viking, 1973), 1–13; Lisa Lindquist Door, "Bootlegging Aliens: Unsanctioned Immigration and the Underground Economy of Smuggling from Cuba During Prohibition," *Florida Historical Quarterly* 93 (Summer 2014): 47–57.

16. Paul Hendrickson, *Hemingway's Boat: Everything He Loved in Life, and Lost* (New York Random House, 2011), 245; Thomas and Witts, *Shipwreck*, 31, 51–52, 234; "Blaze Laid to Reds by Cuban Official," *New York Times*, September 11, 1934.

17. "Ship Fire Pictured On Sister Vessel, Oriente, Duplicate of Burned Liner, Arrives From Havana With 311 Passengers," *New York Times*, September 12, 1934; "Sister Ship Sails, Oriente Departs With More Passengers Than Year Ago," *New York Times*, September 16, 1934.

18. "Notes of Interest in Shipping World," *New York Times*, July 21, 1935; Kobler, "Triumph and Tragedy," 122; Clifford Odets, "What Happened to Us in Cuba," *New Masses* 16, no. 3 (July 16, 1935): 9–11; "Shipboard Friendship," *Time* 26, no. 3 (July 15, 1935): 31; Carleton Beals and Clifford Odets, *Rifle Rule in Cuba* (New York: Provisional Committee for Cuba, 1935), 11, 19; Richard M. Leighton and Robert W. Coakley, *The War Department—Global Logistics and Strategy, 1940–1943. United States Army in World War II* (Washington, DC, Center for Military History, United States Army, 1995), 157; *Thomas H. Barry*, http://www.shipscribe.com/usnaux/AP/AP45.html, retrieved October 5, 2019. In his *Fortune* article "U.S. Ambassadors" (April 1934), *Complete Journalism*, 136–37, Agee describes Caffery as "a lynx-eyed, tough-brained, subtle Louisianian (anti-Long) with a twitchy face and a taste for hard-driving work, sombreros and green socks, and bad puns."

19. Paul Fussell, *Abroad: British Literary Traveling Between the Wars* (New York: Oxford UP, 1980), 38, 40, 51, 71, 218–19; Alec Waugh, *A Year to Remember: A Reminiscence of 1931* (London: W.H. Allen, 1975), 18.

20. Fitzgerald, "A Memoir," 52; Bergreen, *James Agee*, 32, 65; Agee, "The American Roadside," 175–87; "Saratoga," 227–43, *Complete Journalism*; *Collected Short Prose*, 61–75.

21. James Agee Collection.

22. "Havana Cruise," 292–93. Arthur Treacher (1894–1974) was an English actor known for playing butlers. Agee may have seen Treacher in *Step Lively, Jeeves!*, which was playing in movie theaters in April and June in 1937. Treacher also played Jeeves in the 1936 film *Thank You, Jeeves!* Both films were based on characters in the Bertie Wooster stories written by P.G. Wodehouse. Hicks, *When the Dancing Stopped*, 5.

23. James Agee Collection; "Havana Cruise," 293–94.

24. Ibid., 294–95.

25. Ibid., 295–98.

26. Ibid., 296–300; James Agee Collection.

27. "Havana Cruise," 300–01; Ernest Hemingway, "On the Blue Water: A Gulf Stream Letter," *By-Line: Ernest Hemingway*, 237.

28. Louis A. Pérez Jr., *On Becoming Cuban: Identity, Nationality, and Culture* (Chapel Hill: U of North Carolina P, 1999), 166–74; The Aeromarine Website, https://www.timetableimages.com/ttimages/aerom.htm, accessed November 4, 2019.

29. Pérez Jr., *On Becoming Cuban*, 166–81, 433; James Gould Cousins, *The Son of Perdition* (New York: William Morrow, 1929), 225–26.

30. Estrada, *Havana*, 174–184; Rosa Lowinger and Ofelia Fox, *Tropicana Nights: The Life and Times of the Legendary Cuban Nightclub* (Orlando, FL: Harvest, 2005), 75.

31. Agee, in his notes, appeared to be scribbling impressions of what the Cubans thought of the passengers or what the passengers thought of Havana and the Cubans. But the notes also may represent his own unfiltered thoughts about the passengers as character type, fodder for later works of fiction. The plural pronouns are ambiguous. For example, "Up to this point these people seemed lousy but in an amiable sort of way. Now a sharp and absolute focus, against this city and these people. They are stupid and to be hated." James Agee Collection.

32. James Agee Collection; "Havana Cruise," 301; Jackson Lears, *No Place of Grace:*

Antimodernism and the Transformation of American Culture, 1880–1920 (New York: Pantheon, New York, 1981), 186.

33. James Agee Collection; "Havana Cruise," 301–3.

34. *Fortune* (September 1937), 14, 54–55; Joseph Bonney, "Flashback to 1937: Just Add Zeroes," *American Shipper*, September 1991, 70.

35. "The Passenger Business," *Fortune* (September 1937): 64, 117; "Havana Cruise," *Fortune*, 210.

36. Mellow, *Walker Evans*, 363.

37. *Cotton Tenants: Three Families* and *Brooklyn Is: Southeast of the Island* were written for *Fortune* but rejected, and later published respectively in Davis, ed. *Let Us Now Praise Famous Men*, 565–646, and Ashdown, ed., *Complete Journalism*, 376–94. *Cotton Tenants* evolved into *Let Us Now Praise Famous Men* (1941), which was in progress before and during Agee's work on the cruise story, also a collaboration with Evans. *Brooklyn Is* was written in 1939, but only a single sentence written by Agee was published in the magazine as an epigraph. Agee's concerns in the three pieces are congruent. Richard Oulahan, "A Cult Grew Around a Many-Sided Writer," *Life* 55, no. 18 (November 1, 1963), 69–70, 72; Fitzgerald, "A Memoir," 40–41, 44; Moreau, *Restless Journey*, 157–58; Thomas B. Connery, "Discovering a Literary Form," in *A Sourcebook of Literary Journalism: Representative Writers in an Emerging Genre*, ed. Thomas B. Connery (New York: Greenwood, 1992), 6; Mellow, *Walker Evans*, 360.

38. William Dow, "James Agee's 'Continual Awareness' Untold Stories: 'Saratoga Springs' and 'Havana Cruise'," in *Literary Journalism Across the Globe: Journalistic Traditions and Transnational Influences* (Amherst: U of Massachusetts P, 2001), 230–31; "Havana Cruise," 293–94.

39. Stephen M. Park, *The Pan American Imagination: Contested Visions of the Hemisphere in Twentieth-Century Literature* (Charlottesville: U of Virginia P, 2014), 129–52.

40. *Let Us Now Praise Famous Men*, 38; Park, *The Pan American Imagination*, 154. "Havana Cruise," 301.

41. Josh Roiland, "Literary Journalism in America," annotated syllabus, *Nieman Storyboard*, August 25, 2015, https://niemanstoryboard.org/stories/annotation-tuesday-literary-journalism-in-america/, accessed November 1, 2019.

42. Jack Neely, "Our Man in Havana: James Agee's One Drink at Sloppy Joe's," *The Scruffy Citizen*, March 30, 2016, https://www.knoxmercury.com/2016/03/30/man-havana-james-agees-one-drink-sloppy-joes/, accessed December 22, 2019; Dwight Garner, "Do Not Become Alarmed," *New York Times*, June 6, 2017; Dwight Garner, "Grievous Angel: The Unruly James Agee," *Harper's* (November 1, 2005), 91–96; Stephen Henighan, "Knoxville, Campsites and Cruise Holidays," *Times Literary Supplement*, August 4, 2006.

43. *Letters of James Agee to Father Flye*, 97; *James Agee Rediscovered*, 91–93; "Plans for Work: October 1937," *Collected Short Prose*, 161; *Let Us Now Praise Famous Men*, 867. Jorge is probably Jorge Fernández de Castro, a journalist Evans met in Havana. Madrid fell to General Francisco Franco's forces on March 28, 1939.

44. Robert Coles, *Doing Documentary Work* (New York: Oxford UP, 1997), 53–55.

45. "Havana Cruise," 301; Alan Spiegel, *James Agee and the Legend of Himself* (Columbia: U of Missouri P, 1998), 90–92; Agee to Dwight Macdonald, August 1, 1929, quoted in Bergreen, 66.

46. Baker, *Hemingway*, 295, 320.

47. Thomas Gallagher, *Fire at Sea* (London: Frederick Muller, 1969); Thomas and Witts, *Shipwreck*; Burton, *The Morro Castle*; Hicks, *When the Dancing Stopped*; Gretchen F. Coyle and Deborah C. Whitcraft, *Inferno at Sea: Stories of Death and Survival Aboard the Morro Castle* (West Creek, NJ: Down the Shore Publishing, 2012); McFee, "The Peculiar Fate of the Morrow Castle," 313–38. A passenger and crew list is available at https://www.garemaritime.com/morro-castle-passenger-crew-list/, accessed December 11, 2019.

48. Agee, "Brooklyn Is," *Complete Journalism*, 376.

49. James Agee Collection. MSS 3824, box 7, folder 3 (carbon copy of typescript). Michael Lofaro wrote an introduction to this story and called it to my attention; Rathbone, *Walker Evans*, 240; Hendrickson, *Hemingway's Boat*, 59–68.

50. Peter Neill, ed. *American Sea Writing: A Literary Anthology* (New York: Library of America, 2000), 497–515. The quote is on page 497. David Foster Wallace, "Shipping Out: on the (nearly lethal) comforts of a luxury cruise," *Harper's*, January 1996, 33–56; David Foster Wallace, *A Supposedly Fun Thing I'll Never Do Again* (Boston: Little, Brown, 1997), 261; Garner, "Grievous Angel."

51. Joseph Hergesheimer, "The Casual Ark," *Saturday Evening Post* 206, no. 41 (April 7, 1934): 14–90.

52. "Walker Evans," in Paul Cummings, *Artists in Their Own Words: Conversations with Twelve American Artists*," (New York: St. Martin's Press, 1979), 99; "Captain Oscar L. Seastrom, Captain Seastrom 50 Years a Seaman, *New York Times*, May 11, 1941; "Oscar L. Seastrom, A Mariner for 50 Years," *New York Times*, May 18, 1941; "New York and Cuba Mail Company Hiring Foreign Vessels Exclusively on Route After 65 Years of U.S. Tonnage," *New York Times*, June 1, 1954; "Ward Line Bought By Cuban Company," *New York Times*, June 22, 1956. "New York and Cuba Mail Company Hiring Foreign Vessels Exclusively on Route After 65 Years of U.S. Tonnage, *New York Times*, June 1, 1954; *Ulukau: The Hawaiian Electronic Library Index to the Honolulu Advertiser and Honolulu Star–Bulletin, 1929–1967*, vol.1, chapter 4D, 370–506http://www.ulukau.org/elib/cgi-bin/library?e=d-0ihasb261-000Sec—11en-50-20-frameset-book--1-010escapewin&a=d&d=D0.6&toc=0, accessed December 15, 2019.

53. James R. Hagerty, "Entrepreneur Sold Cruises To Middle-Class America," *Wall Street Journal*, November 16–17, 2019; 2018 Cruise Industry Overview Florida-Caribbean Cruise Association, https://www.f-cca.com/downloads/2018-Cruise-Industry-Overview-and-Statistics.pdf, accessed December 15, 2019; Joseph V. Micallef, "The Cruise Industry's Boom Is Primed To Continue," *Forbes*, September 1, 2018, https://www.forbes.com/sites/joemicallef/2018/09/01/the-cruise-industrys-boom-is-primed-to-continue/#39dc8af02d89, accessed December 15, 2019; "SOS: 'Love Boat' Sails Off to the Junkyard," *Time*, March 10, 2012; "Cruises to Cuba Are Abruptly Canceled, After New Travel Ban," *New York Times*, June 5, 2019; see also Brian J. Cudahy, *The Cruise Ship Phenomenon in North America* (Centreville, MD: Cornell Maritime Press, 2001). Michael Smith and Jonathan Franklin, *Cabin Fever: The Harrowing Journey of a Cruise Ship at the Dawn of a Pandemic* (New York: Knopf Doubleday, 2022).

TEN

A Well-Known Postman

James Agee's Father Before A Death in the Family

PAUL F. BROWN

Sitting in a small village in Panama, more than 1,800 miles from home, Hugh James Agee (1878–1916) was not quite twenty-eight years old in early 1906 when he wrote a letter to a friend back in Knoxville, Tennessee. James, who answered casually to Jim or Jay, had recently left that city after accepting a postmastership in Panama, where he distributed mail and other services to Americans employed on the U.S.-led canal project, still in its infancy. The position was a financial step up for him, but at the loss of comfort and companionship. In his letter, the only extant example of his writing, James included details about the climate and his efforts to protect himself against illness, but he also wrote about the "lonesomeness" of his outpost. He had left his immediate family back in Campbell County, and friends and loved ones, including his fiancée, back in Knoxville. Although he would soon begin new phases of life as a husband and a father, it seemed that a particularly rich period of activity, connection, and advancement in his life had ended. He was lonely in Panama, much more so than he had been five years earlier when he stepped off the train in Knoxville as a newly hired postal employee.

Hugh James Agee is remembered as a literary character through the writings of his famous son, James Rufus Agee. The 1957 novel *A Death in the Family* and, to a greater degree, the 2007 "restoration" of Agee's original manuscript represent the writer's "first 6 years, ending the day of my father's burial."[1] Jay, the father in the novel, is a strong, comforting presence in young Rufus's life. His face is rough and tanned; he wears scratchy clothes and "smell[s] like dry grass, leather and tobacco" (36). He seems comfortable living in a Southern city, more so at times than his refined wife does. Compared with Laura, Jay is the more permissive parent. He laughs heartily at jokes that Laura thinks are inappropriate, and she often

FIGURE 10.1 Hugh James Agee, probably in Panama, circa 1906. *Nashville Tennessean Magazine*, February 8, 1959. Submitted photo.

scolds him for it; when doing something Laura would disapprove of, Jay often takes Rufus into his confidence. Jay is impulsive and adventurous, "full of great energy and a fierce kind of fun, but also a feeling that things might go wrong" (36). He tries hard to master his thirst for alcohol, but imbibes on occasion. His temper and use of profanity erupt in times of frustration, and he is quick to defend himself when he feels wronged. Yet by contrast he is also tender, fond of singing, and he cherishes moments of quiet solitude.

Although the novel provides significant clues about Jay's appearance, personality, and relationships, it is mostly silent about what he does for a living. Aside from passing remarks about Jay working at his father-in-law's "office" (198) or "shop" (142), his occupation is a mystery. Readers know only what his children, Rufus and Emma, see: that on weekdays Jay disappears around a certain street corner on his way to work, and then reappears around the same corner on his return home. But there are hints that Jay would rather work outdoors than in an office; when crossing the river by ferry on his last trip to LaFollette, Jay watches the ferryman work: "Must be a nice job, Jay reflected, as he nearly always did; except of course winter" (172).

The novel divulges more about Jay's previous occupation. During the family's car excursion to visit his great-grandmother, Jay estimates that he "had not been there in nearly thirteen years; the last time was just before he came to Knoxville" (129). Dialogue reveals that he "quit working for the post office a long time back," and that his postal service had included a stint in "Cristobal, Canal Zone, Panamaw [*sic*]" (134). These details are intriguing, but never explained.

Jay's unknown occupation is but one example of the character's anonymity in the novel. Although plenty of scenes show him interacting with his wife, children, and various relatives, he is almost never recognized by anyone outside of his family.[2] Jay knows a few of his closest neighbors on Highland Avenue, and briefly chats with Mr. Tripp and Mr. King on the day Jay drives home his new Ford Model T.[3] But beyond Highland Avenue and members of his own family, he seems to be otherwise unknown in Knoxville. In scenes at Chilhowee Park and the L&N Depot, he encounters no one he knows. He is particularly familiar with downtown establishments that entertain and offer refreshments; however, he moves throughout the city without being recognized as a resident, worker, or business patron. After watching movies at the Majestic Theatre one evening, Jay and Rufus walk past Gay Street storefronts to Market Square, where they enter an unnamed saloon. Jay scans the "country bodies" within the saloon for acquaintances from "the Powell River Valley," but "found, tonight, no one he knew" (148). On their walk home, father and son sit for a moment on a rock in a vacant lot, looking out toward North Knoxville. While they enjoy this time of bonding, it becomes clear that Jay is lonely and not completely settled in Knoxville, and that he longs to be back in the Powell River Valley, north of the city, where he is known. As this scene concludes, so do Jay's experiences in Knoxville—for the next chapter brings a family emergency and a car trip north for Jay, who leaves home in the early morning hours, unaware that he will never see his wife and children again. Miles beyond the city, Jay arrives at the river, which he must cross into his "home country" (175); here he is finally recognized, when the ferry operator sees his face: "Oh, howdy thur. . . . You genally all ways come o'Sundays, yer womurn, couple o' young-uns" (172). But the following evening, Jay dies in an automobile wreck on his journey back to Knoxville. During the funeral scene several chapters later, it is not obvious that the non-family characters named as pallbearers and guests were particularly close to the deceased. Only Arthur Savage—an Englishman who in real life co-owned Ty-Sa-Man Machine Company, where Hugh James Agee worked—seems to have been a genuine friend; and yet he admits to Rufus, "Somehow I never got a chance to know Jay—your father—well as I wish" (328). Readers of *A Death in the Family* may share Arthur's sentiment.

Agee intended the novel as a tribute to his father, and one that would represent him exactly as Agee remembered,[4] which may explain why in the novel Jay is rarely known outside of domestic contexts. Agee was only six when his father died, so while drafting the novel Agee filled in memory gaps by asking relatives for information or by inventing certain conversations and incidents. Perhaps Agee held back information about Jay's occupation so that readers would see his father primarily through Rufus's eyes. But the factuality of much of the novel prompts a closer look at Hugh James Agee and the character he inspired. Was Agee's father as anonymous a citizen as the novel depicts? How well was he truly known in Knoxville, and in which social circles did he move? Until recently, these questions were difficult to answer, as the obscurity of contemporary newspaper accounts about Hugh James Agee prevented a deeper understanding of his years in Knoxville and how he contributed to local society. But newly digitized archives of Knoxville newspapers are now revealing information about his life that otherwise would have been inaccessible.

This essay expands the limited information available about Hugh James Agee, and therefore enriches the biography of his famous son, by shedding light on the question of Jay's anonymity. It challenges the novel's portrayal of Jay as a relatively unknown citizen by focusing on an earlier period in the character's life—before he "quit working for the post office" (134). Jay's previous postal employment is significant, because through it he would have served an important civic role in the community and been acquainted with many of his fellow citizens. With this in view, the essay explores the roughly five years that Hugh James Agee was becoming increasingly known throughout the city as a single man associated with Knoxville's post office: from his civil service exam in May 1900 to his transfer to Panama in late 1905. This essay also considers the social and civic disconnection he experienced after returning to Knoxville as a married man. By the time Rufus was old enough to remember him, Hugh James Agee more closely resembled his later fictional counterpart.

The use of "James Agee" rather than "Jay Agee" throughout this essay may confuse readers. Although Hugh James Agee answered to nicknames among his family and close friends, he invariably used "James Agee" on all official documents, including employment and census records. Contemporary newspaper articles almost always identified him as such; alternatives like "J. Hugh Agee" and "Jim Agee" were rare, while "Jay Agee" did not appear in any article about him until 1962.[5] With surprising frequency, local newspaper writers also misnamed him as

"J. W. Agee" and "J. A. Agee," even once as "Jas. J. Agee"; likewise, Knoxville city directories listed him variously as "James A. Agee" and "James E. Agee." The fact that one of his uncles, pension clerk Jesse E. Agee, and a postal clerk named James J. Ashe worked in the same building surely confused matters, as did frequent visits to Knoxville by another uncle, James W. Agee, then sheriff of Campbell County.[6] To help distinguish father from son, Hugh James Agee is "James" and James Rufus Agee is "Agee" throughout much of the following text.

"My father was from the mountains forty miles upstate from town," Agee wrote in a journal in the late 1930s. "Had at length, through civil service examinations, got out of that country into town in the postal service."[7] His father's family had postal connections in Tennessee going back at least half a century. Clergyman Alfred Agee, a great uncle to James, served as the first postmaster in the Morgan County community of Crooked Fork, where a post office opened in 1850.[8] In Campbell County, the defunct Grantsboro post office was renamed Agee in late 1882, in honor of Dr. James Harris Agee, James's paternal grandfather and brother to Alfred.[9] And in 1898, another uncle, Joseph H. Agee, was appointed postmaster of Jacksboro, seat of Campbell County.[10] Perhaps through Joseph's influence, James learned in the spring of 1900 that Knoxville's post office was hiring new clerks and would soon test applicants for placement. By April 25, he submitted his application to the post office board of examiners, which reserved him a seat for the test date: May 2, 1900.[11] James arrived at Knoxville's Custom House that Wednesday morning, and at 9:00 a.m. in the federal courtroom, on the building's third floor, James and twenty-eight other prospective postal clerks and carriers began the four-hour civil service exam. Candidates were tested on seven skills: "spelling, arithmetic, letter-writing, penmanship, copying from plain copy, geography of the United States and reading addresses." Completed tests were sent to Washington, DC, later that day for processing, and James returned to LaFollette.[12] He was there awaiting news of his score on June 20, the day a federal census taker visited Henry C. Agee's seven-member household and recorded James's occupation as "teaching school."[13] Five days later, the civil service exam results were announced. With scores ranging from 90.88 to 71.15, James's score of 83.83 fell above the average. But three individuals performed better than he did on the exam, and were therefore placed higher on the list of eligible applicants. And at the moment, the post office had few openings.[14] So James again bided his time in LaFollette.

On May 7, 1901, the *Knoxville Sentinel* announced: "J. Hugh Agee, of Campbell county, is in the city on business."[15] Whether or not this business related to the

FIGURE 10.2 Postal clerks, carriers, and supervisors posed outside Knoxville's Custom House, circa 1910s. "Knoxville Postmen," 200-071-006, Knox County Two Centuries Photograph Project, McClung Historical Collection, Knox County Library.

post office, by the end of June Knoxville's postmaster, W. L. Trent, was looking to fill a vacancy, and recommended James as "a substitute clerk" because "he is next on the eligible list."[16] Trent telephoned James on July 1, fourteen months after the civil service exam, to offer him the general utility clerk job. James accepted and "at once went to work."[17] His new job began midway through what historian Winifred Gallagher has called the "glory days" of the U.S. postal service: the period from 1880 to 1920, during which the agency exercised its greatest influence over "America's public and private life."[18] As in any city or town, Knoxville's post office was its communication hub, sending and receiving information by railway, on the shoulders of mail carriers, and in wagons assigned to the new and expanding Rural Free Delivery service.

After a few weeks in the position, James was asked to cover the general delivery clerk's duties while she was on vacation.[19] This shuffling of employees was normal practice, but becoming more frequent. By February 1902, the volume of regular incoming mail had swamped the staff, requiring clerks to work well past their eight-hour shifts—some up to twelve hours.[20] And illness-related leave compounded the need for additional help. On March 1, the *Journal and Tribune* reported that three postmen, including James, were absent due to illness, though "Mr. Agee is not ill but was called to his home in LaFollette on account of the illness of relatives."[21] Local newspapers never named those ailing relatives; but a year and nine months later, they would report James's own illness, and the LaFollette relative who traveled to Knoxville on his account.

Meanwhile, both the *Journal and Tribune* and the *Sentinel* were carrying daily updates on the South Carolina Inter-State and West Indian Exposition, which had opened the previous December in Charleston. News of special exposition events like "Tennessee Day" in March and President Theodore Roosevelt's visit in April kept interest high in Knoxville, and excursion trains to Charleston departed twice every day—at 1:50 a.m. and 8:25 a.m.—from the old Southern Station (the company's new passenger depot was then under construction).[22] James Agee and two other postmen, Eli Skaggs and Thomas Shipley, were among the several hundred Knoxvillians who traveled there for the May 16 "Knoxville Day" celebration. Although several factors, including bad weather and lack of sponsorship, would ultimately stymie the six-and-a-half-month exposition, journalists deemed "Knoxville Day" a success. Many Knoxvillians explored the grounds that day while proudly wearing white ribbons bearing the name of their city. It is not known whether James spent the entire trip in the company of Skaggs and Shipley, but when the three returned to work on May 20, they reported having "a great time" on the excursion.[23]

Just under a month later, the *Sentinel* announced that "the clerks in the post-office have caught the fever and organized a baseball team, which they say has much promise in it. . . . This team will be ready in a short time to cross bats with any of the local teams, barring [Frank] Moffett's Indians"—an amateur team that many Knoxvillians considered the region's best. Chosen by substitute mail carrier Ed Doyle, the team roster included James Agee at right field.[24] James had taught baseball to his youngest brother, John—who was now fifteen but gaining "quite a reputation on town lots in LaFollette" as a "southpaw," and would be "touted as a wonder" even before pitching for the University of Tennessee under coach Frank Moffett in 1908.[25] But Doyle's team of postmen apparently played few, if any, games in 1902, as the newspapers carried no further mention of it that year. (Doyle led another post office team in 1903, but with a different lineup.)[26]

Whether James had developed camaraderie with his coworkers or not, he would find social opportunities elsewhere in the city.

In July, he marked one year at the post office and received his first salary increase, from $600 to $700 per year.[27] He had been renting a room at 513 Oxford Place, a boarding house run by widow Stella Shetterly. Once considered "one of the largest, if not the star boarding house of Knoxville," it inspired a dramatic headline in July 1895 when six tenants became "violently ill" with symptoms that suggested poisoning; however, all individuals recovered from what was probably a foodborne illness.[28] The house sat two doors west of the James S. Hall home, where around 1870 a young, burgeoning female writer briefly roomed with the Andrew Campbell family; her later children's novels, including *Little Lord Fauntleroy* and *The Secret Garden*, brought Frances Hodgson Burnett worldwide fame.[29] The same year that James resided on Oxford Place, another future literary father lived three blocks to the south on Church Avenue. Cornelius Coffin Williams carried a locally prestigious surname but none of the family's former wealth; in 1902, he worked as an assistant manager for the East Tennessee Telephone Company. One wonders how often he crossed paths with James, one year his senior, in the few years before Williams left to join a St. Louis shoe company. His later alcoholism, and the family havoc it wreaked, would inspire a corpus of Southern Gothic fiction in the writings of his own famous son, Thomas "Tennessee" Williams.[30]

Before Knoxville collected addresses for its 1903 city directory, James moved about a block east to 407 Wall Avenue, the McCoy Building, where he rented room eighteen. The address put James close to Market Square, to the visiting farmers who regularly sold produce there from wagons outside the market house—a scene reflected in *A Death in the Family*. And in those years before Knoxville turned dry, the McCoy Building was well situated for tenants needing an occasional drink: four of Knoxville's sixty-seven saloons in 1903 operated on Market Square's west side. Still, it was not the Bowery district on South Central, and James likely had personal betterment and fraternal association in mind, not his thirst, when he chose that location. The building's owner, John McCoy, had arrived in Knoxville during the Civil War, operated a general store on Gay Street, gained an education under the Reverend James Park, worked as a clerk for Peter Kern, and more recently served two of his three terms as a city alderman. He was also a past master and current member of Master's Lodge No. 244, a masonic fraternity that assembled every third Monday of the month at the nearby Borches Building.[31]

James had no immediate connections to Masonry back in LaFollette; neither his father nor his late paternal grandfather had ever joined, and his brother Frank would not become a member until 1911.[32] Perhaps James learned of McCoy's association with Master's Lodge and spoke with the esteemed mason about it. He may have already known that Millard Kitts and Robert Loftis, who both worked at the Custom House, were also lodge members.[33] Whatever the case, James absorbed enough about the lodge's obligations and benefits that he eventually petitioned for membership. Among the qualifications to be a mason, one had to believe in God, even if religiously unaffiliated, and avoid excess, whether drink or otherwise. Lodge representatives interviewed James and investigated his background, and judged him to be qualified physically, morally, and spiritually. Voting by secret ballot, the lodge's almost three hundred members unanimously approved him as a degree candidate, and the date of his degree ceremony was set.[34] Even if James's clerical position had not put him into close, daily contact with hundreds of Knoxvillians, he likely would have recognized the names of many members, including James S. Hall Jr., his former Oxford Place neighbor who co-owned J. S. Hall & Sons, a men's clothing and furnishings store; John W. Hope, co-owner of Hope Brothers Jewelers; Peter Kern, the confectioner, baker, and former Knoxville mayor; Gustavus R. Knabe, who taught and conducted music in Knoxville years after performing in Leipzig, Germany, under Felix Mendelssohn; and J. C. Sterchi, co-owner of Sterchi Brothers Furniture Company, the Gay Street business later referred to in *A Death in the Family* as "Sterchi's"—which young Rufus correctly pronounces "Sturkeys" (147).[35] Despite his comparative lack of prominence, James would come to learn that "Masonry regards no man on account of his worldly wealth or honors," that once he became a mason, he would be both an equal and a brother to these men.[36]

The degree ceremony began on November 24 with James being blindfolded and led by cable-tow into the lodge room, where the Worshipful Master directed him through the various steps of the first-degree ritual: praying, walking in circles, kneeling before the altar, taking a vow of obligation, receiving the degree's lambskin apron and working tools, and hearing the lecture and its emphasis on "the four cardinal virtues of Temperance, Fortitude, Prudence and Justice." After the charge to fulfill his duties as a mason, James's blindfold was lifted; he had become an Entered Apprentice Mason. For weeks he studied masonic texts, read about Masonry's symbols (including its forms, vestures, tools, and Three Great Lights) and patron saints (Saint John the Baptist and Saint John the Evangelist), and memorized the catechisms that led him toward advancement as a mason. He would earn his Fellow Craft Mason degree on December 23, and his Master Mason degree on February 18, 1903.[37]

On New Year's Day, 1903, James received a raise and a promotion to mailing clerk.[38] Postal staff worked only until noon that day. Reports were coming in that December had been a record month for Knoxville's post office, with more revenue collected than in any previous month.[39] But as the volume of mail increased, so did the workers' shifts, and Postmaster Trent recognized the need for additional clerks and carriers. He also noted that with various government agencies and the university all sending postage-free mail from Knoxville, the local post office "is doing a very large business but the revenue is below the offices of cities of the same class." The U.S. pension office alone "sends out more than a million" pieces of mail each year, Trent said.[40]

The overworked staff was also at the mercy of Southern Railroad, which chronically ran late. Southern's new, elaborate passenger station was set to open along Depot Street on February 2, and would eventually be the departure point for Knoxville's first rail excursions into the Smoky Mountains. More than a decade down the road, James and his wife and children would leave from the Southern Station en route to the Wonderland Hotel in the resort town of Elkmont—though, as fictionalized in *A Death in the Family*, the family preferred the Louisville & Nashville Station "because there were so many country folks" there (100).[41] But for now James and the other clerks often found themselves sitting around for hours awaiting Southern's mail delivery, as on January 10, when not one of the company's trains arrived on time. The *Journal and Tribune* reported: "All schedules were annulled and the trains ran as they could, while the mails went to the dogs and the clerks loafed, for there was nothing to do until late. Then the clerical force had to work overtime to catch up with the time they had been forced to [lose] by the Southern."[42] It was even worse on the evening of January 26, with one westbound train pulling into the station "five hours late, not arriving here until after 7 o'clock. . . . The clerks of the local office are 'kicking' strenuously against the irregular schedule or lack of schedule which the Southern is now operating under." According to the *Journal and Tribune*, this latest delay marked Southern's "twenty-sixth time this month."[43]

Things had not improved by mid-February, when the overworked clerks faced about eight thousand holiday packages as well as a power outage. "Just as the pension office's mail closed for the quarter, St. Valentine came in with a rush that lasted for about two days and a half, and just as that increased quantity of mail is gotten out of the way the electric lights go out," read a *Journal and Tribune* article. "For about three hours yesterday afternoon, with the skies cloudy on the outside, and the interior barred and arranged so as to make it almost dark, even if the sun had been shining, the force of clerks had to work the incoming and outgoing mails without lights. About 4 o'clock, however, the incandescents again got in their work."[44]

In addition to overwork, train delays, and electrical troubles, the thirty-year-old post office was cramped. Even prior to the new century, Knoxvillians agreed that the Custom House—which held the post office, federal court, and other government offices—was terribly undersized considering the population increase since the building's construction. Proposed solutions, from adding onto the current building to erecting a new post office on a nearby lot, had circulated for more than a year before the issue finally reached the U.S. Senate.[45] The postmaster general, secretary of the treasury, and the government board produced their own assessment of the building's deficiencies, and in February forwarded their findings to the Senate president:

> The court house and postoffice at Knoxville, Tenn., is a three-story, basement and attic building, constructed of East Tennessee marble, and fireproof throughout except the roof.
>
> The postoffice is located on the first or principal floor, and of this there is an available working space of 3,960 square feet. This working space is entirely inadequate for the transaction of the postal business, and each branch of the postoffice is so crowded that there is scarcely space for the employees to move about between the furniture and fixtures. This condition may seem not unreasonable when it is considered that the population of the city has increased to 32,637, according to the last census, from about 9,000 when the building was completed, in 1874, and this is still further increased to about 55,000 by the adjacent towns included within the free delivery from this postoffice.[46]

This report and its recommendations must have raised hopes, especially for James and the other workers packed into those dreary office spaces, that conditions would improve. It was eventually decided to expand the Custom House eastward toward Gay Street. However, this project stalled in the planning phase and would not be completed until 1909, the year of James Rufus Agee's birth.[47]

A few employee complaints were soothed in March with Trent's announcement that two clerks would be added to the local force, and news from Washington that in July postal salaries would increase by $100.[48] But Trent had complaints of his own. On March 26, the morning Chattanooga mail train arrived late, and when the mailbags were finally brought to the post office, only one clerk was there to receive them. "All but one of [the] distributing force went to dinner at 11:30 a.m. and the mail was more than one man could attend to," a *Sentinel* reporter wrote, without naming the lone clerk. "The postmaster [later] told them that evidently some clerks cared more for their boarding house keepers than they did for the interest of the postoffice and the public. . . . He promised that if the delay occurred again there might be a long wait for dinner hereafter."[49] On the other hand, Chief Clerk John Kidd, in a *Journal and Tribune* interview, responded to complaints of slow service by requesting more patience from the public. He described the daily challenge of distributing the mail on time:

> The public will not give us time to do it before it begins to kick. When a mail comes in we put all the clerks that can work at it without being in each other's way to the distribution, and we have some of the best box clerks in the country. Still there is some dissatisfaction all the time.
>
> It takes forty-five minutes, the very best we can do, to put up the Louisville and Cincinnati mails which come in here at 8:15. It takes about thirty minutes to get the mail into the office after the train pulls in. The Chattanooga mail gets to Knoxville by 9:15 and it takes a half hour to get it here. Then we get through with it in twenty minutes. It takes in the neighborhood of an hour or more in some cases, to get the mail distributed after the train arrives. If the patrons of the office would only bear this in mind it would save them considerable worry and criticism.[50]

The post office, perhaps to boost public confidence, agreed in April to test the mail delivery potential of a new machine: a two-seat automobile built in part by Cowan Rodgers of Rodgers & Company, a bicycle and Oldsmobile dealer at the corner of Vine Avenue and Gay Street.[51] The auto would haul a mail load twenty-six miles from Knoxville to Sevierville—trailed by a regular horse-drawn wagon in case of a breakdown. (Delayed until August, the experiment successfully transported mail by auto "from the custom house in [Knoxville] to the post office at Sevierville in two hours and twenty minutes.")[52] But despite this positive press, one incident in April cast a dark shadow over Knoxville's post office for the rest of 1903.

On April 25, just over a week after James turned twenty-five, he and six other clerks were working the evening shift when, around 8:00, a bag of registered mail

FIGURE 10.3 Post office loading dock, at left, on the east side of the Custom House, late 1800s. A later addition to the building, completed in 1909, would take up much of this open area. "Post Office & Custom House, Knoxville, TN," N-0591, Thompson Photograph Collection, McClung Historical Collection, Knox County Library.

went missing. The bag contained letters and "a number of checks" estimated at "more than $500 in value."[53] When it was later found in the building's basement "with a hole cut in its side and the contents gone," police concluded that the crime must have been committed by one of the postal workers on duty that night.[54] James was one of several clerks who, under interrogation, told investigators they had witnessed a coworker leaving his post without permission that night and returning a short time later. Inspectors felt they had enough circumstantial evidence to arrest mailing clerk Andrew P. Russell, a nine-year employee whose reputation was "spotless."[55]

With no hard evidence against him, and a defense team that included popular attorney and multiple-term mayor Samuel G. Heiskell, Russell was acquitted in a preliminary hearing on April 29.[56] But investigators, lacking another suspect, continued questioning James and the other clerks. Almost three months had passed since the theft, and Russell remained the most likely culprit. Postmaster Trent fired him in July and filled the position by shuffling employees, including James, who was promoted to general delivery clerk.[57] In September, about a week after a grand jury indicted Russell, James operated a temporary post office branch inside the First Methodist Church at Clinch and Locust during the six-day Holston Conference of the Methodist Episcopal Church.[58]

When Russell's criminal trial convened in the federal courtroom on November 5, the prosecution named James Agee as one of forty-five government witnesses, and called him to testify the following day about Russell leaving the post office the night of the theft. The *Sentinel* summarized James's testimony as follows: "The tried witness called was J. W. [*sic*] Agee, a clerk in the postoffice. He told of the defendant, Russell, leaving the postoffice on the Monday evening following the theft, and that Mr. Russell told him that he would step out a few minutes. He said Mr. Russell returned in fifteen or twenty minutes and said he had failed to get his brother whom he wanted to talk to about some cattle. He said Mr. Russell was perspiring as he came in."[59] The *Journal and Tribune*'s account differed slightly: "The examination of witnesses was resumed yesterday with the introduction of James Agee by the prosecution. He testified that on the Monday night when an investigation was being made by the postoffice inspectors, Russell went out and as he went told him that he would be back in a few minutes. He said that Russell was out 15 or 20 minutes and that when he returned he was perspiring. On cross examination he said that it would take very rapid walking for one to go to Highland avenue and back in twenty minutes." During that interval, Russell had supposedly returned to his room at "John Cox's residence on Highland" to retrieve a pair of opera glasses.[60] James was familiar enough with that neighborhood in 1903 to know roughly how long it took to walk there from downtown; nine years later, he would move to that street with his wife and two young children after purchasing the former boarding house—1505 Highland Avenue—where Russell had lived.[61]

But James's testimony did little to bolster the prosecution's case. After two days of testimony and arguments, the jury deadlocked and the judge declared a mistrial.[62] A second jury found Russell not guilty the following March. Though vindicated, Russell still felt stung by the accusation and "the fight which was made on me by the people connected with the postoffice."[63] Whether Russell held a personal grudge against James and the other clerks who testified or not, the case took a toll on everyone involved and left the mail department "in a demoralized state" for almost a year.[64]

Fall 1903 had been a particularly taxing season for James. The day in November before he testified in court, someone broke into his apartment at the "McCoy building, and stole his overcoat." James reported the theft to police headquarters on Market Square.[65] But the incident was trivial compared with what hit him three weeks later. James became ill the night of November 29, and missed work the next day. The *Sentinel* reported on December 1 that he was still off work, and that he was "seriously sick at his room in the McCoy building" and would "be sent to his home at LaFollette as soon as he is able."[66] Three days later, James was "slightly improved, and can now sit up a short time each day. He is not yet able to go to his home in LaFollette, which he intends to do as soon as he recovers sufficiently."[67] But James remained in too much discomfort to travel, and instead "summoned" his father, Henry, to Knoxville. The *Sentinel* announced on December 7 that Mr. Agee had arrived at "the bedside of his son . . . who has been ill for several days . . . [and] is now slightly improved."[68] Sometime during Henry's few days in town, a local journalist asked him about Campbell County's "congressional race," knowing Henry's strong Republican ties in LaFollette. Henry opined that Richard W. Austin and James F. Baker were the strongest candidates, but favored Austin, an attorney and U.S. marshal at Knoxville's Custom House. "He is considered as the ablest man for the place and the only man who would stay out of combine and scheme that pervert the interests and will of the people," Henry stated. "We feel that if he should go to congress that we would have a man there who would do something."[69]

James had been ill for almost two weeks when, on December 12, the *Journal and Tribune* published the first clue about his ailment. "James Agee has kidney trouble and is no better," the article stated, though James's specific diagnosis—whether kidney stones, a urinary tract infection, or something more serious—remained undisclosed.[70] Concerned masonic brothers at Master's Lodge sent the *Journal and Tribune* a brief update that ran on December 13: "Brother Agee is quite sick at his apartments in the McCoy building."[71]

As Christmas neared, the *Sentinel* also printed letters that children from Knoxville and surrounding towns had written to Santa. One arrived from a girl in Campbell County who knew she could count on her brother "Jim" to deliver a holiday package:

> LaFollette, Tenn.,
> Dec. 10, 1903.
> Dear Old Santa Claus:
> I am a little girl ten years old and I live in LaFollette. Bring me whatever a little gerl my age desires.
> Your little friend,
> MOSSIE AGEE.
> P S If you cant bring it you can send it by my brother "Jim"[.] You neednt bring John or Paralee anything they are too big.[72]

During the first half of the month, Mossie and siblings Frank, John, and Paralee likely wondered whether they would see their eldest brother for Christmas. But as the latter part of December brought no further reports of his illness, James evidently recovered in time to spend the holiday in LaFollette. He still counted himself among the citizens of that company town, home of the LaFollette Coal, Iron and Railway Company and its expanding network of mines, coke ovens, and rail lines. Campbell County's industry and geography centered there, but its government headquartered in Jacksboro. James had traveled to the courthouse back in March and voted on a referendum to move the county seat, but the issue remained unsettled in May 1904, when James relayed the devastating news that LaFollette's business district had turned to ash.[73]

The fire was said to have started at five in the morning, May 10, inside the oil room of the Cumberland Inn, the town's main hotel and the site of a deadly shoot-out the previous summer. The flames quickly spread through the building, one of only three brick structures in LaFollette—which had no fire department.

By the time the blaze was extinguished, three hours later, thirty-five buildings had been destroyed or damaged.[74] Back in Knoxville, the *Sentinel* consulted James for its front-page story about the disaster:

> James Agee, of the postoffice, a member of the clerical force, lived at LaFollette before he went to work in the Knoxville postoffice, and he has relatives who are in business in the town. . . .
>
> [He] telephoned to LaFollette early this morning for the latest information in regard to the fire. The information which he received was that the fire started in the Cumberland inn, and then spread to buildings on Tennessee avenue. The entire business section was swept on both sides of the street. Mr. Agee states that the property owners of LaFollette, especially in the present fire district, offered the fire insurance writers 8 per cent to write their property. This offer was refused, the companies claiming the risk was too great owing to a lack of fire apparatus and the congestion of the houses as to location.[75]

James, already an important component in Knoxville's postal communication system, was here being cited as a source for a major news story, which newspapers from Wisconsin to Florida capsulized over subsequent days. Here also James received tragic information from LaFollette via telephone, as Jay does in *A Death in the Family* when his brother Frank calls about their father's illness.[76] Several years after the fire, Frank Agee would establish a durable mortuary and furniture business, Agee & Carden, in this rebuilt section of downtown LaFollette. (He would also serve as the town's postmaster from 1922 to 1933.) When LaFollette was later named in *A Death in the Family*, many citizens spurned the novel and its author for fictionalizing Frank Agee as the alcoholic mortician (renamed Ralph Follet in the novel's original publication), and for associating such an unsavory character with their hometown.[77]

By the summer of 1904, James had moved about five blocks south from the McCoy Building to a room at 810 ½ South Gay Street. Located above the Knoxville Traction Company's streetcar shed, it must have ranked among the city's noisiest apartments.[78] But James's new address also placed him within a few doors of Knoxville's premier entertainment venue. Staub's Theatre booked its share of relatively anonymous touring vaudeville and minstrel acts, and its auditorium hosted school graduations and civic events as well, but it occasionally drew some of the country's finest actors to the city. The year James relocated to that block, Ethel Barrymore graced the stage in *Cousin Kate*, and Maude Adams also starred there in J. M. Barrie's *The Little Minister*. (Adams would be remembered for originating an iconic role on Broadway the following year, as the lead in Barrie's *Peter Pan*.)[79]

Elsewhere in the city a striking, twenty-year-old woman, whose life would soon intersect with James's, was treading the boards as an amateur thespian. Laura Tyler's family had moved to Knoxville from Michigan when she was seven. Educated in the city schools, she later joined the Chi Omega sorority while attending the University of Tennessee. By 1904, she was no longer a student, having withdrawn partway through her junior year, but she found other involvements in the city that year.[80] On May 24, as a member of the Girls' Friendly Society at St. John's Episcopal Church, Laura performed in a one-act farce, *A Precious Pickle*, by George M. Baker. Her role in the play is not known, but the scenario places three vacationing city girls in the rural household of Mrs. Gabble and her daughter.[81] A few weeks later, Laura took part in a "leap year cotillion" on June 13 at Chilhowee Park along with other "members of the younger set."[82] And the University Drama Club invited her back to campus to act in another theater production, Arthur W. Pinero's four-act comedy *Trelawny of the "Wells."* Laura was cast as Miss Trafalgar Gower, one of the "non-theatrical" characters in the play; Miss Gower is the sister of Sir William Gower and described as "a spare, prim lady, of gentle manners, verging upon sixty." The July 19 performance was held on campus at Jefferson Hall.[83] Little else is known of her activities in 1904. But scholar Alfred Barson may be correct that this was the year Laura Tyler met postal clerk James Agee.[84]

After A. P. Russell's acquittal in March, the post office was enjoying a respite from major news coverage. The newspapers carried few updates about James that year, aside from him relaying information about LaFollette's devastating fire, filling in for a co-worker at the general delivery window in mid-September, and then taking vacation leave. He was earning an annual salary of $900. Presumably, he still attended monthly meetings at Master's Lodge every third Monday.[85]

Perhaps tired of living above the streetcar barn, in 1905 James relocated again and found a room at the imposing, five-story Vendome Apartments at 417 West Clinch. Opened as a hotel in 1890 with a French café on the top floor, the Vendome afforded the street "an air of metropolitan significance." From its "pressed brick" and "Kentucky sandstone" exterior to the "rich gleam of polished mahogany" and "brown and white inlaid" tiles of its long foyer, the building had lost little of its original elegance.[86] Aesthetics aside, for James it was a very convenient place to live, just one block west of the Custom House, and only five blocks from L&N's new passenger station at Asylum and Broadway.

FIGURE 10.4 Laura Whitman Tyler, about age nineteen, as a member of the Chi Omega sorority, University of Tennessee. *Volunteer*, 1903, UT Libraries Digital Collections.

Despite his upscale apartment, James nevertheless lived in a city that, on occasion, seemed more like the Wild West than a modern metropolis. He was, after all, a Knoxville resident in December 1901 when train robber Harvey "Kid Curry" Logan shot two men in a Central Street saloon, and in June 1903 when Logan escaped from Knox County's jail and fled across the Gay Street Bridge.[87] Thus far, James had personally been the victim of only one minor crime in Knoxville: the theft of his overcoat at the McCoy Building. But on the brisk evening of March 15, 1905, he was walking through L&N's rail yard below Clinch Avenue—perhaps after departing the train from LaFollette, or just taking a shortcut home—when "an unknown man stepped from behind a telegraph pole and pointed a pistol in his face." Escaped convict Ernest Miner, who had been sent to Brushy Mountain Penitentiary last spring for holding up C. M. McClung's store, demanded James's belongings, which amounted to a scarf, a knife, and $1.50. After handing over the items, James "thanked the footpad for letting him go at this"—a somewhat unexpected reaction considering that Jay, his fictional counterpart in *A Death in the Family*, proves himself to be both quick-tempered and unafraid of physical confrontation, as when arguing with a man at Chilhowee Park: "Just watch out who you try to boss around, next time" (99). Whether or not Agee could have imagined his father thanking a man who had just robbed him, Miner's pointed gun was the key difference. That night the convict also mugged attorney Clarence Barber near St. John's Episcopal, getting away with $9, and attempted to rob a man on Church Street and hold up a Wall Avenue saloon. Miner evaded police until the following night, when they caught him in the alley behind Peter Kern's establishment with stolen items on him, including James's knife and scarf.[88] Two months later, the circuit court sentenced Miner to twelve years in addition to time not yet served on his previous conviction, and sent him back to Brushy Mountain's prison mines in Morgan County.[89]

James, now a paper distributor at the post office, vacationed in early April and missed workdays the following month due to illness. In June, his salary increased from $900 to $1,000.[90] The extra income proved especially useful as James began to see Laura Tyler more frequently. They had met each other at a dancing class in the city, and by the summer of 1905 were attending events hosted by the Twentieth Century German Club. On the evening of July 24, Laura accompanied James to the Neubert Springs Hotel, a resort about eight miles from town that was known for its mineral spring water. The club sponsored an "open air dance" there after supper, with music provided by William Crouch's orchestra.[91] The club held its "initial fall dance" on September 19 at the Woman's Building, across Main Street from Knoxville's courthouse. Many of the same individuals, including James, were there, but Laura was not listed among that night's participants. It now seems probable that James joined the Twentieth Century Club by way of fellow Master's Lodge member James Hall Jr., who had been with the group at least three years and was skilled at leading "the figures of the German."[92]

That fall, Laura and James talked of marrying. An obscure reference in *A Death in the Family* suggests that Laura's parents asked her not to marry Jay but that she "resisted" their request (222). This agrees with a later anecdote, perhaps from Laura herself, that Joel and Emma Tyler initially frowned on the relationship and judged James's "situation" to be "too unstable."[93] If in fact they objected to the engagement, it seems unlikely that James's occupation was the issue. He had a respectable government job and was making better money and connections in Knoxville than he might have back in LaFollette. Perhaps the Tylers sensed in James a tendency to vacillate between two spheres. His Campbell County connections were very strong; and after experiencing crowded workspaces, a criminal trial, serious illness, and armed robbery in Knoxville, it would seem natural for James to desire

FIGURE 10.5 Clinch Avenue, looking west toward the Custom House (lower left), the turreted Vendome Apartments (upper right), and the viaduct spanning L&N's rail yard. Laura Tyler's family lived at 1115 West Clinch, about two blocks beyond the viaduct. In this detail of a circa 1915 photograph by Laura's brother, Hugh Tyler, street traffic includes at least one horse (bottom right). "Clinch Avenue View, Knoxville, TN," Tyler Album 057, Hugh Tyler Collection, McClung Historical Collection, Knox County Library.

a simpler, more rural life. As Jay does in the novel, James may have experienced occasional pangs of homesickness and, finding a quiet corner of the city, passed minutes gazing northward toward his ancestral home.[94] On October 31, 1905, he purchased the old Henry Myers homestead, a hundred-acre farm at the foot of Cumberland Mountain, in Campbell County's Powell River Valley.[95] If any indication of how James had voted in the county seat referendum two years earlier, his farm sat half the distance to downtown Jacksboro as it did to downtown LaFollette. The acquisition appeared to be part of a long-term plan to leave Knoxville and settle in his native county, where his family and civic ties were strongest.

But he knew well enough that farming was a gamble, and that he needed a larger cash cushion—more than his parents had had—to make it work. So when James heard about a potentially lucrative opportunity, he adapted his plan to include a short-term job transfer to a foreign country. It is not known when he applied, but his acceptance came much sooner than expected, and put his marriage to Laura on hold. He visited LaFollette relatives around Thanksgiving, carrying important news that the *Sentinel* would sum up in a November 27 headline: "James Agee Will Go to Panama Mail Service." (The article's writer called him "one of the best known of the clerks at the postoffice."[96]) To James, the opportunity made perfect financial sense: he would operate a small post office for American contractors on the Panama Canal project, and earn more than $1,500 per year. He knew that living in Panama would be a new experience; but considering the heat, torrential rain, and diseases there, he may have worried that it could be a miserable one—especially for Laura, should she later join him there. So he accepted the overseas position on a trial basis, with Postmaster Trent's assurance that if James bailed out of Panama, his old job would be waiting for him in Knoxville. The *Sentinel* revealed this agreement in early December, about two days into James's ocean voyage from New York to Panama: "[James Agee] has not resigned as a clerk in [Knoxville's] office and will not do so until after he has reached Colon and investigated the character of the work that he will do and the climate."[97]

In mid-February, a twenty-year-old Knoxville man received a much-anticipated letter. Affixed to the envelope was a monochrome Panama stamp overprinted in black with "CANAL ZONE."[98] Until recently, George J. Tauxe had been a special delivery carrier at the post office, and had become acquainted with James as his own duties took him in and out of the clerks' offices.[99] Before leaving

Knoxville, James assured Tauxe that he would write to him from Panama. This excerpt, preserved only because the *Sentinel* published the letter "in part" shortly after Tauxe received it, is the only example of Hugh James Agee's writing known to exist:

> Dear George: You are thinking, I guess, that I've forgotten that I promised to write you, telling you something of conditions down here, but I've delayed principally because I wanted to be here long enough to know something before I wrote.
>
> The worst thing about the whole business that I have been up against is the "cussed" lonesomeness of the place. So far as the sickness and the heat are concerned, I've suffered from neither so far. Malaria is the greatest drawback in the way of diseases. It doesn't kill very many, but fully half, I should think, of the employes [*sic*] of the commission have had it in a form severe enough to lay them off from work. I, as yet, haven't felt any symptoms of it. I take quinine regularly—from six to twelve grains per day. There has been only one case of yellow fever here since I came down.
>
> The wind blows all the time strong enough to keep one cool in the shade during the day and the nights are cool enough to require the use of a blanket. Everything in the way of furniture is furnished free with the quarters. All you have to get is sheets, blankets and pillow cases for the bed. Oil is also furnished for the lamps. Washing is about the same as in the states. Board costs 30 cents per meal. Your friend,
>
> JAMES AGEE,
> Corozal,
> Isthmus of Panama.
> Canal Zone.[100]

The letter's abrupt conclusion suggests that the newspaper editor cut material of a more personal nature from the end. While one can only guess how well James knew Tauxe (who would relocate to Los Angeles by late 1913), James's informal closing is evidence that he had developed at least one friendship in Knoxville.[101]

From December 1905 to November 1908, James worked as postmaster in the village of Corozal, "one of the most American of the many new towns that have sprung up along the Mosquito gulf."[102] Laura lived with him there for two years, beginning June 20, 1906—the day James watched her steamship dock in Cristobal and then took Laura to be his wife.[103] This period in the couple's life is reflected in *A Death in the Family*, when Jay's Aunt Paralee remembers mailing him a postcard, addressed to "'Post Office, Cristobal, Canal Zone, Panamaw'" (134).[104] When the couple left the isthmus for good, "tired of life in the tropics," James returned home only to face malarial infection and job instability. Laura became pregnant, and divided her time between Campbell County—where James farmed his property near Jacksboro with slim hope of making a living—and her parents' home in Knoxville.[105] Fatherhood rapidly approached, and in desperation James asked then-Congressman Richard Austin, whom he knew from his years at the Custom House, for assistance getting rehired in Panama. On November 13, 1909, exactly one year after James ended his overseas employment, the *Journal and Tribune* announced that he "will accept" the reappointment and "leave for his new duties very soon." However, he never returned to the Canal Zone, and instead took a temporary job in Knoxville's post office. Perhaps the approval for reappointment had come too late, for James chose to remain with Laura in the city for a most important delivery: a son, James Rufus, born November 27.[106]

In a few years, Hugh James Agee would find work as a bookkeeper for his father-in-law's company, Ty-Sa-Man, see the birth of a daughter, Emma Farrand, and settle the family on Highland Avenue. He seemed resigned to city life, and in 1913 deeded most of his Campbell County farmland to his father, who had lived on the property longer than James had.[107] For whatever reason—whether him being a private sector employee, a West Knoxville suburbanite, or a father of two—James's social and civic presence in Knoxville shrank. He no longer worked in the heart of the city, no longer spoke to hundreds of Knoxvillians each week as a window clerk. By the time Rufus was old enough to form memories of him, James lacked many of the associations that, a decade earlier, had marked his first years in the city. He eventually stopped attending masonic meetings, and Master's Lodge suspended his membership in December 1914 for "nonpayment of dues."[108] His name seldom appeared in the local newspapers after his son was born; the handful of times it did appear, it mostly referenced "Mrs. James Agee" or the family's changes of address. Then on May 19, 1916, the *Journal and Tribune* and *Sentinel* carried his name in two devastating headlines: "James Agee, of This City, Pinned Under Automobile"—"Accident Fatal for James Agee." James, in a reversed role from his own serious illness thirteen years earlier, had visited his ailing father's bedside in LaFollette, but then wrecked while driving back to Knoxville on the night of May 18. Both articles noted that the thirty-eight-year-old victim left a wife and two children behind, and that he was "well known" in Knoxville.[109] A marble slab chiseled with "JAMES AGEE" marks his Greenwood Cemetery gravesite.

James's sudden death influenced the course of young Rufus's education, which in turn included Highland Avenue School, then St. Andrew's School for

FIGURE 10.6 Emma Farrand Agee and James Rufus Agee, photographed at the Knaffl & Brakebill studio in Knoxville, circa 1915. QSPC 2020.005, McClung Historical Collection, Knox County Library.

Mountain Boys in Middle Tennessee, Knoxville High School, Phillips Exeter Academy in New Hampshire, and finally Harvard University. One of James Rufus Agee's first and strongest literary impulses was to write about his father's death and how it affected the family. Themes of death and family loss infused his earliest published fiction (as in his short story "The Circle") and poetry (as in "Ebb Tide" and "Widow"). In two poetic pieces from the 1930s, "In Memory of My Father (Campbell County, Tenn.)" and "Knoxville: Summer of 1915," Agee created impressionistic representations, respectively, of his father's rural and suburban homes.[110] But the personal tragedy would not explicitly surface in Agee's writing until the late 1940s, when he began work on what would become *A Death in the Family.*[111] While preparing the novel, he wrote in a "letter" to his deceased father that by attempting "to recall and understand my life, as well as I can, and [trying] to write it down as clearly and well as I can . . . I am bound to be writing, mainly, about you."[112] Elsewhere he stated, "I find that I value my childhood and my father as they were, as well and as exactly as I can remember and represent them."[113]

In *A Death in the Family*, Hugh James Agee emerges in fictional form as Rufus's brave father and symbol of strength, but also as a mostly anonymous city dweller longing to be back in his "home country." In the short novel *The Morning Watch*, he appears in young Richard's recurring memory of death—"his father's prostrate head and . . . the mortal blue dent in the impatient chin . . . a head of wax immense upon this whole rich waxen air"—and the father's absence is the reason for the boy's lonely, boarding-school existence.[114] And though mentioned only in passing—"My father, my grandfather, my poor damned tragic, not unusually tragic, bitched family"—in *Let Us Now Praise Famous Men*, the father was the ancestral link to tenant farming that charged the writer's journalistic quest to be "as faithful as possible," to represent the cotton farmer "as the human being he is; not just to amalgamate him into some invented, literary imitation of a human being."[115]

If faithfully depicting his father was of great importance to Agee, it seems odd that he said almost nothing in his fiction about Jay's vocation as a postal clerk or bookkeeper. However, the father might have figured more prominently in the work of his son had the latter survived well beyond May 16, 1955. For Agee's notes reveal that the novel published as *A Death in the Family* was actually the third in a sequence of autobiographical novels that he intended to write, beginning with "The Ancestors," which would have included his father's postal employment in Knoxville and ended with his parents meeting at the dancing school. The next book, all about "The Father and Mother," would have included his parents' years in Panama and ended with Rufus's birth.[116] Agee's other major prose works, *The Morning Watch* and *Let Us Now Praise Famous Men*, figure into this chronological sequence as well.

Today Hugh James Agee is little remembered as a postal clerk within Knoxville's old Custom House building, where the Museum of East Tennessee History now fills the former post office space and the McClung Historical Collection's third-floor reading room occupies the former federal courtroom.[117] He would not be recognized in the halls of Master's Lodge No. 244, which now meets at the Masonic Temple in Fountain City. All of his known Knoxville residences, from Oxford Place to Highland Avenue, are long gone. The significance of his brief life in Knoxville might also have vanished over time, leaving little besides obscure

FIGURE 10.7 The original columns, beams, and barrel-vaulted ceiling can be seen inside the former post office space, now part of the Museum of East Tennessee History. In Hugh James Agee's day, the wall to the left in this photograph was part of the building's main entrance, with three doors that opened to Prince (Market) Street. Photo by the author, 2020. Courtesy of Cherel Henderson and the East Tennessee Historical Society.

newspaper references and a weathered headstone behind. Such was the fate of most Knoxvillians from that era, postmen or otherwise. But as James Rufus Agee had faithfully documented three tenant families in Alabama, so he elevated his father from anonymity into literature, and assigned him to the ranks of those "famous men" whom the apocryphal psalmist praised: those "who perished, as though they had never been born; and are become as though they had never been born; and their children after them. . . . Their bodies are buried in peace; but their name liveth for evermore."[118]

Acknowledgments

I am grateful to Michael Lofaro, Paul Ashdown, and Jack Neely, whose advice and suggestions vastly improved this essay.

Notes

1. James Agee, *A Death in the Family* (New York: McDowell, Obolensky, 1957); James Agee, *A Death in the Family: A Restoration of the Author's Text* (hereafter *ADITF-R*), ed. Michael A. Lofaro (Knoxville: U of Tennessee P, 2007); James Agee, *Letters of James Agee to Father Flye* (New York: George Braziller, 1962), 170–71. I have chosen to cite only the restored version of the novel because it presents a fuller depiction of Jay's character and more closely preserves Agee's intentions for the novel, including the names of real people and places. Quotations from this source (*ADITF-R*) are cited parenthetically in the present text.

2. Kenneth Curry, "The Knoxville of James Agee's *A Death in the Family*," in *Tennessee Studies in Literature*, vol. 14 (Knoxville: U of Tennessee P, 1969), 7.

3. Agee, *ADITF-R*, 114–16.

4. James Agee, "Now as Awareness," in *ADITF-R*, appendix 8, 581.

5. See Pat Fields, "Knoxvillian Nostalgically Recalls Visit with Agee in NY," *Knoxville Journal*, November 2, 1962.

6. Much of the source material for the present text comes from archives of the *Knoxville Journal and Tribune* (hereafter *KJT*) and *Knoxville Sentinel* (hereafter *KS*) newspapers, whose pre-1920 issues have only recently been digitized. Archives accessed through Newspapers.com.

7. James Agee, Journals, circa 1930s, undated, University of Tennessee Library, James Agee Collection, MS.2730, box 8, folder 15.

8. "New Post Offices," *Knoxville Register*, August 29, 1850.

9. Paul F. Brown, *Rufus: James Agee in Tennessee* (Knoxville: U Tennessee P, 2018), 30; "From Wa[s]hington," [Knoxville] *Daily Chronicle*, January 18, 1883.

10. "A New Postmaster," *KJT*, August 11, 1898.

11. "For Clerk and Carrier—Civil Service Examination Will Be Held May 2nd," *KJT*, April 4, 1900.

12. "For Clerk and Carrier"; "Twenty-Nine Applicants—Take the Civil Service Examination for Clerks and Carriers," *KJT*, May 3, 1900.

13. 1900 U.S. Census, Campbell County, Tenn., population schedule, LaFollette (fifth district), p. 240 (stamped), dwelling 155, family 159, Henry C. and Mossie Agee (digital image, Ancestry.com).

14. "Clerks and Carriers' Grades—Results of Civil Service Examination Held May 5 [*sic.*] Made Known Today," *KS*, June 25, 1900.

15. "Personal Mention," *KS*, May 7, 1901.

16. "Two Local Postoffice Jobs," *KS*, June 26, 1901. Knoxville newspapers from this period invariably compounded "post office" as "postoffice," a usage that the present text preserves when quoting these sources.

17. "Miss Ida Davis Dismissed," *KS*, July 1, 1901; "Miss Davis Dismissed," *KJT*, July 2, 1901.

18. Winifred Gallagher, *How the Post Office Created America* (New York: Penguin, 2016), 181.

19. "General Delivery Clerk Returns," *KS*, August 9, 1901.

20. "Postoffice Clerks—Forced to Work Several Extra Hours to Perform Their Tasks," *KJT*, February 25, 1902.

21. "At the Custom House. Postoffice Force is Now Short Three Men on Account of Sickness," *KJT*, March 1, 1902.

22. "Tennessee Day at Charleston," *KJT*, March 25, 1902; "President Roosevelt at Charleston Receives a Genuine Southern Welcome," *KJT*, April 9, 1902; "Charleston Exposition" advertisement, *KS*, April 9, 1902.

23. "Knoxville Day at the Charleston Exposition," *KJT*, May 1, 1902; Bruce G. Harvey, "South Carolina Inter-State and West Indian Exposition," *South Carolina Encyclopedia*, http://www.scencyclopedia.org; "Knoxville People Seeing the Exposition," *KS*, May 19, 1902; *KJT*, May 21, 1902, p. 8.

24. "Postoffice Ball Team Ready," *KS*, June 18, 1902.

25. Brown, *Rufus*, 34; "First Game of the Season," *KJT*, March 14, 1908; "Frank Moffett to Coach Team," *KS*, Dec. 30, 1907.

26. "Lively Baseball Game Scheduled for Saturday," *KS*, July 30, 1903.

27. "Got Raises—Employes [*sic*] of Local Postoffice are Favored," *KS*, June 28, 1902; "Employes [*sic*] Taking Vacations," *KS*, July 21, 1902.

28. Knoxville city directory, 1902; "Were They Poisoned?" *KJT*, July 27, 1895.

29. Sanborn insurance map, Knoxville, 1903, sheet 21; Paul F. Brown, "'The Dryad Days': Frances Hodgson Burnett in East Tennessee, Part 1," *Journal of East Tennessee History* 90 (2018): 36–37.

30. Knoxville city directory, 1902. For a definitive account of Williams's Knoxville connections, see Jack Neely, "A Family Drama in Three Acts: Tennessee Williams in Tennessee," in *Knoxville Lives* (Knoxville: Knoxville History Project, 2020), 16–61.

31. Knoxville city directory, 1903; "Hard Problems for New City Officials," *KS*, January 25, 1908; "Masonic Directory of Knoxville, Tennessee (1905): Master's Lodge, No. 244," *Knox County, Tennessee Genealogy & History*, http://knoxcotn.org/old_site/directories/masonic/knoxvillle1905/masterslodge.htm; Knoxville city directory, 1902. The Borches Building on the northwest corner of Wall and Prince housed the Masonic Temple, and in 1902 six lodges met there—Master's

Lodge No. 244, Maxwell Lodge No. 433, Oriental Lodge No. 453, Pearl Chapter No. 24, Knoxville Council No. 75, and Coeur de Lion Commandery No. 9—each on a different night each month.

32. Philip M. Hamer, "A. Frank Agee," in *Tennessee: A History, 1673–1932*, vol. 4 (New York: American Historical Society, 1933), 564. As researched by Walter E. Seifert Jr., historian, Grand Lodge of Tennessee, Nashville, no masonic records were found for Henry Clay Agee (James's father) or James Harris Agee (James's grandfather). Seifert emailed membership information for Alfred Frank (A. F.) Agee (James's brother) to the author, June 9, 2020. Frank was a member of LaFollette Lodge No. 623; he received his Entered Apprentice degree on May 11, 1911, his Fellow Craft degree on June 1, 1911, and his Master Mason degree on August 17, 1911.

33. "Masonic Directory of Knoxville, Tennessee (1905)"; Knoxville city directory, 1902.

34. Information here and below about masonic requirements and degree rituals is drawn from two websites: "The Three Degrees of Freemasonry," *North Raleigh Masonic Lodge*, http://www.jjcrowder743.com/threedegrees.html; and "Freemasonry Revealed," *Grand Lodge of North Carolina*, http://grandlodge-nc.org/freemasonry-revealed.

35. "Masonic Directory of Knoxville, Tennessee (1905)." At one time, Sterchi Brothers "was reported to be the world's largest furniture chain"; see National Register of Historic Places Inventory—Nomination Form, Stratford/Sterchi Mansion, Knoxville, Tenn. (National Register no. 135816894).

36. George E. Simons, *Standard Masonic Monitor of the Degrees of Entered Apprentice, Fellow Craft and Master Mason* (New York: Macoy Publishing and Masonic Supply Co., 1901), 28.

37. Masonic records for Hugh James Agee were researched by Seifert and emailed to the author by Erick H. Tuck, secretary, Oriental Lodge No. 453, F&AM, Knoxville, February 25, 2020.

38. "Postoffice Promotions Have Been Made," *KS*, December 29, 1902; "Postoffice Changes," *KJT*, January 1, 1903.

39. "New Year's Day—Was Observed by the Banks and Postoffice Force," *KJT*, January 2, 1903; "Report of Postoffice," *KJT*, January 6, 1903.

40. "More Carriers and More Clerks are Needed," *KS*, January 28, 1903; "Much Free Mail," *KS*, April 3, 1903.

41. "Fine New Passenger Station of the Southern Railway was Opened to the Traveling Public This Morning," *KS*, February 2, 1903; "Society Personals," *KS*, October 9, 1914.

42. "Not a Train on Time—Postal Clerks Have Their Worries Piled in Large Bunches," *KJT*, January 11, 1903.

43. "Southern's Late Trains—Put the Local Postoffice Clerks in the Air Again," *KJT*, January 27, 1903.

44. "Troubles at Postoffice," *KJT*, February 17, 1903.

45. The following assessment of the building appeared in "Need of Room for Postoffice," *KS*, January 11, 1899:

> The small postoffice outside of the rooms of the postmaster, assistant postmaster and superintendent of the money order office, is only 68x52 feet. Out of this space is cut the stamp clerk's office, the registry of the carriers' department, besides the desk room for superintendent of mails and superintendent of carriers. . . .
>
> At present the safe, desk and cases fill up [the money order office] so that only one man can work in it. . . .

> At least seventy-five additional square feet of space is needed in the general delivery, and the clerks are crowded so a good service is almost impossible. The case[s] are set behind each other and are jammed together so there is hardly room to turn around.
>
> The stamp clerk's office is too small by half, in view of future growth. The office can get along fairly well while there is only one clerk there but with two clerks . . . the present space would be too small. . . .
>
> [T]he carriers' department . . . has now about 225 square feet of space, with seventeen carriers . . . [who] need a place to sit while waiting for mails. They are obliged to stand in the way of other clerks. . . .
>
> The general mailing room is 30x50 feet and is not near large enough. This is what is left of the large room, after taking out registers, general delivery, stamp clerk's office and carriers' space. The present service is greatly hindered for want of room. . . .
>
> There is not sufficient light at any time, without burning artificial lights, which burn from year to year and are never out.

See also "New Postoffice Building," *KS*, October 26, 1901; "Will Entertain Schley in Usual Good Style," *KS*, January 1, 1902; "Public Opinion Favors a Separate Postoffice," *KJT*, January 5, 1902; "Separate Building," *KJT*, January 23, 1902; "Postmaster Trent Talks," *KJT*, January 9, 1903.

46. "Senate Calls for Report on Knoxville Federal Building," *KS*, February 12, 1903.

47. "Office Arrangement in Custom House Addition," *KS*, April 14, 1909.

48. "Postoffice Affairs," *KJT*, March 20, 1903.

49. "Postmaster Trent Stirred Things Up," *KS*, March 26, 1903.

50. "Distribution of Mail is a Tedious Job—Chief Clerk Kidd Talks of the Impatience of the Public," *KJT*, April 5, 1903.

51. Knoxville city directory, 1903.

52. "Will Try the Auto," *KS*, April 20, 1903; "Test Auto Run—Made to Sevierville Yesterday by a Local Machine," *KJT*, August 4, 1903.

53. "Registered Mail Sack Stolen from Postoffice," *KJT*, April 26, 1903; "Registered Mail—Stolen from Door of Knoxville Postoffice," *KS*, April 27, 1903.

54. "Clerk Suspected," *KS*, April 28, 1903.

55. "Russell Arrested—As Author of Registered Mail Pouch Mystery," *KJT*, April 29, 1903.

56. "Clerk Russel [*sic*] Accused; Preliminary Hearing Today," *KS*, April 29, 1903; "Russell was Acquitted on Preliminary Hearing," *KS*, April 30, 1903.

57. "Three More Letters Gone," *KJT*, May 9, 1903; "After Russell—Postoffice Authorities Continue to Investigate," *KS*, May 19, 1903; "Russell Removed—From the Postoffice Department Service," *KJT*, July 17, 1903; "Clerks Make Temporary Change," *KS*, July 14, 1903; "Four Clerks Promoted in the Postoffice," *KS*, July 28, 1903.

58. "Former Clerk Russell was Indicted Today," *KS*, September 15, 1903; "Branch Postoffice Opened at Conference Headquarters," *KS*, September 23, 1903; "Fifty-Ninth Session of Holston Conference," *KJT*, September 24, 1903; "Conference Ends Monday Morning," *KS*, September 26, 1903.

59. "Witnesses in Russell Case Giving Their Testimony," *KS*, November 5, 1903; "Rather Weak Testimony Produced Against Russell," *KS*, November 6, 1903.

60. "Russell's Case Given to the Jury at 10 P.M.," *KJT*, November 7, 1903.

61. Knoxville City Directory, 1903; Brown, *Rufus*, 57, 244. Robert T. Wardrep, a fellow member of Master's Lodge, sold the house to the Agees on November 27, 1912.

62. "Seven for Acquittal Five for Conviction in 'Tobe' Russell Case," *KS*, November 7, 1903; "Mistrial Resulted—In the A. P. Russell Case in Federal Court," *KJT*, November 8, 1903.

63. "A. P. Russell was 'Not Guilty,'" *KS*, March 19, 1904.

64. "After Russell—Postoffice Authorities Continue."

65. *KS*, November 5, 1903, p. 8.

66. "Clerk Agee Sick," *KS*, December 1, 1903.

67. "Clerk Agee Better," *KS*, December 4, 1903.

68. "A. S. Agee Visiting Son," *KS*, December 7, 1903. The newspaper misnames James's father, H. C. Agee, as "A. S. Agee"—perhaps a typesetter's misreading of the reporter's handwritten notes. It also misnames James, "a clerk in the postoffice," as "J. W. Agee," though there are several other instances of this in *Sentinel* articles from this period.

69. "Hale is Not So Strong in Campbell County," *KS*, December 9, 1903. Here again, Henry and James are given incorrect initials: "H. A. Agee . . . is the father of J. W. Agee, of the local postoffice."

70. "Town Topics," *KJT*, December 12, 1903.

71. "Masonic," *KJT*, December 13, 1903.

72. "Santa Claus Letters from Sentinel Readers," *KS*, December 19, 1903.

73. "LaFollette—An Iron and Coal Center," *KJT*, November 18, 1912; "In the Postal Service," *KJT*, March 30, 1903. For background on county seat referendum see "LaFollette the Winner," *KJT*, March 29, 1903; "Fiat for an Injunction Granted by Judge Kyle," *KJT*, April 3, 1903; "LaFollette Is Winner," *KJT*, November 12, 1903; "Birmingham Architect Here," *KS*, January 2, 1904; "Campbell 'Squires Enjoined," *KS*, January 5, 1904; "Back to Jacksboro Goes County Seat," *KS*, April 30, 1904.

74. "Big Conflagration at LaFollette; Entire Business Section in Ashes," *KS*, May 10, 1904. For shoot-out, see "Full Details of the LaFollette Tragedy," *KJT*, July 26, 1903.

75. "Knoxville People Have L'Follette Interests," *KS*, May 10, 1904.

76. Agee, *ADITF-R*, chapter 18.

77. Brown, *Rufus*, 53, 180, 241–44.

78. Knoxville city directory, 1904; Sanborn insurance map, Knoxville, 1903, sheet 2.

79. "Theatrical Gossip," *KS*, February 27, 1904; "Maude Adams Pleased Large Audience," *KS*, October 18, 1904; Joseph F. Panarello, "Maude Adams: The 'First' Peter Pan," *BroadwayWorld*, December 13, 2011, https://www.broadwayworld.com/article/Maude-Adams-The-First-Peter-Pan-20111213. For further information about Adams at Staub's, see Paul F. Brown, "Somewhere in Time: A Knoxville Theater, and the Actress Who Inspired a Classic Film" (in two parts), *Inside of Knoxville*, October 6 and 7, 2020, https://insideofknoxville.com.

80. Brown, *Rufus*, 39.

81. "Girls' Friendly Society to Give Entertainment," *KS*, May 21, 1904; George M. Baker, *A Precious Pickle: A Farce in One Act for Female Characters Only* (Boston: Walter H. Baker, 1900).

82. "Leap Year Cotillion Given Monday Evening," *KS*, June 14, 1904.

83. "Trelawney [*sic*] of the Wells to Be Given This Evening," *KS*, July 19, 1904; Arthur W. Pinero, *Trelawny of the "Wells": A Comedietta in Four Acts* (London: William Heinemann, 1897), 60.

84. Alfred T. Barson, *A Way of Seeing: A Critical Study of James Agee* (U of Massachusetts P, 1972), 11, 192–93. Father James Harold Flye, whom Barson interviewed in 1970, probably supplied the information about Laura meeting James in 1904, though Barson's notes are not clear about this.

85. "Deputy Marshal Made the Arrest," *KS*, September 14, 1904; "Federal Court Meets Thursday," *KS*, September 28, 1904; "Clerks Get Good Increases," *KS*, June 14, 1905.

86. Knoxville city directory, 1905; "Hotel Vendome. Thrown Open to the Public in a Blaze of Glory," [Knoxville] *Evening Sentinel*, January 28, 1890; "Vendome is Haven of Rest in City Bustle," *Knoxville News-Sentinel*, November 8, 1931.

87. "Montana Train Robber Who Shot Policemen Now Behind the Bars," *KS*, December 16, 1901; "Harvey Logan, the Bandit, Riding Toward the Mountains; Bold Montana Train Robber Escapes from Knox County Jail," *KJT*, June 28, 1903.

88. "Foot Pad Artist Under Arrest," *KS*, March 18, 1905; "Bound to Court in Five Cases," *KS*, March 20, 1905.

89. "Back to the Mines will Earnest [*sic*] Miner Be Sent," *KS*, May 15, 1905. See also "Ernest B. Minor [*sic*]," Minerd.com, https://www.minerd.com.

90. "Agee Returns from Vacation," *KS*, April 13, 1905; "Clerk Agee Recovered," *KS*, May 9, 1905; "Clerks Get Good Increases," *KS*, June 14, 1905.

91. Brown, *Rufus*, 37–38; "Supper and Dance by the Twentieth Century Club," *KS*, July 25, 1905; "Open Air Dance Monday by Twentieth Century Club," *KS*, July 29, 1905; "Neubert Springs Hotel is Totally Destroyed by Fire," *KJT*, February 25, 1924.

92. "Initial Fall Dance by Twentieth Century Club," *KS*, September 20, 1905.

93. Geneviève Moreau, *The Restless Journey of James Agee* (New York: William Morrow, 1977), 32. Although Moreau did not specifically cite that information, she may have learned it from Laura Wright, née Tyler, whom she interviewed in 1964.

94. Agee, *ADITF-R*, 151–52.

95. Brown, *Rufus*, 40; Campbell County, Tenn., Deed Book 46:230, Willie B. Johnston to James Agee, October 31, 1905.

96. "LaFollette," *KJT*, November 27, 1905; "James Agee Will Go to Panama Mail Service," *KS*, November 27, 1905.

97. Brown, *Rufus*, 40; "Agee Has Reached New York," *KS*, December 4, 1905.

98. Robert J. Karrer and David Zemer, "Canal Zone Stamps," *Smithsonian National Postal Museum*, https://postalmuseum.si.edu/exhibition/canal-zone-stamps.

99. Knoxville city directory, 1905; "Back to Old System," *KJT*, November 16, 1903.

100. "Tells of Life in Canal Zone," *KS*, February 20, 1906.

101. "Personal Mention," *KJT*, November 2, 1913, includes the first mention of Tauxe being "of Los Angeles, Cal., formerly of Knoxville."

102. "James Agee Living in the Canal Zone," *KS*, January 5, 1906.

103. Brown, *Rufus*, 42–44.

104. Jay's employment in Panama overlapped that of another Knoxvillian, George Dempster, who operated a steam shovel in the Canal Zone decades before inventing the first "dumpster" in Knoxville and serving a term as mayor. See "Geo. R. Dempster Back from Panama Canal," *KS*, June 6, 1908; "History of Mayors," *City of Knoxville*, https://knoxvilletn.gov/government/mayors_office/history_of_mayors.

105. "L'Follette Man is Visitor in City," *KS*, January 8, 1909; "Society Personals," *KS*, June 17, 1909.

106. "James Agee Will Return to Panama," *KJT*, November 13, 1909. Two documents confirm that James did not accept the reinstatement. The final entry on his "Service Record Card" from Panama indicates that James was reinstated on November 17 as a postal clerk earning $125 per month; however, this entry was subsequently crossed out and noted as "Cancelled Declined." And James Rufus Agee's birth certificate lists the father's residence and occupation, respectively, as "Knoxville" and "Post Office Employee." See "Panama Canal Zone Employment Records and Sailing Lists—Service Record Cards, 1904–1920," FamilySearch.org; "Tennessee, City Birth Records, 1881–1915," Ancestry.com.

107. Brown, *Rufus*, 53–57; Campbell County, Tenn., Deed Book 55:534, James and Laura T. Agee to Henry C. Agee, December 3, 1913.

108. Masonic records for Hugh James Agee, Grand Lodge of Tennessee, Nashville. The exact date of suspension was December 21, 1914.

109. "Found Dead on Clinton Pike," *KJT*, May 19, 1916; "Automobile Accident Fatal for James Agee," *KS*, May 19, 1916. For events surrounding Hugh James Agee's death, see Brown, *Rufus*, chapter 3.

110. James Agee, "In Memory of My Father (Campbell County, Tenn.)," *transition* 26 (Spring 1937): 7; James Agee, "Knoxville: Summer of 1915," *Partisan Review* 5, no. 3 (August–September 1938): 22–25.

111. For Hugh James Agee's influence on his son's work, see Brown, *Rufus*, chapter 5.

112. James Agee, "Unfinished Draft of Agee's Letter to His Father," in *ADITF-R*, appendix 5, 573–74.

113. Agee, "Now as Awareness."

114. James Agee, *The Morning Watch* (1950; reprint, New York: Ballantine Books, 1969), 48–49.

115. James Agee, *Let Us Now Praise Famous Men* (1941; reprint, New York: Ballantine Books, 1978), 349, 216. For Agee's link to tenant farming, see Brown, *Rufus*, 204–5; Andrew Crooke, "A Fraternal Relationship: James Agee and John Berger on Representing the Rural Poor," in *Let Us Now Praise Famous Men at 75: Anniversary Essays*, ed. Michael A. Lofaro (Knoxville: U of Tennessee P, 2017): 205n79.

116. "Outline and Possible Introduction to Agee's Massive Autobiographical Project and the Place of 'This book' in It," in Agee, *ADITF-R*, appendix 8, 579–80.

117. Thanks to Rebecca P'Simer, East Tennessee Historical Society's Curator of Collections, for confirming information about the former Custom House building.

118. Agee, *Let Us Now Praise Famous Men*, 405–6 (quote from Ecclesiasticus 44).

ELEVEN

"Tidmore and the Negro"

An Unpublished Chapter from Let Us Now Praise Famous Men

HUGH DAVIS

When James Agee and Walker Evans were dispatched to the South in the summer of 1936 by *Fortune* magazine, their explicit charge was to document "the daily living and environment of an average white family of tenant farmers."[1] In addition to the many other problems raised by this type of intrusion into the lives of people on the margins of society and the difficulties of accurately representing them, Agee was well aware that the assignment itself was a distortion of the situation, since of the nine million sharecroppers in the South, three million were black. As published in 1941, *Let Us Now Praise Famous Men* does focus on three families of white sharecroppers. However, Agee also hinted at the racial dynamics complicating the assignment in the "Late Sunday Morning" and "Near a Church" chapters of the book, in which his attempts to approach black subjects are frustrated by suspicion and miscommunication. The recent scholarly edition of *Famous Men* contains additional material on race, including "Notes: 'Under Negroes,'" a Freudian analysis of white landowners in "Cotton Tenants," and a long narrative describing the public whipping of a black teenager caught stealing shoes.[2] To these can now be added the previously unknown chapter "Tidmore and the Negro,"[3] which survives in manuscript and appears in several early tables of contents for *Famous Men* but which has heretofore been unavailable to researchers. Although Agee ultimately chose not to include the piece, "Tidmore and the Negro" provides additional insight into Agee's complex view of landowners, tenants, and race relations in the South.

In "Tidmore and the Negro," Agee recounts witnessing a conversation between landowner Christopher (Mr. Chris) Tidmore and one of his tenants in Tidmore's office in the Moundville Mercantile Store. While Mr. Chris and his brother, J. Watson Tidmore, are relatively minor characters in *Famous Men,* their importance to the book's overall meaning is underscored by the fact that the book opens with Walker Evans's portrait of Christopher Tidmore (see figure 11.1), who along with his brother owned the land on which the Tingle and Fields families were tenants and for whom the Burroughs family had previously farmed as well. (In his notes for this photograph, Evans identifies the subject as J. Watson Tidmore, but it is clear from Agee's descriptions and account of the day the photograph was taken that the subject is, in fact, Christopher Tidmore.) In a draft of "Persons and Places," Agee describes the brothers (whose names are given as "Michael" and "T. Hudson Margraves" in *Famous Men*) as follows:

> Among the strongest men of their town. One serves in the state legislature. They own twenty-two hundred acres locally, of which about six hundred are in cultivation, and eight hundred acres more in Texas. They have controlling interests in one of the gins and in the town's main store. They began as the sons of small farmers, came to Moundville, married money, and have gained their basic wealth chiefly through skilful uses of mortgages to the disadvantage of just such farmers as those of whom they came. They are in their early fifties.[4]

Not only were the brothers substantial landowners, but J. Watson Tidmore was also a locally powerful politician, serving as an Alabama state legislator for twelve years and as the mayor, a councilman, the treasurer of the local Masonic lodge, and the justice of the peace of Moundville. In "Landlords," an unpublished description of the brothers, Agee writes that J. Watson was more interested in the farming aspect of the business and personally supervised the tenants and their activities. As Agee explains, "He seems to drive around to the farms a fair amount. What little I can of this, I gather he often does so not for any urgent reason, but because he mistrusts the intelligence and steadiness of any tenant as you can only if you want to do the work yourself, and because he likes at least to be near this work and production, and at least to boss it, and to warm himself at it as if at a fire."[5] On the other hand, Mr. Chris "has little or no interest in farming; a good deal in business and money." Agee continues:

> He spends a good deal of his day in a small latticed office in the centre of the Vergil Davis store, at a rolltop desk, getting a certain steady sensual and egoistic pleasure out of the squeaking of his swivel chair. He is large, bony, full-bodied, with a paunch; a large round cannonball head, soft white hair close-clipped, big shoulders and long heavy arms; the face florid; the triangular eyes bright blue and small, lively

> and calculating, the mouth that of a moderate sensualist whose sensuality is entirely absorbed into shrewdness and acquisition, the hands strongly shaped, white, hard but not calloused, the large thighs spread, confident, and in a small way regal as he sits. He wears a white shirt, a foulard tie, sleeve-gaiters, pale blue suspenders, ill-fitting cream-colored summer trousers, recently pressed but already much wrinkled, black shoes. A creamcolored coat and a slightly soiled panama hat hang next the office door.[6]

Although this description certainly complements "Tidmore and the Negro," allowing the reader more readily to sense Tidmore's imposing physical presence, Agee may well have omitted it from *Famous Men* because he realized that it was redundant, given that Evans's portrait captures many of the same details, including the more intangible qualities of self-assurance, ruthlessness, and institutional power and privilege. However, the draft continues with a short account of the taking of the photograph, which provides context that complicates it considerably. Agee writes:

> His house is not overshaded, and is painted a pure strong white; the jigsaw work among the thick leaves is beautiful at night in the light of a streetlamp. We came there once at a wrong time of Sunday, to see whether he would have himself photographed. His wife answered the door, a plump woman with glasses who looked a little like a rabbit and who looked as if for twenty years she had suspected that there is something sad in sexlessness but that it is best not to think about it: she was courteous to us in a curious mixture of coldness and warmth and asked us to step inside the door. There was a strong odor of flour, butter, and boiled chicken and I realized they were nearly ready for dinner, and a man and wife in their fifties and a sullen man in his thirties sat waiting in the parlor with Tidmore and kept looking at us. It was dark and heavy suite furniture in an odor of cedar and wax and seemed as if steam-heated in the middle of winter, and there was a heavy feeling of tasteful choice, careful housekeeping, and sterility. In spite of our apologies and withdrawals, Tidmore without either unctuousness or show of annoyance, put on his coat and came out into the side yard and stood for his photograph.[7]

The uncaptioned, "straight-style" documentary portrait is Evans at his best, and it says everything about the power dynamic between landlords and tenants that needs to be said. But does it lose something (or gain something) through the realization on the part of the viewer that the most important consideration for Christopher Tidmore at the moment it captures is that his dinner is getting cold?

FIGURE II.1 Walker Evans's portrait of Christopher Tidmore, which opens *Let Us Now Praise Famous Men.*

In "Tidmore and the Negro," a black tenant comes to cash in a gin slip on cotton he is taking to deliver to Tidmore's warehouse. Tidmore takes the slip but reminds the tenant that he has an outstanding debt; unspoken is the fact that Tidmore would be completely within his rights, legally and culturally, to take the money owed out of the payment and leave the tenant with nothing to show for this year's crop and, more devastatingly, no seed money for next year's. As the tenant fully recognizes, he has no recourse except to appeal to Tidmore's "good Christian heart." After letting the situation sink in for a moment, Tidmore decides to pay for the cotton and defer the debt but warns the tenant that he won't get much money, leaving him with this advice: "Try to get heavier bales from now on."

Although fairly brief, this exchange clearly reveals the absolute power imbalance of the landowner-tenant relationship as well as the casual cruelty through which it is perpetuated. Agee states that he wrote the conversation down immediately after witnessing it and that it is a nearly verbatim record of the encounter. As such, it can stand without elaboration as what William Stott calls a "human document,"[8] one that obviates the need for argument, making its appeal directly to the conscience of the reader. However, rather than letting the scene speak for itself, Agee cannot resist probing it for deeper significance (as when he interrupts his otherwise objective description in "Landlords" to claim that Tidmore gets "a certain steady sensual and egoistic pleasure out of the squeaking of his swivel chair"[9]). For Agee, the performance of a type of social dance—the script of which dictates when the tenant may speak and must remain silent, whether or not he can take off his hat, and how he must stand and whether he may sit—is the most interesting aspect of the encounter, with the two men as ritualistically locked into their roles as in the most formal Balinese drama. As in other episodes from *Famous Men*—for instance, when a group of black singers is summoned to perform for Agee and he realizes his desire to connect authentically with them is compromised by the role he has been forced into—Agee refuses to present the scene as unmediated by his presence. Although he admits that the situation would have probably played out much the same way if had not been there, he nonetheless filters it through an exacting self-consciousness that complicates the possibility of knowing altogether. Rather than a human document that communicates its meaning directly, Agee reframes the encounter so that it now depends on the perspective of the tenant: unstated, unknowable, and irrecoverable.

Finally, Agee emphasizes that the tenant "was not by any means servile, but was in a favorable sense of the word 'self-respecting' to the farthest degree he could be short of yielding any impression whatever of sullenness, impudence, or 'independence.'" Within the rules of the game he is forced to play, he maintains a certain level of dignity. However, Agee seems finally to see him primarily in aesthetic terms. He writes:

> He was hot and his odor as he waited in silence, which seemed to intensify or even embody his waiting and the strength of his subsequent silences and patiences in the course of the dialogue, is emotionally and "esthetically" important to me both in my recollection of the scene, and to any attempt fully to communicate it. Not at all that it was extraordinary. It was simply the odor of a tired strong country negro male body that had been awake since before dawn and in the hot sun for some hours, and which now, standing still in a close and shadowy place, awaiting and later trying not to be deprived of its reward for months of work, had for a little while nothing to do but stand and sweat.

As is typical in *Famous Men,* there is almost a compulsive need to aestheticize the scene, and Agee again makes his perception of it and anxiety about precisely presenting it central to his description. Despite its relevance to the published text, in the end, it is probably unfair to read too much into a draft that Agee never revised and did not use. However, in approaching his treatment of the black tenant farmer and his "patiences and silences," it may serve the reader well to focus not so much on what Agee reveals about the limits of his own understanding but rather what the tenant may have known but could not tell.

Notes

1. James Agee and Walker Evans, Let Us Now Praise Famous Men: *An Annotated Edition of the James Agee–Walker Evans Classic, with Supplementary Manuscripts,* ed. Hugh Davis, vol. 3 of *The Works of James Agee,* gen. ed. Michael A. Lofaro (Knoxville: U of Tennessee P, 2015), vii. Subsequent references to this edition will be abbreviated in the notes as Davis, *LUNPFM.* The method for editing this manuscript follows the procedures initiated in Michael A. Lofaro and Hugh Davis, eds., for *James Agee Rediscovered: The Journals of* Let Us Now Praise Famous Men *and other Manuscripts* (Knoxville: U of Tennessee P, 2005), xli–xlv, and continued in *The Works of James Agee.*

2. See Davis, *LUNPFM* for "Notes: 'Under Negroes,'" 881–82; "Appendix or Box on LANDOWNERS," 629–33; and "Notes on 1) Music 2) Alabama," 852–62.

3. The manuscript of "Tidmore and the Negro" is housed in the University of Tennessee Special Collections in the James Agee Manuscript Collection, MS-3824, box 5: *Let Us Now Praise Famous*

Men Drafts. It has been edited in accordance with the principles outlined in Davis, *LUNPFM*, "General Textual Method," 513–16.

4. Davis, *LUNPFM*, "Draft: 'Persons and Places,'" 817–18.

5. "Landlords: J. Watson Tidmore. Christopher Tidmore.," University of Tennessee Special Collections in the James Agee Manuscript Collection, MS-3824, box 5: *Let Us Now Praise Famous Men* Drafts. Subsequent references to this three-page manuscript will be abbreviated as "Landlords."

6. "Landlords," 2–3.

7. "Landlords," 3.

8. William Stott, *Documentary Expression and Thirties America* (1973; Chicago: U of Chicago P, 1986) 6.

9. "Landlords" 2.

Tidmore and the Negro

[1]

Tidmore and the Negro

While I was talking with Tidmore, in his office in the store, at his desk, a negro came up softly with his hat in one hand and his ginning slip between the fingers of the other, held lightly, not to soil it, and waited at the door. Tidmore looked up at him, without nodding; (the negro ducked his head); and continued to talk with me, unconsciously (I think) raising his voice a little. At the first place for a pause I said I didn't want to interrupt his business. "Oh, he can wait," he said, not looking at the negro. The negro stirred a very little. He continued talking until our conversation was at a point where the interruption of it would hang it up, and would in his terms insult me by desertion midstream in favor of a nigger, and leaned back, and swung in his swivel chair, looking up at the negro and saying, "all right now; what's on <u>your</u> mind." The negro shuffled a couple of paces forward, so that he was just inside the door, saying yes sir, to Tidmore and me, and held out his slip. The following is not the complete conversation but is accurate as far as it goes. Some of it I copied on the spot under pretense of revising and amplifying my notes; the rest I took down immediately after leaving Tidmore.

<u>Tidmore:</u> I get half of this don't I.

<u>Negro:</u> No sir, you get a fourth.

<u>Tidmore:</u> I thought you was working on halves.

(A pause. The negro does not speak. He swings back in the chair again, knees apart.)

<u>Tidmore:</u> Well now you owe me some money don't ye.

Negro: Sir?

Tidmore: I give ye some money, while back, didn't I.

Negro: Yes sir but you wouldn't take my cottonseed money on that sir, you got a good Christian heart.

Tidmore: Cottonseed money's good as any other.

(The negro does not speak.)

Trouble thyew fellers, ye'll promise anything when ye want suh[1] and then you won't keep your promise.

(The negro is somewhat supposed to say yes, sir, but he does not say anything. But to make his silence as nearly all right as possible he shrinks his body a little more, and sticks out his foot and looks at it. Tidmore turns away leaning, and takes a couple of ledgers out of a black iron safe on whose door flowers are painted. The negro does not speak while his back it turned, he is waiting for Tidmore to turn back and look up at him. But when Tidmore turns back he does not look up at him, he looks in the book instead. At length the negro speaks. At the sound of his voice Tidmore looks up quickly and coldly, and immediately examines the ledger again; are you speaking? I am not hearing you.)

Negro: I'll pay that later on, sir. I'll git some money then and git clair.

(Tidmore continues to look in the ledger. He is figuring with a pen. The negro waits, looking no longer at his foot but a little to one side of Tidmore.)

Tidmore (not looking up): You won't get much money. I wish you would but you won't get much.

[2]

(The negro does not speak. Tidmore studies and figures in the books a little longer, then puts them on the desk. He takes money out of a cash box and counts it out slowly into the palm of one hand. He takes it between the fingertips of the other hand, and reaches this hand over to the negro. The negro extends his hand, palm up, then reverses and reorganizes it, for he sees that the money is not to be laid in his palm but taken with the fingers.)

Tidmore: Well, it's six fifty four but here's six fifty five.

(The negro takes the money in his fingertips. Their hands do not touch; not even on the narrowness of the nickel.)

(Tidmore looks at the slip again.)

1. Something

Tidmore: You want to put this in my warehouse don't ye.

Negro: Yes sir. You sell it for me when it

Tidmore: What's price now.

Negro: Twelve cents on inchlong stuff.

Tidmore (to me): He knows they ain't going to be no inchlong stuff.

(He takes a locked key ring from his pocket and slips a key from it. The keys make an iron quiet noise of property more strong than that of coins.)

Tidmore: Here's the key to the back door.

Negro: (taking it, shuffling backward through the door, stooping his shoulders and head in a half bow) Yes sir.

Tidmore: Now mind you set that cotton up on end with the tag up.

Negro: Yes sir.

Tidmore: Don't go in there smokin.

Negro: No sir. (He has backed through the door and is turning away.)

Tidmore: (more loudly) You be sure and bring that key back, don't go off with that key.

Negro: (arrested in his turning:) No sir. (He relaxes and starts on.)

Tidmore (louder): Try to get heavier bales from now on.

Negro: (halted once more, nodding deeply, his whole spine in it) Yes sir.

Tidmore: (loud again, again halting the negro before he has managed to straighten): Don't let that cotton git warm.

Negro: No sir.

(He walks on. When he has come near the door he begins to put on his hat. It is not fully on before he steps through the door into the sun.)

---

[3]

Notes of analysis and comment.

softly: he must not disturb our conversation even by the sound of his approach and presence. The approach was not at all on tiptoe, or fearful, but a softshoed, tactful shuffle; not the loose walk with which he had entered the store.

the hat: this was removed as he came within emanation of the office.

the ginning slip: All men who are hard workers are liable to be gingerly with fragile and clean substances. This is one of the reasons why they seem so delicately uneasy in sunday clothes. // The slip was mutual property, and was sacred two ways: One, because it was Tidmore's. Two, because it was the negro's and represented work done and money earned. The respect would be automatic and instinctive more than conscious. // A negro's hands are thought of as dirty, even rather foully so, and capable at their cleanest of spotting and streaking. I believe that many negroes share some of this belief, which of course would be sharpened in them in any white context. // Again, this is hardly a considered belief, but an "instinctive" one. As such, I believe it is sharp.

at the door: meaning, just outside the door. The sense of these symbols and of the meanings of placement and gesture is strong and delicate between negroes and whites. If the negro had stepped in before it was full time for his own personal business, that would have been an astonishing piece of affrontery. (If the office had been larger, and had been a room to itself, rather than the small latticed-in affair it was, different movements would have held. He would have entered by the screen door slowly and shyly, giving his employer plenty of time to gesture or order him to stay out, and if there was lack of gesture either way, would risk coming the rest of the way in, and would even shut the door behind him: for though this shutting might indicate a certain overconfidence, not-shutting would be discourteous and careless, letting flies in. He would then stand near the door, looking at calendars, or his hands, or the floor, or out the window but taking care to give no appearance of looking at anything pertaining to money or his employer's business. Conceivably; depending entirely on his relationship with his employer, he might sit down, if there was a chair far enough withdrawn against the wall, which could be reached with very little movement, and by backing into it as if by accident rather than walking or by deliberation.)

without nodding: also without any sign of greeting save, temperatureless, in the eyes: oh. you. There would have been the same look to a white tenant, but probably also a very slight jerk of the head. The "ducking" is a sort of bow, with a slight tinge in it of dodging a blow. A certain and fairly common kind of negro would also have smiled, or even make soft nearly wordless noises.

Throughout this "scene," Tidmore was aware of me, and that he was showing me how a nigger is handled, and that a nigger is not handled badly, and that a nigger is not "loved." In other words he was aware of, and enjoying, insulting or correcting or reinforming what he believed my beliefs and opinions to be. I do not believe their dialogue would have been essentially, or even hardly in detail, different, if I had not been there: yet my presence was a pressure on the consciousness and conduct of them both; to Tidmore as an enemy; and to the negro as an unexplained white stranger of whom he had, it now occurs to me, just conceivably heard.

This negro was I believe in his middle thirties. He was hot and his odor as he waited in silence, which seemed to intensify or even embody his waiting and

[4]

the strength of his subsequent silences and patiences in the course of the dialogue, is emotionally and "esthetically" important to me both in my recollection of the scene, and to any attempt fully to communicate it. Not at all that it was extraordinary. It was simply the odor of a tired strong country negro male body that had been awake since before dawn and in the hot sun for some hours, and which now, standing still in a close and shadowy place, awaiting and later trying not to be deprived of its reward for months of work, had for a little while nothing to do but stand and sweat.

This negro was not by any means servile, but was in a favorable sense of the word "self-respecting" to the farthest degree he could be short of yielding any impression whatever of sullenness, impudence, or "independence." In the interests of yielding no such impressions he was extremely careful of his motions and demeanors and of this language and tones of voice.

Some [of] the elements possible of analysis in the dialogue are so self-evident, and others are [so] subtle, ambiguous and complex, that, rather than blur what may be perfectly clear to a thoughtful reader, I will let it alone as it is.

A suggestion, about the hat. A negro may wear his hat in a store; this man had worn his in. But leaving, the whole of the store had become symbolically identical, for the moment, with Tidmore's office; and he knew also that Tidmore's eyes might be following him. The influence was weakened by the time he was halfway to the door, but not so removed that he set the hat firmly on his head. He did this only as he stepped into the open air.

All this, and all those relations of gesture, motion, tones of speech, and rhythm, which are extremely elaborate and delicately defined, are between half and fully unconscious in the negro and in the white man; but both are exceedingly sensitive to their meanings and still more to any even very slight variation or infringement: and these are the centers of the whole negro-white relationship, and the essential strength of it.

Textual Notes

274.5	softly] (Inserted from top margin.)
274.5	his hat in one hand and] (Inserted from top margin.)
274.8	unconsciously (I think) raising his voice a little.] (Inserted from top margin.)
274.22	The negro does not speak. He swings] The negro does not speak. ~~says No, sir, I ain't working on halves; but Tidmore, penciling among some papers, gives no appearance of hearing him.~~ He swings
275.16–17	immediately examines . . . hearing you.] (Inserted from left margin.)
275.27	reverses and reorganizes] ~~reverses~~ reverses and reorganizes
276.26–27	his approach and presence] his ~~presence~~ approach and presence
277.9	an astonishing] an ~~extreme~~ astonishing
277.12	employer plenty of time] employer ~~full time~~ plenty of time
277.14	door behind] door ~~to~~ behind
277.15	indicate a certain] indicate a ~~very~~ certain
277.36–278.1	heard. / This negro] heard. / ~~This negro would have been I believe in his middle thirties. He was not at all of a servile or fawning kind. His lack of speaking where this is mentioned in the dialogue~~ /This negro
278.7	had been awake] had been ~~up for~~ awake
278.8	now, standing] now, ~~arrested~~ standing
278.9–10	nothing to do] nothing do to
278.18–19	as it is. / A suggestion] as it is. ~~A very few suggestions only.~~ / A suggestion

APPENDIX ONE

Three New Poems

James Agee's "The Darkened Cage," "[A deer went down to water]," and "Eureka"

JESSE GRAVES

The forthcoming *Complete Poems of James Agee*, edited by Michael A. Lofaro and me as part of the scholarly edition of The Works of James Agee, will present many previously unpublished, and in fact previously unknown, poems and fragments written through every phase of Agee's life. A casual reader of Agee, if such reader exists, might assume that he essentially gave up the writing of poems after the publication of his Yale Younger Poets Prize–winning volume, *Permit Me Voyage*, at age twenty-five. While his publishing ambitions shifted to prose fiction, journalism, and film, at least partly directed by financial obligations, Agee continued to compose poems, sometimes in the form of such imaginative experiments as automatic writing and sometimes in regular rhyming and metrical verse. If a signature quality exists for a writer as various and "myriad-minded"[1] as James Agee, surely his immense range of voice (which I use here as repository for all manner of stylistic elements such as tone, diction, syntax) would rank highly on the list of contending qualities.

Here are three "new" poems by James Agee, uncollected in any previous volume of his poetry: "The Darkened Cage," "[A deer went down to water]," and "Eureka." Each of these represents some quality of Agee's voice, some style or formal manner he pursued. In the "Introduction" to the 1968 volume of *The Collected Poems of James Agee*, which he edited, Robert Fitzgerald says that certain of Agee's poems "are in a direct line of descent from English achievements of the period between 1550 and 1640, and yet it would be foolish to consider them merely imitative; they are poems in their own right, new increments to the tradition."[2] Agee's poem "The Darkened Cage" demonstrates some of the sensibilities Fitzgerald refers to with the finely tuned iambic pentameter line, the rhymed quatrains and concluding couplet, and the courtly, old-fashioned language of a poem despairing the emptiness of romantic love in favor of religious devotion. Agee struggled with how to balance his beliefs with the paradoxes of his experience, and if the "One" in the final couplet may be interpreted as God, then this poem shows an instance of the speaker finding comfort in embracing "remembered tunes afresh." The second poem, "[A deer went down to water]," maintains some of the formal elements of "The Darkened Cage" while modifying others. This poem employs a tighter iambic trimeter form but loosens the formality of the diction for a poem that is more meditative in its perspective and more pastoral in setting. Agee shows the remarkable range and facility for which he is known, adapting his tone to suit the material of the poem. The third poem, "Eureka," displays an altogether different side of Agee's voice: animated, sarcastic, and biting. Agee is known for his sweepingly poetic descriptive language, and for the depths of his empathy for the abused and uncared-for, but in "Eureka" he shows a lesser-remarked-upon gift for satire and cutting wit. Agee was often prescient in his youthful writings, and the future appears to have revealed itself to him as he assesses the risk of one of the early twentieth century's most dangerous political tendencies. The three "new" poems presented here invite the reader to take a fresh look at Agee's poetry, and to discover there a seam of his immense talent that deserves greater recognition and celebration.

THE DARKENED CAGE

I looked on love, and love was meaningless,
No meaning more had music to my ear,
Nor knowledge, other than my mind's distress,
Nor beauty's self to me, other than fear:

Nothing had power to move me or to wrest
Speech from my lips, who stood irresolute,
Knowing the measured perturbation in my breast
Of one who lived, but was bestunned and mute.

Then One twitched off that shroud of flesh,
And my heart sang remembered tunes afresh

(University of Tennessee Special Collections, MS 2730 B5 F12)

[A DEER WENT DOWN TO WATER]

A deer went down to water.
And we walked under night.
She stood there with her daughter.
And night was over us all.

She lifted from the leafmold
Into the wetted air
Her listening snout and heard us
Because we were right there.

There by that talking water
Before her knees were sprung
The bullet spread inside her.
Her mouth spilled out her tongue.

Her child is in the oakwoods.
We saw it: it was gone.
It gasps in the far oakwoods.
Her child is hoof and bone.

And therefore was some sorrow
For salt for that red steak.
Therefore, long since, in dead of nights,
I find I am awake.

(University of Tennessee Special Collections, MS 2730 B5 F32)

EUREKA

Fellows by the living Jingo
Nationalism's a damn fine thing-o!
We can prop the crumbling state
By properly directing hate.

(University of Tennessee Special Collections, MS 2730 B5 F14)

Notes

1. David Madden, in print in multiple sources.

2. Robert Fitzgerald, "Introduction," *The Collected Poems of James Agee* (Boston: Houghton Mifflin, 1968), x.

APPENDIX TWO

A New Story

On the Brooklyn Waterfront—James Agee's "Freighter's Sailing Day"

MICHAEL A. LOFARO

When the future Pulitzer Prize winner James Agee (1909–1955) moved to the Flatbush neighborhood of Brooklyn for two months in early March 1939, it was to research an article for *Fortune* magazine. The article was slated to appear in a special July issue on New York City to commemorate its hosting of the 1939 World's Fair.[1] Like his previously rejected article "Cotton Tenants"[2] that ultimately became the influential *Let Us Now Praise Famous Men* (1941), "Southeast of the Island: Travel Notes" would also be vetoed for publication to later appear in *Esquire* in November 1968, and then in 2005 in book form as *Brooklyn Is. Southeast of the Island: Travel Notes.*[3]

Likely during this same period he authored this newly discovered gem of a short story, "Freighter's Sailing Day,"[4] a narrative likely inspired by Agee's proximity to all the commercial shipping traffic using the many piers of Brooklyn, which all took great advantage of the location's access to the East River, the Bay of New York, and the Atlantic. Unlike the section of *Brooklyn Is* that treats the waterfront in a panorama of Whitman-like scope, however, "Freighter's Sailing Day" bores down into the space of just a few late afternoon and evening hours to immerse the reader in the realistic details of the men, their characters, the ship, and the rhythm of their lives and work. As creative nonfiction, it likewise gives evidence of Agee's evolving journalistic style, one that drastically departs from the personal and experimental style of *Let Us Now Praise Famous Men*, and of his continued ability both to incorporate accurate dialect speech and, in this instance, to use precise nautical terms as ways to enhance realism. That he authors such different texts essentially at the same time highlights the diversity of his talent.

Although Agee's story does not deal with the crime and criminals on the New York City docks, it reveals an atmosphere and context that are similar to both Malcolm Johnson's Pulitzer Prize–winning series of articles for the *New York Sun* (November 2, 1948, through February 2, 1949), and to the film developed from them by Budd Schulberg—*On the Waterfront* (1954)—which won eight Academy Awards.[5]

Welcome aboard Agee's representative ship, the S. S. Typicus, as she prepares to shove off from the Brooklyn docks on her journey to Rio.

Notes

1. A sample of Agee's work on New York for the World's Fair can be seen in his original typescript "Foreword," reproduced in *the Paris Review* 229, with a short introduction by Michael A. Lofaro (Summer 2019): 100–103.

2. For both "Cotton Tenants" and *Let Us Now Praise Famous Men*, see Hugh Davis, ed., Let Us Now Praise Famous Men: *An Annotated Edition of the James Agee–Walker Evans Classic, with Supplementary Manuscripts* (Knoxville, TN: U of Tennessee P, 2015). It is volume 3 of The Works of James Agee, General Editor, Michael A. Lofaro, Associate General Editor, Hugh Davis.

3. James Agee, *Brooklyn Is: Southeast of the Island; Travel Notes* (New York: Fordham UP, 2012). For the standard scholarly edition, see Paul Ashdown, ed., *Complete Journalism: Articles, Book Reviews, and Manuscripts* (Knoxville: U of Tennessee P, 2013), 376–94. It is volume 2 of The Works of James Agee, General Editor, Michael A. Lofaro, Associate General Editor, Hugh Davis. Agee was likely also working on "Southeast of the Island" at the same time as his pieces for the World's Fair. For Agee's notebook for "Southeast of the Island," see his notebook located in the University of Tennessee Special Collections MS 1998 box 1, folder 6. For background on the literary culture of Brooklyn from Whitman forward (although it does not mention Agee, likely because of his brief residence there), see Evan Hughes, *Literary Brooklyn: The Writers of Brooklyn and the Story of American City Life* (New York: Henry Holt, 2011).

4. "Freighter's Sailing Day" is located in the University of Tennessee Special Collections, MSS 3824, box 7, folder 3. It is a carbon copy of Agee's typescript; the original has not been found.

5. For a helpful edition of the newspaper stories, as well as additional material by Schulberg, see, Malcolm Johnson, *On the Waterfront: The Pulitzer Prize–Winning Articles that Inspired the Classic Movie and Transformed the New York Harbor* (New York: Chamberlain Bros., 2005). See also, William DiFazio, *Longshoremen: Community and Resistance on the Brooklyn Waterfront* (South Hadley, MA: Bergin & Garvey, 1985). And on the film, among others, see Joanna E Rapf, *On the Waterfront* (New York: Cambridge UP, 2003) and Leo Braudy, *On the Waterfront* (London: British Film Institute, 2005).

Freighter's Sailing Day

JAMES AGEE

The S. S. Typicus, freighter in the South American trade, is lying at Pier 34 in Brooklyn. Her Blue Peter[1] has been flapping in the raw February breeze since early in the forenoon. Chalked up on her gangway board is: "Rio de Janeiro, 4 P.M." It is quarter past four and the stevedores are still working in four of the holds.

The Typicus has divided thirty days between Boston, Philadelphia and New York. Both ship and the crew are beginning to show the effects of so much contact with civilization. The Second Mate has seen his wife and three children. After five days of intense family life, he is inwardly content to be among men again. The skipper is back from a flying trip to Vassar with a new picture of his daughter. She has confused him considerably by ordering him to appear next trip in his uniform. In the foc'sle[2], the watches have been set and the twelve to four are congratulating themselves over a common bottle. The new Ordinary[3], making his first trip to sea, is piteously and hopelessly looking for a place where he may relieve himself—hopelessly because he does not know whether to use the vulgar or polite term in asking for it.

The Bos'n[4], a nutbrown Russian-Finn with big ears, mournful eyes and a jutting nose, is sitting on a bitt[5], oblivious to the yammering winches, and apparently regretting something. Two firemen and an oiler come down the dock and swarm over the ship's side with cat-like grace. Safe in their mess-room, they release into helpless drunkenness. Amidships, the Steward is walking up and down talking to himself in a violent manner. It is quarter past four and the laundry hasn't arrived yet. In the shambles of his pantry, notable mainly for a six days' collection of garbage, the Saloon[6] Messboy fervently prays to his heathen gods that she'll sail before midnight.

The last slingload of cargo for number one hatch hurtles into the lower hold as a fine Scotch mist begins to impregnate everything, turning the dun-colored snow into coffee-colored slush. "Awright, Bos'n, get the watch-on-deck and batten down number one!" bawls the Mate.

The Bos'n quivers slightly and heaves himself up from his bitt. "OY." he says.

"And get the cluster lights ready for number three."

"Oy."

"Better get the off-shore lines in too."

"Oy." The last "oy" is a hopeless murmur. The watch-on-deck has been across the street since two o'clock drinking up three shirts and a suit of oilskins[7]. The long-suffering Bos'n knows and expects that. But he also knows that, by some uncanny instinct, they will turn up at five minutes to sailing time, work very efficiently for the twenty minutes necessary to cast her off, and then pass out quietly in their bunks. The Bos'n motions to the new Ordinary Seaman, now in fearful agony and still in his best suit. "Come forrad and we batten down number one now."

"Yes sir!" agrees the Ordinary, all bright-eyed and eager. He rushes after the Bos'n, who has already disappeared in the gathering murk, nearly gets his head cut off by a cargo runner at number five, and becomes lost for a half hour in the 'midship alleyways.

It is totally dark now, and the mist has become a fine sleet. The ship's stores, the laundry, and the Steward's wife arrive almost simultaneously. The Steward becomes a foaming madman. The Chief Engineer, leaning over the after 'midships rail, turns a jaundiced eye upon his first assistant and observes, "Everything is lovely in the garden, now."

A meek little man in an old green mackinaw, carrying a Saturday Evening Post in one hand and a wrinkled Boston bag in the other, trundles up the gangway. With the imperturbability of all pilots he says nothing to anybody but makes undeviatingly for the bridge. He retires to the quietness of the chart-room and, unfurling his Post, is heard of no more until the Typicus is clear of the dock. He then becomes a font of omnipotence, barking orders at all and sundry.

In the radio shack, Sparks is stolidly fumbling for a gum-drop with one hand while, with the other, he is interpreting the peevish clickings[8] that are raining into his ears. His pencil sprawls across the page: "Winds rising to gale force at Fire Island." His hand finds the gum-drop and conveys it to his mouth. "Storm warnings up from Nantucket to Hatteras." He munches speculatively on the gum-drop. "Early this morning Miss Barbara Ferris of 60 West 54th Street was set upon by two men and—." Sparks stops munching and, listening with avid interest, ceases to write.

The Mate is striding up and down by the fiddley door[9] howling for the Bos'n. He sights the Ordinary halfway into the Officer's Lavatory and, after giving him a brief but sulphurous scathing for that horrible breech of ship's etiquette, sends him to tell the Bos'n that number two is ready to be battened down.

The crew's Mess slips and slithers aft with an early supper. He is short, bow-legged, with one crossed eye, and the mouth of a petulant goat. The three tiered mess-kits are too long for him and they bump on the deck with every other step sending a spray of hot stew over his ankles. He curses continuously in a low monotone with a small, sharp crescendo when the stew penetrates to this flesh. Sailing Day makes him acutely conscious that he is the lowest man on the ship upon whose head all passed bucks inevitably fall.

He sets one kit in the fireman's mess-room and the other in the sailor's. "Onatabul!"[10] he roars, and vanishes amidships where he remains, deaf to prayers and threats alike. Two A. B.'s[11] who have been storing up sleep against the eight to twelve watch, emerge from a cocoon of blankets and smell suspiciously of the fish hash. They discard it with drowsy grunts and stack their plates with fried potatoes and an alleged salad of cabbage and tomatoes. The old Ordinary Seaman who, with the immense sophistication of one trip, has been lying low in the Bos'n's room, comes out and takes an apple. "Hey, Mess," he bellows, "Tea!"

The Bos'n comes in from the deck and throws his sodden gloves on the radiator. "Oy," he sighs, "Fish hash." Behind him trails the new Ordinary, bedraggled but beatific in expression. He has taken advantage of the darkness.

The Irish dayman, a genial giant of a man, arrives laden down with bundles and lumpy in his shore clothes. He has had two days off and the odor of domesticity still hangs about him. He tosses one of his bundles on the table and says, "Scoff up, lads, the gud wife made thim for yex special." They are two apple pies, still warm. The offending fish hash is forgotten but not forgiven.

There is a commotion outside. The watch-on-deck, all their vendible property drunk up, are coming aboard. They are wide-eyed, their hats are very much on the back of their heads, and they are now endowed with the tender sensitivities of

Princes of the Blood. One is tall and rather good looking with a calm and cynical cast of eye. The other is short and immensely self-important. He has a thumb-shaped nose and is inclined to be noisily watchful of his rights. It seems that the tall one took the cautious course and came aboard over the side, in the traditional sailing day manner. The shorter one, coming arrogantly up the gangway, has evidently been spoken to sharply by the Mate.

"___ the rat-eater sees me comin up the gangway an he looks at me like I was a bad dog. Well, he starts to give me a growl so I tells him straight out: 'Look here, mister,' I sez, 'you may be Mate of this rat-eatin wagon but you got no right to bark at me,' I sez."

"An what did he say?"

"He gives me another growl about it bein sailing day and ___"

"And what did you say?"

"I sez, 'Look here, Mister, when it comes to the point that a man can't step ashore an have a sociable drink on a rat-eatin day like this, it's time he got off, you can be rat-eatin sure of THAT!'"

"And what did he say?"

"'Aw right' he sez, 'Aw right,' an walks away."

"And what did you say?"

"Well, I speaks right up to him, 'An what's more,' I sez, 'what about all this rat-eatin overtime we're putting in today, what about that?'"

"AND WHAT DID HE SAY?" the whole table wants to know in chorus. It's an old game that never loses its savor with them.

"Aw, go pound sand in your rat-eatin ears! And that goes for the rat-eatin Mate, too." says the shorter one relapsing sullenly under the knowledge that he has been made game of.

At this point the Mate sticks his head in the Mess-room and, after one intent look at the Shorter One which causes that one to grovel in his fish-hash, says, with a tinge of regret for the unfinished supper, "Fore and aft, lads, we'll be letting go in a couple of minutes now. Give the tugs the new lines and break out all the cork fenders[12]. Bose, you come forward."

"Oy." Says the Bos'n, downing his coffee at a scalding rate, "Hey, Ordinary, what name have you got?"

The Ordinary, quite overcome by such a personal turn in the conversation, flushes and stammers, "Er—my name is Carstairs but my—that is, they call me Slim, Sir."

"Well, Mr. Slim," says the Bos'n, unmoved by this revelation, "You come forward and stand by on the foc'sle head. And don't 'Sir' me. I'm yoost the mule driver."

The Skipper comes out of his room and mounts slowly to the bridge. He is muffled in oilskins which are already stiffening with the cold. His face is long and his mouth is worrying the tattered stump of a cigar. Glumly he looks first at the sky and then at the immediate surroundings of the Typicus. Between the Typicus and open water are two other freighters and, directly across with about thirty yards of water between them, is a large Grace Line passenger ship. Even this meagre expanse is generously populated with a variety of barges. The two tugs are doing their best with these but are having some trouble finding an out of the way place to put them all. At the end of the pier, the Skipper knows with melancholy certainty, that he will find tide, current, and wind all running vigorously in the same direction. The Pilot appears at his side like a gloomy wraith. "It ain't nothing here, Cap'n," he observes, "To what you're going to get outside."

Across the street, the fly-specked Bar and Lunch is closing up for the day. The old Swede carpenter steps unsteadily out into the snow, a phenomenon he notes with some surprise. It had been high and sunny noon when he entered the Bar and Lunch. He tacks across the street towards the ship. A street light reveals a great yellow cat nesting comfortably in his arms. He makes his way with some difficulty up the steep and slippery gangway and aft to his room, always with more solicitude for the cat than for his own footing. Shifting the animal under one arm, he gets out his key and, after a good deal of fumbling, unlocks the door. He puts the cat on his bunk where there are already three other cats, comfortably curled, but with heads inquisitively aloft at this new arrival. "Here iss come a new shipmate, aint it, Yoolya." he says, putting Yoolya down amongst them. "You be goot chums wit Yoolya." he adds admonishingly. After looking at them fondly for two or three minutes—a look which the four cats return with a smug and blinking complacence, he heaves a sigh of contentment and says, "I ban turn in now." He stretches his bulk precariously on the wooden settee and, stuffing a boot under his head, falls immediately into a heavy slumber.

The tugs are fast, now, fore and aft, waiting, with slack lines for the Typicus to cast off. She is singled up—only two lines and a spring wire are holding her. The tug-boat skipper is on the bridge shrilling cryptic blasts on his whistle. "Let everything go forard, Cap'n, but hold your stern line."

"All right, mister" says the Captain and bellows the order towards the foc'sle head. The wind plays havoc with the words almost before they leave the megaphone, but the Mate Senses the maneuver and shortly screams back, "All gone forrard!" The propellers of the bow tug commence to churn the water into angry cream and the Typicus starts to slant imperceptibly towards the centre of the slip. The after tug bunts blindly against the stern, holding her there. When the bow is in open water, the tug captain keens on his whistle and the first tug makes haste to escape from the narrowing gap between the Typicus and the Grace Liner. The tug takes the strain dead ahead, now, and the order is given to let go aft. The second tug reverses vigorously pulling the stern out and slightly back. Slowly, and with the overpowering impression of irresistible weight, the Typicus comes parallel to the Grace Liner not six feet from it. The seaman hovering at the break of the forward well-deck with a cork fender will not be needed.

The Typicus begins to quiver with her own life now. She is carrying very little cargo and a third of her propeller blade shows at every revolution. The blade beats upon the water with a noise like the slow hooves of a tired drayhorse walking through a covered bridge. As her nose sticks out into the current and wind beyond the slip's end, both tugs strain mightily to hold her up against the stream. The clomping of the propeller increases its beat as her bow begins to fall off towards the corner of the opposite pier. The seaman with the cork fender is once more attentive. This time it is a four foot margin as her poop-rail[13] swings out and away from the pier-head. All detail of the Typicus is immediately lost. She becomes a black, symmetrical silhouette against the gray of a snow-laden sky. The two tugs cast off and depart across the harbor like two alert and self-satisfied terriers.

By the time the Typicus has reached the lower harbor, the Bos'n and the day-men have performed miracles in the darkness. They have stowed the lines below decks out of reach of the rapacious seas that will be upon them within the hour and they have lowered eight fifty-five foot booms safely and accurately into their cradles—a ticklish job on a calm and sunny day. To the new ordinary, wandering about with a bag of wedges and a hammer, it is awesome magic concocted out of a witches' broth of wind and snow, blocks and ropes, snarling winches, unintelligible shoutings, and impenetrable darkness.

The wind's howl is rising to a roar and gives promise of shortly becoming a scream. The ordinary feels the deck heaving slowly forward toward the sickness and the suffering of the next few days as an acolyte awaits the fast that will make him a priest. He is a New Englander. Although he does not realize it yet, he is coming home. When that first fine fire subdues, all that is sordid about ships and the working of them will have passed from his ken.

The rest of the men have gone aft. Leaving the Bos'n and the Ordinary alone on the forward well-deck. The Bos'n is unrolling the pilot ladder. "Give a hand, lad, we're nearly on to the pilot boat." Watching the frail web dangle and leap as the howling seas snatch at it, the Ordinary starts to ask an incredulous question and then thinks better of it. Instead, a warm admiration for the daily work of the little man in the green mackinaw surges through him.

On the bridge, the little man gives the final course to the helmsman and stuffs his Saturday Evening Post firmly into the top of his Boston bag. "Slow her down, Cap'n, I can see the tender coming up on the lee-side." The Skipper makes a clangor on the telegraph and the pitching of the Typicus settles slowly into a lethargic rolling.

A cluster lamp at the wing of the bridge snaps on, bathing the startled Ordinary in a circle of light that includes the wildly dancing ladder and a small hemisphere of surging water. A pathetically minute rowboat, with a glowworm lamp[14] at its bow, inches its way into the hemisphere as the Pilot swings himself over the rail. Three young apprentice pilots wearing life preservers, turn their damp and glistening faces upwards. The Pilot looks toward the bridge. "Pleasant voyage, Captain." he shouts. The Bos'n makes the Boston Bag fast to a heaving line and lowers it into the rowboat which is directly under the ladder, rising and falling twenty feet in every second. At the zenith of a rise, the Pilot steps lightly into the stern sheets[15]. He makes the whole operation appear deceivingly easy. The three apprentices stroke together and the boat falls fifty feet away to the leeward, leaving no sign but the intensely bobbing lantern.

The Typicus begins to pitch again as she gathers headway. The Ordinary pauses at the foc'sle door and looks aloft. The masts are swaying against the sky like mad metronomes. He feels a happiness like an inward hymn. "Nineteen days to Rio" he says to himself with quiet ecstasy, and goes in, suddenly conscious of exhaustion, to his bunk.

Notes

1. "Blue Peter" is a blue signal flag with a white rectangle in the center that means the ship is ready to sail and all crew and passengers need to board.

2. "Foc'sle" is the abbreviated nautical term for "forecastle" and is the upper deck of a sailing ship forward of the foremast, or the forward part of a ship with the sailors' living quarters.

3. "Ordinary" is an ordinary seaman in the merchant fleet with limited shipboard experience.

4. The "Bos'n" is a warrant officer or petty officer who is in charge of a ship's rigging, anchors, cables, and deck crew.

5. "Bitt" is a mooring bitt, a heavy two-pillar cast cleat around which a crew member can secure a dockline or hawser.

6. "Saloon" is a relatively large compartment used for entertaining guests, mainly on cruise ships.

7. "Oilskins" are waterproof protective foul weather gear, also called "sou'westers."

8. "Clickings" are the sound of Morse Code being transmitted over radio waves to communicate with other operators.

9. "Fiddley door" is likely the door to a hatch that is difficult to open and close.

10. "Onatabul" is a dialect rendering of inedible.

11. "A. B.'s" are able-bodied seamen, another rank above that of the ordinary seaman.

12. "Cork fenders" serve as protective bumpers between ships or between a ship and a dock.

13. A "poop-rail" is the railing that surrounds the poop deck on the stern, or rear elevated portion, of a ship.

14. "Glowworm lamp" is a small lantern.

15. "Stern sheets" are the inboard part of an open boat aft of the thwarts and is often used for storage. "Thwarts" are any feature that lie side-to-side across the deck.

CONTRIBUTORS

PAUL ASHDOWN, Professor Emeritus of Journalism and Electronic Media at the University of Tennessee, Knoxville, is the editor of *Complete Journalism: Articles, Book Reviews, and Manuscripts*, the second volume in the scholarly edition of The Works of James Agee. He edited *James Agee: Selected Journalism* (1985 and 2005) and contributed essays on Agee to *James Agee: Reconsiderations* (1992), *A Sourcebook of American Literary Journalism* (1992), the *Encyclopedia Americana* (1996), *Agee Agonistes: Essays on the Life, Legend, and Works of James Agee* (2007), *Agee at 100: Centennial Essays on the Works of James Agee* (2012), and Let Us Now Praise Famous Men *at 75: Anniversary Essays* (2017). His latest book is *Imagining Wild Bill: James Butler Hickok in War, Media, and Memory (2020),* the fifth volume in a Civil War–era series written with Edward Caudill.

CAROLINE BLINDER, Professor of American Literature and Culture at Goldsmiths University London, has published widely on the intersections between literature and photography. Her latest monograph, *The American Photo-Text: 1930–1960* (EUP, 2019) traces documentary collaborations and creative endeavors between photographers and writers, including Agee and Evans. Blinder has previously written on Agee and cinema in her edited collection *New Critical Essays on James Agee and Walker Evans: Perspectives on* Let Us Now Praise Famous Men (2010); in Let Us Now Praise Famous Men *at 75* (2017); and in *Moments of Moment: Aspects of the Literary Epiphany* (1999). She has also co-edited an issue on photography for the *Journal of American Studies* (2020), *US Topographics: Imaging National Landscapes,* and various publications on film and television: "Smokescreens to Smokestacks: True Detective and The American Sublime," in *Popular Modernism and its Legacies* (2017), and on Jim Jarmusch's *Paterson* "No Ideas but in Seeing" in *Poetry and Film–Kiarostami and Jarmusch* (2020).

PAUL F. BROWN is a freelance writer in Knoxville, Tennessee, and a former K-12 educator. He authored *Rufus: James Agee in Tennessee* (2018), winner of the Tennessee History Book Award. His essay "'The Dryad Days': Frances Hodgson Burnett in East Tennessee" appeared in the *Journal of East Tennessee History* (vols. 90–91). He also writes for regional and higher education publications and has given talks on Agee for the East Tennessee Historical Society, Knoxville History Project, Rose Glen Literary Festival, Southern Festival of Books, and other organizations.

JEFFREY COUCHMAN teaches screenwriting at the College of Staten Island. He has collaborated on screenplays for Hollywood studios, and his fiction has appeared in various literary quarterlies. Couchman wrote book and lyrics for the musicals *Battleship Potemkin* and *Blood and Fire*. For Florida Studio Theatre, he wrote the play *Master of the Revels*, about the Shakespeare forger William Henry Ireland. He is co-author of the play *Three Wise Guys*, based on Damon Runyon Christmas stories (Broadway Play Publishing). He is editor of "*The African Queen" and "The Night of the Hunter": First and Final Screenplays* (2017), volume 4 in The Works of James Agee, and is author of "*The Night of the Hunter": A Biography of a Film* (2009). His articles on film have appeared in *American Cinematographer* and the *New York Times*, and he has contributed essays to other volumes on Agee published by the University of Tennessee Press.

ANDREW CROOKE teaches American literature and creative writing courses at Moravian University in Bethlehem, PA. He has also taught at several other institutions in his native eastern Pennsylvania as well as at the College of New Jersey. He earned a BA in English (summa cum laude) from Cornell University and a PhD from the University of Iowa, where he was a Presidential Fellow. His dissertation focused on photo-textual representations of rural poverty, particularly in the works of James Agee, Walker Evans, John Berger, and Jean Mohr. Crooke previously contributed an essay to *Agee at 100: Centennial Essays on the Works of James Agee* (2012), along with two essays and his own photographs from Alabama to Let Us Now Praise Famous Men *at 75: Anniversary Essays* (2017).

HUGH DAVIS, Professor of English and Chair of Humanities at Piedmont University in Demorest, Georgia, is the general editor of *The Works of James Agee*, coeditor, with Michael A. Lofaro, of *James Agee Rediscovered: The Journals of* Let Us Now Praise Famous Men *and Other New Manuscripts* (2005), author of *The Making of James Agee* (2008), and editor of The Works of James Agee, volume 3: Let Us Now Praise Famous Men: *An Annotated Edition of the James Agee-Walker Evans Classic, with Supplementary Manuscripts* (2014).

JEFFREY FOLKS has taught in Europe, America, and Japan, most recently as Professor of Letters in the Graduate School of Doshisha University. He has published numerous books and articles on American literature, including *In a Time of Disorder* (2003), *Damaged Lives* (2005), and *Heartland of the Imagination* (2012). His articles on American literature and culture have appeared in many journals, including *Modern Age*, *Southern Literary Journal*, and *Papers on Language and Literature*.

JESSE GRAVES is the author of four poetry collections, the latest of which is *Said-Songs: Essays on Poetry and Place*. His work received the James Still Award for Writing about the Appalachian South from the Fellowship of Southern Writers and the Philip H. Freund Prize for Creative Writing from Cornell University. Graves has been an editor on several volumes of poetry and scholarship, including *Jeff Daniel Marion: Poet on the Holston* and the forthcoming *The Complete Poems of James Agee*. He teaches at East Tennessee State University, where he is Poet-in-Residence and Professor of English.

MICHAEL JACOBS is Dean, Humanities and Social Sciences, at Monroe Community College in Rochester, New York. He has contributed essays and articles on documentary literature, humanities education, high-impact teaching practices to *Literary Journalism Studies*, Let Us Now Praise Famous Men *at 75: Anniversary Essays*, *Community College Humanities Review*, and the Association of American Colleges and Universities. He is also the founding Director of Monroe Community College's Institute for the Humanities and currently serves as deputy director, National Conferences, for the Community College Humanities Association. Prior to his position at MCC, Michael was co-chair of English at Berkeley College in New York City, where he taught courses in writing, literature, and film from 2002 to 2017.

MICHAEL A. LOFARO is Professor Emeritus of American Literature and American Studies at the University of Tennessee. His book-length work on Agee includes the editing of *James Agee: Reconsiderations* (1992), coediting *James Agee Rediscovered: The Journals of* Let Us Now Praise Famous Men *and Other New Manuscripts* (2005) with Hugh Davis, and editing volume 1 of The Works of James Agee—*A Death in the Family: A Restoration of the Author's Text* (2007); *Agee Agonistes: Essays on the Life, Legend, and Works of James Agee* (2007); *Agee at 100: Centennial Essays on the Works of James Agee* (2012); and Let Us Now Praise Famous Men *at 75: Anniversary Essays* (2017). Other recent editions include *Boone, Crockett, and Black Hawk in 1833: Unsettling the Mythic West* (2019), *The Life and Adventures [or Sketches and Eccentricities] of Colonel David Crockett of West Tennessee* (2020), and *Life of Ma-ka-tai-me-she-kia-kiak, or Black Hawk* (2021).

DAVID MADDEN is Robert Penn Warren Professor Emeritus at Louisiana State University. Poet, playwright, critic, and novelist, he has published many short stories, several of which were reprinted in numerous college textbooks. Two of his novels, *Sharpshooter* (1996) and *The Suicide's Wife* (1978), were nominated for the Pulitzer Prize. He has edited two editions of *Remembering James Agee* and contributed to five previous Agee volumes. As an historian, he is founding director of the United States Civil War Center and author of *The Tangled Web of the Civil War and Reconstruction* (2015). A book about him is *David Madden: A Writer for All Genres* (2006). His eleventh novel, *London Bridge in Plague and Fire*, appeared in 2010, his fourth book of stories, *The Last Bizarre Tale*, in 2014, and in 2017, *Marble Goddesses and Mortal Flesh*, four related novellas, appeared. His most recent book is *The Voice of James M. Cain* (2020), an innovative biography.

Index